Admiral of the Ocean Sea

CHRISTOPHORVS·COLVMBVS.

Ideal Portrait of Columbus
From the Henri Lefort etching
of the modern portrait in
the Naval Museum of Madrid.
Courtesy M. Knoedler & Co., N.Y.

VOLUME 1

Admiral of the Ocean Sea

A LIFE OF CHRISTOPHER COLUMBUS

BY SAMUEL ELIOT MORISON

TIME Reading Program [RTP] Special Edition

TIME INCORPORATED / NEW YORK

TIME INC. BOOK DIVISION

EDITOR *Norman P. Ross*
COPY DIRECTOR *William Jay Gold*
ART DIRECTOR *Edward A. Hamilton*
CHIEF OF RESEARCH *Beatrice T. Dobie*
EDITOR, TIME READING PROGRAM *Max Gissen*
RESEARCHER *Seena G. Harris*

PUBLISHER *Jerome S. Hardy*
GENERAL MANAGER *John A. Watters*

TIME MAGAZINE

EDITOR *Roy Alexander*
MANAGING EDITOR *Otto Fuerbringer*
PUBLISHER *Bernhard M. Auer*

Maps by ERWIN RAISZ

Drawings by BERTRAM GREENE

An Atlantic Monthly Press Book
© 1942 by Samuel Eliot Morison
Reprinted by arrangement with Little, Brown and Company, Boston

Editors' Preface

"At 2 a.m. October 12 the moon, past full, was riding about 70° high over Orion on the port quarter, just the position to illuminate anything ahead of the ships. Jupiter was rising in the east; Saturn had just set, and Deneb was nearing the western horizon, toward which all waking eyes were directed. There hung the Square of Pegasus, and a little higher and to the northward Cassiopeia's Chair. . . . On speed the three ships, *Pinta* in the lead, their sails silver in the moonlight. A brave trade wind is blowing and the caravels are rolling, plunging and throwing spray as they cut down the last invisible barrier between the Old World and the New. Only a few moments now, and an era that began in remotest antiquity will end.

"Rodrigo de Triana, lookout on *Pinta's* forecastle, sees something like a white sand cliff gleaming in the moonlight on the western horizon, then another, and a dark line of land connecting them. '*Tierra! tierra!*' he shouts, and this time land it is."

If there is a freshness, an immediacy of vivid personal experience in these lines about a great event that took place almost five centuries ago, it is because the author of *Admiral of the Ocean Sea* lived them. Samuel Eliot Morison, who thus describes Columbus' first landfall in the New World, himself sailed the same midnight sea, saw the same stars, strained his eyes toward the land which he felt sure must lie ahead and finally made out, with a surge of deep emotion, that distant glimmering of silver sand. Morison "discovered" the islands of the Caribbean the way Columbus did—sailing by the charts of that amazing seaman, retracing on the Admiral's "Ocean Sea" the historic voyage which changed the world forever.

Few biographers—certainly none of the many others who have written about Columbus—have gone to such lengths to reconstruct for themselves the actuality of their subject's life. In fact, the literature on Columbus has been generally distinguished by a lack of understanding of both who he was and precisely what he did. The literature was mostly the work of what Morison scornfully calls "armchair admirals," scholars with little or no knowledge of the sea. And the legends of Columbus were even more cluttered with confusion—a confusion which finally provoked Morison, a man who uniquely combined the abilities of seaman, historian and writer, into action.

He was, and remains, an unabashed admirer of the Discoverer: he was convinced that Columbus knew what he was doing when he sailed westward across the Atlantic to find land. School children are still told that Columbus was one of the few men of his age who believed the world was round; that when his sailors mutinied and tried to turn back, they did so because they were afraid they were at the edge of the world and would fall off into an unthinkable abyss. Nonsense, says Morison: like many seamen of his time, Columbus knew that the world was a globe. Furthermore, as a man who had studied map making, he believed that by sailing westward he would find the rich and storied Orient. And so he would have—eventually. The error in his thinking was one of distance: he believed that Japan (which he knew as Cipangu) was only some 750 leagues, or about 2,400 nautical miles, away, and he did not know that a continent and then another ocean lay between.

But he did feel certain that land of some sort lay across the Atlantic, and toward this land, after incredible difficulties and frustrations in financing and mounting his expedition, he steadfastly set sail. He headed south and then turned west to sail along in the favorable trade winds. He knew that the trade winds existed, and he counted on them. He knew, too, of the dread Sargasso Sea, with its frightening mysterious weed growths. He did not know of the doldrums, and on the Third Voyage he languished in them as sailboats without power still do today. But eventually the fresh winds caught him once again, filled out his sails and sped him to his great achievement.

Four and a half centuries later his distinguished biographer, armed with a scholar's detailed knowledge of all that Columbus knew, repeated that third epic voyage. And what did he learn? He learned from ancient books and journals the art of navigation as Columbus had learned it in his day. He learned about the behavior of different types of compasses. He learned that the Admiral was not much good at longitude, only a little better at latitude, but was a whiz at dead reckoning, with an uncanny sense of navigation among uncharted shoals and islands.

Morison learned, too, how a sailor lived at sea aboard the Admiral's ships, and the ships and the men aboard them come alive with vivid detail in this book: "There is no need to give the new watch time to dress, for nobody has undressed; when they 'went below' at 3 a.m. each man simply sought out his favorite soft plank, anywhere that he could brace himself against the rolling and pitching. They are soon awake, rubbing their eyes and grumbling, and each man grabs a ship biscuit, with some garlic cloves, a bit of cheese, a pickled sardine or what-have-you for breakfast and shuffles aft to the break in the poop. The helmsman gives the course to the master who is captain of his watch, he repeats it and gives it to the new helmsman, and he repeats it again. No chance for error! And most of the time on this outward passage the course is simply

"Oeste: nada del noroeste, nada del sudoeste."

"West: nothing to the northward, nothing to the southward."

And thus it went, day after day, for more than a month of sailing into the unknown. "Columbus was not accurate," Morison says. "He never knew exactly how fast his vessel was sailing, because he had no fixed standard and no check." But even though he traveled farther than he had originally figured he would have to go, his confidence was never shaken. His detailed technical knowledge was erroneous to a colossal degree, and yet when he found land where he knew that it must be, he was elated but not surprised.

The true measure of the Discoverer's achievement is not merely that he found land where he knew that land must be, but that he brought his entire company safe home again from that remote and unknown region—and then went back to it again, not once but three more times. That, says seaman Morison with the honest admiration of one navigator for another, was sailing—not blind sailing into the unknown, but sailing of a high degree of skill.

Samuel Eliot Morison, born in Boston in 1887, is official historian of United States naval operations in World War II. He was educated at Harvard and has been on the faculties of the University of California, Harvard and Oxford, where he was the first incumbent of the new chair of American history. He is now professor emeritus of history at Harvard and a retired rear admiral of the U.S. Naval Reserve. His many books, from *The Maritime History of Massachusetts* to his monumental 15-volume *History of U.S. Naval Operations in World War II,* have brought him high honors, including two Pulitzer Prizes (1943 and 1960), the Bancroft Prize (1949), the Loubat and Jusserand Prizes, the Theodore Roosevelt Medal (1956), the Edison Award (1957), the Gold Medal for History and Biography of the National Institute of Arts and Letters (1962). *The Admiral* won him honors and much more: adventure, fulfillment of a seaman's passion nurtured from boyhood summers on the coast of Maine and the satisfaction of setting straight the record of a great and much maligned man.

In his own Introduction to this special edition, historian Morison recalls the genesis of the book with great gusto, and he plainly relishes the fact that it has been translated into many foreign languages. One suspects that of the entire prodigious output of this seaman-scholar-writer's life, this book is probably his favorite.

—THE EDITORS OF TIME

R|T|P *Introduction*

This book, which first appeared in 1942, took a long time to germinate. I may say that the seed was sown in 1893, when I stood weeping on a platform of the old Boston & Albany "deepo" at Kneeland Street, Boston, seeing off my parents and a party of gay young married people. They were going to visit the great White City at Chicago, where the World's Columbian Exposition was commemorating (one year late) the 400th anniversary of the discovery of America. To match the imitation-marble buildings designed for the exposition by McKim, Mead and White, the railroads put on special white trains: parlor car white, glistening with brass trimmings; locomotive white; tenders white; conductor and brakemen in uniforms like the summer whites of the Navy.

I was considered too young—six years—to go to Chicago, but I devoured and stowed away all kinds of information about Columbus and the great discovery. I'm sure Dr. Freud would have said that this book is my revenge on my parents for not taking me to the exposition. And although I missed the white train, I was able to make my Columbian explorations in white-winged ships.

We now skip to the year 1916, when Professor Edward Channing turned over to me, an instructor in history at Harvard College, his course on the colonial period of America. I spent the greater part of the summer at home in Concord with the intention of preparing all the lectures for "History 10," but the vast and highly controversial literature on the Discovery of America so fascinated me that by the time college opened, I had not yet worked through Columbus. So then I decided that if the opportunity occurred, I would sail to the West Indies and check on Columbus' landfalls and coastings. That seemed to be the only way to find out what kind of seaman and navigator he was—and exactly where he did sail.

About 20 years elapsed before it was possible to fulfill this ambition, but in the meantime I read practically every bit of the printed sources and secondary works on the Discovery. In the winter of 1937 it was now or never. Obtaining leave of absence from the university, I chartered the yawl *Ptarmigan* and sailed to the Windward and Leeward Islands with a party of friends. Our brief excursion to a small portion of Columbus' discoveries was an eye opener. Returning from the voyage, I went on to study in the libraries of Lisbon, Paris and London and made plans for a more thorough coverage of Columbus' voyages in preparation for a biography of my hero as seaman, explorer and navigator.

Ellery Sedgwick, editor of the Atlantic Monthly Press, accepted the idea with great enthusiasm and put me in touch with Paul Hammond, a Harvard man slightly older than myself. In addition to being a distinguished blue-water sailor, Paul is a financier and a great organizer. He fell in heartily with my plans, raised most of the money and organized the Harvard Columbus Expedition, as we called it. We purchased an old three-masted schooner yacht, gave her the dignified Columbian name of *Capitana,* and rerigged her as a barkentine with spars and sail donated by several of our yachting friends. The expedition was saved from being an all-Harvard affair by my cousin William D. Stevens, Yale 1923, who joined us with his 44-foot ketch *Mary Otis,* making a *Niña,* as it were, to our *Santa María.*

Our voyage is described briefly in my original Preface, reprinted in this special edition. There is still more detail in my compilation of essays entitled *By Land and By Sea.* In voyages through the Bahamas and around Cuba in *Mary Otis,* and in various short trips in native sloops and a motor craft of the Garde d'Haiti, I covered all the coasts and islands in the New World visited by Columbus in the course of his four voyages, with the exception of Honduras and Nicaragua. In order to cover them, we were just preparing to embark once more in *Mary Otis* when America entered World War II and Bill Stevens and myself were called to other duties. Thus, for the Honduras-Nicaragua leg of the Fourth Voyage I have had to depend on other observers who know that region, notably Wolfgang von Hagen and Samuel K. Lothrop. The war also prevented me from finishing my translations of Columbus' journals and other documents, which will occasionally be referred to in the following narrative. That task, however, has now been accepted by the Limited Editions Club of New York.

The original two-volume 1942 edition of *Admiral of the Ocean Sea* included numerous footnotes and appendices. They were omitted for a shortened version which came out simultaneously and which is the basis for the present edition. In one version or another, *Admiral of the Ocean Sea* has been translated into Spanish as *El Almirante de la Mar Océano,* into German as *Admiral des Welt-meeres* and into French as *Christophe Colomb l'Amiral de la Mer Océane.* An Italian edition is scheduled. A shorter biography of the Admiral, called *Christopher Columbus, Mariner,* published in the U.S. and in England in the 1950s, has been translated into Italian, Dutch, Hungarian and Persian, and into other languages beyond my ken behind the Iron Curtain.

Very little of importance about Columbus has appeared in the last 20 years. Salvador de Madariaga's *Christopher Columbus* (1940), the whole object of which was to prove the Discoverer to have been a Catalan Jew, was somewhat mordantly reviewed by me in *The American Historical Review.* I had particular fun with some of Señor Madariaga's "evidence," notably the fact of my hero's beating to windward along the Hispaniola coast proving him to be a "wandering Jew." Madariaga got back at me in his 1949 edition by warning his readers to disregard Morison as a mere "yachtsman." Despite abundant evidence to the contrary, certified by the Spanish historian Angel de Altolaguirre y Duvale, Madariaga persists in maintaining that the 1498 *mayorazgo* (right of succession), in which Columbus states that he was a Genoese, was "fabricated." Since that time, new evidence of Columbus' Genoese nationality has appeared. Hernán Pérez de Oliva of Cordova (1494-1530), a noted Spanish writer of his day, wrote an early Columbus biography which only recently came to light, and he had no doubt of Columbus' Genoese origin.

The only other important works on Columbus that have appeared since 1942 are those of the Mexican historian Edmundo O'Gorman. In his *La Idea del descubrimiento de América,* published in Mexico in 1951, and in *The Invention of America,* published in the United States in 1961, this author attempts to prove, mainly by dialectic, that Columbus should not be called the Discoverer of America because he was not looking for a New World and did not recognize it as such when he saw it. Amerigo Vespucci, therefore, was the real discoverer of America because he recognized it as the New World—*Mundus Novus*. But Columbus called Venezuela an Other World—*Otro Mundo*—in the course of his Third Voyage, made in 1498, one year before Vespucci went there. He called it *Nuevo Mundo* in his letter of 1500 to Doña Juana de Torres, and by *Otro Mundo* and *Nuevo Mundo* Columbus meant exactly what Vespucci did by *Mundus Novus*—a world unknown to Ptolemy and the ancients.

Both of Señor O'Gorman's works teem with sarcastic jibes at poor me, particularly at my presumption in trying to find out anything about Columbus by sailing over his routes. Fair enough, since I have made plenty of cracks at "armchair admirals" and "library navigators," of whom O'Gorman is an outstanding example.

The Discovery of America was such a supremely important event in history that we cannot expect to establish finality, unless in an "Other World" where we hope that Columbus, Vespucci and all the other great navigators are now at peace. Historians will rearrange bits of evidence, make revisions and fresh estimates, and perhaps find more contemporary sources. Since Pérez de Oliva's biography was discovered after four centuries, and the Dead Sea Scrolls after two millennia, it is perhaps not too much to expect that Columbus' original Journal of his First Voyage, which we know only from Las Casas' abstract, may still turn up in some obscure monastic library or muniment room in Spain.

The reader will not have to wait for that document to learn what manner of man Columbus was, what sort of a navigator, and what islands and shores of the New World he discovered. Here, if you will, you may follow the Admiral in his little caravels over tropic seas and share his wonder over the people and the beauty of this strange New World, of which we shall never wholly complete the exploration.

—S. E. MORISON

To my shipmates of the
Harvard Columbus Expedition

BARKENTINE *Capitana*
KETCH *Mary Otis*

1939–1940

Contents

VOLUME TWO

THE SECOND VOYAGE TO AMERICA

THE THIRD VOYAGE TO AMERICA

List of Maps, Charts and Illustrations

Spanish Coins of the Columbian Era
and Their Equivalents

	In maravedis	Number to the mark *	Weight of gold content in grams	Value in U.S. pre-1934 dollars
Copper blanca	0.5			$0.0035
Copper maravedi	1.	96		.007
Silver real (1475)	30.	67		.133
Gold ducat	375.	65⅓	3.48	$2.32
Gold castellano or peso d'oro	435.	50	4.55	$3.025
Gold excelente (1475)	870.	25	9.1	$6.05

The above figures are based on the monetary legislation of 1475 and 1497.
* The mark (Sp. *marco*) was a weight equivalent to 230.04½ grams.

GOLD PIECE OF 20 EXCELENTES OF FERDINAND AND ISABELLA

Admiral of the Ocean Sea

Preface

This book arose out of a desire to know exactly where Columbus sailed on his Four Voyages, and what sort of seaman he was. No previous work on the Discoverer of America answers these questions in a manner to satisfy even an amateur seafarer. Most biographies of the Admiral might well be entitled "Columbus to the Water's Edge." The authors either cared little about the Discoverer's career on his chosen element, or expended so much space on unprofitable speculation about his birth, character and early life that no room was left to tell where and how he sailed. The earliest writers, such as Peter Martyr, Oviedo, Ferdinand Columbus and Las Casas, have more sense of proportion, but take too much knowledge for granted, and of course do not identify places by their modern names. Von Humboldt, Murdock and Irving cleared up a few points, and Charcot sized up Columbus's seamanship correctly, but neither Irving nor Charcot visited the West Indies, and the great Von Humboldt, with the universe for his field, had little time for this subject.

Popular interest in Columbus, which was slight in the colonial era, became progressively greater as the Americas won their independence and forced Europe to recognize their importance. The entire Western World joined in celebrating the four hundredth anniversary of 1492. European libraries and archives were searched for any and every scrap of contemporary information about the early voyages, and the Italian government's monumental source collection, the *Raccolta di Documenti e Studi,* was the imposing result. Navarrete's *Colección de los Viages* had, early in the century, presented the most important documents from Spanish archives, and from time to time investigators like Harrisse, Gould, Assereto, and the Duchess of Berwick and Alba made significant finds. Thus, material for the Four Voyages is both abundant and available; yet little of it has been used to any advantage. For no biographer of Columbus appears to have gone to sea in quest of light and truth. And you cannot write a story out of these fifteenth- and sixteenth-century narratives that means anything to a modern reader, merely by studying them in a library with the aid of maps. Such armchair navigation is both dull and futile. It may be compared with those ancient books on natural science that were compiled without field work or experimentation.

Francis Parkman, the greatest North American historian, was not content to study the documentary history of Canada in his Boston library. He followed the routes of the French explorers, camped in the primeval forest, and lived among primitive Indians. This field work, combined with historical imagination and a lively narrative style, gives Parkman's *History of France in the New World* a peculiar depth and vividness. It is no more flat land made of words out of other words on paper, but a fresh creation in three dimensions, a story in which the reader is conscious of space and light, of the earth underfoot, the sky overhead, and God in His Heaven.

That, in a modest way, is what I have tried to do for Columbus. One winter's sail in a chartered yawl along the line of the Windward and Leeward Islands provided me with a living commentary on the contemporary narratives of Columbus's Second Voyage, and proved that Parkman's outdoor methods could profitably be applied at sea. So I sought ways and means for following the routes of Columbus's other voyages under sail. Paul Hammond and a number of his friends and mine organized for that purpose the Harvard Columbus Expedition. We purchased and fitted out the barkentine *Capitana,* near enough to Columbus's larger ships in rig and burthen to enable us to cross the ocean under conditions very similar to those of his day, and to view islands and coasts as through his eyes. William D. Stevens contributed his 45-foot ketch *Mary Otis* as the *Niña* of our expedition. Departing separately in August and September, 1939, we dropped down near enough to the latitude of Columbus's first homeward passage to check his observations of weather, birds and gulfweed. At the Azores we met, and examined very thoroughly the island of Santa Maria where Columbus had unhappy experiences; then sailed by the track of his First Voyage to Lisbon, Cape St. Vincent and Palos. Thence by way of Sanlúcar and Cadiz we caught the winter northerlies to Porto Santo, Madeira and the Canary Islands, all associated with Columbus. Our ocean crossing from

Gomera to Trinidad was approximately on the route of his Third Voyage, and we made exactly the same Trinidad landfall on December 12, 1939, as he did on July 31, 1498. With somewhat more trepidation than his Journal exhibits, we sailed through the Boca de la Sierpe into the Gulf of Paria. On the northern (Venezuelan) shore of that gulf we ascertained the place where Columbus first made contact with the American continent, and where he took possession *por Castilla y por León*. Passing out through the Bocas del Dragón, we followed the route of the Third Voyage to Margarita, visited Cartagena, and joined the route of Columbus's Fourth Voyage at the entrance to the Gulf of Darien, where he took his last departure from the mainland. The somewhat confused accounts of the Fourth Voyage became clear as we reconnoitered the Caribbean shores of Panama and Costa Rica; and with the aid of a native sloop we effected the difficult landing at the mouth of the Rio Belén, where Columbus attempted a mainland settlement. After identifying the passage between Almirante Bay and Chiriqui Lagoon which Columbus expected would lead to the Indian Ocean, we called at his "Cariai" in Costa Rica, and proceeded to Jamaica, where our *Capitana* paid homage to the ghost of his, at her last resting place in St. Ann's or Santa Gloria Bay.

During the summer of 1940 Captain Stevens and I sailed *Mary Otis* along Columbus's course of the First Voyage from the San Salvador landfall through the Bahamas to Cuba, and along the beautiful Oriente Province to Cape Maisi. There we picked up the route of his Cuban exploring voyage of 1494. *Mary Otis* took us into Guantanamo Bay and Santiago de Cuba, around Cape Cruz, through El Jardín de la Reina and past the Sierra de Trinidad to Cienfuegos. We drew too much water to follow the remainder of that Columbian Voyage, and my reconnaissance of the "Province of Mangi" was successfully completed aboard a shoal-draught and hospitable Cuban gunboat.

On other occasions in 1938 and 1939 I sailed in government patrol boats, native sloops, or anything I could pick up, along the shores of Hispaniola, the Virgin Islands and Puerto Rico. Nicaragua and Honduras I had reserved for another voyage; but war conditions have indefinitely postponed that pleasure, and it seemed best to conclude this biography without completing the work of re-exploration.

Although I have not neglected the problems connected with the
nationality, birth, early life and objectives of Columbus, the emphasis
in this book is on what he did, where he went, and what sort of
seaman he was. I am greatly indebted to the works of marine archeologists such as Ernesto D'Albertis, Cesare Fernández Duro, my
patient correspondent D. Julio Guillén y Tato, and my late lamented
friend Capitão A. Fontoura da Costa, for a knowledge of the technical side of seafaring in 1492—the design and rig of vessels, how
they sailed, methods of navigation, and the routine and ritual of the
sea. I trust that my chapters on these subjects are clear and simple
enough so that anybody, seaman or landsman, can understand the
conditions of navigation in those days and appreciate the excellent
work that Columbus and his shipmates performed.

The reader may be disappointed at finding no "authentic portrait"
of Columbus; but none there is. He may also wonder why I have no
general chart showing the Four Voyages of Columbus out and home,
since other and less ambitious biographies of the Admiral generally
provide one. The reason again is that no authentic materials exist for
tracing the ocean crossings, except those of the First Voyage, and,
with some approximation, the outward passage of the Third. Of
these, especially the First, a careful study has been made by the
expert navigators of the Expedition, and new charts provided. For
the five other ocean crossings we know only the point of departure
and the landfall; any attempt to trace the actual course, considering
that the vessels were propelled by sail, would be pure guesswork.
But our sailing experience in the Caribbean has made it possible to
follow Columbus's routes along American coasts and among the
islands with reasonable accuracy, to mark his anchorages and identify the points that he named. A complete series of charts of Columbus's Caribbean voyages has been drafted under my direction by
Dr. Erwin Raisz of the Harvard Institute of Geographical Exploration and by my nephew Bertram Greene. These charts and diagrams,
representing an immense amount of labor and research, are copy-
righted and may not be reproduced without my permission.

Outside the monumental *Raccolta*, accurate printed texts of the
sources of Columbus's voyages are not easy to find, and trustworthy
translations (bad ones are plenty) do not exist. Accordingly I have
made my own translations, and these, with selected texts, will be

published separately in a volume entitled *Journals of Columbus and Other Documents on His Life and Voyages.*

The persons and organizations who have helped this work of historical reconstruction are so numerous that I cannot name them all. President Franklin D. Roosevelt and the Foreign Service of the United States; President Augusto S. Boyd and the government of the Republic of Panama; President Larcdo Diu and the government of the Republic of Cuba; the foreign offices and naval officials of Portugal, Spain, Colombia, Costa Rica, Haiti and the Dominican Republic; the Governors and Administrators of the Azorean Islands, Madeira, the Grand Canary, Gomera, Trinidad, Jamaica, the Virgin Islands, St. Croix, and of several islands in the Bahamas; the Historical, Scientific, Geographical and Columbian Societies of Lisbon, the Niebla, Las Palmas, Trinidad, Panama, Santiago de Cuba, Havana, and San José; and the United Fruit Company, all gave assistance of various kinds. Many port officials, scholars, antiquarians, and other gentlemen in these countries and islands co-operated in the most generous manner to aid us in acquiring the information that we sought, and entertained us splendidly ashore. The Carnegie Corporation, the Mellon Educational Foundation of Pittsburgh, the Milton Research Fund of Harvard University, and several firms and individuals contributed money, labor and materials to the Harvard Columbus Expedition. Among the individuals to whom I am particularly indebted are Mr. and Mrs. Paul Hammond for organizing the Expedition, William D. Stevens for the indispensable and ubiquitous *Mary Otis,* and my "staff" of secretaries—Captain John W. McElroy and Albert Harkness, Jr. (both seagoing), Dr. Milton V. Anastos (research), and Miss Florence Berlin (permanent). I wish also to thank collectively and severally the gentlemen of the Press in the United States, Portugal, Spain, Latin America and the British possessions in the West Indies, for their sympathetic and abundant publicity, which enabled us to meet local experts, and to acquire many important facts.

The present volume is a condensation of my two-volume *Admiral of the Ocean Sea,* published at the same time. All the notes have been omitted, and a good many pages of navigational data; a chapter on Ships and Sailing and one on the origin of syphilis have been summarized. Otherwise the two editions are identical. Readers who wish to learn my authority for this or that statement, or the exact source of a quotation, are respectfully referred to the two-volume edition, which is liberally annotated.

S. E. MORISON

HARVARD UNIVERSITY
1942

THE FIRST FORTY YEARS

— Así es — replicó Sansón —; pero uno es escribir como poeta, y otro como historiador: el poeta puede contar o cantar las cosas, no como fueron, sino como debían ser; y el historiador las ha de escribir, no como debían ser, sino como fueron, sin añadir ni quitar a la verdad cosa alguna.

I am of your opinion, said Samson; but it is one thing to write like a poet, and another thing to write like an historian. The poet can tell or sing of things, not as they were but as they ought to have been, whereas the historian must describe them, not as they ought to have been but as they were, without exaggerating or suppressing the truth in any particular.

— *Don Quixote* PART II CH. 3

CHAPTER I

Prologue

At the end of the year 1492 most men in Western Europe felt exceedingly gloomy about the future. Christian civilization appeared to be shrinking in area and dividing into hostile units as its sphere contracted. For over a century there had been no important advance in natural science, and registration in the universities dwindled as the instruction they offered became increasingly jejune and lifeless. Institutions were decaying, well-meaning people were growing cynical or desperate, and many intelligent men, for want of something better to do, were endeavoring to escape the present through studying the pagan past.

Islam was now expanding at the expense of Christendom. Every effort to recover the Holy Sepulchre at Jerusalem, touchstone of Christian prestige, had been a failure. The Ottoman Turks, after snuffing out all that remained of the Byzantine Empire, had overrun most of Greece, Albania and Serbia; presently they would be hammering at the gates of Vienna. For half a century each successive pope had proclaimed a new crusade, but Europe regarded these appeals to duty as a mere device to raise money; and no wonder, since papal diplomacy was as cynical as any. Innocent VIII even used a Turkish prince as hostage to extort money and support from the sultan in order to checkmate France, whose king was showing unmistakable signs of embarking on the easy adventure of invading Italy instead of the hard one of fighting Turks. One great scandal of Christendom, the great schism, had indeed been overcome, but only at the cost of suppressing reforms within the Church, thus rendering the greater and more permanent Protestant schism inevitable; and in 1492 the papacy touched bottom when Rodrigo Borgia, a corrupt ecclesiastical politician, was elected to the throne of Saint Peter as Alexander VI.

If one turned to the Holy Roman Empire, secular counterpart to the Catholic Church, the picture was no brighter. The amiable

but listless Emperor Frederick III, driven from his Austrian lands
by the king of Hungary, had finally retired to dabble in astrology
and alchemy; his son Maximilian was full of promise but short in
performance. In England the Wars of the Roses were over, but few
expected the House of Tudor to last long. Only in the Iberian
peninsula, in Portugal and Castile, were there signs of new life;
but these kingdoms were too much on the periphery of Europe to
alter the general picture of degeneracy and decay.

With the practical dissolution of the Empire and the Church's
loss of moral leadership, Christians had nothing to which they might
cling. The great principle of unity represented by emperor and
pope was a dream of the past that had not come true. Belief in
the institutions of their ancestors was wavering. It seemed as if the
devil had adopted as his own the principle "divide and rule."
Throughout Western Europe the general feeling was one of pro-
found disillusion, cynical pessimism and black despair.

One may catch the prevailing mood by reading the final pages
of the *Nuremberg Chronicle*. The colophon of this stately old folio,
dated July 12, 1493, declares that it contains "the events most
worthy of notice from the beginning of the world to the calamity
of our time." Lest any reader feel an unjustified optimism, the
Nuremberg chroniclers place 1493 in the Sixth or penultimate Age
of the world, and leave six blank pages on which to record events
from the date of printing to the Day of Judgment. Then begins a
prophecy of the Seventh and final Age, "in comparison with which
our age, in which iniquity and evil have increased to the highest
pitch, may be regarded as happy and almost golden." Only the
wicked will prosper, good men will fall into contempt and penury;
there will be no faith, no law, no justice, no peace, no humanity,
no shame and no truth. Gog and Magog "shall go out to deceive
the nations which are in the four quarters of the earth . . . to
gather them together to battle" (Revelation xx 8), war and civil
tumults will spread over the whole world, neighboring cities fall
to fighting one another, and conditions become so abominable that
no man can lead the good life. Then will be fulfilled the whole
screed of the Apocalypse: flood, earthquake, pestilence and famine;
crops will not grow nor fruit ripen; the springs will dry up and
waters flow with blood and bitterness, so that every fowl of the air,

beast of the field and fish of the sea will perish. The seventh angel will pour out the seventh vial, and the awful Day of Judgment, painted in the lurid colors of the Vision of Saint John, will conclude the history of a wicked world.

Such was the burden of the imprecatory sermons that Savonarola was then preaching to a complacent Florence. Such, one may say, was the common expectation of serious thinkers in 1492. Yet, even as the chroniclers of Nuremberg were correcting their proofs from Koberger's press, a Spanish caravel named *Niña* scudded before a winter gale into Lisbon, with news of a discovery that was to give old Europe another chance. In a few years we find the mental picture completely changed. Strong monarchs are stamping out privy conspiracy and rebellion; the Church, purged and chastened by the Protestant Reformation, puts her house in order; new ideas flare up throughout Italy, France, Germany and the northern nations; faith in God revives and the human spirit is renewed. The change is complete and astounding. "A new envisagement of the world has begun, and men are no longer sighing after the imaginary golden age that lay in the distant past, but speculating as to the golden age that might possibly lie in the oncoming future."*

Christopher Columbus belonged to an age that was past, yet he became the sign and symbol of this new age of hope, glory and accomplishment. His medieval faith impelled him to a modern solution: expansion. If the Turk could not be pried loose from the Holy Sepulchre by ordinary means, let Europe seek new means overseas; and he, Christopher the Christ-bearer, would be the humble yet proud instrument of Europe's regeneration. So it turned out, although not as he anticipated. The First Voyage to America that he accomplished with a maximum of faith and a minimum of technique, a bare sufficiency of equipment and a superabundance of stout-heartedness, gave Europe new confidence in herself, more than doubled the area of Christianity, enlarged indefinitely the scope for human thought and speculation, and "led the way to those fields of freedom which, planted with great seed, have now sprung up to the fructification of the world."

In his faith, his deductive methods of reasoning, his unquestioning acceptance of the current ethics, Columbus was a man of the

* Sir Charles Oman *On the Writing of History* p. 117.

Middle Ages, and in the best sense. In his readiness to translate thought into action, in lively curiosity and accurate observation of natural phenomena, in his joyous sense of adventure and desire to win wealth and recognition, he was a modern man. This dualism makes the character and career of Columbus a puzzle to the dull-witted, a delight to the discerning. It unlocks most of the so-called Columbus "mysteries," "questions" and "problems," which were neither mysteries, questions nor problems to his contemporaries, but recent creations of dull pedants without faith who never tasted the joy of sea adventure.

My main concern is with the Columbus of action, the Discoverer who held the key to the future in his hand, and knew in exactly which of a million possible keyholes it would turn the lock. I am content to leave his "psychology," his "motivation" and all that to others. Yet, as the caravels sail on tropic seas to new and ever more wonderful islands, and to high mountain-crested coasts of terra firma where the long surges of the trade winds eternally break and roar, I cannot forget the eternal faith that sent this man forth, to the benefit of all future ages. And so, writing in a day of tribulation both for Europe and for America, I venture to close my prologue by the prayer with which Columbus began his work: —

Jesus cum Maria
Sit nobis in via.

CHAPTER II

Genoa

1451–1473

"Et in fines mundi uerba eorum." Saltem temporibus nostris quibus mirabili ausu Christophori Columbi genuensis, alter pene orbis repertus est Christianorumque cetui aggregatus.

"And their words unto the ends of the world" (Psalm xix 4). At all events in our time, when by the marvelous daring of Christopher Columbus of Genoa, almost another world has been discovered and added to the company of Christians.

— GIUSTINIANI'S *Psalterium* of 1516

THERE is no mystery about the birth, family or race of Christopher Columbus. He was born in the ancient city of Genoa sometime between August 25 and the end of October, 1451, the son and grandson of woolen weavers who had been living in various towns of the Genoese Republic for at least three generations. As there was a good deal of moving about along the shores of the Mediterranean in the Middle Ages, some of the Discoverer's remote ancestors doubtless belonged to other races than the Italian. His long face, tall stature, ruddy complexion and red hair suggest a considerable share of "barbarian" rather than "Latin" blood, but do not prove anything; and he himself was conscious only of a Genoese origin. There is no more reason to doubt that Christopher Columbus was a Genoese-born Catholic Christian, steadfast in his faith and proud of his native city, than to doubt that George Washington was a Virginian-born Anglican of English race, proud of being an American.

This is not to say that Columbus was an Italian patriot in the modern sense. The people of proud Genoa, *Genova la Superba,* have always held themselves apart from other Italians. Columbus was so loyal a Genoese that he never became a naturalized Spaniard; but for him, "Italy" was a mere geographical expression. In the majorat or entail of his estate that he executed before departing on his Third Voyage to the New World, he charged his heirs "always to work for the honor, welfare and increase of the city of Genoa," and to maintain a house in Genoa for some member of the Colombo family, "so that he can live there honorably and have foot and root in that city as a native thereof . . . *because from it I came and in it I was born.*" And, "being as I was born in Genoa," his executors shall accumulate a fund in the famous Bank of St. George at Genoa, that "noble and powerful city by the sea."

Every contemporary Spaniard or Portuguese who wrote about Columbus and his discoveries calls him Genoese. Three contemporary Genoese chroniclers, and the commentator who is quoted at the head of this chapter, claim him as a compatriot. Every early map on which his nationality is recorded describes him as Genoese. Nobody in the Admiral's lifetime, or for three centuries after, had any doubt about his birthplace.

If, however, you suppose that these facts would settle the matter, you fortunately know little of the so-called "literature" on the "Columbus Question." By presenting farfetched hypotheses and sly innuendoes as facts, by attacking documents of proved authenticity as false, by fabricating others (such as the famous Pontevedra documents), and drawing unwarranted deductions from things that Columbus said or did, he has been presented as Castilian, Catalan, Corsican, Majorcan, Portuguese, French, German, English, Greek, and Armenian. It only remains for some American patrioteer to come forward and claim that Columbus was really an Indian, native to these shores, who was "blown across" (a favorite means of transportation in these fairy tales) and so knew his way home.

The history of Christopher's family and of his early life has to be pieced together from fifteen or twenty notarial records and municipal documents. When illiterate people, such as the Colombos were, made an agreement or settled a dispute or concluded an important business transaction, they went to a public notary, an educated gentleman who wrote down the essential facts and details in Latin. No signatures or marks were made; the notary put down who the witnesses were and what they said; his record was good in any court. Many of these records remained in the same notarial family for centuries, and some are still in private possession; but if the line died out they were deposited in the municipal archives, where most of those relating to the Columbus family have been found.

Giovanni Colombo, the Discoverer's paternal grandfather, was a weaver of woolen cloth from the village of Moconèsi in the Fontanabuona valley above Chiavari, a seaport about twenty miles east of Genoa. We first hear of him in 1429 in the town of Quinto, so called because located at the fifth milestone east of old Genoa. He was then apprenticing his son Domenico (Columbus's father), "aged about eleven," to a clothweaver from Brabant who lived in Genoa.

By 1440, several years after completing his apprenticeship, Domenico Colombo has become a master weaver, and hired a house just inside the Porta dell'Olivella, the eastern gate of Genoa. About 1445 he marries Susanna Fontanarossa, daughter of a weaver who lived in the valley of the Bisagno River, which the Olivella gate overlooks. She brought Domenico a little dowry, and (unless this was another Domenico Colombo, which is quite possible) he was appointed warder of the Porta dell'Olivella, at a salary of 84 Genoese pounds a year (about $160 in gold), out of which he had to pay assistants. It must have been in this house near the gate, in a quarter so rebuilt that the site cannot now be definitely fixed, that Christopher was born in September or October of 1451.

So Columbus's forty-first birthday fell during his great voyage of discovery. Very likely he did not remember the exact date, since boys and girls in Catholic countries celebrated the feast day of their patron saint rather than their own birthday. It would have been on June 25, the feast of Saint Christopher, that young Cristoforo attended Mass with his mother and received a little pocket money and a glass of wine from his father.

The story of Saint Christopher, familiar to every child in the Middle Ages, made Columbus's baptismal name far more significant to him than his patronymic. The famous saint was a great hulk of a pagan who, hearing of Christ, went forth in search of Him. A holy hermit said, "Perhaps Our Lord will show Himself to you if you fast and pray." "Fast I cannot," said Christopher, "and how to pray I know not; ask me something easier." So the hermit said, "Knowest thou that river without a bridge which can only be crossed at great peril of drowning?" "I do," said Christopher. "Very well, do thou who art so tall and strong take up thine abode by the hither bank, and assist poor travelers to cross; that will be very agreeable to Our Lord, and mayhap He will show Himself to thee." So Christopher built him a cabin by the riverbank and, with the aid of a tree trunk as staff, carried wayfarers across on his broad shoulders.

One night the big fellow was asleep in his cabin when he heard the voice of a Child cry, "Christopher! come and set me across." Out he came, staff in hand, and took the Infant on his shoulders. But as he waded through the river the Child's weight increased so that it became almost intolerable, and he had to call forth all his mighty strength to avoid falling and struggle through to the other bank. "Well now, my little fellow," said he, "thou hast put me in great danger, for thy burden waxed so great that had I borne the whole world on my back, it could have weighed no more than thou." "Marvel not, Christopher," replied the Child, "for thou hast borne upon thy back the whole world and Him who created it. I am the Christ whom thou servest in doing good; and as proof of my words, plant that staff near thy cabin, and tomorrow it shall be covered with flowers and fruit." The saint did as he was bid, and found his staff next day transformed into a beautiful date palm.

This story would certainly have gone home to the boy Christopher who was father to Columbus the man we know. He conceived it his destiny to carry the divine word of that Holy Child across the mighty ocean to countries steeped in heathen darkness. Many years elapsed and countless discouragements were surmounted before anyone would afford him means to take up the burden. Once assumed, it often became intolerable, and often he staggered under it; but never did he set it down until his appointed work was done. We may fairly say that the first step toward the discovery of America was taken by the parents of Columbus when they caused him to be baptized Cristoforo in some ancient church of Genoa, one day in the late summer or early fall of 1451.

As Domenico and Susanna had now been married six years, it is probable that Christopher was not the eldest child; but if he had any older brothers and sisters they died young. Bartholomew, the future Adelantado of the Indies, was at least a year or two younger than Christopher. There was a brother named Giovanni Pellegrino who died when a young man, and a sister named Bianchinetta about whom almost nothing is known. The youngest brother, Giacomo, must have been Christopher's junior by seventeen years; for there is record of his apprenticeship to a clothweaver in 1484 at the age of sixteen. Toward Giacomo, better known as Diego (the Spanish equivalent), Christopher felt the affection that an elder brother often does for the baby of the family. He took him on his Second Voyage, and after ascertaining the young man to be a failure as a seaman and a colonist, helped him to obtain holy orders, and made futile efforts to procure a Spanish bishopric for him from the Queen. Columbus's son Diego was probably named after this uncle.

In 1455, when Christopher was four years old, his parents removed to a house with a courtyard and garden near the Porta Sant' Andrea. A modern house on the same foundation is now marked as the *Casa di Colombo*.

Domenico Colombo was not a journeyman weaver dependent on wages, but a master clothier (to use the old English term), who owned one or more looms, bought his own wool, sold the finished cloth, and taught apprentice boys their trade. As a citizen of Genoa and member of the local gild of clothiers, he had a respectable position in the lower middle class. On ceremonial occasions, when the brethren marched to a corporate Mass in their own chapel of the Cathedral, he probably displayed the arms (blue bend on a gold field with red chief) which the Admiral afterwards quartered with the arms of Castile; members of trade gilds in the Italian cities often used just such a simple coat as this.

Christopher's mother is a shadowy figure, but the personality of his father emerges from the dry records. Domenico had his son's optimism, without his will. He was always making promises that he was unable to fulfill, buying goods for which he was unable to pay, starting sidelines like cheese and wine instead of sticking to his loom. We happen to know the name of the cheesemonger who married his daughter Bianchinetta, because he had to sue Domenico for the promised dowry. Although a poor provider for his family, Domenico must have been a popular and plausible sort of fellow to obtain so much property as he did on credit, and to be appointed on committees of his gild. He was the kind of father who would shut up shop when trade was poor and take the boys fishing; and the sort of wine seller who was his own best customer.

For fifteen years the records tell us nothing of the Colombos. Christopher grew tall and his red hair made him very conspicuous around his eighteenth birthday; Bartholomew was in his early teens. These two famous brothers were wool carders rather than weavers in their youth according to the Genoese chroniclers. Very likely they carded raw wool that their father bought, and their mother spun it into yarn, ready for the loom when properly dyed. Then, like as not, it was mother and boys who had to do the weaving, while Domenico sat drinking with boon companions.

Early in 1470 Domenico Colombo was placed on a committee by his gild to examine the rules and regulations of the master clothiers of Savona, with a view to adopting them in Genoa. Apparently this investigation convinced him that trade was better in Savona, since by the first of March he had removed thither with loom and family and an apprentice. We know that his side business there was retailing wine, for he is described in one document as *tabernarius*, and on October 31, 1470, son Christopher, "over 19 years of age," acknowledged a debt of over forty-eight Genoese pounds in settlement of a bill for wines delivered to him and his father. Christopher had attained his majority according to Genoese law, and as a hard-working, steady-going young man he was considered better security than his father.

The next traces of Christopher in the notarial records are on March 20, 1472, when he witnessed a will at Savona, and on August 26, 1472, when he and his father jointly contracted with a wool merchant to purchase a considerable quantity of wool, and pay for it in cloth. Possibly Christopher had been at sea in 1471; if so, he was now standing by at the parental loom. He certainly lived at Savona long enough to make one good friend in a superior class, Michele de Cuneo, who accompanied him on the Second Voyage; the island of Saona off Hispaniola is a record of their friendship.

On August 7, 1473, Christopher joined with both parents and his brother Giovanni Pellegrino in an agreement to sell the house near the Olivella gate at Genoa, and in 1474 "Dominicus de Quinto Ianue, habitator Savone, lanerius" leases land from the cathedral chapter of Savona. After that, we have no trace of the family for nine years. During the interval Susanna and Giovanni Pellegrino died, and Domenico moved back to Genoa with little Giacomo and Bianchinetta, taking up his residence in the Porta Sant' Andrea house. The old man, through with weaving, and living on remittances from his sons in Portugal, found the house was too big for him. So "Domenico Colombo son of Giovanni, citizen of Genoa, formerly clothweaver," leased the garden and most of the house to a shoemaker in 1483, reserving for himself the garret and some space on the ground floor. A few years later, Domenico's creditors put pressure on him to sell the house, which a certain cheesemonger offered to purchase for 250 Genoese pounds. But as Susanna had held the title, Christopher and his brothers had an interest in the property, and Domenico in his capacity as "father and legal administrator of Christopher, Bartholomew and Giacomo, sons to the said Domenico and heirs of the late Susanna their mother," was able to resist a sale on the ground that the price was insufficient. His name as witness to a document of September 30, 1494, is the last trace that we have of Christopher's father. Giacomo by that time had left home to follow his brother's fortune, Bianchinetta was married, and the old fellow probably died within a couple of years; for he is not mentioned in Christopher's majorat of 1498. But Domenico was not forgotten, for Christopher and Bartholomew named the new capital city of Santo Domingo after the patron saint of their father.

Besides these documents from which we may glean facts on Christopher's early life, there are others which identify the Discoverer as the son of Domenico the wool weaver, beyond the possibility of doubt. For instance, Domenico had a brother Antonio, like him a respectable member of the lower middle class in Genoa. Antonio had three sons: Matteo, Amigeto and Giovanni, who was generally known as Giannetto, the Genoese equivalent of "Johnny." Johnny like Christopher gave up a humdrum occupation to follow the sea. In 1496 the three brothers met in a notary's office at Genoa

and agreed that Johnny should go to Spain and seek out his first
cousin "Don Cristoforo de Colombo, Admiral of the King of
Spain," each contributing one third of the traveling expenses.
This quest for a job was highly successful. The Admiral gave
Johnny command of a caravel on the Third Voyage to America,
and entrusted him with confidential matters as well.

Such are the bare facts that we have of the life of Christopher
Columbus to the age of twenty-two, and of his family. It gives
us little on which to base conclusions as to his early home and
character. Assuming that the boy whom we do not know was
father to the man of recorded history, he was a proud and sensitive
lad, faithful in his religious duties, following a humble trade in
order to help support his parents, but eager for adventure and
mystically assured of his high mission. We may picture him if we
like as a poet did, a little fair-complexioned, red-haired boy dreaming the long thoughts of youth: —

> Now watching high on a mountain cornice,
> And steering now from a purple cove,
> Now pacing mute by ocean's rim.

Or we may imagine him as a leader in the rough-and-tumble street
life of Genoa, and a flaming spark in his early twenties at Savona.
One thing is certain, he had very little if any schooling.

Ferdinand's assertion that his father studied at the University
of Pavia is disproved not only by the well-preserved matriculation
records of that ancient foundation, but by the internal evidence
of Christopher's Latin, which shows that it was learned after
Spanish had become the language of his thought. The absence of
Italian in the preserved writings of Columbus, excepting for a
stray word or phrase, is a great talking point of the *Colón Español*
sect. The earliest bit of writing that can possibly be his, a postil or
marginal note dated 1481 on one of his books, is in bad Spanish
mingled with Portuguese; all his letters, even those to Genoese
friends and to the Bank of St. George, are in Spanish; and when
he annotated an Italian translation of Pliny's *Natural History* in
later life, all but one of his postils are Spanish translations of the
Italian text; that one is in very bad Italian. None of the authors

to whom he alludes wrote in Italian; the beauty of the *Divine Comedy*, with Ulysses' last voyage and the play of light on the ocean, apparently was unknown to Columbus.

Actually the lack of Italian in Columbus's writings is good evidence of a Genoese birth, rather than the contrary. The Genoese dialect of his day, even more than in ours (when a Genoese speaking it in a trial at Rome around 1910 had to have an Italian interpreter), was very different from Tuscan or classical Italian; even more than the Venetian and Neapolitan dialects. It was a language of common speech that was never written. A poor boy of Genoa would not have known Italian, unless he had learned it at school. Christopher undoubtedly left home almost if not completely illiterate, and when he finally learned to read and write used the Castilian language because it was that of his new associates. Many thousands of peasant Italian emigrants have done just that. Arriving in their New World home illiterate, they learn to read and write in English, Spanish or Portuguese, according to the country of their residence, and eventually forget the dialect which they were brought up to speak.

A careful analysis of Columbus's writings has recently been made by the most eminent living Spanish philologist, Ramón Menéndez Pidal. The Discoverer did not write Jewish-Spanish, or Italian-Spanish, but Portuguese-Spanish. To the end of his life, he wrote Castilian with Portuguese spellings, especially in the vowels, which prove that he spoke Portuguese before he learned Castilian. During the decade when he based his voyages on Lisbon, Castilian was the favorite language among the educated classes of Portugal, into which Columbus married; a little later Gil Vicente wrote his plays in Castilian, and even Camoëns used that language for his sonnets. So an ambitious young man such as we know Christopher to have been would naturally have chosen the more literary and widely expanded language. Possibly he wrote Portuguese as well; but only short notes of his have been preserved for the period before he went to Spain, and they are all in Castilian.

What effect if any did Christopher's residence of some twenty-two years on Genoese territory have on his future career? Genoa was certainly a place to give any active lad a hankering for sea adventure. The Ligurian Republic bathes her breasts in the sea, and spreads her arms to embrace it, one toward Savoy and the other toward Tuscany. *Genova la superba* looks southward to a clean horizon, drinking in the sun which circles seaward all winter and sets behind Monte Beguia at the summer solstice. The *libeccio* or southwest wind comes in freshened by a long journey across the Mediterranean, and gives the terraced hills above the coast sufficient moisture for tillage, vineyards and pastures. Shipbuilding went on in little coves and harbors all along the shore; great galleys and carracks were constantly clearing for and arriving from the Aegean, the Levant and Northern Africa. Although the Republic had seen better days (as had most republics at that time), she cherished traditions of navigators like the Vivaldi who sought the ocean route to India by way of Africa as early as 1291, of Malocello, one of the discoverers of the Canaries; and Andrea Doria was not yet born. Genoa had a noted school of map makers who supplied portolan charts to half the Mediterranean, and to whom the Portuguese came when they wanted their new African possessions charted. One can well imagine young Christopher picking up the rudiments of map making in one of these shops, for he and his brother later plied that art in Lisbon. One may picture him looking wistfully out on the harbor from the weave-room in the Porta Sant' Andrea house, or letting his eyes linger on the broad sweep of Mediterranean from the home in Savona where he worked at a loathed trade. Here, too, he may even have conceived his grand enterprise; for the achievements of a great man are often but the fulfillment of his youthful dreams.

Such speculations are for the poet or novelist, not the historian. All we now know and all we shall probably ever know of Columbus's life to the age of twenty-two is that he helped his parents at Genoa and Savona in their respectable trade of woolen weaver, that he had no schooling and no privileges; yet his youth was neither so hard nor his life so bitter as to cause him to forsake allegiance to "that noble and powerful city by the sea."

CHAPTER III

Cheerfully at Sea

1473–1477

And cheerfully at sea
successe you still entise
to get the pearle and gould . . .
— MICHAEL DRAYTON
To the Virginian Voyage (1606)

WHEN did Christopher first go to sea? His own statements seem contradictory. "At a very tender age," he wrote to the Sovereigns about 1501, "I entered upon the sea sailing, and so have I continued to this day. That art [of navigation] inclines him who follows it to want to know the secrets of this world. Already 40 years have passed that I have been in this employment." In his Journal for December 21, 1492, he remarks, "I have followed the sea for 23 years without leaving it for any time worth reckoning." And in another place, according to Ferdinand, "he says that he began to sail at 14 years of age." Antonio Gallo, a Genoese chronicler who knew the Columbus family, says that Christopher and his brother Bart "puberes deinde facti" (which may mean anything from fourteen to twenty-one years old), "set forth on voyages after the manner of their people."

So, according to Columbus's own statements, he went to sea in 1461, 1465, or 1469–1470; according to Gallo's, at some date between 1465, when he was fourteen, and 1472, when he was twenty-one. Yet as we have seen, there is documentary evidence of his having been at Genoa on September 22 and October 31, 1470, at Savona on March 20 and August 26, 1472, and also on August 7, 1473. What about it?

Suppose we accept Madariaga's invitation for once, and "leave the dusty papers and come back to flesh and spirit." We are not

to hold a seaman rigidly to these memorial additions and subtrac-
tions, or to assume that Christopher's foot never crossed a gun-
wale when he was a weaver. At what point would a seacoast-bred
boy who eventually becomes a sailor, say that he first went to sea?
When he began to play about with boats, made his first overnight
sail, received his first pay for bearing a hand, or departed on his
first long voyage? The writer might boast (and doubtless has) of
having followed the sea "these forty year" if he counted back to
his first cruise in a catboat around Mount Desert. But the forty
years would have to be cut down to four, if his first real voyage
in the wake of Columbus were meant. He recalls one old shell-
back in a Maine post office, reading aloud a postcard from a lad
who had just left home in a coasting schoonor. "Arrived safely in
Boston," it said, "had a fine voyage." "Voyage!" snorted the old
Cape Horner — "Two nights out!"

Christopher was living in a seafaring community, where every
healthy boy took all the sailing he could get. Fishing trips, out at
evening with the land breeze, net sardines all night by flaring
torches under the stars, and race the fleet home at dawn with the
fresh *libeccio* to be first to market with your catch. Short trips in a
packet *fusta* eastward to Nervi, Portofino, Rapallo; westward to
Cogoleto and Savona. Maybe a run over to Corsica and back; a
great adventure, and his first taste of that lovely experience of
seeing a high, jagged island rise above the ocean's rim like a row
of little islands, watching them run together into one island, and
the color change from blue to green, and the white specks on the
shore become houses, and anchoring in a strange harbor where the
men jabber at you in a weird dialect and (so Skipper says) are all
pirates anyway if you give them a chance, and the wonderful girls
ashore, so much more beautiful and outgoing than those of the
old home town.

Most of the commerce along the Ligurian littoral was sea-borne;
and if Christopher liked sailing, it would have been natural for his
father to send him along the coast to buy wool, wine and cheeses,
and sell his cloth. Perhaps Domenico kept at Savona and Christopher commanded a little lateen-rigged packet, which ran up to
Genoa every week or two and carried freight for the neighbors. This

kind of coastwise experience is not to be despised. Whoever can
handle a small sailboat is on his way to command a great vessel; he
who can cope with a sudden squall off the mountains is half prepared to meet a storm at sea.

Ferdinand, the Admiral's son, did not pretend to know when
or under what circumstances his father first went to sea; for the
Admiral died, says he, "before I made so bold as to ask him to give
an account of such matters; or, to speak more truly, at that time
I as a lad was far from being troubled by such thoughts." But in
that *omnium gatherum,* his fourth chapter, Ferdinand quotes from
a now lost letter to the Sovereigns, written from Hispaniola in
January 1495. In order to illustrate the chances and errors of
pilotage, Columbus says: —

"It happened to me that king René (whom God hath taken)
sent me to Tunis to capture the galleass *Fernandina;* and being off
the island of S. Pietro near Sardinia I was told there were two ships
and a carrack with the said galleass, which disturbed my people,
and they resolved to go no further, but to sail right back to Marseilles and pick up another ship and more people. I, seeing that
nothing could be done against the force of their wills without
some stratagem, yielded to their desires, and then, 'changing the
feed' of the needle, made sail when night fell, and on the following
day at sunup we found ourselves off Cape Carthage while all aboard
were certain we were on our way to Marseilles."

To a mariner, this is one of the most intriguing passages in all
the writings of Columbus. The Admiral declares that as a young
captain he doctored the compass in some way so that when the
card read NW by N (the course for Marseilles), his ship was really
sailing SE by S (the course for Tunis). Is that possible? I should
say it was, although there is no record in all marine literature, to
my knowledge, of such a hoax being pulled on seamen; Columbus's
"phony" reckoning on the First Voyage was nothing in comparison.
Common seamen are very dumb about telling the stars, and the
wind might have changed so that they would have noticed nothing
wrong about the ship's direction with reference to the waves. On
the dry-card compasses of that day the needle, fastened below,
could be reversed; or the captain with his lodestone could have
destroyed its polarity and remagnetized the other end.

Another difficulty is the distance. From S. Pietro Island to Cape Guardia, which the ship would have to pass before Cape Carthage, is 130 nautical miles; and from Toro Island south of S. Pietro to the nearest point of Africa in a southeasterly direction is 110 nautical miles. No ship of that day could have made Cape Carthage in a night's sail. But we may allow Columbus a little exaggeration; perhaps they did not raise the African coast until noon. One forgets these things after a few years. Always make an old sailor verify phenomenal day's runs and ocean passages from his log!

The story does fit in with the history of René d'Anjou, *le bon roi René* of happy memory. Although his troops were thrown out of Genoa in 1461, he continued to charter Genoese galleys for the defense of Provence against the Barbary corsairs, and for his various enterprises against Catalonia. Down to 1472 he was supporting a Catalan rebellion against Juan II of Aragon, whose throne was claimed by his son; and the name *Fernandina* of the galleass suggests that she was Aragonese. As we have seen in the previous chapter, there is no record of young Christopher between October 31, 1470, when he acknowledges a bill for wine in Genoa, and March 20, 1472. Again there is no record of him between August 26, 1472, and August 7, 1473. During the first interval of fifteen months, when René was still at war with the King of Aragon, Christopher could have made this voyage aboard a Genoese armed ship in the Angevin service. The one impossible circumstance is Columbus's claim to have been the captain. No young fellow of about twenty who had been carding and weaving wool most of his life could so quickly have risen to command. I suspect that Christopher was really a foremast hand on René's ship, and one of those who discovered the trick played on them when Cape Carthage hove into sight. When relating the incident a quarter-century later in a letter to his Sovereigns, he promoted himself to captain, as more appropriate to his then dignity of Admiral.

If serving René afforded Columbus his first sea adventure, an expedition of his native city for the relief of Chios was the next. Twice on his First Voyage of Discovery, in Cuba and in Hispaniola, he describes the local gumbo-limbo tree (quite inaccurately) as the lentisk, "which I have seen in the island of Chios in the Archipelago," from which the profitable gum mastic was (and still is) extracted.

Chios had been captured in 1346 by a fleet of Genoese privateers, whose owners were compensated by the Republic with a monopoly of the land, trade and revenues of the island. These concessionaires formed a corporation called the Maona, which governed and exploited Chios exactly as the seventeenth century joint-stock companies of France, England and the Netherlands exploited their several portions of North America. Control of Chios gave the Maona a virtual monopoly of mastic, which at that time, owing to its reputed medicinal qualities, was relatively far more valuable than today. The Maona made immense profits until the Turks appeared. Thereafter, what with tribute money and defense, the corporation had to borrow large sums from the Bank of St. George.

Three of the five Genoese individuals or families to whom Columbus made legacies in his last will and testament were Luis Centurione, "merchant of Genoa," his son-in-law Battista Spinola, and the heirs of Centurione's partner, Paolo di Negro. The house of Centurione was one of those merchant-banking concerns which were so important in the early development of finance. It had branches throughout the Mediterranean, in Spain and Portugal, and had even sent an expedition to the interior of Africa in search of gold. Columbus is known to have been employed by them in 1478–1479, and it seems likely that they took him to Chios. For in 1474 Gioffredo Spinola fitted out at Savona a ship named *Roxana* for trade with Chios and defense against the Turks; and her records, still preserved, mention that she carried besides seamen and soldiers a number of "workmen of Savona" including *tessitori*, weavers. Surely Columbus was one of these. How could he have passed up the chance? And in 1475 another and more formidable expedition, including ships of Nicolò Spinola and Paolo di Negro, left Genoa for Chios.

On one or the other of these voyages Columbus must have sailed. We may picture him in the crew of a Genoese carrack or galleass, passing Scylla and Charybdis in the Straits of Messina, stretching across the Ionian Sea to Cape Matapan and through the Cervi Channel behind Cythera, picking up the white columns of the Temple of Poseidon on Cape Sunium, negotiating the difficult currents

in the D'Oro channel between Andros and Euboea, and then with
luck catching a fresh norther for the last leg to Cape Mastika,
Chios. It was on these voyages, if not under René, that he learned
to "hand, reef and steer," to estimate distances by eye, to let go
and weigh anchors properly, and all the other elements of seamanship. Christopher learned seamanship the old way, the hard way
and the only way, in the school of experience. Book-larnin' such as
arithmetic and a few notions of "astrology" would come later and
ashore.

Not long after he had returned from Chios, Columbus joined a
fleet that played into the hands of destiny by casting him up on
the shore of Portugal. In May 1476, when most of the Mediterranean
nations were at war, Genoa organized a big convoy in order to
market a quantity of Chian mastic in Lisbon, England and Flanders.
Three galleasses and a big armed ship, belonging to the Spinolas,
Di Negro and one of their associates, made up the bulk of this
fleet. A fifth vessel named *Bechalla,* a Flemish *urca* (the type the
English called "cog"), manned largely by men of Savona, was
probably the one on which Columbus sailed. His name is not found
on the list of officers or passengers, so he must have been a common
seaman. The fleet set sail from Noli on May 31, worked its way
westward and passed safely through the Straits. On August 13,
1476, when they were off the southern coast of Portugal near
Lagos, not far from Cape St. Vincent, they were suddenly attacked
by a Franco-Portuguese war fleet of thirteen or more vessels commanded by a famous naval hero, Guillaume de Casenove. Genoa
and France were supposed to be at peace, but as *Bechalla* flew
the flag of Burgundy with which Louis XI was at war, Casenove
regarded the whole fleet as his legitimate booty. The Genoese
proved no easy prey. Three ships grappled with their opposite
numbers, the other two engaged the rest of the enemy, and all day
the battle raged hot and heavy. By nightfall three Genoese ships
and four of the enemy had gone down, hundreds of men were
drowned, and the surviving vessels were glad to sheer off and seek
the nearest friendly port for repairs. Columbus fought on one of
the vessels, presumably the *Bechalla,* that went down; he leaped
into the sea, grasped a sweep that floated free, and by pushing it
ahead of him and resting on it when he was exhausted (for he had

been wounded in the battle) he managed to reach the shore, over six miles distant. The people of Lagos treated the survivors kindly, and Columbus eventually made his way to Lisbon where he was taken in by some member of the local Genoese colony, and cured of his wounds.

One more adventurous voyage Christopher made before he entered a new career in the country on whose hospitality he had been so fortuitously cast. In one of the Admiral's notes, says Ferdinand, which he wrote to prove that the torrid and the arctic zones were inhabitable, he says: —

"I sailed in the year 1477, in the month of February, a hundred leagues beyond the island of *Tile,* whose northern part is in latitude 73° N and not 63° as some would have it be; nor does it lie on the meridian where Ptolemy says the west begins, but much further west. And to this island, which is as big as England, come English with their merchandise, especially they of Bristol. And at the season when I was there the sea was not frozen, but the tides were so great that in some places they rose 26 *braccia,** and fell as much in depth."

Now, what are we to make out of this? Tile (Thule) meant Iceland, that is certain. Christopher, arriving penniless in Lisbon, would naturally have shipped at the first chance that offered. There is known to have been a lively trade between Lisbon, the Azores, Bristol and Iceland at that time. Latitude 63° 30', not 73°, is right for the southern coast of Iceland; but Columbus never was much good at finding latitude, and presumably his captain on this voyage was no better. Columbus certainly visited Galway in Ireland, a natural port of call on Iceland voyages, for on the margin of his copy of Aeneas Sylvius's *Historia Rerum* he wrote, "Men of Cathay which is toward the Orient have come hither. We have seen many remarkable things, especially in Galway of Ireland, a man and a woman of extraordinary appearance in two boats adrift" — flat-faced Finns or Lapps, probably. "The author says that the northern ocean is neither frozen nor unnavigable."

The only incident in this Iceland voyage that sticks in one's crop is the 50-foot tides. Such can be found at only two or three

* A Genoese *braccio* was equivalent to 22.9 inches.

places in the world; the spring range at Reykjavik is only 13 feet.
It would be time and effort wasted to find an explanation of this.
"They who go down to the sea in ships, and occupy their business
in great waters" see many incredible "wonders in the deep." Old
seafarers know that the psalmist spoke the truth. We do not talk
about such things nowadays because we know they are just not so.
In Columbus's day anything was possible, and every apparent
monster or marvel was reported. There is no more reason to reject the Iceland voyage because of this "whopper" on the tides
than to reject Columbus's third transatlantic voyage because he
reported an enlarged polar distance of the North Star, as he was
sailing over a breastlike swelling in mid-ocean.

One more question remains unanswered. Did Columbus gather
any information in Iceland that was useful for his Great Enterprise?
A new "Nordic" myth to that effect is now in the process of being built up. Columbus, it is hinted (then argued, finally asserted
as a proved fact), obtained information in Iceland about Greenland and Leif Ericsson's Vinland; that was his "secret." Vinland,
the Norsemen's land of wild grapes, was what he proposed to re-
discover by cutting across the Atlantic.

Information about Vinland would certainly have been welcomed by Columbus; but any such would assuredly have been
inserted by Ferdinand in his tenth chapter, where all the mythical
and "reported" islands mentioned in his father's notes are thrown
together. Since Vinland is not there, we may be sure that Columbus
never heard of it. In other words, if we accept Ferdinand's positive
evidence of the Iceland voyage, we must also accept his negative
evidence that Columbus found no useful information there. The
Vinland story was not likely to come his way, unless he had learned
Icelandic and attended saga-telling parties ashore. Greenland,
however, he would most probably have heard of, for Iceland had
only recently lost touch with the Norse colony there, and there
are a few mentions of it in pre-1492 literature. Part of the new
"Nordic" build-up is to point out that Greenland is America,
Greenland lies west of Iceland; so Greenland showed Columbus the
way. But Greenland is always represented on pre-Columbian maps
as a peninsula of Northwest Asia coming out over Iceland, and as
such it had no significance for Columbus. Nor was he interested

in Greenland's leading products, white falcons and walrus tusks. Consequently there is no reason to suppose that Columbus got anything out of his Iceland voyage but experience and adventure, plenty of both.

Christopher had certainly not been idle since leaving the paternal loom. A voyage from Genoa to Marseilles and Tunis, one or two from Genoa to Chios, a voyage outside the Straits that ended in a sea fight and swimming ashore, and a voyage to Ireland, Iceland and parts north. He was now prepared for bigger things; perhaps the Great Enterprise was already simmering in his active brain.

CHAPTER IV

Lusitania

1477-1485

Eis aqui, quasi cume da cabeça
De Europa toda, o reino lusitano;
Onde a terra se acaba e o mar começa,
E onde Febo repousa no oceano.

Behold her seated here, both head and key
of Europe all, the Lusitanian queen;
where endeth land and where beginneth sea;
where Phoebus goeth down in ocean green.

— CAMOËNS *Lusiads* iii 20

B Y THE spring of 1477 Columbus was back in Lisbon, where he had first arrived the previous fall, after drying his clothes and recovering from the sea fight off Cape St. Vincent.

This lucky landing in Portugal was the turning point in Christopher's career, for chance had washed him ashore in the world-center of oceanic voyaging and discovery. He was among people who could teach him everything he was eager to learn: Portuguese and Castilian, the languages of far-ranging seamen; Latin to read the geographical works of the past; mathematics and astronomy for celestial navigation; shipbuilding and rigging; and above all, discovery.

Portugal, the ancient Lusitania, was then the liveliest and most go-ahead country in Europe. She alone had been enlarging the bounds of the known world during this tag end of the Middle Ages. Portugal not only discovered and peopled the Azores, where no human beings had ever lived before; for almost half a century she had been sending vessels further and further south along the West African coast. *Os rudos marinheiros,* the rough mariners of

Camoëns, had proved that tropic seas were navigable and lands on the equator habitable. They had dispelled the myth of *mare tenebrosum,* the "green sea of gloom" of the Arabs. They were learning to find their way by the stars, and had acquired such confidence in ocean navigation that every few years a fresh attempt was made to discover new lands beyond the Azores.

INCIDENT IN A VOYAGE OF SAINT BRENDAN
From the Piri Reis Map of 1513

The Infante Dom Henrique* was the initiator of this forward movement. Men before him had the spirit of discovery; he organized discovery. His headquarters were on Cape St. Vincent, the

---

* Prince Henry the Navigator to English writers, a title invented in the nineteenth century.

southwestern promontory of Portugal and of Europe, only a few
miles from where Columbus swam ashore. As the prevailing winds
there are northerly, galleys and sailing vessels bound from Southern to Northern Europe used to anchor in Sagres roadstead just
south of the cape, awaiting a favorable slant. On the desolate wind-
blown cliffs overhanging Sagres Roads, a natural exchange post
for marine information, the prince built himself a town that included everything needed to supply and attract seamen, including
an information service that made this lonely settlement ancestor
to every marine observatory and hydrographic office of today.
D. Henrique procured all the charts and *roteiros* or sailing directions
that he could find of the known world, mathematicians who encouraged seafarers to strike out from the shore into deep water,
and pilots who were competent to find their way back. Young,
daring and enterprising masters were encouraged to enter his
service, and from the harbor of Lagos, a few miles down the
coast, their ships were dispatched to destinations unknown.

On the Catalan and Majorcan maps that he procured, Prince
Henry found a chain of islands well out in the ocean beyond Portugal. These represented nothing more definite than the legend of
Saint Brendan, the seagoing Irish saint of the sixth century whose
saga of ocean voyaging was one of the most popular stories of the
Middle Ages. Much as Columbus stumbled on a New World when
in search of the Indies, so the captains of the Infante, when searching for the mythical St. Brendan Isles, found the Azores. Seven of
them had been discovered by 1439, and in 1452 far-flung Flores
and Corvo, the latter only a little over a thousand miles from
Labrador, were discovered by Diogo de Teive with a Spanish
pilot who lived long enough to encourage Columbus. These beautiful and fertile islands, seven hundred to almost a thousand miles
offshore, were promptly settled by Portuguese and Flemings.
Madeira and the near-by Porto Santo, which had been discovered
in the previous century, were colonized by order of the Infante in
1418; and the proprietor of the smaller island, Bartholomew Perestrello, was the father-in-law of Columbus. The Cape Verde Islands
were discovered by a Venetian and a Genoese in the service of the
Prince between 1456 and 1459.

Even more closely integrated with the discovery of America were the African voyages made under Prince Henry's direction. For "above all," says his admiring chronicler Azurara, "was this prince bound to attempt the discovery of things which were hidden from other men, and secret." His first objective was to find out what lay around Cape Não or Nun on the western bulge of Africa; but that was no easy matter.

"Although many set out — and they were men who had won fair renown by their exploits in the trade of arms — none dared go beyond this cape. . . . And this, to tell the truth, was not by reason of any lack of courage or good will, *but because they had to do with a thing entirely novel,* which was yet mingled with ancient legends which had existed for generations among the mariners of the Spains.* And although these legends were deceitful, the idea of discovering if they were seemed full of menace; and it was doubtful who would be the first to be willing to risk his life in such an adventure."

Year after year vessels were dispatched by the Prince with orders to find what lay beyond Cape Nun; year after year they returned to Lagos with one excuse or another for not passing it. But "the Infante always welcomed with great patience the captains of the ships which he had sent to seek out these countries, never showing them any resentment, listening graciously to the tale of their adventures, and rewarding them as those who were serving him well. And immediately he sent them back again to make the same voyage." Princely persistence was finally rewarded when Gil Eannes rounded the cape in 1434, and found that the reputed terrors of the ocean south of 28° North Latitude did not exist. Within a few years ships had gone far enough to capture Negro slaves and trade for gold dust. The Portuguese erected a fort and trading factory on Arguin Island near latitude 20° N a few years later, and by 1460, when the Infante died, his caravels had passed

---

* A punning proverb of the Portuguese put it neatly: —

Quem passar o Cabo de Não
Ou voltera ou não.

When old Cape Nun heaves into sight
Turn back me lad, or else — good night!

This was not the modern Cape Nun, but either Cape Bojador, or the one next south of it. "The Spains," as used before 1500, meant all the kingdoms of the Iberian Peninsula.

the site of Dakar, and were within hailing distance of Sierra Leone, only ten degrees above the equator.

It is still a matter of controversy whether or not D. Henrique looked toward reaching India by circumnavigating Africa, and whether the Pope, when granting Portugal in 1456 exclusive jurisdiction over the coast of Guinea "and past that southern shore all the way to the Indians," meant the real India or only the "Hither India" of Prester John. That mythical Christian potentate was supposed to hold sway somewhere in Asia or Africa. The substance behind this legend was Abyssinia; but in the imagination of Europeans Prester John was a more wealthy and powerful monarch than any of their own princes, and contact with him was ardently desired in order to kindle a Christian backfire against the infidel Turk. Columbus once thought he was hot on the trail of Prester John in Cuba!

For almost a decade after Prince Henry's death the Portuguese made no further progress southward, except to settle the Cape Verde Islands. Then, in 1469, King Afonso V gave a Lisbon merchant named Fernão Gomes the monopoly of trading with the Guinea coast, on condition that he explore it a hundred leagues further every year. And there is no doubt that by this time the crown was seeking a southern sea route to India. Gomes's vessels promptly swung around the bulge and opened up the richest part of West Africa: the Gold and Ivory Coasts and Malagueta, where a variety of pepper almost as hot as the East Indian variety was found. By 1474 when his monopoly expired, Fernão Gomes had sent ships clean across the Gulf of Guinea and reached the island of Fernando Po on latitude 3° 30′ N, where the African coast again turns southward.

Commerce with Africa then became a crown monopoly, under the direction of the Infante D. João, who succeeded to the throne in 1481 as D. João II. So it was precisely at the moment when Columbus settled in Lisbon that Portuguese maritime enterprise was producing its richest fruits. Every spring fleets of lateen-rigged caravels, the type of vessel especially designed for this trade, were bringing into the Tagus bags of Malagueta pepper, cords of elephant tusks, coffles of Negro slaves, and chests of gold dust. In the autumn they set forth again with holds full of red caps, hawks' bells, Venetian beads and assorted trading truck that the Negroes bought for gold; and deckloads of horses, for which the native chiefs paid extravagant prices. Along the quays and in the narrow streets of the old town all the languages spoken from Iceland to the Cameroons could be heard; seamen from Scandinavia, England and Flanders jostled Spaniards, Genoese, Moors, Berbers and converted Negro potentates. From his palace windows on the Praça do Comércio Dom João could watch ships of a dozen different nations straining at their cables in the swift Tagus, while the royal nostrils were tickled with the odor of unloading spices, and the princely appetite was whetted by scents from the near-by ship-biscuit ovens. New churches and palaces were being built, Italian bankers and Jewish moneychangers had offices all around the square; Lisbon was enterprising, opulent and sanguine. All this in marked contrast to stagnant Genoa, whose possessions the Turks were plundering with impunity.

Lisbon, the *nobres Lisboa* of Camoens, still the most beautiful of the world's greater seaports, was then the most stimulating place in all Europe for an ambitious young seaman like Columbus. Lisbon looked out and not in, forward to world dominion instead of backward to the glories of past centuries. From her quays there was no long and tedious sail to open water. Drop down the Tagus with the ebb tide, cross the bar with an east wind, and the whole western quadrant of 180 degrees lies open. Columbus and many others had sailed thence north, to Iceland and beyond. The Portuguese were sailing southward, along Africa. Why not try sailing west, to Japan, China and India?

What would prevent it? No flat-earth theory certainly; for of all the vulgar errors connected with Columbus, the most persistent and the most absurd is that he had to convince people "the world was round." Every educated man in his day believed the world to be a sphere, every European university so taught geography, and seamen, though they might doubt the practical possibility of sailing "down under" or holding on when you got there, knew perfectly well from seeing ships "hull-down" and "raising" mountains as they approached, that the surface of the globe was curved. Aristotle was reported to have written that you could cross the ocean from the Spains to the Indies *paucis diebus,* in comparatively

few days; and Strabo, the Greek geographer who died about A.D.
25, hinted that it had actually been tried. "Those who have returned
from an attempt to circumnavigate the earth do not say that they
have been prevented from continuing their voyage by any opposing
continent, for the sea remained perfectly open, but through want
of resolution and the scarcity of provision."

Shortly before Columbus arrived in Portugal it occurred to King
Afonso V that his people were perhaps seeking passage to India
the hard way, that the Western Ocean route might prove shorter
and less dangerous; and a Florentine scholar assured him that it
would.

A canon of the Cathedral of Lisbon named Fernão Martins had
met in Italy a Florentine physician and humanist named Paolo dal
Pozzo Toscanelli. Physicians in the fifteenth century were apt to
be good mathematicians and astronomers, since the stars helped
their medicine to "take"; and from astronomy it was a short jump
to geography and estimating the size of the globe. That happened
to be Toscanelli's hobby.

Early in the fourteenth century Marco Polo and his elders
had brought home their marvelous tale of the glories of the Grand
Khan, of China, and of the island kingdom of Cipangu (Japan)
which lay off the Chinese coast — 1500 miles off, said Marco; some
wish he had been right. "The Book of Ser Marco Polo" spread
around in countless manuscript copies before the invention of printing, and kindled the imagination of Columbus, among many others.
But the indoor geographers of the fifteenth century generally regarded Marco Polo as a liar, because he gave a far greater eastward
extension to Asia than they found in the geography of Ptolemy.
So great then was the veneration for the ancients that if any discovery conflicted with Ptolemy, so much the worse for the discoverer. American cartography for almost half a century after
Columbus is marked by the amusing attempts of map makers to
combine the new explorations with Ptolemaic Asia. Now, Toscanelli was one of the few men of science who accepted Marco
Polo. Consequently he believed that the eastern edge of Asia lay
much closer to Portugal than other men supposed. His friend Canon
Martins broached this idea to the king of Portugal, who asked
Martins to procure a letter from Toscanelli developing his views.

Toscanelli replied to the canon in a letter from Florence dated June 25, 1474, a copy of which was later obtained by Columbus and used as "exhibit A" in his "case." Paul the Physician is delighted to hear that the king is interested in a "shorter way of going by sea to the lands of spices, than that which you [the Portuguese] are making by Guinea." He has made a chart to demonstrate the course, with parallels of latitude and meridians of longitude, and sends it along for the king. On this chart he has marked divers landfalls that a ship sailing westward from Portugal might make, so that she may be able to identify the land and convince the natives that she "has some knowledge of that country, which will surely be no little pleasure to them" — a pleasure that Columbus was never in a position to afford. A course due west from Lisbon will take you in about 5000 nautical miles to Quinsay, capital of the Chinese province of Mangi. In the next province, Cathay, resides the Emperor of China, the Grand Khan, "which name in Latin means king of kings." (We shall hear more of this potentate later.) An alternate route to China passed by "the island of Antillia which is known to you," and after 2000 miles hits the "noble island of Cipangu" (Japan), "most fertile in gold, pearls and precious stones, and they cover the temples and the royal residences with solid gold." "Thus by the unknown ways there are no great spaces of the sea to be passed." Many more things Toscanelli might explain, but he expects that the king would rather work these out for himself.

Neither Afonso V nor his son did anything about this extraordinary letter, whose echoes we shall find in Columbus's journals of every major voyage. Portugal was content with her promising advance along West Africa, the immense profits that exploration in that direction was bringing to the crown, and the expectation that any day a southward-pressing caravel might open up the sea route to India.

Columbus's exact movements during the eight or nine years that he spent under the Portuguese flag can never be cleared up, for the Lisbon earthquake destroyed notarial and court documents where we might have found some trace of his activities. According

to the contemporary Genoese chronicler, Antonio Gallo, Bartholomew Columbus established himself in Lisbon before Christopher,
opened a chart-making establishment, took his elder brother into
partnership, and imparted to him the ideas that led to the great
discovery. Andrés Bernáldez of Seville, who knew Columbus
well, describes him in his contemporary history as "a hawker of
printed books, who carried on his trade in this land of Andalusia,
. . . a man of great intelligence though with little book learning,
very skilled in the art of cosmography and the mapping of the
world." That Columbus was a skilled chartmaker is seen by the
sure touch in his free-hand sketch of Northern Haiti, the only
map indubitably his that has survived; but that Bartholomew taught
him the art may be questioned. For, if Bartholomew's later statement about his age may be trusted, he was still in his teens when
Christopher reached Lisbon. He had, to be sure, left home earlier
than his elder brother, and might well have reached Lisbon first and,
through the good offices of some Genoese compatriot there, gone
through the apprentice stage of chart making before Christopher
arrived. Or he may have learned the rudiments at one of the numerous ateliers of portolan charts in Genoa, and merely sought
Lisbon as a promising opening. Men over fifty, like women over
thirty, are apt to be forgetful about their birthdays; so it seems
more likely that the Adelantado was nearer sixty than fifty years
old in 1512, than that the Genoese chronicler got his facts wrong.
Let us assume that Christopher did find Bartholomew, only a year
or two younger than himself, already making charts at Lisbon in
1477, and that the two brothers became partners in providing
articles for which the Portuguese maritime expansion created a
great demand.

There was nothing new about Genoese working in Lisbon. Fifty
years or more earlier, a group of them had offered to buy up the
establishment of the Infante D. Henrique on Cape St. Vincent,
"and the Genoese, as you know, are people who do not make
employ of their money without great hope of gain," says Azurara.
A number of Genoese captains like Usodimare and Antonio da
Noli had entered the service of infante or king, and made important
discoveries. There was even a *Rio de Ginoves* on the early map
of West Africa. The contraction of Genoa's sphere of influence

in the Levant forced many of her best seafarers and business men to emigrate. There were so many of them in Portugal that the Cortes in 1481 petitioned the king to exclude them from his dominions, alleging that they were good for nothing except to steal important secrets of the African and Western Island trade. Eventually the crown adopted a policy of exclusion as regards Africa; but when Columbus arrived in Lisbon the city had an important colony of Genoese. They cared for young Christopher when a castaway; and now, presumably, they patronized his chart-making business, and put him in the way of filling out his scanty education. We may suppose that it was in his first year or two in Portugal that Christopher learned to read and write Castilian, and that he began to get the hang of Latin. For Latin he must have if he wished to mingle with gentlemen and scholars; Latin alone could unlock the learning of the past.

How long Columbus stayed ashore we do not know; but he was at sea again in the summer of 1478. Paolo di Negro, the associate of Centurione who had employed Christopher on the Chios voyages, engaged him at Lisbon to visit Madeira and purchase 2400 or more *arrobas* (about 60,000 pounds) of sugar for Centurione's account. Centurione had given Di Negro 1290 ducats for this purpose, but Di Negro gave Columbus only 103½ ducats. With this small portion of the purchase money in hand, Columbus took passage to Funchal and there made a contract for the full amount, to be shipped when the balance was paid. But by the time a vessel arrived to load the sugar, the balance had not been paid, and the Madeira merchants refused to deliver sugar on credit. So Columbus was forced to proceed to Genoa with a short consignment. This proved embarrassing to Ludovico Centurione, who perhaps had already contracted to deliver the whole; and on August 25, 1479, he had Columbus and other witnesses examined in court and the facts placed on record. Columbus, described by the notary as a citizen of Genoa, further declared his age ("27 or thereabouts"), admitted that he had 100 florins on him, and expressed his intention to depart for Lisbon the next morning.

Obviously this young man had won the confidence of his Genoese employers, to be entrusted with a business transaction involving several thousand dollars. And the next important event in his life, marriage to Dona Felipa Perestrello e Moniz, indicates that he was considered a good prospect by one of the first families of Portugal.

Christopher met his wife, according to Ferdinand, when attending Mass at the chapel of the Convento dos Santos in Lisbon. This convent belonged to the knights of the military order of St. Iago. Originally intended as a retreat for their womenfolk when the cavaliers were away fighting, it had by this time become a fashionable boarding school for daughters of the Portuguese aristocracy. In the convent, which overlooked the Tagus not far from Christopher and Bartholomew's chart-making establishment, there was a chapel to which the public were admitted, and where young men in search of a good match found it agreeable to perform their religious duties. How Christopher's wooing was managed we are not told. Presumably it was one of those sidewalk-to-window affairs; the process that the modern Spanish and Portuguese young men call "eating iron," or "gargling." The biographer merely says, "forasmuch as he behaved very honorably, and was a man of such fine presence, and withal so honest," Dona Felipa "held such converse and friendship with him that she became his wife." Date and place of the wedding we do not know; but as their son seems to have been born in 1480, we may assume that Christopher and Felipa were married in the latter part of 1479, after he returned from Madeira and Genoa, and in the chapel where they first met. It is quite possible, however, that the wedding took place earlier, and that Dona Felipa accompanied Columbus when he went to Madeira to buy the sugar.

To some writers this marriage appears to be a great mystery. How could a foreign chartmaker of low birth who had been literally "on the beach" a few years before, marry into one of the noble families of the kingdom? Dona Felipa was the daughter of D. Bartholomew Perestrello and of his third wife, Dona Isabel Moniz. Perestrello, son of a noble family of Piacenza that had emigrated to Lisbon in the previous century, accompanied the second colonizing expedition to Porto Santo and Madeira in 1425, received the hereditary captaincy of the smaller island from the Infante D. Henrique, and died there about 1457. Dona Isabel's father, Gil Ayres Moniz, belonged to one of the oldest families of

the Algarve, and had fought with the Infante D. Henrique at
Ceuta. After the death of her husband, Dona Isabel sold her widow's rights in the captaincy of Porto Santo to Pedro Correa da
Cunha, husband of one of her stepdaughters, and retired to Lisbon.
Her own son Bartholomew caused this act of cession to be an-
nulled when he reached his majority, and himself took over the
captaincy of Porto Santo in 1473. That left his mother with slender
means to support her rank; and as Dona Felipa was the elder of
two daughters, already about 25 years old when she caught young
Christopher's roving eye, her mother was glad enough to have no
more convent bills to pay, and as son-in-law to secure an up-and-
coming young man of gentlemanly manners, who asked for no
dowry.

Ferdinand Columbus, who was not the fruit of this marriage but
of a later connection, informs us that Columbus lived for a time
with his mother-in-law, who, observing his great interest in the
sea, broke out the old yarns her late husband had spun. She told
the amusing tale of how Dom Bartholomew had ruined Porto Santo
for years by taking ashore on his first arrival a she-rabbit with her
litter. The rabbits bred so fast that within a year they completely
covered the island and ate up every green thing on it; the Portuguese had to shift to Madeira, and settlement of Porto Santo was
postponed until the balance of nature was re-established. Since
"these stories and voyages pleased the Admiral much," writes his
son, Dona Isabel "gave him the writings and sea-charts left by her
husband, by which the Admiral was the more excited, and he informed himself of the other voyages and navigations that the Portuguese were making."

Not the slightest hint has come down to us of the appearance
or disposition of Columbus's only wife; Dona Felipa is as shadowy
a figure as the Discoverer's mother. We do not even know when
she died, only that it was before Columbus left Portugal in 1485,
and that she was buried in the church of the Carmo, whose earth-
quake-shaken ruins still overlook the old city of Lisbon. Little
definite information is preserved of Columbus's movements during
the next few years. Apparently, after a short sojourn with Dona
Isabel at Lisbon, he and his wife went to Porto Santo, where

Dona Felipa's brother Bartholomew Perestrello II was captain and governor; their only child Diego Colón was born there about 1480.

Porto Santo, 30 miles northeast of Madeira, has the same high, jagged appearance as most of the Western Islands, and is visible from a great distance. Approaching Porto Santo from Cape Blanco in Africa, we sighted the island at 10.45 A.M., November 14, 1939; but although our sturdy cutter was doing her 5 knots in a fine NE trade wind, it was not until 4.45 P.M. that we came to an anchor in the roadstead off the town, Villa Baleira. Our hosts were quite certain that the charts and documents given to Columbus by his mother-in-law lie buried somewhere on the island, as that was what the people did with their valuables in the seventeenth century when raided by the Moors. The church where D. Diego must have been baptized is still standing, and a modest house near by, according to tradition, is where Columbus and Dona Felipa lived. I suspect, however, that the tradition was created for the benefit of an American who visited the island over fifty years ago looking for Columbian relics. Porto Santo is less beautiful close at hand than at a distance; it has the air of never having recovered from the depredations of Perestrello's rabbits.

Again probably (and no reader can be more tired than I am of these interminable probabilities), the Columbus couple spent most of the next few years in the island of Madeira. When he called at Funchal on his Third Voyage in 1498, Columbus wrote in his Journal (as paraphrased by Las Casas): "In the town he was given a very fine reception and much entertainment, for he was well known there, having been a resident thereof for some time." As Funchal was already a flourishing town of some fifty years' standing, rising proudly up the mountainside to the famous vineyards, Columbus must have located there as a merchant. With his Centurione connections and his new ones by marriage, he should have done well. Local tradition presents several candidates for the house where the couple lived.

In 1481 the old king died and was succeeded by his son D. João II, "the complete prince." Young and energetic, wise and learned, politic and ambitious, D. João was equal in ability to any prince of his age. Just before his accession, a long and fruitless war with Castile was concluded with the Treaty of Alcáçovas, in which

Spain recognized Portugal's exclusive rights to the African coast and islands south of the Canaries, which were retained by Spain. D. João, who as infante had managed the crown monopoly of African trade, determined to build a castle or fortified trading factory on the Gold Coast, sufficiently strong to beat off any European rivals, and to keep the natives in order. A fleet of nine caravels and two *urcas* (cargo carriers like Columbus's ill-fated *Bechalla*) was fitted out at Lisbon, with several hundred soldiers, stonemasons and other artisans; the Pope conceded a full indulgence for their sins to all Christians who might die in this enterprise; and the fleet set sail from Lisbon late in 1481, under the command of D. Diogo d'Azambuja. On the Gold Coast the men worked hard and well that winter, erecting a great stone castle of medieval design, complete with turrets, moat, chapel, warehouse, and market court; and a garrison was left in charge. São Jorge da Mina (St. George of the Mine), as this castle was named, upheld Portuguese sovereignty and protected her trade on the Gold Coast as long as she remained independent. The site and the ruins today are called Cape Coast Castle.

Columbus either took part in D'Azambuja's expedition or made a voyage to Mina shortly after the castle was built. This is proved by the postils he jotted down on the margins of his favorite books. In his copy of Aeneas Sylvius's *Historia Rerum*, opposite a passage where Eratosthenes is quoted as to the climate below the equator being temperate, Columbus writes, "Perpendicularly under the equator is the castle of Mina of the most serene King of Portugal, which we have seen." With Pierre d'Ailly's statement that the Torrid Zone is uninhabitable because of excessive heat, Columbus disagrees: "It is not uninhabitable, for the Portuguese sail through it today, and it is even very populous, and under the equator is the castle of Mina of the most serene king of Portugal, which we have seen." Moreover, in his famous note to Pierre d'Ailly's speculations on the size of the Earth, Columbus says, "Note that often, in sailing from Lisbon to the southward into Guinea, I observed carefully the course . . ."

This word "often" has led some to infer that Columbus made more than one Guinea voyage; but it clearly refers to the frequency of taking sun sights, not to voyages. When was this Guinea voyage made? Nowhere does Columbus mention Diogo d'Azambuja, which presumably he would have done had he sailed under so distinguished a captain. I therefore conclude that he visited São Jorge da Mina in 1482–1483 or 1483–1484, perhaps both years, as master or officer of a trading expedition, or of royal ships sent to reinforce the garrison. An undated incident of Columbus's early voyages, when he had command of two ships and left one at Porto Santo while he proceeded to Lisbon with the other, would have fitted in perfectly with a return passage from the Gold Coast.

Columbus was much impressed by West Africa. In the journal of his First Voyage to America he frequently compares people and products of "The Indies" with those of Guinea; he is always talking about finding a "mine" in Hispaniola; and his Third Voyage had particular reference to the supposed latitude of Sierra Leone The experience of a passage to the Gold Coast and back, in company with Portuguese pilots, must greatly have improved his seamanship, although it may be doubted whether it gave him any competence in celestial navigation.

Columbus learned many useful things from his Portuguese shipmates, who were the world's finest mariners of that era: how to handle a caravel in head wind and sea, how to claw off a lee shore, what kind of sea stores to take on a long voyage and how to stow them properly, and what sort of trading truck goes with primitive people. Every voyage that he sailed under the flag of Portugal made it more likely that he would succeed in the Great Enterprise that was already in his brain. Above all, he learned from the Portuguese confidence that with a good ship under him and God's assistance, the boundaries of the known world might be indefinitely enlarged; that the Age of Discovery had only just begun. From his own experience he had learned that the ancients did not know everything; the Torrid Zone *was* habitable; he, Christopher Columbus, had been in regions never seen by Roman or described by Greek.

By the time he was home from the Guinea voyage, Columbus was ready to make an amazing proposition to the king of Portugal.

CHAPTER V

The Man Columbus

Christophoro Colombo Zenovese homo de alta et procera statura rosso de grande ingegno et faza longa.

Christopher Columbus, Genoese, a tall man and well built, ruddy, of great creative talent, and with a long face.
— ANGELO TREVISAN

C HRISTOPHER Columbus, thirty years old, an experienced seaman and trusted factor, having business connections with one of the leading merchant-banker houses of Italy, related by marriage with two important families of Portugal, had "arrived," according to the standards of the day. He needed but to follow the upward curve of merchant shipping to be a success, if that was what he wanted. Maybe at times his family and friends wished that was all he wanted. Maybe Dona Felipa tried to persuade her husband to forget his youthful dreams and pay more attention to business. You are a father, now, my lord, and should settle down as my father did. A neat house and garden overlooking the Tagus where you can watch the pretty ships come and go . . . No! Never! Christopher I was baptized, and as Christoferens I shall die.

So let us pause and find out if we can what manner of man was this Columbus at the dangerous age of thirty — dangerous that is to youthful ambition, to ideals and visions; the age that makes rovers settle down, drains the fire from ardent youth, turns men into tabby-cats content to sit by the fire. Hear what was said about Columbus by men who knew him, and whose lives crossed his.

No description of Columbus at this precise period exists; we have to work back from what people said of him after the great achievement. Oviedo, who witnessed the Admiral's triumphant entry into Barcelona in 1493, says this of him in a work that was printed forty years later: "A man of honest parents and life, of good stature and appearance, taller than the average and strongly limbed: the eyes lively and other parts of the face of good proportion, the hair very red, and the face somewhat ruddy and freckled; fair in speech, tactful and of a great creative talent; a nice Latinist and most learned cosmographer; gracious when he wished to be, irascible when annoyed."

Ferdinand Columbus, who was with his father constantly between the ages of twelve and eighteen, has this description in his biography: —

The Admiral was a well built man of more than medium stature, long visaged with cheeks somewhat high, but neither fat nor thin. He had an aquiline nose and his eyes were light in color; his complexion too was light, but kindling to a vivid red. In youth his hair was blond, but when he came to his thirtieth year it all turned white. In eating and drinking and the adornment of his person he was always continent and modest. Among strangers his conversation was affable, and with members of his household very pleasant, but with a modest and pleasing dignity. In matters of religion he was so strict that for fasting and saying all the canonical offices he might have been taken for a member of a religious order. And he was so great an enemy to cursing and swearing, that I swear I never heard him utter any other oath than "by San Fernando!" and when he was most angry with anyone, his reprimand was to say, "May God take you!" for doing or saying that. And when he had to write anything, he would not try the pen without first writing these words, *Jesus cum Maria sit nobis in via,* and in such fair letters that he might have gained his bread by them alone.

Las Casas, who saw the Admiral in Hispaniola in 1500, and whose father and uncle had been shipmates and colonists under him, amplifies Ferdinand's description in the *Historia de las Indias:* —

As regards his exterior person and bodily disposition, he was more than middling tall; face long and giving an air of authority; aquiline nose, blue eyes, complexion light and tending to bright red; beard and hair red when young but very soon turned gray from his labors; he was affable and cheerful in speaking, and, as says the abovesaid Portuguese history,° eloquent and boastful in his negotiations; he was serious in moderation, affable with strangers, and with members of his household gentle and pleasant, with modest gravity and discreet conversation; and so could easily incite those who saw him to love him. In fine, he was most impressive in his port and countenance, a person of great state and authority and worthy of all reverence. He was sober and moderate in eating, drinking, clothing and footwear; it was commonly said that he spoke cheerfully in familiar conversation, or with indignation when he gave reproof or was angry with somebody: "May God take you, don't you agree to this and that?" or "Why have you done this and that?" In matters of the Christian religion, without doubt he was a Catholic and of great devotion; for in everything he did and said or sought to begin, he always interposed "In the name of the Holy Trinity I will do this," or "launch this" or "this will come to pass." In whatever letter or other thing he wrote, he put at the head "Jesus and Mary be with us on the way," and of these writings of his in his own hand I have plenty now in my possession. His oath was sometimes, "I swear by San Fernando"; when he sought to affirm something of great importance in his letters on oath, especially in writing to the Sovereigns, he said, "I swear that this is true."

He observed the fasts of the Church most faithfully, confessed and made communion often, read the canonical offices like a churchman or member of a religious order, hated blasphemy and profane swearing, was most devoted to Our Lady and to the seraphic father St. Francis; seemed very grateful to God for benefits received from the divine hand, wherefore, as in the proverb, he hourly admitted that God had conferred upon him great mercies, as upon David. When gold or precious things were brought to him, he entered his cabin, knelt down, summoned the bystanders, and said, "Let us give thanks to Our Lord that he has thought us worthy to discover so many good things." He was extraordinarily zealous for the divine service; he desired and was eager for the conversion of these people [the Indians], and that in every region the faith of Jesus Christ be planted and enhanced. And he was especially affected and devoted to the idea that God should deem him worthy of aiding somewhat in recovering the Holy Sepulchre. . . .

He was a gentleman of great force of spirit, of lofty thoughts, naturally inclined (from what one may gather of his life, deeds, writings and conversation) to undertake worthy deeds and signal enterprises; patient and long-suffering (as later shall appear), and a forgiver of injuries, and wished nothing more than that those who offended against

° João de Barros *Da Ásia* (1552), as we shall see.

him should recognize their errors, and that the delinquents be reconciled
with him; most constant and endowed with forbearance in the hardships
and adversities which were always occurring and which were incredible
and infinite; ever holding great confidence in divine providence. And
verily, from what I have heard from him and from my own father, who
was with him when he returned to colonize Hispaniola in 1493, and
from others who accompanied and served him, he held and always kept
on terms of intimate fidelity and devotion to the Sovereigns.

So Columbus appeared to those who knew him, and who took
pains to study his character and set it down a few years after his
death. The reader will have ample opportunity to judge the
Discoverer's character for himself. Physical courage, which the
early historians took for granted, he will find in plenty; and un-
tiring persistence and unbreakable will. Certain defects will appear,
especially lack of due appreciation for the labors of his subordinates; unwillingness to admit his shortcomings as a colonizer; a
tendency to complain and be sorry for himself whenever the
Sovereigns, owing to these shortcomings, withdrew some measure
of their trust in him. These were the defects of the qualities that
made him a great historical figure. For he was not, like a Washington, a Cromwell or a Bolivar, an instrument chosen by multitudes to express their wills and lead a cause; Columbus was a Man
with a Mission, and such men are apt to be unreasonable and even
disagreeable to those who cannot see the mission. There was no
psalm-singing New Model, no Spirit of '76, no Army of Liberation
with drums and trumpets behind Columbus. He was Man alone
with God against human stupidity and depravity, against greedy
conquistadors, cowardly seamen, even against nature and the sea.
Always with God, though; in that his biographers were right;
for God is with men who for a good cause put their trust in Him.
Men may doubt this, but there can be no doubt that the faith of
Columbus was genuine and sincere, and that his frequent communion with forces unseen was a vital element in his achievement.
It gave him confidence in his destiny, assurance that his performance would be equal to the promise of his name. This conviction
that God destined him to be an instrument for spreading the faith
was far more potent than the desire to win glory, wealth and
worldly honors, to which he was certainly far from indifferent.

An incident of the Second Voyage proves how in the midst of active seafaring Columbus could be completely absorbed in worship. Off Portland Bay in Jamaica, one morning as *Niña* was ghosting along with the land breeze, the Admiral was praying in his cabin when a native cacique with a large retinue boarded the caravel. This must have created no small excitement on deck; but none of the loud talking and tumult disturbed the Admiral's prayers, and he finished his devotions with no suspicion that anything unusual was going on.

The physical description of Columbus shows that he was of a North Italian type frequently seen today in Genoa; tall and well-built, red-haired with a ruddy and freckled complexion, hawk-nosed and long of visage, blue-eyed and with high cheekbones. Unfortunately no portrait of him was painted in his lifetime, for the great age of Spanish portraiture was yet to come; there are no contemporary portraits of Ferdinand and Isabella except on coins. No less than seventy-one alleged original portraits of Columbus or copies were exhibited at the Chicago Exposition of 1893. They showed lean-faced, long-jowled Columbuses and fat-faced, pudgy Columbuses; blond Columbuses and swarthy, olive-tinted Columbuses; smooth-visaged Columbuses and Columbuses variously mustached, bearded and whiskered; Columbuses garbed in all manner of costume, lay and ecclesiastical, noble and vulgar, from the Franciscan robe to the courtier's dress, and in styles ranging over three centuries. Most of them tallied in no way with the contemporary descriptions, and the jury who examined them could find no satisfactory evidence that any one was authentic.

The portrait which has the greatest claim to authenticity is the so-called Giovio belonging to Count Alessandro Orchi. Count Orchi is a descendant of the humanist Paolo Giovio, who is known to have included Columbus in his portrait gallery of famous men, as early as 1550. But Giovio did not begin this collection until thirty years after Columbus's death, and the portrait is probably nothing more than a fancy posthumous sketch by some second-rate Italian painter who never saw the Admiral. Inscribed COLOM-BVS LYGVR NOVI ORBIS REPERTOR, it shows the head and shoulders of an elderly man with thin gray hair, downcast *brown* eyes, a round rather than a long face, and a somewhat dejected expression. His most prominent feature is an obstinate straight mouth, with a protruding lower lip. An engraving of the original Giovio portrait, published in 1577, is very different from the Orchi portrait, and even less convincing; for it shows a "Columbus" with an amiable and rather weak expression, looking straight at the observer.

Every biographer of Columbus finds among the eighty or more so-called portraits of the Admiral one that most appeals to him, and chooses that as "his" Columbus. An ideal portrait painted in the nineteenth century for the Naval Museum of Madrid follows closely the personal descriptions of Columbus, and gives an impression of force, dignity and integrity. This I have selected for the frontispiece to this volume.

Four early authorities on Columbus and his voyages will be quoted frequently in the course of this work: Ferdinand Columbus, Las Casas, Peter Martyr and Oviedo. These four I have relied upon probably more than any biographer of Columbus since Washington Irving; for the "scientific" historians of the last century tended to regard their predecessors either as hopeless amateurs or as incorrigible liars upon whom no dependence should be placed. My own experience in studying and writing history has impelled me almost to the opposite pole: to rely on contemporaries unless they are demonstrably false. *Contemporanea expositio fortissima est,* said the famous Justice Coke; the judgment of a man's peers may not be final, but it is based on a myriad of facts (and fancies too), on things both seen and heard that are now forever lost. Contemporary biographers and historians should be controlled by documents, if you have them, and discounted for bias, if bias can be detected. They are often irritatingly silent on questions that we moderns particularly wish to have answered. But for a body and background of knowledge about Columbus and his work, these four are as indispensable as the Discoverer's own writings and the Spanish documentary sources.

Ferdinand Columbus (Don Hernando Colón) was the son of the Discoverer and of Beatriz Enríquez de Harana, born at Cordova in August or September, 1488. At the age of ten he was appointed a page to the Queen; between the ages of twelve and sixteen he accompanied his father on the Fourth Voyage. Returning with him to Spain in order to continue his education, he went out to Santo Domingo with his half-brother D. Diego the second admiral in 1509, returned six months later, and thereafter led the life of a scholar, collector, traveler and man of letters. He inherited his father's tall stature and ruddy complexion, but grew extremely corpulent; an amiable disposition won him a host of friends.

Ferdinand was a man of wealth. He enjoyed several lucrative sinecures by royal appointment, and the revenue from four hundred slaves in Hispaniola, besides a share of the paternal estate. This enabled him to collect a library, and to travel extensively in Italy, France and the Low Countries, where he met Erasmus and received a presentation copy of one of his works. Learned men corresponded with Ferdinand and regarded him as one of themselves; he was the first European intellectual to bring fresh air from the New World into European letters. In 1525 "Don Hernando" settled down at Seville, in a house beside the river with a large garden that he planted with trees and shrubs from America. He accumulated a large and splendid library which numbered over 15,000 volumes at the time of his death in 1539, and which eventually went to the cathedral chapter of Seville. In their hands it suffered a shameful neglect and dilapidation, so that not more than 2000 of Ferdinand's own volumes remain. Yet this Biblioteca Colombina, adjoining the great cathedral where the Admiral worshiped and where his sons lie buried, is today an inspiration for every American scholar; an alembic as it were where a new civilization was distilled from classical scholarship, medieval piety and modern science. There one may see books annotated in the Discoverer's own hand, his magazines of intellectual ammunition for the Great Enterprise. There, too, one may read Seneca's famous prophecy of the Discovery,* in an early edition of his Tragedies that belonged to Ferdinand, and next it this simple but glorious annotation in the son's hand: —

Haec profetia impleta est per patrem meum . . . almirantem anno 1492.

---

* See head of next chapter.

This prophecy was fulfilled by my father . . . the Admiral in the year 1492.

How early Ferdinand began the biography we do not know, but it was not finished until shortly before his death. The manuscript, which has since disappeared, was taken by D. Luis Colón the Admiral's grandson to Italy in 1568, before any Spanish edition had been printed; and the sole surviving text is an Italian translation by Alfonso Ulloa printed at Venice in 1571. The title is so lengthy that it is generally referred to by the first word, *Historie*.

Although the authenticity of the *Historie* was attacked by Harrisse, he lived to confess his error; even Vignaud the great iconoclast admits that this work is "the most important of our sources of information on the life of the discoverer of America." A first printing in Italy was natural enough, for in Italy the keenest interest was shown in voyages and exploration, during the second half of the sixteenth century, and Ulloa made faithful translations of such works as Castanheda's *History of India*. Ferdinand's *Historie* needs no more discounting than does any biography of a distinguished father by a devoted son. It is particularly valuable for the First Voyage, and for the Fourth, in which Ferdinand took part.

Bartolomé de Las Casas wrote *Historia de las Indias*, the one book on the discovery of America that I should wish to preserve if all others were destroyed. This lengthy work was begun about 1527 in Hispaniola, but mostly composed between 1550 and 1563, after the author's return to Spain. It was not printed until 1875. Las Casas had all Columbus's papers at hand, including the Journals and the lost Spanish original of Ferdinand's biography; his room in the College of San Gregorio at Valladolid was reported to be so full of manuscripts that one could hardly get in and out.

Las Casas's father and uncle came to Hispaniola as colonists on Columbus's Second Voyage. He himself arrived there in 1500, a brisk young university graduate of 26 ready to make his fortune like the others. Conversion came instead, and in 1510 Las Casas was the first priest to be ordained in the New World. Out of his experience as a missionary in Cuba arose a passionate conviction that the Indians were men and brothers who should be converted and treated as fellow Christians; and he devoted the rest of his life to this cause. At all times he was the Indians' apostle, protector and friend; and at various times their advocate at court, governor on the Pearl Coast, and bishop of Chiapa in Mexico. The *Historia de las Indias,* written by a scholar and divine who was also a man of action over a wide field, is at once solid, spiritual and robust. Las Casas admired Columbus with reservations, and had no hesitation in reproving his policy towards the natives. His critical sense in the handling of texts is seen in his chapter on Vespucci; and although at times he is disappointingly vague on matters we are now eager to know, and not altogether reliable on subjects very close to his heart, such as the Indians, he left us a great and noble history of the discovery and first conquest of America.

Peter Martyr has the distinction of being the earliest historian of the New World. An Italian born on the shores of Lake Maggiore in 1457, he had a humanist education, and at the age of thirty went to Spain, where his learning and accomplishments made him a welcome member of the court. He lectured to enthusiastic students at Salamanca, took part in the war against the Moors, and with the court at Barcelona welcomed Columbus on his return from the New World. Peter Martyr was intensely curious about "The Indies," pumped Columbus and other shipmates for information, helped to spread the good news in his letters to Italian friends, and as early as 1494 decided to write a history of the discovery and conquest of the New World, a term coined by him. In this design he persisted, though diplomatic appointments and tutoring the young nobles of the court interrupted it constantly. He took holy orders in order to enable him to enjoy ecclesiastical revenues in absentia, including those of a monastery in Jamaica, and lived magnificently in Valladolid.

The first Decade *de Orbe Novo* came out in 1511, and the English translation by Richard Eden, first published in 1555, has all the freshness of our speech in the Elizabethan era. The value of Peter Martyr's letters and of his Decades is very great, for he had a keen and critical intelligence which pierced some of the cosmographical fancies of Columbus that the less erudite Las Casas was inclined to accept, and he gives us more information about the Second Voyage than any other contemporary historian. He never visited the New World, and apparently did not particularly admire Columbus, but gives a fair and straightforward account of his work.

El Capitán Gonzalo Fernández de Oviedo y Valdés, Oviedo for short, was a young hidalgo of fifteen in Barcelona when Columbus arrived there in 1493. An intimate friend of the Infante D. Juan, he fought in the war of Naples under Gonsalvo de Cordova, and after various adventures and employments sailed to America in 1513 with Pedrarias Dávila as comptroller of the gold diggings of Darien. Oviedo spent thirty-four years in different parts of the Caribbean. A brief description of America, which he wrote on a visit home in 1526, proved so good that he was made official chronicler of "The Indies," and in 1535 appeared the first volume of his *Historia General y Natural de las Indias*. Oviedo had uncommon powers of observation, and his descriptions of West Indian fauna and flora are illustrated by his own sketches. His chapters on navigation and the like are excellent. In narrative history he is inferior to Las Casas, but his account of Columbus's voyages, though somewhat meager, was written earlier than those of Ferdinand and Las Casas, and drew on oral sources to which they did not have access.

Thus we have four contemporary and fairly comprehensive accounts of Columbus and his voyages; one by a pious and scholarly son, one by the passionate Apostle to the Indians, one by a sophisticated Latinist and courtier, and the fourth by a *caballero*, artist and man of action. All four had seen Columbus, Ferdinand on terms of filial intimacy and as shipmate on a long voyage; all but Peter Martyr visited the New World, lived there for some years, and were familiar with the scenes of Columbus's exploits. In addition to what they and less important contemporaries wrote, a considerable body of Columbus's own letters, manuscripts and annotated books have been preserved, and the contemporary documents published by Navarrete and in the *Raccolta Colombiana* fill out the story. We still have but slender information about his life to the age of forty, but there is no excuse for regarding Columbus as a man of mystery. His life and voyages are better documented than those of any great navigator or discoverer previous to the seventeenth century.

CHAPTER VI

The Enterprise of the Indies

1474–1492

> *Venient annis*
> *Secula seris; quibus Oceanus*
> *Vincula rerum laxet, et ingens*
> *Pateat telus tiphisque novos*
> *Detegat orbes nec sit terris*
> *Vltima tille.*

An age will come after many years when the Ocean will loose the chains of things, and a huge land lie revealed; when Tiphys will disclose new worlds and Thule no more be the ultimate.

— SENECA, *Medea*

WE MUST now face the crucial question of what Columbus was trying to do, where he got the idea, and how he went about it.

La Empresa de las Indias, the Enterprise of the Indies, as Columbus called his undertaking in after years, was simply to reach "The Indies," that is, Asia, by sailing westward. That was the main idea to which everything else was subordinate. He expected to get gold, pearls and spices by trade or conquest when he reached "The Indies." He expected to find one or more islands on the way, which might prove convenient as ports of call, if not profitable in themselves. But he had no thought or intention of finding the continent which we call America; no suspicion of its existence. America was discovered wholly by accident, and only on his Third Voyage did Columbus admit that he had found a new continent.

These statements may seem too downright in the eyes of readers who have followed the so-called Columbus literature of the last fifty years; but they are made advisedly. Nobody doubted them until around the four hundredth anniversary of the discovery. They are derived from Columbus himself, from his son Ferdinand, from Las Casas, from Peter Martyr the first historian of the New World, Oviedo the first official historian of the Spanish Empire, and the Portuguese historian João de Barros. All these agree explicitly or implicitly; the Asiatic objective of Columbus was so taken for granted as to need no exposition or proof. It did not make sense otherwise. The whole gamut of historians from 1600 to 1892 – Benzoni, Herrera, Muñoz, Von Humboldt, Washington Irving, Henry Harrisse, Justin Winsor, Cesare de Lollis – agreed that Columbus was looking for some portion of "The Indies" such as Japan or China, or both, and hit America by chance, or by divine guidance.

Around 1900 men began to write about Columbus who were so bright as to "discover" what had been hidden for centuries; even though they had but a small fraction of the documentary evidence, and none of the oral and visual evidence available to Columbus's contemporaries. Henry Vignaud in two stout volumes and numerous pamphlets built up the hypothesis that Columbus was not looking for "The Indies," had no idea of sailing to China; he was simply searching for new Atlantic islands of whose existence he had secret information, in order to found a valuable estate for himself and his family. Having passed the position where he expected to find these lands, and made land much further west, he concluded that he had reached Asia. Then, with his son Ferdinand and Las Casas as fellow conspirators, Columbus falsified the Journal, forged the Toscanelli letter, even annotated the margins of his books, to prove that he had been looking for Asia all along!

No satisfactory motive has ever been alleged for this gigantic conspiracy to distort the truth, but the Vignaud hypothesis has been the theme of numerous "debunkers," and others have taken up the story where Vignaud left off.

It would require a larger volume than this to follow Vignaud and his successors point by point, and I am as eager as I hope the reader is to leave this stagnant harbor of idle speculation and get out into blue water. My interest is in what Columbus did rather than what he proposed to do. But I may say here that unless his enterprise had been to sail westward to Asia, no long sessions with experts and princes would have been necessary, no elaborate equipment would have been wanted, no honors and privileges demanded, no obstacles encountered, no objections raised. For forty years before 1492 the kings of Portugal had been granting undiscovered islands to specific explorers, if they could find them; and Columbus could have obtained a similar grant on the same simple conditions. Unless he proposed to do something more novel and important and eventually more profitable, there was no sense in his demanding three ships, hereditary titles, profits of trade and all that.

Whilst no valid ground exists to question the traditional concept that Columbus's purpose was to reach Asia by sailing west, there is plenty of room for argument as to where he got the idea, and when.

These questions can never be answered with any certainty; Columbus apparently never told anybody, and perhaps did not himself remember. Any philosopher or scientist who has built his life about one idea would be hard put to it to say when the first germ of it entered his mind. Sailing west to the Orient may have come to Columbus in childhood as he pondered the story of his namesake; or in youth at a season of fasting and prayer, which makes the mind receptive to inspiration; or in manhood as he watched a glorious sunset from the deck of a ship. It may have come silently, like the grace of God, or in a rush and tumult of passionate and emotional conviction.

Certainly the theory was not original with him. We have already seen what Aristotle was reputed to have said, and what Strabo did say, about the possibility of sailing west to the Orient. Since there was no doubt of the world being a sphere, almost everyone admitted that Columbus's theory was valid; his originality lay in proposing to do something about it. A concept of sailing west to China in 1480 was much like that of flying in 1900 or of reaching the moon today; theoretically sound, but impractical with existing means. And the people who opposed Columbus were in a sense more right than he; for nobody could have sailed west to Asia in 1492, even if America had not been in the way.

Among scholars, the favorite explanation of Columbus's great idea is that he read it in some book; for scholars find it difficult to imagine ideas coming in any other way. Ferdinand Columbus, who was a scholar and a collector, emphasized his father's study of ancient authors, such as Aristotle, Ptolemy, Marinus of Tyre, Strabo and Pliny. Certainly Columbus took much comfort from the ancient and medieval geographers (as we shall see in good time), most of whom he read in popular compilations; but it is much more likely that he used their words to support his theory, rather than deriving his theory from them. As one much addicted to prophecies, and who had already voyaged beyond Thule (Iceland), Columbus was much impressed by the passage in Seneca's *Medea* quoted at the head of this chapter. An age will come when the Ocean will break his chains, a huge land will lie revealed, Tiphys (Jason's pilot) will discover new worlds, and Thule no longer be the ultimate.

Ferdinand admits that "the third and last motive the Admiral had to undertake the discovery of the Indies was the hope of finding, before he arrived there, some island and land of great utility, whence he might the better pursue his principal design." From his father's notebooks, he completed a list of reputed islands and other evidence that seemed significant.

This search for more islands had been pursued by the Portuguese almost continuously since Prince Henry's time. It took them over twenty years to collect the nine Azores, and they had no reason to suppose that Corvo, discovered in 1452, would end the list; for on Corvo there was a natural rock statue of a horseman pointing westward. Columbus is said to have seen this on one of his early voyages, and to have taken it as meant for him. The rock formations on Corvo are fantastic indeed; as we sailed around the island in our *Capitana,* the early morning sun lighted up the figure of a grim crusader with visor down and arms resting on his sword. Grim enough for us, with Newfoundland only 1054 miles distant. *Absit omen!*

Diogo de Teive and his pilot Pedro Vasques sailed northeast from Corvo in 1452 to the latitude of Cape Clear, Ireland. They felt certain that land lay near to the westward of them, but turned back. Ten years later, Afonso V granted two of the mythical St. Brendan Isles, Lovo and Capraria, to one Vogado, if he could find

them; and the same year an island was sighted WNW of the
Canaries and Madeira. In 1473 San Borondon, the principal St.
Brendan's isle, was searched for from the Canaries, and people
went on sighting and losing it until the eighteenth century. Next
year the king granted to one Teles "whatever islands he shall
find," including Antillia or the Island of the Seven Cities.

Antillia, reputedly the largest of the mythical islands, whose
existence Toscanelli took for granted and whose name is still on
the map, was supposed to have been settled by seven Portuguese
bishops with their followers who fled before the barbarian in-
vasions of the eighth century. Columbus heard that a storm-driven
Portuguese ship had landed there in the time of the Infante D.
Henrique. The crew were welcomed ashore in good Portuguese
and invited to stay; but, fearing foul play, made sail when the
wind turned west. On their return voyage to Portugal, they found
gold in the sand they had taken aboard for the firebox. Another
island was sighted between Madeira and Terceira, and several
fruitless searches were made for it. A Madeiran told Columbus
about three islands that he had sighted west of Madeira; he
thought they were only rocks, or floating islands such as Pliny
mentioned, but Columbus believed that they must have been some
of the St. Brendan chain. In England the men of Bristol began in
1480 to search for the mythical island of O'Brasil off Ireland,
which people have sworn that they saw even in the last century.

Why did not some of these navigators reach America; or did
they? Modern Portuguese historians have convinced themselves
that they did. But there is no record of any of these voyagers finding anything, and there is no reason to suppose that they found
anything. One and all struck out into the Atlantic at seasons and
in latitudes where strong westerly winds, even today, make navigation full of danger and uncertainty for sailing vessels. Portuguese caravels were weatherly craft, but they could not cope
with a head wind and a rough head sea. John Cabot was the first
mariner to cross the Atlantic by the short northern route; yet in
spite of taking off from Bristol, where he had a better chance for
easterlies than from the Azores, and at the best time of year, he
required almost eight weeks for the passage to Cape Breton Island;
and Cabot sailed after Columbus had made two successful voyages.

So it is no discredit to the Portuguese mariners that they turned back, discouraged by their buffetings, before reaching America. Even the islands that some of them imagined they saw encouraged Columbus; and if he succeeded where they failed, it was because he had the sense or the luck to follow a latitude where northeast trade winds prevailed.

As for the islands reported west of the Azores, only a person who has never been to sea would believe in their existence. Sighting phantom islands and disappearing coasts is a commonplace of ocean voyaging. A line of haze, a cloud on the horizon (especially at sunset) often looks so like an island as to deceive even experienced mariners who know that no land is there. In Columbus's day, when anything was possible, a shipmaster sighting an imaginary island at sunset would set a course for it if the wind served, and when day broke and no land appeared, he would conclude that by some compass or other error he had passed it in the night. Columbus made two such false landfalls on his First Voyage. Consult any terrestrial globe a century or more old, and you will find the Atlantic fairly peppered with imaginary islands, rocks and "reported breakers." Brazil Rock, last of these phantoms, was not removed from Admiralty charts until 1873. If every island were real that some mariner has thought he sighted during the last four centuries, they would be as close together as the Florida keys.

More substantial evidence of exotic lands to the westward was collected by Columbus during his residence in Portugal and the islands. A Portuguese pilot named Vicente picked up "a piece of wood ingeniously wrought, but not with iron," out beyond the Azores. Columbus's brother-in-law Pedro Correa da Cunha collected a similar piece of carved driftwood on Porto Santo, and canes so thick that each joint would hold a couple of quarts of wine; no such canes were known in Africa, and Columbus thought these must be the bamboo described (though not by that name) in Ptolemy. Two dead bodies had been cast up on Flores, not like Christians but broad-faced like the "Chinese" that Columbus had seen in Galway.

The driftwood was really a substantial clue. The Gulf Stream fans out so broadly northwest of the Azores that very little flotsam reaches them or the Madeiras, except objects of a low specific gravity which are helped across by the westerly winds. After every tempest the people in these islands pick up on their beaches specimens of the common horse-bean, which they call *fava do mar*, "sea bean."* This is the seed of *Entada gigas*, a woody climber related to the mimosa that grows all along the shores of the Caribbean. Its skin has the same color and texture as that of a horse chestnut, and inside there is a large median air space, which enables the bean to float long distances. Tropical rains carry them to streams and rivers, the Gulf Stream and the winds take them across the Atlantic and they have been picked up alongshore all the way from the Shetlands to Madeira. I was given a *fava do mar* by an Azorean fisherman, in which he had drilled a little hole so that it served him as a snuffbox; four months later, while searching for the site of Columbus's attempted settlement of Belén on the coast of Panama, I found hundreds of similar beans on the beach.

Large driftwood rarely comes ashore on the outer Azores, but an old gentleman recalled that after the great storm of 1869 he saw cast up on the beaches of São Miguel a number of tree trunks, "bluish, horizontally striped with black." These are easily identified as the Cuipo tree (*Cavanillesia platanifolia*) which grows in Central America; the wood is superlatively light so that it floats high and catches the wind.

Columbus, then, had definite physical clues of transatlantic lands with an exotic flora, as well as indefinite rumors of islands. Did he have any definite information? Not long after his great discovery a story began to circulate that Columbus was merely carrying out someone's sailing directions. As Oviedo, the first to publish this story of the Unknown Pilot (in 1535), says: —

Some say that a caravel that was sailing from Spain to England charged with merchandise and provisions, such as wine and other things which are usually shipped to that island . . . was subjected to such mighty and violent tempests and foul winds that she was forced to run westward for so many days that she picked up one or more of the islands of these regions and Indies; and [the pilot] went ashore

---

* In Porto Santo they are called *favas de Colom*, Columbus beans, for the people think that these are what gave him the clue.

and saw naked people . . . and when the winds moderated which had driven him thither against his will, he took on water and wood to return to his first course. They also say that the better part of the cargo which this vessel carried consisted of provisions and things to eat and wines, whereof they were able to sustain life on so long a voyage. . . .

But it took four or five months to return. Everyone but three or four mariners and the pilot died en route, and all save he arrived in so bad a condition that they died shortly after.

Moreover, it is said that this pilot was a very intimate friend of Christopher Columbus, and that he understood somewhat of the latitudes, and marked the land which he found, and in great secrecy shared it with Columbus, whom he asked to make a chart and indicate on it the land which he had seen. It is said that Columbus received him in his house as a friend and sought to cure him, as he too landed very weak; but that he died like the rest, and thus Columbus was informed of the land and navigation of those regions, and he alone knew the secret. Some say that this master or pilot was Andalusian, others have him Portuguese, others Basque; some say that Columbus was then in the island of Madeira and others in the Cape Verde Islands, and that there the aforesaid caravel came to harbor, and in this way Columbus learned of the land. Whether this was so or not, nobody can truly affirm; but so the story ran among the common people. As for me I hold it to be false; and as St. Augustine says, *Melius est dubitare de ocultis, quam litigare de incertis* — "Better to doubt what is obscure, than dispute about things uncertain."

Few later writers on Columbus took Augustine's excellent advice. Las Casas, who says that the story was current in Santo Domingo on his first arrival in 1500, repeats it in almost the same words as Oviedo. Other versions are given by Gomara (1553), the Inca chronicler Garcilaso de la Vega (1609), Orellana (1639) and later historians. Some name the unknown pilot Alonso Sánchez and give his home as Palos, Huelva, Galicia or Portugal; the fugitive caravel was engaged in commerce between the Peninsula and Madeira or the Canaries or the Gold Coast; she is "blown across" in 28 or 29 days by an "east wind of great fury and relentlessness" in 1484; she returns to Graciosa, Terceira, Madeira, Porto Santo or the Canaries, in each of which Columbus performs his well-rewarded act of charity.

Certain modern pundits, whose critical standards are so severe that they reject Columbus's sea journals as unauthentic, snap at this Tale of an Ancient Mariner and swallow it, hook, line and sinker. The real objection to the story is meteorological. It is impossible for a vessel to be "blown across" the North Atlantic from east to west: I challenge anyone to produce a single instance. She might drift across in the trades after a storm that blew all her sails to ribbons; but if she had any sails left there would have been no need to drift westward, she could have worked her way home after the storm subsided. In August–October, 1940, two boys, survivors of the torpedoed *Anglo-Saxon,* sailed in an eighteen-foot jolly boat from a point about 800 miles SW by S of the Azores to Eleuthera in the Bahamas in 70 days; but they arrived half dead and could not possibly have returned unaided. Supposing the Unknown Pilot's ship had lost her sails in an easterly storm and then drifted to the Antilles. There she would have stayed, without means to make new sails. Never could she have worked her way north to the zone of westerlies and then home, unless by such supernatural aid as sent Coleridge's Ancient Mariner zooming along in a flat calm.

Why then did the story appear credible to so many people in the sixteenth century? Because, for one thing, the winds had not been charted, nor would they be until the nineteenth century; so, for aught anyone knew, there might have been a sufficient spell of easterly storm to blow a ship to hell or Hispaniola. Perhaps some aged and mysterious seaman did die in Columbus's house, and after the great discovery people whispered, "That old fellow must have told him the way!" More probably the Unknown Pilot tale was made up by some malcontent in Hispaniola, where Las Casas first heard it in 1500, and gained currency because of an unfortunate human tendency to pluck at the laurels of the great. As Von Humboldt cynically remarked, there are three stages in the popular attitude toward a great discovery: first men doubt its existence, next they deny its importance, and finally they give the credit to someone else.

Just when Columbus matured his plans to the point of doing something about them, it is impossible to say. The gathering of "evidence" must have gone on for some years, and the Toscanelli correspondence must have been concluded not later than 1481, for the Florentine died in May 1482. Somehow or other, Columbus got wind of the fact that Toscanelli had the same idea as he that a westward voyage from Spain to Asia was practicable. Obtaining an introduction to him from a Florentine at Lisbon named Gerardi or Berardi, he wrote to the sage requesting particulars. Toscanelli replied enclosing a copy of his letter of 1474 to Fernão Martins, with this covering note: —

"To Cristóbal Columbo, Paul the Physician, greeting:

"I observe thy great and noble ambition to pass over to where the spices grow, Wherefore in reply to thy letter I send thee a copy of another letter which some time ago I wrote to a friend of mine, a servant of the most serene king of Portugal, before the wars of Castile, in answer to another which by command of his highness he wrote to me on this subject; and I send thee another sea-chart like the one which I sent to him, wherewith thy demands may be satisfied."

The letter enclosed to his friend Martins, we have already examined in Chapter IV. Although it and the chart (now irretrievably lost) gave Columbus the gist of the Florentine's ideas, he wanted more, and wrote again. Toscanelli's second letter to Columbus, also undated, exhibits some impatience at the young man's importunity, and merely repeats some of the observations in the 1474 letter to Martins. The concluding sentence, "I am not surprised that thou, who art of high courage, and the whole Portuguese nation who have always been noble men in all great enterprises, should be inflamed and desirous to prosecute the said voyage," indicates that Toscanelli supposed his correspondent to be Portuguese.

The important thing that Columbus obtained from Toscanelli, apart from the prestige of having an eminent scholar approve his enterprise, was the Florentine's approval of Marco Polo. For the Venetian traveler had added some 30° of longitude to the easternmost point of China described by Ptolemy. And beyond Mangi, Cathay, Quinsay and Zatun, 1500 miles out to sea, Marco Polo placed the fabulously wealthy island of Cipangu (Japan) with its gold-roofed and gold-paved palaces. Even at that, Toscanelli predicted a sail of some 5000 nautical miles from Spain to China, although the voyage could be broken at the mythical island of Antillia

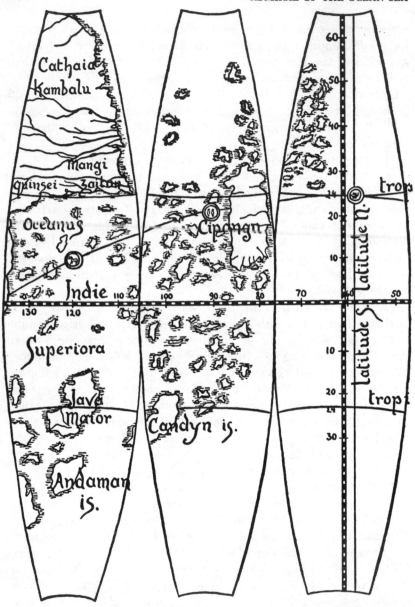

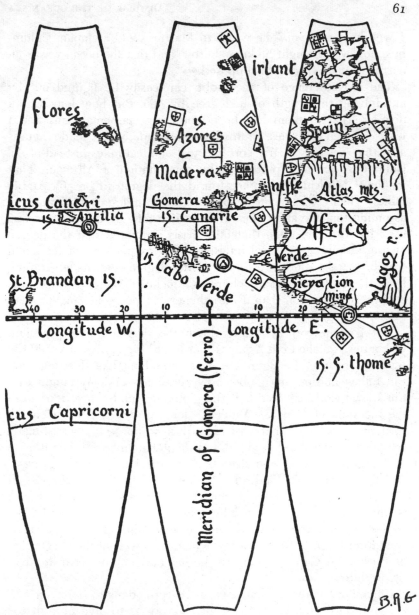

flores

Irlant

15.
Azores

Madera

Spain

niffe

Atlas mts.

cus Canđri

Gomera

15. Canarie

Africa

15. Antilia

E. Verde

15. Cabo Verde

St. Brandan 15.

Sieva Lion
mina

Lagos

40   30   20   10   0   10   20

Longitude W.   Longitude E.

15. S. thome

cus Capricorni

Meridian of Gomera (ferro)

B.R.G

BEHAIM'S GLOBE OF 1492
Original. Degree Numbers Added.

("well known to you," he wrote to Martins) and at Japan. Columbus, however, thought he knew better, and that the ocean was even
narrower than Toscanelli supposed.

The circumference of the globe can easily be figured out by
multiplying the length of a degree by 360. But how long was a
degree? That problem had been bothering mathematicians for at
least eighteen centuries. Eratosthenes around 200 B.C. made a guess
at it that was very nearly correct: 59.5 nautical miles instead of 60.
Columbus, however, preferred the computation of Alfragan. That
medieval Moslem geographer found the degree to be 56⅔ Arabic
miles, which works out at 66.2 nautical miles; but Columbus,
assuming that the short Roman or Italian mile of 1480 meters was
used by Alfragan, upon that false basis computed that the degree
measured only 45 nautical miles, roughly 75 per cent of its actual
length, and the shortest estimate of the degree ever made. Arguing
from this faulty premise, Columbus concluded that the world was
25 per cent smaller than Eratosthenes, 10 per cent smaller than
Ptolemy, taught.

Not content with whittling down the degree by 25 per cent,
Columbus stretched out Asia eastward until Japan almost kissed the
Azores. The way he figured it was something like this; and you
can follow him on any globe, however small. Ptolemy taught that
the known world covered half the globe's circumference, 180° from
the meridian of Cape St. Vincent (long. 9° W of Greenwich) to
"Catigara" in Asia. That was already a 50 per cent overestimate,
but Columbus insisted it was all too small. He preferred the estimate
of Marinus of Tyre, who stretched out the known world to 225°.
To that Columbus added an additional 28° for the discoveries of
Marco Polo, and 30° for the reputed distance from eastern China
to the east coast of Japan. The total width of Europe and "The
Indies" thus measured 283°, and as Columbus proposes to start
west from Ferro in the Canaries, which is 9° west of the "beginning
of Europe" at Cape St. Vincent, he has only 68° of ocean to cross
before hitting Japan.

Columbus, moreover, had two more corrections to be taken into
account, and applied them in such a way as to give him all the
breaks. (1) Assuming that Marinus of Tyre's already exaggerated
linear distance from Cape St. Vincent eastward to the end of Asia

was correct, the distance in degrees was too small, because Marinus's degree (so Columbus thought) was oversize. So, instead of 68° of open water to be crossed between the Canaries and Japan, there were only 60° of longitude to cover. (2) As Columbus estimated a degree of longitude on the equator to be 45 nautical miles, it would measure only 40 miles on latitude 28°, which he proposed to follow for his ocean crossing. Therefore he had only 60 × 40 or 2400 nautical miles (750 leagues) to sail. As we shall see, he expected to hit land at exactly that distance from the Canaries on his First Voyage. In other words, his calculations placed Japan about on the meridian of the Anegada Passage, Virgin Islands.

A brief table will exhibit the colossal errors of these fifteenth-century optimists, the distances being reduced to nautical miles, and assuming Behaim's length of a degree to be the same as that of Columbus: —

	Toscanelli	Martin Behaim	Columbus	Actual air-line*
Canaries to Cipangu (Japan) . . .	3000	3080	2400	10,600
Canaries to Quinsay (Hangchow) . .	5000	4440	3550	11,766

Of course this calculation is not logical, but Columbus's mind was not logical. He *knew* he could make it, and the figures had to fit. To anticipate a bit, the Portuguese king's committee of mathematicians will have no difficulty in seeing the flaw in his reasoning; for even if he were right and Ptolemy wrong about the length of a degree (which they would hardly be disposed to admit), he had applied the corrections both ways in order to narrow down the ocean as much as possible. One can well imagine him explaining it, his eyes sparkling and his ruddy complexion flaming, with Bartholomew standing by to back him up; and one can anticipate the committee's reply. No bogy terrors of shoals and sea monsters, no flat-earth nonsense, but good solid arguments like this: —

Unfortunately, Captain Colombo, we deny the validity of your calculation of the globe, we suspect the accuracy of your compatriot Marco Polo, we doubt the existence of his Cipangu; Ptolemy mentioned no such place. According to the close calculations of our

* Between the respective meridians, measured on latitude 28°.

mathematical experts, who were already studying the heavens when you were plying the shuttle, it would be necessary to sail at least 10,000 nautical miles due west before reaching Catigara, the eastern verge of the known world. Master Paul, on your own showing, makes it 5000 miles to Quinsay, if such a place there be. Even assuming that you find favorable winds over that vast expanse of ocean (which we strongly doubt), and that you can sail an average of four knots, which is what our best caravels can do on long voyages, your passage would require a hundred days. Over fourteen weeks beyond sight of land! We should not feel justified in risking the money of the king our lord (whom God preserve), or the lives of his subjects, on so dubious an enterprise. . . . You may go.

Whether or not Columbus first tried to interest his native city in the Enterprise of the Indies, the first definite offer known to us is the one that he made to D. João II, king of Portugal.

These were busy years for the energetic young king and his navigators. In 1484 he appointed a *Junta dos Mathemáticos* or Maritime Advisory Committee to deal with matters of navigation and discovery. Its principal members were Diogo Ortiz de Vilhegas, a churchman high in the king's favor, and two learned Jewish physicians: Master Rodrigo the king's physician, and Master José Vizinho, a pupil of the famous Rabbi Abraham Zacuto who was professor of mathematics at Salamanca. Their first assignment was to provide instruments and tables by which navigators would ascertain their position in the low latitudes where the North Star was invisible. To this end Rodrigo simplified the astrologers' astrolabe and made it an effective instrument for taking a meridional altitude of the sun,* José Vizinho translated Zacuto's ephemerides and was sent by the king in 1485 to fix the latitude of important places in Africa. Columbus was present when he returned and reported that the Los Islands lay on latitude 5° N, a mistake of 4° 30'.

At home, D. João II was faced with privy conspiracy and rebellion. The Duke of Bragança was executed for treason in May 1483, and the Duke of Viseu, the Queen's brother, was personally assassinated by D. João II in August 1484. Now the king was ready to

---

* See illustration in Chapter XIII, below.

consider what Columbus had to offer, as the Spanish Sovereigns were after the conquest of Granada. We may assume that the Enterprise of the Indies was laid before him in the later months of 1484.

João de Barros, "the Portuguese Livy," is our first authority for the negotiations between Columbus and the king, and he had unusual means of information. In his *Decades of Asia*, begun in 1539 and first published in 1552, Barros says: —

As all men declare, *Christovão Colom* was of Genoese nation, a man expert, eloquent and good Latinist, and very boastful in his affairs. And since at that time the Genoese nation was one of the powers of Italy which navigated more by reason of their merchandise and commerce, he, following the custom of his country and his proper inclination, went a-sailing over these seas to the eastward for a very long time until he came to these regions of Spain, and gave himself to the navigation of the Ocean Sea, following the same profession. And, seeing that the king D. João frequently ordered the coast of Africa to be explored with the intention of going by that route to reach India, and as he was a Latinist and curious in matters of geography, and since he read a good deal in Marco Polo who spoke moderately [!] of Oriental matters of the kingdom of Cathay, and of the mighty Isle Cypango, he reached the conception that over this Western Ocean Sea one could sail to this Isle Cypango and other unknown lands. For, since in the time of the Infante D. Henrique the Azores were discovered, so there should be other islands and lands to the westward, since nature could not have made so disorderly a composition of the globe as to give the element of water preponderance over the land, destined for life and the creation of souls.* With these fancies, given to him by his continual voyaging and the conversation of men proficient therein, who in this kingdom were very knowing in past discoveries, he came to demand of the king D. João that he give him some vessels to go and discover the Isle Cypango by this Western Ocean, not confiding so much in what he had come to know (or rather dreamed) of some Western Islands, as in the experience he had that in these matters foreigners would be much accredited. . . .

---

* That six sevenths of the globe were land was the favorite medieval geographical notion which Columbus shared, and referred for authority to the apocryphal Book of 2 Esdras vi 42, "six parts hast thou dried up."

Barros alludes to some of the foreigners like Antonio de Noli who had made discoveries for Portugal, and takes time out to refute what Cardan had written about the connection of Columbus's voyages with those of the Carthaginians. He then continues:—

The king, as he observed this *Christovão Colom* to be a big talker and boastful in setting forth his accomplishments, and full of fancy and imagination with his Isle Cypango than certain whereof he spoke, gave him small credit. However, by strength of his importunity it was ordered that he confer with D. Diogo Ortiz bishop of Ceuta and Master Rodrigo and Master José, to whom the king had committed these matters of cosmography and discovery, and they all considered the words of *Christovão Colom* as vain, simply founded on imagination, or things like that Isle Cypango of Marco Polo. . . .

Note the emphasis on Japan and on Marco Polo's story, which was the foundation of Columbus's ideas regarding the accessibility of Asia, and of the Toscanelli letter. Columbus's strongest point was the practical possibility of reaching gold-roofed Japan. And there must have been something mathematical about Columbus's proposition, or the king would not have submitted it to his maritime commission.

Ferdinand hints that his father's price to the king of Portugal was too high. "For the Admiral," says he, "being a man of generous and lofty thoughts, would covenant to his great honor and advantage, in order to have his own reputation and the dignity of his house conform to the grandeur of his work and of his merits."

Las Casas, who wrote the *Historia de las Indias* after Barros's account had been published, repeats in substance what the Portuguese historian wrote, but adds considerable detail. Columbus proposed, he said, to sail to "the land of India and the great island of Cipango and the realms of the Grand Khan, which means in our vernacular Great King of Kings." And the materials and conditions he demanded were as follows: —

(1) That the king equip three caravels manned and provisioned for one year, and loaded with trading goods such as hawks' bells, brass basins, glass beads, red caps and colored cloth. (2) That the king make Columbus *caballero,* so that he and his descendants could be styled *Don;* that he create him "Great Admiral of the Ocean," with all rights and privileges appertaining to admirals of Castile;

and appoint him perpetual Viceroy and Governor of all islands and mainlands that he might discover. (3) That Columbus retain a tenth part of all revenues and precious metals derived from these lands, and have the privilege of freighting an eighth part of all ships trading with the countries he discovers.

These are exactly the same conditions that Columbus later demanded and obtained from the Sovereigns of Castile. The almost word-for-word similarity arouses the suspicion that Las Casas simply read back into the Portuguese negotiations the known conditions of the Spanish "capitulations" of 1492. Especially suspect is the statement that Columbus demanded of the king of Portugal the rights of an admiral of Castile. Why of Castile? In Portugal the office of admiral was hereditary in the Genoese family of Pessagno or Pessanhas. Surely that would have been the obvious model for another would-be Genoese admiral. It looks very much as if Las Casas picked up from Ferdinand the hint that his father's negotiation with Portugal was wrecked by asking too much, and that he merely assumed that the same conditions were set as in 1492. I very much doubt whether his inference was correct. Columbus had doubtless observed that Diogo Cão, a man of the people like himself, was ennobled for merely discovering a big river and planting a stone column "furthest South." He may well have decided in his own mind that he must have something very substantial for making a far more original and significant discovery than that of the Congo. Son of a shiftless father in the lower middle classes, he had known poverty and struggle, the indifference of the great and the contempt of the secure; he would naturally have resolved to barter his enterprise for titles, honors, and riches which his descendants could inherit. But it is very doubtful whether he ever got to the point of stating these conditions to the king, and the question of rewards and honors was no business of the maritime committee.

Only this is certain about the Portuguese negotiations of 1484–1485: Columbus required the king to provide him with more than one ship, and Japan was his proposed destination. The proposition was rejected by a commission of experts on technical grounds. Now, Japan was oriental, a part of Asia or of "The Indies" as then commonly understood; Columbus's intention to reach "The Indies," and not merely to pick up Antillia or other reported islands, may then be considered proved. And we may fairly infer that the experts' objection to his enterprise was their knowledge that his estimate of the distance was impossibly small. How old Neptune must have laughed at this eager navigator and the skeptical experts, both in a sense right, yet both so completely wrong!

Yet Columbus had made an impression on the king. They parted friends, and very likely D. João encouraged him to call again, in case Diogo Cão's second voyage failed to round Africa.

In 1485 the king made a bargain with two of his own subjects to perform at least part of Columbus's and Toscanelli's project, the discovery of Antillia, which the Portuguese called the Island of the Seven Cities. Fernão Dulmo of Terceira, who applied for permission to sail in two caravels "to seek and find a great island or islands or mainland by its coast, which is presumed to be the Isle of the Seven Cities, and all this at his own proper charge and expense," was given a royal donation of anything he might discover. The king promised to confer on him, if successful, suitable "titles of honor"; a reflection, doubtless, of Diogo Cão's knighthood. Unable to swing it alone, Dulmo takes in João Estreito of Funchal as partner, and the king confirms the grant to both, with the interesting proviso that Dulmo shall command the fleet during the first forty days of their volage from Terceira, and possess all lands discovered in that space of time, after which Estreito shall fly the commodore's pendant and keep everything discovered thereafter, until their return home. And, whilst the kings had contributed nothing to earlier Atlantic explorers, D. João now promises naval assistance in case the inhabitants of Antillia forcibly resist annexation to their former mother country.

So it is clear that D. João had become strongly interested in Atlantic exploration, if not in a western route to the Indies. Dulmo had given him a much better bargain than Columbus offered. The outfitting of Dulmo's fleet will not cost the crown a maravedi. Dulmo and Estreito agree to sail westward at least forty days, which they may have figured out to be the maximum time required to reach Cipangu. If they discover Antillia, why not continue to Cipangu? Portugal would then have an alternate route to the Indies. If not, the crown would lose nothing.

The date set for the start of this interesting voyage was March 1, 1487. Absolutely nothing about it can be found in Portuguese sources; but from an oblique reference of Ferdinand Columbus's to the land which Fernão Dulmo "sought to discover," and whose story he proposed (but forgot) to relate, Dulmo and Estreito evidently set sail. Their proposed starting point, Terceira in the Azores, is the key to their failure. Like earlier Portuguese explorers of the Atlantic, they had to buck the westerlies in high latitudes. Had Columbus made the same mistake, we should probably know as little of him as we know of Dulmo and Estreito.

Columbus and D. João II, as we have said, parted friends after his enterprise had been rejected, and the possibility of their eventually coming to terms was held open. Columbus went to Spain in 1485; but he made very little progress there. Early in 1488 he wrote to D. João II from Seville expressing a desire to renew his application, and to visit Lisbon if he could have a safe-conduct from arrest; for he had probably left unpaid bills behind. The king replied in the most cordial terms, addressing Columbus as "our particular friend," lauding his "industry and good talent," urging and even begging him to come immediately, guaranteeing his freedom from arrest or detention for whatever cause, and assuring him that he would be highly grateful for his coming. What cause can be assigned for the king's amazing forthcomingness, save Dulmo's return empty-handed, and the lack of news from Bartholomew Dias, then searching for the African route to India?

Columbus proved a little less eager than the king, for he did not come to Portugal immediately. Possibly he expected a report from the Spanish committee that had had his proposition under advisement for over two years. But by December Columbus had reached Lisbon, in time to witness the dramatic conclusion of a great voyage.

Bartholomew Dias sailed from Portugal in the summer of 1487 with two caravels and a storeship, and India as his destination. Passing the furthest south of Diogo Cão's second voyage (22° south latitude), he felt his way along the coast, and at Christmas tide reached Angra Pequeña, a point south of Orange River at latitude 26° 38′ S. There he left the storeship. As the wind was freshening from seaward the two caravels clawed offshore, and were overtaken by a heavy NW gale (a rarity in those latitudes) which drove them to the southward; and on January 6, 1488, Dias lost sight of, land. When the wind moderated and shifted he turned east and, having failed in the course of several days to sight land, altered the course to the northward. On February 3, 1488, the lookouts reported land on the larboard bow. They were actually about 200 miles east of the Cape, at Mossel Bay. Dias followed the coast northward, about to the Great Fish River, where his seamen refused to go further, and he was forced to return. On the homeward passage Dias called at the Cape, which either he or D. João II named *Cabo de Boa Esperança*, Cape of Good Hope.

Columbus was in Lisbon in December 1488, when the Dias fleet came proudly sailing into the Tagus. In one of the postils written in his copy of Pierre d'Ailly's *Imago Mundi*, in order to refute Ptolemy's notion that only one sixth of the globe is land, he says: —

"Note that in this year '88 in the month of December arrived in Lisbon *Bartholomaeus Didacus* captain of three caravels which the most serene king of Portugal had sent to try out the land in Guinea. He reported . . . that he had reached a promontory which he called *Cabo de Boa Esperança*, which we believe to be in *Agesinba* (Abyssinia). IIe says that in this place he discovered by the astrolabe that he was 45° below the equator.* He has described his voyage and plotted it league by league on a marine chart in order to place it under the eyes of the said king. I was present in all of this."

Now that Africa had been circumnavigated and the eastern sea route to India was open, the king of Portugal had no more use for Columbus, who returned to Spain.

One more Portuguese postscript before we follow him thither. In 1484 there came to Lisbon a young Nuremberger named Martin Behaim, who by passing himself off as a pupil of the mathematician Regiomontanus managed to enter the most learned and courtly circles. D. João appointed him to the royal maritime commission (apparently he was absent when Columbus's scheme came up); he visited the Azores and married a daughter of the captain of Fayal, and received knighthood from the king in 1485. The next year he was proposed as a member of the Dulmo-Estreito voyage,

---

* The Cape is in latitude 34° 21' S, and Dias could not possibly have been below 37° S; another instance of the unreliability of celestial observations made in the era of Columbus.

but possibly did not go; in 1490 he returned to Nuremberg and there in 1492 constructed his famous globe, in time to receive complimentary mention in the *Nuremberg Chronicle*. The scale, the eastward extension of Asia, and the narrow ocean on this globe are so similar to the false geographical notions on which Columbus based his voyage, as to suggest that Columbus and Behaim were collaborators. But there is no positive evidence of their trails ever crossing.

Nevertheless, we have another strong connection between Behaim and Columbus, in an extraordinary letter from a German astronomer named Hieronymus Müntzer to D. João II. Müntzer writes from Nuremberg on July 14, 1493, in complete ignorance that Columbus had returned from "The Indies" four months earlier. He maintains that the East is very near the West by sea; numerous arguments demonstrate that by crossing the ocean, eastern Cathay can be reached in a few days. This is proved by the presence of elephants in Asia and in Africa, and by the canes that drift ashore in the Azores. Your Highness's seamen have proved that habitable land lies in the tropic zone of Africa; so it follows that similar land will be found on the same parallel in Asia. "You possess means and ample wealth; as also able mariners, eager to acquire immortality and fame. O what glory you would gain, if you made the habitable Orient known to the Occident, and what profits would its commerce give you, for you would make those islands of the Orient tributaries, and their kings amazed would quietly submit to your sovereignty!" And furthermore (here's what he is leading up to), our young man Martin Behaim is ready to take charge of such a voyage and set sail from the Azores whenever you say the word.

Here is Columbus's Enterprise of the Indies, complete even to the driftwood evidence and the naïve supposition that kings of the Orient will passively submit to the first European who reaches their coasts. It does not matter whether Behaim obtained this idea from Columbus, or worked it out independently from the same sources; Müntzer's letter is the last term of a cycle that began with the Toscanelli letter of 1474. Columbus's scheme of reaching the East by sailing West was in the air for eighteen years before he put it into execution; and if he had faltered or failed, another was ready to embark on the same bold adventure.

Martin Behaim, however, would have made the same old error of starting a transatlantic voyage from the Azores, in the teeth of westerly winds.

NOTE ON THE TOSCANELLI CORRESPONDENCE

Readers who have followed Columbian controversial literature of the last forty years may be surprised that I accept as genuine Toscanelli's letters to Canon Martins and to Columbus, since Henry Vignaud devoted a whole volume and parts of several others to arguing that they were false. If any still accept the Vignaud hypothesis, they are referred to the able, scholarly and critical discussion of the Toscanelli question by Dr. Diego Luis Molinari in the University of Buenos Aires' co-operative *Historia de la Nacion Argentina* II (1937) 398–425. Dr. Molinari's chapter in that volume is the best account of the Grand Enterprise of Columbus that has appeared in any language.

CHAPTER VII

In Castile

1485-1490

Dimitte populum meum ut sacrificet nihi.

Let my people go, that they may serve me.

— EXODUS ix 1

ABOUT the middle of the year 1485 Christopher Columbus with his five-year-old son Diego took passage from Lisbon for the port of Palos in Andalusia, with the purpose of offering his Enterprise of the Indies to the Sovereigns of Castile. He left Lisbon furtively and in haste, probably because he feared arrest for debt. Living expenses during the many months of promotion in Lisbon, and the cost of giving Doña Felipa a burial commensurate with her rank, must have consumed all Columbus's savings from his Guinea voyage and his Funchal business. Bartholomew remained in Lisbon for at least three years, supporting himself by making and selling charts.

The ship that took Columbus and his little son from Lisbon rounded Cape St. Vincent, crossed the bar of Saltés and anchored off the town of Palos on the Rio Tinto. It was rather a melancholy region of Spain to which Columbus had come, by design or by chance. The ancient Condado de Niebla is an undulating coastal plain traversed by two tidal rivers, the Odiel and the Tinto, which unite a few miles from the sea to form the Saltés. Around the seaports there was a great waste of marshland. An even more optimistic temperament than that of Columbus would have felt a sinking of the heart on first viewing the sleepy little seaports of Huelva and Palos, comparing them with bright, brisk Lisbon or tidy Funchal surrounded by vineyards. Actually the stagnation of Huelva, Palos and Moguer was only temporary. The Niebla had been the center of Castile's African slave trade, and her men were only less skilled than the Portuguese in making long African voyages; but Castile had renounced her African trade in the treaty of 1481 and it was now forbidden. Columbus knew nobody in Spain except his Molyart brother- and sister-in-law, who lived at Huelva, but they were in no position to do anything for him.

When his ship rounded the promontory at the entrance to the Rio Tinto, Columbus noted on a bluff the buildings of the Franciscan friary of La Rábida. These suggested a solution of his first problem, what to do with Diego while he sought friends and ways and means. The Minorites were noted for their hospitality, and often conducted schools for young boys; perhaps this house would take charge of his son. Soon after landing at Palos, father and son set out for La Rábida.

On this occasion took place the pretty incident of the alms at the monastery door. García Fernández, physician of Huelva, testified at Palos in 1513 "that the said Admiral Don Cristóbal Colón with his son Don Diego now admiral, came on foot to La Rábida, a monastery of friars in this town, and asked the porter to give him bread and a drink of water for that little boy who was his son." No doubt this happened. It is a long and dusty walk to La Rábida from Palos, and the little fellow would have been hungry and thirsty. But Dr. Fernández places the incident about six years too late, implies that Columbus was down and out, and proceeds to tell how Fray Juan Pérez, who came to the gate, talked with the future Admiral, understood his project, and arranged an audience with the Queen. Hence this chance encounter and timely charity set the wheels rolling that led to the great discovery.

That part of the story belongs to 1491; Dr. Fernández combined two visits of Columbus to La Rábida in one. It is certain that Columbus left his boy at La Rábida very soon after landing in Spain; but the friar who helped him then was Antonio de Marchena, *custodio* of the Franciscan sub-province of Seville, a man of spirit and intelligence, and of high repute as an *astrólogo* (astronomer). Fray Juan Pérez, *guardian* or head of La Rábida, helped Columbus in 1491; on this first visit he perhaps sent Columbus to Seville with a letter of introduction to Fray Antonio, or the *custodio* may have been visiting the friary when it received this unexpected visit from two future admirals of the Indies.

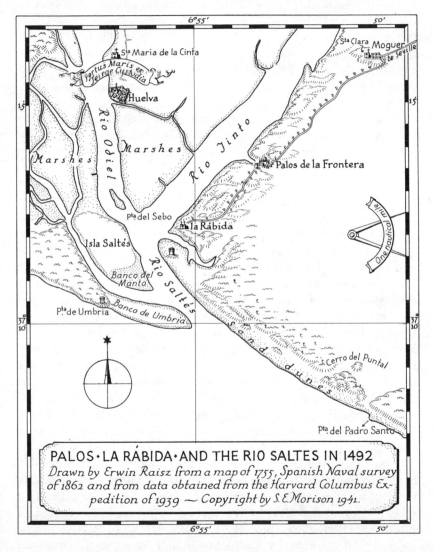

PALOS·LA RÁBIDA·AND THE RIO SALTES IN 1492
Drawn by Erwin Raisz from a map of 1755, Spanish Naval survey of 1862 and from data obtained from the Harvard Columbus Expedition of 1939 — Copyright by S. E. Morison 1941.

Antonio de Marchena was not so set in his ideas of the size of the globe as to be impervious to argument; Columbus later gave him credit for being one of the few Spaniards who believed he was right and furthered his enterprise. A man of imagination and human sympathy, he decided that Columbus had something, and became his advocate. On Fray Antonio's advice, application was first made to the very magnificent Don Enrique de Guzmán, Duke of Medina Sidonia, grandee of Spain and wealthiest subject of the Sovereigns. The duke became definitely interested, and was at the point of promising to equip a fleet for Columbus when, owing to an unseemly brawl with the Duke of Cadiz, the Sovereigns ordered him to leave Seville and the negotiations were broken off. Columbus then turned to Don Luis de la Cerda, Count of Medina Celi, who had a large establishment at Puerto Santa María and owned a merchant fleet.

At this point we have definite and contemporary evidence. A few days after the Admiral's return from his First Voyage, Medina Celi (who in the meantime had been created duke) wrote to the Grand Cardinal of Spain declaring that he had received Columbus on his first arrival from Portugal, and that he then decided to underwrite the Enterprise and provide the Genoese "with three or four well equipped caravels, for he asked no more." Thinking that royal permission was desirable for so important an affair, he applied to the Queen; she then ordered the man to come to court. After hearing Columbus, Isabella decided to submit his proposal to an advisory commission, but agreed that Medina Celi might outfit the fleet and invest in it if her decision was favorable. Later she decided to undertake the entire expense herself. In the meantime the duke had entertained Columbus for two years. Accordingly, on the ground that this great voyage was indirectly due to him, Medina Celi begs the cardinal to ask the Queen to permit him to send a few caravels annually to the newly discovered lands.

Most interesting is the statement that Columbus then demanded nothing more than three or four caravels, suitably equipped. Obviously a mere nobleman could not confer hereditary titles or offices or promise a tithe of the revenues and trade of the Indies. Following Portuguese precedent in the Western Islands, "The Indies" if discovered by Columbus under ducal auspices would have been conferred by the Sovereigns on the duke, who might reward the discoverer with a hereditary captaincy, and whatever share of the revenues he saw fit. So, if Las Casas's account of the Portuguese negotiation of 1484–1485 is correct, Columbus had come down tremendously in his price. It seems much more likely that Las Casas made a mistake, and that Columbus never demanded titles, honors and revenues until 1491.

Columbus was so much the man of action, looked so constantly ahead and not astern, that the reminiscent passages in his writings are very few. One of these fixes the date of his arrival at the royal city of Cordova as January 20, 1486. He was too late to catch the King and Queen (they had left for Madrid at the end of 1485); but he always regarded himself as having been constantly in their service from the day of his arrival.

In that interval of waiting Columbus entered into relations with a young woman of Cordova named Beatriz Enríquez de Harana, who became the mother of his son Ferdinand in the late summer of 1488. Many and diverse have been the speculations about this girl, ranging all the way from a noble lady of Cordova down to chambermaid of the inn where Columbus stayed. Fortunately, the researches of my good friend D. José de la Torre, in the municipal archives of Cordova, have discovered exactly who Beatriz was, and how Columbus happened to meet her.

The Haranas were a family long established in Cordova and the vicinity as peasants, wine pressers and gardeners. Beatriz, daughter of a peasant named Pedro de Torquemada (a remote cousin of the grand inquisitor) and of Ana Núñez de Harana, was born about 1465 in the hamlet of Santa María de Trasierra up in the hills northwest of Cordova. Both her parents died when she was a child. With her elder brother, Pedro de Harana, who subsequently commanded a caravel on Columbus's Third Voyage, she went to live in Cordova with her mother's first cousin, Rodrigo Enríquez de Harana.

Rodrigo, though a wine presser by trade, was a man of culture and intelligence who married above his station and lived beyond his means. He had a son Diego de Harana, second cousin to Beatriz and subsequently marshal of the fleet on Columbus's First Voyage. These Haranas were friends and neighbors of Maestre Juan Sánchez, subsequently surgeon of the *Santa María*, and of a Genoese apothecary named Leonardo de Esbarraya whose shop was near the Puerto del Hierro of Cordova. In those days apothecary shops were informal clubs for physicians, surgeons and amateur scientists. Columbus probably drifted into the *botica* because it was kept by a compatriot, and frequented it as the place where local scientists foregathered. He made friends with Diego de Harana, a member of this informal club, was invited to his father's house, and there met the young orphan who became his mistress.

Although the sentimental and ecclesiastical biographers of Columbus insist that a clandestine marriage took place between him and Beatriz, nothing in his life is more certain than that he did *not* marry her, secretly or otherwise. Las Casas and Oviedo declare that Ferdinand was born out of wedlock. Columbus refers to Beatriz twice in his extant writings, in 1502 and 1506, and by her maiden name, not as his wife. She survived him fourteen years, and in sundry documents signs herself or is referred to by the notary as Beatriz Enríquez de Harana, never as Doña Beatriz Colón y Enríquez, or as widow of the great Admiral.

These documents prove incidentally that Beatriz knew how to read and write, but nothing is known of her appearance, personality or character. We do not even know how long Columbus lived with her; perhaps not after his First Voyage. But he had her on his mind all his life; for in 1502 he ordered his legitimate son Diego to give her the annuity of 10,000 maravedis which he took as reward for first sighting the New World, and in a testamentary codicil of 1506 he charged Diego to see that "Beatriz Enríquez, mother of Don Fernando my son, is put in a way to live honorably, as a person to whom I am in so great debt, and thus for discharge of my conscience, because it weigheth much on my mind."

Why he never married her, although his wife was dead, may easily be inferred. It was not to his advantage. Doña Felipa had been a lady of rank who helped him up in the world; if he married again, it must be to another lady of rank, like Doña Beatriz de Peraza, whom he is said to have wooed at Gomera. A peasant's daughter, unpresentable at court, would have been a bar to his ambition when still a suppliant, and an unsuitable match for an admiral and viceroy. The moral aspects of the relationship need not trouble us, since they did not bother his contemporaries. In an era when grandees, bishops and princes of the Church openly paraded their mistresses and procured honors and titles for their bastards, nobody criticized Columbus for not marrying the mother of his second son. Her family were evidently proud of the connection, since the cousin and the brother of Beatriz accepted responsible offices in the Admiral's fleets. Relations between them and the legitimate Colons remained intimate for at least three generations. D. Diego the second admiral of the Indies not only paid the annuity to Beatriz as his father had commanded, but remembered her in his will; and his widow, the Virreina Doña María de Colón y Toledo, made generous bequests to Beatriz's nephew Pedro de Harana and to Pedro's daughter Catalina. Moreover, it was Ferdinand, the son of this illicit union and biographer of the Admiral, who worked hard and successfully to protect the hereditary rights of his legitimate half-brother D. Diego.

.   .   .   .

In late April, which is almost summer in Andalusia, the Sovereigns again took up their residence in the Alcazar of Cordova, just over the Guadalquivir from the Moorish stone bridge and hard by the magnificent mosque, which had been rededicated as a cathedral church. For the first time Columbus was brought into the presence of Ferdinand and Isabella, to whose reign his achievements were destined to lend the brightest luster.

The marriage in 1469 of Isabella of Castile with Ferdinand of Aragon united modern Spain, the kingdom which became mistress of Europe in the next century through her own valor, implemented by the vast wealth that Columbus was now asking permission to pour into her lap. When he first appeared before *los Reyes Católicos,* "the Catholic Sovereigns," as Ferdinand and Isabella were generally called, they had been joint rulers of Castile, León and Aragon for twelve years. In this period they had curbed the power of the nobles and strengthened that of the crown, restored internal order, and "succeeded in arousing the economic energies of Castile in a variety of directions, and to an extent previously unknown." They had liquidated the secular struggle with Portugal by renouncing West Africa and securing the Canaries, whose conquest, a

dress rehearsal for that of America, was already under way. Since
the Canaries were Columbus's destined point of departure, that
was all to the good; but a nearer conquest then being pressed, of
the Moorish kingdom of Granada, was using so much energy and
money as to hinder his chance of interesting the Sovereigns in an
oceanic enterprise. It was as if a polar explorer had tried to interest
Lincoln in the conquest of the Antarctic about the time of the
Battle of Gettysburg.

Ferdinand of Aragon was not an agreeable person, and the contrast in this respect with the Queen has tended to obscure his
abilities. His great and consuming interest was diplomacy: to deceive an old fool like Louis XII of France, which he boasted having
done no less than ten times, was his greatest delight; and there was
no league or combination of states on the continent in which he did
not have a hand. His Catalan and Valencian kingdoms, bordering on
the Mediterranean, had maritime interests and traditions, but looked
eastward rather than westward. Columbus could not expect much
from him.

Isabella of Castile was a strikingly handsome woman with regular
features, a fresh, clear complexion, blue eyes and auburn hair; the
coloring particularly admired in Spain because of its rarity. Her
manners were gracious, dignified and affable, and she showed such
tact in dealing with people as to gain an ascendancy over her
turbulent subjects that no king of Castile could boast. She was
simple in her tastes, temperate in her diet, and only tolerated
frivolous entertainments at her court in the hope of weaning young
ruffians of the nobility from their savage amusements. For the
internal problems of Castile, which were many and complicated,
she showed a statesman's grasp, and pursued a policy with tenacity
and skill. When once she had given her confidence to a man, he
could count on her unvarying support. Her piety and exemplary
moral conduct were such that even in the corrupt court of her
brother and predecessor, no scandal was ever breathed against her
name. Unfortunately, too, she had the common defect of that
quality, intolerance and bigotry; her expulsion of the Jews entailed
a loss to her kingdoms that counterbalanced the gain from the conquest of Granada.

Christopher Columbus and Isabella the Catholic were of the same physical type, and very similar in character. She was his senior by only four or five months. Surely some spark of mutual comprehension and understanding passed between them when Columbus was first presented to her in the audience chamber of the Alcazar of Cordova, about the first day of May, 1486. She listened graciously to his ardent exposition of his desires. But before giving him further encouragement, several questions had to be settled. Did her counselors who were expert in such matters think a westward journey to the Indies practicable? Could the crown afford to underwrite it at that juncture? Or should Medina Celi be allowed to undertake it? In the meantime, she placed Columbus in charge of her comptroller of finances, Alonso de Quintanilla, who put him up at his house, and introduced him to the very magnificent Don Pedro González de Mendoza, Archbishop of Toledo, Grand Cardinal of Spain, first minister of the crown of Castile.

After this one burst of royal sunshine the clouds gathered once more, and the next five or six years were the hardest in Columbus's life. It would have been so much simpler had he been allowed to accept Medina Celi's offer. Las Casas says, "He began to sustain a terrible, continued, painful and prolonged battle; a material one of weapons would not have been so sharp and horrendous as that which he had to endure from informing so many people of no understanding, although they presumed to know all about it, and replying patiently to many people who did not know him nor had any respect for his person, receiving insulting speeches which afflicted his soul." For Columbus was not merely a mariner. He was proud and sensitive, he knew that he was right; and the clownish witticisms and crackpot jests of stupid and ignorant people were almost more than he could bear. Again and again in later life he alluded bitterly to those years, when almost everyone *fazen burla*, made game of him and his enterprise. Often, and most unwisely, he went out of his way to remind the Sovereigns and others how everyone had been wrong and he right.

Fray Hernando de Talavera, Prior del Prado (a Jeronymite monastery near Valladolid), the Queen's confessor and subsequently Archbishop of Granada, was chosen to organize a commission to examine Columbus's project. It first met at Cordova in the early summer of 1486, and adjourned to Salamanca where the court spent Christmas.

Salamanca was then a university of residential colleges, following the usual late-medieval organization that is now preserved only in Oxford and Cambridge. One of these colleges, that of St. Stephen, was presided over by the Dominican father Diego de Deza, later Bishop of Palencia and Archbishop of Seville. Columbus found in him one of his warmest and most useful advocates in Spain. In this college the Talavera commission sat. For, in 1515 a city councilor named Dr. Rodrigo Maldonado testified that he was there present when Talavera "with other wise and learned men and mariners, discussed with the said Admiral about his going to the said islands, and that all of them agreed that what the Admiral said could not possibly be true, and that contrary to what appeared to the most of them the Admiral persisted. . . ."

Obviously the thing that "could not possibly be true" was the Admiral's theory of a narrow ocean between Spain and the Indies. It was not true. Yet, owing to the feeling of Diego de Deza, perhaps also of Talavera, that there might be something in Columbus's project nevertheless, the commission postponed rendering a report.

What, then, becomes of the celebrated sessions of the University of Salamanca, before whose professors of mathematics, geography and astronomy Columbus argued his case, and was turned down because he could not convince them that the world was round? That is pure moonshine. Washington Irving, scenting his opportunity for a picturesque and moving scene, took a fictitious account of this nonexistent university council published 130 years after the event, elaborated on it, and let his imagination go completely. The result is that wonderful chapter where "an obscure navigator, a member of no learned society, destitute of all the trappings and circumstances which sometimes give oracular authority to dullness, and depending on the mere force of natural genius," sustains his thesis of a spherical globe against "pedantic bigotry" of flat-earth churchmen, fortified by texts from the Bible, Lactantius and Saint Augustine, until he began to feel nervous about the Inquisition. And how Columbus "met them upon their own ground, pouring forth those magnificent texts of Scripture, and those mysterious predictions of the prophets, which, in his enthusiastic moments, he considered as types and annunciations of the sublime discovery which he proposed." A gripping drama as Irving tells it, this has become one of the most popular Columbian myths; for we all love to hear of professors and experts being confounded by simple common sense.

Yet the whole story is misleading and mischievous nonsense. The University of Salamanca was not asked to decide. Columbus and Talavera merely held committee hearings in the College of St. Stephen, at which neither side was able to convince the other. The sphericity of the globe was not in question. The issue was the width of the ocean; and therein the opposition was right.

These informal conferences and hearings were presumably held around Christmastide 1486, when the court was at Salamanca. Not long after, Columbus was put on the royal payroll. The records of the treasury of Castile show that "Cristóbal Colomo, extrangero" (foreigner) was paid 3000 maravedis on May 5, 1487, the same amount on July 3, 4000 on August 27, 1487, "to go to the royal encampment" (then investing Malaga), the same on October 15, and 3000 maravedis on June 16, 1488. In other words he was given a retaining fee of about 12,000 maravedis a year, roughly eighty to ninety dollars, the pay of an able seaman. Not exactly princely, but enough for a man of his simple tastes to keep body and soul together.

Of Columbus's own movements this year we have no hint, except the payment to enable him to visit the royal camp before Malaga, the last important Spanish seaport held by the Moors. Malaga had capitulated on August 18, 1487, and Columbus doubtless expected that this would be an opportune juncture to interest the Sovereigns. If so, he failed; for there were still strong cities in the hands of the infidel. The Sovereigns' overwhelming interest in this war was an even greater obstacle to him than the doubts of scientists. Apparently the court lost interest in him the next year, for his retaining fee was not renewed after June 1488. In August or September of that year Beatriz gave birth to Ferdinand at Cordova. The Talavera committee had not yet reported, nor had Columbus been formally dismissed; but with his small income cut off he thought it wise to accept D. João's invitation and renew negotiations with Portugal.

These fell through, as we have seen, after Bartholomew Dias returned from the Cape of Good Hope; D. João II had found one ocean route to India and needed no other. Columbus then returned to Spain, and sent his brother Bartholomew to London.

The movements of Bartholomew are even more obscure than those of Christopher. He probably had stayed on in Lisbon after his elder brother's first departure in 1485, and did not leave until the return of Bartholomew Dias had spoiled the proposed deal with Portugal. The most meticulous research in English sources and archives has uncovered no trace of Bartholomew in England; but this is not surprising, for scarcely anything can be found about John Cabot. According to Ferdinand Columbus, his uncle obtained an interview with Henry VII and presented him with a world map containing an interesting but provokingly vague Latin inscription, to the effect that "you who wish to learn of the coasts of countries must learn by this map what Strabo, Ptolemy, Pliny and Isidore taught." Ferdinand adds that Henry VII became definitely interested, and was still dickering with Bartholomew in his parsimonious Tudor manner when news of the great discovery arrived; but Oviedo, who wrote earlier than Ferdinand, says that the proposition was rejected by the counselors of the king, who "made game of what Columbus said, and held his words to be vain."

Not later than 1490 Bartholomew proceeded to the court of France, where his proposition proved to be no more acceptable than in England. Again, we have the same provoking silence of the archives, but several statements from French sources of the next century say that Charles VIII thought no more of the Enterprise than did Henry VII. Bartholomew, however, found a protector and patroness in Anne de Beaujeu, the king's elder sister and regent during his minority. From her his hopes of French support must have been kept up, since Christopher himself was on the point of going to France in 1491. Bartholomew was still living at Fontainebleau as a retainer of Anne de Beaujeu, unhappily employed in making maps, when news of his brother's great discovery arrived.

Christopher Columbus, we may suppose, was back in Spain early in 1489, waiting, hoping and praying for a favorable report from the Talavera committee, and for a swift conclusion of the last campaign against Granada. He had two more years to wait. Until the latter part of 1491, when he reappears at La Rábida, his movements are purely conjectural. Presumably part of this time he put in at Cordova with Beatriz, who was bringing up their child Ferdinand; he certainly regarded Cordova as his home in 1493. He probably visited La Rábida from time to time to keep in touch with young Diego. Possibly he sold books and charts at Seville. And, as the slender pittance from the Queen was cut short in June 1488, he may have been supported by the hospitable Duke of Medina Celi.

In any event, he had plenty of time for reading. Between 1485 and 1490 Columbus did some heavy combing through ancient and medieval authorities on geography in order to gather ammunition for his next bout with the experts. Let them throw Ptolemy at him, he would pay them back in their own coin and better. Four of these books that Columbus owned (three of them elaborately annotated) have been preserved: a 1485 Latin translation of the *Book of Ser Marco Polo;* an Italian translation of Pliny's *Natural History* printed in 1489; Pierre d'Ailly's *Imago Mundi* and minor treatises, all in Latin and printed at Louvain between 1480 and 1483; and a 1477 edition of the *Historia Rerum Ubique Gestarum* by Aeneas Sylvius (Pope Pius II).

Two in particular, the *Imago Mundi* and *Historia Rerum,* show by their multitude of postils or marginal notes, made with a variety of pens and inks with minor differences of handwriting, that Columbus and probably his brother Bartholomew also read them over and over again. The *Imago Mundi* seems to have been Christopher's bedside book for a number of years, and he used the blank leaves at the back of the *Historia Rerum* as a catch-all for miscellaneous observations. These postils have been studied by Columbus's biographers, beginning with Ferdinand and Las Casas. There has been much discussion by self-styled handwriting experts as to whether this or that note is by Christopher or Bartholomew. It really does not matter,* for the two brothers worked together with the same ideas and on the same project.

---

* Excepting as regards the three relating to Bartholomew Dias and José Vizinho, which serve to date the Discoverer's (or his brother's) movements.

The *Imago Mundi* of Pierre d'Ailly, Cardinal of Cambrai, was a comprehensive world geography composed around the year 1410, before Ptolemy's Geography had been rediscovered by Western Europe. That is one reason why Columbus preferred D'Ailly to Ptolemy. The French cosmographer followed the system of Marinus of Tyre, who made Eurasia long and the Atlantic narrow. Incorporated in Columbus's copy of the *Imago Mundi* were two of the Cardinal's later cosmographical tracts, written after he had read Ptolemy; but they served Columbus even better, since D'Ailly ventures to disagree with the Alexandrian sage. For instance, he says, "The length of the land toward the Orient is much greater than Ptolemy admits . . . Arim° is not merely a distance of 90° from the [end of] the Orient, it is much farther, because the length of the habitable Earth on the side of the Orient is more than half the circuit of the globe. For, according to the philosophers and Pliny, the ocean which stretches between the extremity of further Spain (that is, Morocco) and the eastern edge of India is of no great width. *For it is evident that this sea is navigable in a very few days if the wind be fair,* whence it follows that the sea is not so great that it can cover three quarters of the globe, as certain people figure it." Heavy underscorings and long postil by Columbus; mental note to bring this up whenever anyone mentions Ptolemy's 180° of land.

Columbus notes every mention of the length of a degree, and sometimes writes in the margin, "Not so. A degree is 56⅔ Roman miles," or words to that effect. We have already cited the notes from his own experience in Africa, proving that the Torrid Zone is inhabitable. Any statement in the *Imago Mundi* about the narrowness of the ocean is eagerly picked up and copied or commented on by Columbus. For instance: —

The end of the habitable earth toward the Orient and the end of the habitable earth toward the Occident are near enough, and between them is a small sea.

Between the end of Spain and the beginning of India is no great width.

An arm of the sea extends between India and Spain.

° Aryim, the terrestrial umbilicus according to the ancients, should be halfway on Ptolemy's 180° length of the habitable world.

India is near Spain.

The beginnings of the Orient and of the Occident are close.

From the end of the Occident to the end of India by land is much greater than half the globe, viz. 180°.

Water runs from pole to pole between the end of Spain and the beginning of India.

Aristotle [says] between the end of Spain and the beginning of India is a small sea navigable in a few days . . . Esdras [says] six parts [of the globe] are habitable and the seventh is covered with water. Observe that the blessed Ambrose and Austin and many others considered Esdras a prophet.

Julius [Solinus] teaches that the entire sea from India up to Spain behind (*per dorsum*) Africa is navigable.

The end of Spain and the beginning of India are not far distant but close, and it is evident *that this sea is navigable in a few days with a fair wind.*

As complement to the narrow ocean, Columbus grasps at every bit of "evidence" as to an excessive length of Asia.

Note that the king of Tarshish came to the Lord at Jerusalem and spent a year and 13 days on the way, as the blessed Jerome has it.

From a harbor of the Red Sea to India is a sail of one year. And Solomon took three years to make the round voyage. . . . From the end of the Occident (Portugal) to the end of the Orient (India) by land is a tremendous distance.

D'Ailly's chapter on India (Asia) is heavily annotated by Columbus. The mighty rivers, the gold, silver, pearls and precious stones, the elephants, parrots, gryphons and monsters excite him. One postil accompanied by an index finger calls attention to the innumerable islands around India, full of pearls and precious stones. Disappointed at the meager mention of Ophir in *Imago Mundi*, Columbus writes a postil so long as to be almost a supplement, referring to the third book of Kings and second of Chronicles for the movements of Solomon and Jehoshaphat. He adds, "See our maps on paper where the sphere is represented." Naturally a cartographer would have made maps to demonstrate his theory of the narrow ocean.

The *Historia Rerum Ubique Gestarum* (1477) of Aeneas Sylvius, although printed a few years earlier than the *Imago Mundi,* was written some thirty years later. Largely potted Ptolemy, it was more accurate and informing than *Imago Mundi*, but by the same token less acceptable to Columbus. Yet there was plenty in Ptolemy and the other ancient authors quoted by Aeneas Sylvius that Columbus could use.

Study and analyze as we will these "subtle shining secrecies, writ in the glassie margents of such bookes,"* all point to one object and one only of the Great Enterprise: to reach the Orient by sailing west. Pierre d'Ailly's chapter "On the other celebrated islands of the Ocean" aroused no interest on Columbus's part, except to note that the Insulae Gorgades and Fortunatae were the modern Cape Verdes and Canaries, and that the terrestrial paradise was certainly not located there. Thus, the postils afford very cold comfort to those trying to prove that Columbus was seeking nothing more important than new Atlantic islands, that his interest in the Orient arose only when he missed Antillia. Writers of this description either ignore the unmistakable evidence in the postils or blandly assert that they were all made *after* the First Voyage either (1) to mislead posterity as to Columbus's real object, or (2) to gather material for the Book of Prophecies. The first charge is too frivolous to be worth a reply; the Book of Prophecies contains nothing but prophecies, mainly from the Bible, with only a few incidental gatherings from the *Imago Mundi, Historia Rerum* and Marco Polo. Three postils dated 1481 and "in hoc anno '88" prove that Columbus at least began reading the *Historia Rerum* well before 1490. These and others, as well as the detached postils preserved by Ferdinand, mention facts gathered from Christopher's experience on voyages to Africa, Ireland and Iceland, in order to refute something in the text.

Can anyone for a moment believe that Columbus could have made these annotations after 1492 and not inserted a single fact from his infinitely more marvelous experience in America?

---

* Shakespeare, *The Rape of Lucrece.*

CHAPTER VIII

The Queen Consents

1489–1492

Et erunt reges nutritij tui, et reginae nutrices tuae.

And kings shall be thy nursing fathers, and their queens
thy nursing mothers.

— ISAIAH xlix 23

O
NLY one certain trace of Columbus exists for the year 1489.
On May 12 the Sovereigns furnished him with an open letter
to all municipal and local officials, ordering them to furnish free
board and lodging to "Cristóbal Colomo" who "has to come to this
our court." The king was then directing the siege of Baza. A great
fortified camp was built outside the Moorish city, the "flower of
Spanish chivalry" were present, and everything was done in the
most magnificent manner. Why the Sovereigns wished to see Columbus at this juncture we do not know. Possibly Talavera, who had
not yet reported, suggested an interview; more likely Columbus
himself, as soon as he returned from Portugal, renewed his application to the Queen, who graciously permitted him to come into her
presence. And as he had no money, provision had to be made for
his transportation.

How long Columbus stayed with the court in camp, and what
if anything he accomplished, are unknown. He is said to have joined
the army as a volunteer, and to have "given demonstration of the
conspicuous valor which accompanied his wisdom and high desires." Considering his zeal against the crescent, he would naturally
have welcomed an opportunity to strike a few blows for the
cross; and a curious incident of this siege served to implement his
highest desires. An embassy arrived from the Sultan of Egypt, who
threatened to persecute the Christians in his dominions and raze

the Holy Sepulchre unless Ferdinand and Isabella stopped fighting
the Moslems of Spain. Columbus most certainly took occasion to
point out to the Queen how precarious were the sacred places of
Palestine under the infidel, and to beg her to send him westward in
search of new sources of wealth for financing a crusade. But Isabella's attention could not be attracted to the Enterprise of the
Indies while the Moorish kingdom of Granada still held out. When
Baza capitulated, on December 4, 1489, Columbus was again turned
out to grass.

This was the period when he suffered real distress; when, according to Bishop Geraldini, he applied to a Franciscan monastery
near Marchena in Andalusia for hospitality. How did he manage
to live, and where? Was he selling books and maps, as Andrés
Bernáldez of Seville reported to be his occupation when first he
met Columbus? Had he exhausted the hospitality of Medina Celi?
Did he lodge with the Haranas in Cordova? Almost any conjecture is possible, since no facts have survived. It was not a period
that Columbus cared to talk about in later years.

The court spent part of 1490 in Seville, and it was probably there
late in the year that Talavera finally rendered a report. The committee "judged his promises and offers were impossible and vain
and worthy of rejection," says Las Casas, and advised the Sovereigns "that it was not a proper object for their royal authority
to favor an affair that rested on such weak foundations, and which
appeared uncertain and impossible to any educated person, however
little learning he might have." Ferdinand and Las Casas give six
arguments used by Talavera to prove that Columbus was wrong.
(1) A voyage to Asia would require three years. (2) The Western
Ocean is infinite and perhaps unnavigable. (3) If he reached the
Antipodes (the land on the other side of the globe from Europe)
he could not get back. (4) There are no Antipodes because the
greater part of the globe is covered with water, and because Saint
Augustine says so. (According to Las Casas, *duda Sant' Agustin,*
"Saint Augustine doubts," became a sort of refrain of the Talavera
committee.) (5) Of the five zones, only three are habitable. (6) So
many centuries after the Creation it was unlikely that anyone
could find hitherto unknown lands of any value.

Although this set of reasons is denounced by Vignaud and others as frivolous and fabricated (for they help to prove Columbus's Asiatic objective, and are no great credit to the Spanish intellect of 1490), there seems no good reason to doubt Las Casas's word. They are exactly the sort of objections anyone would have made in 1490, in the then state of geographical knowledge in Castile, a country not so far advanced in such matters as Portugal. After all, the Portuguese had been merely pushing coastwise along a continent known to the ancients. Striking out westward to the Orient was a very different matter, novel, risky and uncertain. The postils in Columbus's books prove that he had been accumulating answers to the first five points, and Seneca's *Medea* was a sufficient answer to the sixth. It certainly did not take much learning to see that Columbus's 60° ocean was all wrong. Why then, we may ask, did the committee require four and a half years to report on it? Simply the custom of the country.

Ferdinand and Isabella neither accepted nor rejected the Talavera report. They caused Columbus to be informed, says Las Casas, that his Enterprise might again be brought to their attention at a more propitious moment, when the war with Granada was over.

Columbus waited another six to nine months, possibly at the house of Medina Celi. By the end of that time he swore "by San Fernando" he would wait no longer on the Queen's pleasure. He had had more than enough Castilian procrastination. Whether or not Bartholomew encouraged him from Fountainebleau we do not know; but Columbus determined to go to France and offer his Enterprise to Charles VIII.

In the summer of 1491 Columbus visited La Rábida to call for his son Diego, now ten or eleven years old. Perhaps the boy was unhappy with the friars, maybe Columbus wished to be under no further obligation to them; in any case he proposed to leave the lad at Huelva with his mother's sister, the wife of Miguel Molyart, before departing for France.

Now occurs the second half of the well-known La Rábida story. Fray Juan Pérez, head of the friary, deplored Columbus's intention to quit Spain forever. Dr. Fernández, who as a physician was the local authority on astronomy and cosmography, was called into consultation; as (in all probability) was Martín Alonso Pinzón, a leading shipowner of Palos. Fray Juan, who many years before had been confessor or comptroller to the Queen (perhaps both), promised to obtain for Columbus another royal audience if he would stay. The Queen was then at the fortified camp of Santa Fe, a city which was especially constructed in July 1491, in order to serve as Castilian headquarters during the siege of Granada. Fray Juan sent her a letter by Sebastián Rodríguez, a pilot of Lepe, and in two weeks' time received a favorable reply. Isabella commanded Fray Juan to come to court, to encourage Columbus, and tell him to await a summons of his own. The friar departed at once on a mule chartered for him by Columbus, and probably paid for by Martín Alonso Pinzón. Before long the Queen wrote directly to Columbus, commanding him to proceed to court. Either she recalled his shabby appearance on a former occasion, or Fray Juan excited her compassion by describing his state of extreme penury; for the Queen sent with her letter the sum of 20,000 maravedis in order that Columbus might procure some decent clothing and a mule.

Not before August, and probably somewhat later in the year 1491, Columbus in his new suit of clothes appeared before the Queen. And again his Enterprise was put in the hands of a committee; for Las Casas says that *astrólogos* (astronomers), mariners and pilots as well as *filósofos* were consulted. From this *ad hoc* committee (like the Ortiz one in Portugal and the Talavera one in Spain) which examined and reported on the technical aspects of the case, the Enterprise was referred to the Royal Council of Castile, composed of grandees and higher ecclesiastics. There, presumably, the technical aspects were reviewed. Bishop Geraldini, who was present, remembered the old "duda Sant' Agustin" being dragged out again; he observed to the Cardinal of Spain that, whilst Saint Augustine was undoubtedly a great theologian, navigators like Columbus who had sailed beyond the Line probably knew somewhat more about antipodean geography.

Columbus of course demonstrated his narrow ocean hypothesis with a *mappemonde*. We know that he had one or more among the "exhibits," and a keen search has been made in every depositary of old maps in Europe for one that might have been his. An entry in a library catalogue of 1629, "Declaratio chartae nauigatoriae Domini Almirantis," proved a false lead, as the last two words were a later interpolation. In the present century Charles de la Roncière thought he had found Columbus's very map among the collections of the Bibliothèque Nationale, and reproduced it in a sumptuous volume; but there is really nothing in this map to connect it with Columbus, for it does not demonstrate his Q.E.D., the narrow ocean and proximity of Asia to Spain.

Ferdinand and Las Casas both infer that the reason the Enterprise was rejected again was the enormous price Columbus demanded in honors, titles and revenues, as a reward for success. This suggests that the Enterprise was approved by the special committee and rejected by the Royal Council. For no committee of *astrólogos*, mariners and the like had any business to recommend what honors and titles their Sovereigns should accord to a successful discoverer. Their job was to report whether or not the project was feasible; and only if they favored it was there any need for the Council to take it up. The Council naturally would review the case, and decide whether to take the risk and pay the price. So, after sifting the various and conflicting statements by contemporaries, it seems probable that Columbus was now turned down for the third and last time, simply because his contingent demands were considered exorbitant.

This is the earliest occasion when we may be certain that Columbus stated his expected reward. Possibly he had settled in his own mind some years before what he intended to demand, but as yet there had been no occasion for him to let it out. The Ortiz commission in Portugal, the Talavera committee in Spain, were charged only with the technical aspects of Columbus's project. Las Casas does indeed say that Columbus's price to Portugal was the same as that which he demanded and obtained from Spain, but we suspect his accuracy. Columbus would certainly have retained enough peasant bargaining instinct to hold back what he expected in the way of titles and emoluments until his Enterprise was accepted in principle; his strategy was to have it pronounced scientifically correct, technically feasible, and likely to bring in money to the crown. Then and then only would he bring up the subject of rewards to King, Queen or Royal Council.

One may speculate endlessly as to when Columbus settled in his own mind that nobility and a coat of arms, a resounding title, high offices and substantial revenues should be his proper reward for success in the Enterprise of the Indies. Medina Celi's letter indicates that in 1485 his ambitions in this direction were still modest; and, in my opinion, the final schedule of honors and emoluments was not formulated before 1491. He had then made up his mind to go to France, and anticipated that Charles VIII would treat him handsomely (in which expectation he would certainly have been disappointed). He was under a sense of outrage and wrong over six wasted years in Spain. On a thousand occasions he had smarted under the insults which a "somebody" with no brains could inflict with impunity on a "nobody" with an idea. Columbus resented this treatment all his life long, frequently adverted to it bitterly. So, thought he, if those proud Castilians want my services after all, they will have to pay through the nose, God take them! I will not glorify Spain for nothing. If the Sovereigns will grant me appropriate titles and honors to found a noble family, and the means for my descendants to keep up their rank, well and good. If not, I go to France.

Granada capitulated on January 2, 1492, and Columbus had the joy of marching in the procession that entered the last stronghold of the Moslem in Catholic Spain. Then the axe fell for him. Before many days he was informed that his Enterprise was absolutely and definitely rejected. The Sovereigns themselves confirmed this at an audience which they meant to be final, and in which they wished him *bon voyage*.

So that was the result of six and a half years' watching and waiting in Spain. "By San Fernando" he was through!

Columbus saddled his mule, packed the saddlebags with his spare shirt, world chart, *Imago Mundi* and *Historia Rerum,* and in company with the faithful Fray Juan set forth on the road to Cordova. He had saved enough of the Queen's present to take passage for France, no doubt. In any case, he could work his way.

Suddenly the whole picture changed. Columbus had made another friend at court, Luis de Santangel, *escribano de ración* (keeper of the privy purse) to King Ferdinand. The very day that Columbus departed from Santa Fe, Luis de Santangel "went to find the Queen, and with words which his keen desire to persuade her suggested, told her that he was astonished to see that her Highness, who had always shown a resolute spirit in matters of great pith and consequence, should lack it now for an enterprise of so little risk, yet which could prove of so great service to God and the exaltation of His Church, not to speak of very great increase and glory for her realms and crown; an enterprise of such nature that if any other prince should undertake what the Admiral offered to her, it would be a very great damage to her crown, and a grave reproach to her." If money were a consideration, Santangel would be glad to finance the fleet himself. Isabella, much impressed by his warmth and sincerity, said that she would reconsider the case as soon as she had a little breathing space; or, if there were any haste, pledge her jewels for the expenses, which Santangel assured her would be unnecessary. The Queen then sent a messenger for Columbus, who overtook him at the village of Pinos-Puente, about ten miles from Granada and four from Santa Fe, where the court was then residing.

Royal commands must be obeyed. The fellow travelers came about, and caught a fair wind that lasted to America.

Why this sudden change of mind? One may speculate that personality had much to do with it. The most impressive thing about Columbus's presentation of his case had not been the facts and the arguments, but the man. His dignity, sincerity and absolute certainty must have left their mark on the Queen. "When he had made up his mind," wrote Las Casas, "he was as sure he would discover what he did discover, and find what he did find, as if he held it in a chamber under lock and key."

His character was very similar to that of the Queen, and he reasoned much in the same way, from fixed ideas and religious preconceptions. So, if Isabella still hesitated when she sent for Columbus, his presence gave her confidence. Moreover, Santangel's reasoning was irresistible. So little risk for so vast a gain! What if the experts or some of them did laugh at the Enterprise and say that the geographical notions of this Genoese were absurd, impossible, ridiculous? How did they know, these closet cosmographers and Mediterranean mariners? The Queen had seen a good deal of experts in her reign of eighteen years, and realized that half the time they did not know what they were talking about. This man Colomo or Colón appealed not only to her reason, but to her instincts.

Let us give feminine intuition due credit, but not all. The King had to consent to everything the Queen did, Santangel was his official, not hers; and Santangel found at least half the money. Exact figures as to the expense of the First Voyage are not available; but from various hints and indications it seems to have cost around 2,000,000 maravedis (say $14,000) to fit out. Isabella had proposed to raise the money on her crown jewels, but this was not necessary; the fable that she actually pawned them for Columbus dates from the seventeenth century. Santangel and Francisco Pinelo, who were joint treasurers of the Santa Hermandad, an efficient police force that had its own endowment, borrowed from that treasury 1,400,000 maravedis, which was eventually repaid by the crown. Columbus himself invested 250,000 maravedis in the enterprise, which he must have borrowed from his friends and supporters, such as Juanoto Berardi the Florentine merchant-banker of Seville, or the Duke of Medina Celi. The balance was probably advanced by Santangel on his own account, or from the treasury of Aragon. This sum of two million maravedis did not include the payroll, which came to a quarter of a million monthly.

.   .   .   .

Almost three months were required to negotiate with the Sovereigns after the Great Enterprise was accepted in principle; yet of these negotiations we have no information. We only know that Fray Juan Pérez acted as Columbus's attorney, and Juan de Coloma represented the Sovereigns. Very likely the delay was due to chancery red tape, copying and recopying documents, greasing the right palms, and all that. Crown officials must have been very busy liquidating the Moorish kingdom of Granada, demobilizing the army and preparing to expel the Jews — another and less happy enterprise that was under way at the time.

The main documents of the Great Enterprise are seven in number: the Capitulations or Articles of Agreement of April 17; the

Título or Title of April 30, 1492 (sometimes called the Commission); the Letter of Credence to foreign potentates, dated April 30; the Passport, undated; and three Orders of the Sovereigns dated April 30 about fitting out the fleet.

The Capitulations of April 17 are in five articles, each signed "It pleaseth their Highnesses, Juan de Coloma," and the whole signed by the King and Queen. The preamble of the oldest copy we have, made in 1495, describes this document as "the things supplicated and which your highnesses give and grant to *Don Cristóbal de Colón* in some satisfaction for what he hath discovered [*que ha descubierto*] in the ocean seas and for the voyage which with God's help he is now about to make thereon." (The past tense has aroused no end of conjecture; but as it did not trouble contemporaries it need not trouble us.) Their Highnesses appoint the said Don Cristóbal Colón their Admiral in and over all islands and mainlands "which shall be discovered or acquired by his labor and industry," and that title with all rights and prerogatives appertaining thereunto shall be enjoyed by his heirs and successors perpetually. (2) The said *Don Cristóbal* is appointed Viceroy and Governor-General over all such mainlands and islands as he shall discover or acquire in the said seas, and he may nominate three candidates for each office, from whom the Sovereigns will select one. (3) He shall take and keep a tenth of all gold, silver, pearls, gems, spices and other merchandise produced or obtained by barter and mining within the limits of these domains, free of all taxes. (4) Any case involving such merchandise or products will be adjudicated by him or his deputy, as Admiral. (5) He is given the option of paying an eighth part of the total expense of any ship sailing to these new possessions, and taking an eighth of the profits.

The *Título* or Title of April 30 is a solemn but still contingent confirmation of the titles and offices: —

"Whereas you, *Cristóbal Colón,* are setting forth by our command . . . to discover and acquire certain islands and mainland in the ocean sea . . . it is just and reasonable that, since you are exposing yourself to this danger in our service, you be rewarded therefor, . . . it is our will and pleasure that you the said *Cristóbal Colón* after you have discovered and acquired the said islands and mainland . . . or any of them, shall be our Admiral of the said islands and mainland which you may thus discover and acquire, and shall be our Admiral and Viceroy and Governor therein, and shall be empowered henceforward to call and entitle yourself *Don Cristóbal Colón,* and his heirs and successors forever may be so entitled, and enjoy the offices of Admiral of the Ocean Sea, Viceroy and Governor of the said islands and mainland."

Now the extraordinary thing about these documents is their failure to refer to a route to the Indies, indeed to mention the Indies in any manner whatsoever; they speak only of discovering and acquiring a mainland and islands in the Ocean Sea. On this negation was built the hypothesis of Vignaud that Columbus never thought of sailing to the Indies, never proposed or intended anything more than discovering hitherto unknown islands and mainlands, such as Antillia and the placed touched at by the Unknown Pilot; that he shifted his whole emphasis and denatured his purpose when, having sailed past the supposed position of these islands, he found others at a longitude which he supposed to be that of China and Japan.

Yet the evidence of Columbus's oriental objective, as we have seen, is abundant, and the Sovereigns' intent to support that objective is unmistakable, despite the equivocal language of the agreement. The phrases "islands and mainlands of the Ocean Sea" meant Japan, China and neighboring islands. This is sufficiently proved by the fact that when Columbus returned in 1493, insisting that he had discovered Cipangu and certain outlying dominions of the Grand Khan, nobody contested his right to be Admiral, Governor and Viceroy thereof, and the Pope freely conceded Spanish sovereignty over them. Moreover, the agreement of April 17 mentions "pearls, precious stones, gold, silver and spices" among the products that the Admiral will be privileged to tithe, and these were of the Orient; there was no tradition or expectation that any such precious things were to be found in Atlantic islands. There is also a significant analogy to the letters-patent of John Cabot, whom we know positively to have been seeking a westward passage to India. His grant of 1496 from Henry VII was couched in terms very similar to the Columbus capitulations. The Indies are not mentioned by name, but the king confers on Cabot power to "conquer, occupy and possess" any "islands, countries, regions or provinces of heathens and infidels, in whatsoever part of the world placed, which before this time were unknown to all Christians."

Surely, the reader will ask, you do not suppose that Ferdinand and Isabella (and Henry VII) were so simple as to suppose that three small vessels (or one still smaller) with ninety (or eighteen) men could sail into a harbor of Japan or China and simply take over? The answer is, yes, they were as simple as that. Remember that letter of Dr. Müntzer to D. João II, which assumes that any and every oriental potentate will be only too glad to swear allegiance to the Christian monarch whose ship first appears in his territorial waters?* That is what had happened to the Portuguese in West and South Africa; and Europe envisaged the kings of the Orient as no better prepared to defend their possessions than the sable potentates of the Dark Continent. The information of the European chanceries about China was so out of date that they even alluded to the Emperor of China as the Grand Khan, a title that became extinct when the Tartar Dynasty fell in 1368.

Moreover, the oriental objective is proved by the next two documents with which the Sovereigns provided Columbus. The first, undated, was a brief Latin passport: —

"By these presents we dispatch the noble man Christoforus Colon with three equipped caravels over the Ocean Seas toward the regions of India [*ad partes Indie*] for certain reasons and purposes."

The other is the Letter of Credence. The record of it, which has been found in the registries of Aragon, may be translated in part as follows: —

"To the most serene prince
our very dear friend, Ferdinand and Isabella, King and Queen of Castile, Aragon, Leon, etc., greetings and increase of good fortune. We have learned with joy of your esteem and high regard for us and our nation and of your great eagerness to receive information concerning our successes. Wherefore we have resolved to dispatch our noble captain *Christopherus Colon* to you, with letters, from which you may learn of our good health and prosperity . . .

   I THE KING   I THE QUEEN
done in triplicate"

---

* End of Chapter vi, above.

Las Casas thus explains the blank, and the subscription "done in triplicate." Columbus carried "royal letters of recommendation for the Grand Khan, and for all the kings and lords of India and of any other region that he might find in the lands which he might discover." Probably in the blank space of one copy the engrosser inserted *Magno Cano,* and the other copies were left blank so that Rodrigo de Escobedo, secretary of the fleet, could insert the correct name and titles of the Emperor of Japan, the Lord of Mangi, or whatever potentate the fleet might encounter. The Grand Khan, moreover, is specifically mentioned in the prologue to Columbus's Journal of his First Voyage.

The alleged high regard of the Chinese Emperor for Spain, and his supposed eagerness to learn of her conquest of Granada, are based on the story of a mysterious oriental traveler, said to be from a Christian nation bordering on China, who visited Florence about 1445 and conversed through an interpreter with Toscanelli. Columbus inferred from the incidental reference to this strange personage in Toscanelli's famous letter, that he was an envoy of the Grand Khan, who was eager to conclude an alliance with Christian princes against the Moslems.

Practical matters of equipment did not enter into the formal agreement; they were probably settled by word of mouth between Columbus and some ministers of the crown before April 30, when the Sovereigns issued what they believed to be the necessary orders for chartering, equipping, provisioning and manning the fleet at Palos.

On May 12, 1492, Columbus left Granada and proceeded to the town where he had first set foot in Spain, and whence he was destined to depart on his great voyage of discovery.

CHAPTER IX

Niña, Pinta and Santa María

1492–1493

Ecce et naues . . .

Behold also the ships . . .
    — JAMES iii 4

Aᴿᴹᴱᴰ with his credentials and contracts, full of energy and eager to be off and away, Columbus arrived on May 22, 1492, at Palos de la Frontera. Why Palos? Seville or Cadiz, the principal ports of Andalusia, would seem to have been the logical places to prepare an important expedition; but Cadiz was out as a port of departure for Columbus, because it had been designated as the embarking place for the Jews who were then being forced into exile; 8000 families are said to have sailed from there in the summer of 1492. Palos very likely would have been chosen in any case, since it had a fleet of caravels and a seafaring population experienced in Guinea voyages. Palos, moreover, was the home of the friendly friars who had done so much to further the enterprise, and Palos had conveniently committed some municipal misdemeanor for which the Sovereigns fined it the use of two caravels for a twelvemonth. If other reasons were good and sufficient, this last was conclusive.

On Wednesday, May 23, "in the Church of St. George of this town of Palos, in the presence of Fr. Juan Pérez" and of the mayor and councilors, "Cristóbal Colón gave and presented to the aforesaid this letter of their Highnesses, the which was read by me, Francisco Fernández, notary public of said town." So reads Francisco's endorsement on a letter of the Sovereigns dated April 30, the same day as the Capitulations and Titles: —

Ferdinand and Isabella, by the Grace of God King and Queen of Castile, León, Aragon, Sicily, etc., etc., to you Diego Rodríguez Prieto and all the other inhabitants of the town of Palos, greeting and grace.

Know ye that whereas for certain things done and committed by you to our disservice you were condemned and obligated by our Council to provide us for a twelvemonth with two equipped caravels at your own proper charge and expense. . . . And whereas we have now commanded Cristóbal Colón to go with three *carabelas de armada* as our Captain of the same, toward certain regions of the Ocean Sea, to perform certain things for our service, and we desire that he take with him the said two caravels with which you are thus required to serve us; therefore we command that within ten days of receiving this our letter . . . you have all ready and prepared two equipped caravels, as you are required by virtue of the said sentence, to depart with the said Cristóbal Colón whither we have commanded him to go, . . . and we have commanded him to give you advance pay for four months for the people who are to sail aboard the said caravels at the rate to be paid to the other people who are to be in the said three [*sic*] caravels, and in the other caravel that we have commanded him to take, whatever is commonly and customarily paid on this coast to the people who go to sea in a fleet, . . . and we forbid the said Cristóbal Colón or any others who sail in the said caravels to go to the Mine or engage in the trade thereof that the King of Portugal our brother holds. . . . Given in our City of Granada on the 30th day of April, year of Our Lord Jesus Christ 1492.

I THE KING   I THE QUEEN

Quite an order! There must have been some long breaths drawn, and significant looks exchanged among the town fathers of Palos when the public scrivener rolled out this royal command in the courtyard of the Church of St. George. And if Columbus imagined that caravels manned and equipped for an ocean voyage would be produced within ten days, he had plenty to learn about the difficulties and delays of fitting out ships in a far from enthusiastic community.

When arrangements were completed for furnishing *Niña* and *Pinta* and chartering *Santa María,* we do not know. The first two, as we have seen, were provided by the municipality at the tax-payers' expense. The letter above does not mean that Columbus was required to pay the wage bill; everyone in the fleet who had to do with working the ships was on the royal payroll. Columbus, perhaps after trying to argue the town fathers into providing a third caravel, himself chartered *Santa María* from her master-owner. Details of equipment and provisioning are wholly wanting,

SHIP WITH SAILS FURLED
From Juan de la Cosa Map of c. 1508

but they seem to have been done fairly efficiently since no complaints of carelessness and ship chandlers' dishonesty are recorded, as on later voyages. It took ten weeks instead of ten days to get ready for sea, but that was not excessive. The delay was fortunate; for if Columbus was lucky in escaping a West Indies hurricane with a September departure from the Canaries, he could not possibly have avoided some sort of "twister" with a June departure.

Three other royal letters of the same date, April 30, Columbus brought with him to Palos. All persons in Andalusia, especially timber merchants, carpenters, ship chandlers, bakers and provision dealers, were ordered to furnish Columbus with everything he required at reasonable prices. No customs or excises must be levied on said provisions, materials or equipment. All civil and criminal prosecutions must be suspended against anyone who agreed to ship with Columbus.

SQUARE-STERNED SHIP SAILING FULL
UNDER FORE COURSE WITH TWO BONNETS
From Piri Reis Map of 1513

My readers will be disappointed that I cannot furnish them with an authentic picture of the three famous vessels, whose preparations for the great voyage were now under way. But there are no data or documents from which it can honestly be done. Nobody knows what *Niña, Pinta* and *Santa María* really looked like. Every picture of them (including ours) is about 50 per cent fancy, and almost all are demonstrably inaccurate in some important respect. We have no contemporary painting or drawing of a single ship in which Columbus sailed. The woodcuts inserted in some of the editions of Columbus's published Letter on his First Voyage had already done duty in a work printed at Mainz in 1486. So-called models, replicas or reproductions of *Santa María* and her consorts are not models, replicas or reproductions, since no plans, drawings or dimensions of them exist; they merely represent what some naval architect, archeologist, artist or ship modeler thinks these vessels ought to have looked like. The best of these, representing an immense amount of research, are (1) Captain Ernesto D'Albertis's plans of 1892, from which models were made for the Marine Museum at Pegli, near Genoa; (2) *Niña II*, *Pinta II* and *Santa María II* constructed after plans made by Fernández Duro and Monléon for the Chicago Exposition of 1893; (3) D. Julio Guillén's *Santa María III*, constructed in 1927 for the Seville Exposition; (4) Mr. R. C. Anderson's miniature model of *Santa María* at the Addison Gallery of American Art, Andover, Massachusetts. My own description of the Columbus fleet is built on what few facts we can glean from the records, and illuminated by abundant data on contemporary vessels that these expert marine archeologists, D'Albertis, Fernández Duro, Guillén and Anderson, have brought to light.

Niña was the Admiral's favorite and so mine. "If she had not been very staunch and well found," he wrote after the February storm of 1493, "I should have been afraid of being lost." *Santa María*, which he never liked, ran aground off Hispaniola, and stayed there. *Pinta* returned home, and disappears from history. But *Niña* — there's a vessel to sing about! Built in the Ribera de Moguer, an estuary (now silted up) of the Rio Tinto, she made the entire First Voyage, bringing the Admiral safely home. She accompanied the grand fleet of the Second Voyage to Hispaniola, and Columbus selected her from seventeen sail for his flagship on an exploring voyage to Cuba, and purchased a half share in her. The only vessel in West Indian waters to survive the hurricane of 1495, she brought back the Admiral and over a hundred passengers to Spain in 1496, and after his return made an unauthorized voyage from Cadiz to Rome, was captured by a pirate off Sardinia, recaptured by her master and crew, and returned to Cadiz in time to sail for Hispaniola early in 1498, as advance guard of Columbus's Third Voyage. She was lying at Santo Domingo in 1500, and we last hear of her making a trading voyage to the Pearl Coast in

1501. Assuming that she reached Spain safely a third time, *Niña* logged at least 25,000 miles under the Admiral's command. One of the greatest little ships in the world's history.

Santa Clara she was named, after the patron saint of Moguer. A Spanish vessel in those days had an official religious name, but was generally known by a nickname, which might be the feminine form of her owner's or master's patronymic, or of her home port or some quality of sailing. Thus, a caravel owned by Gonzales Bachiller was nicknamed *Bachillera;* ship *Santiago de Palos* was called *Bermuda* after her master, Francisco Bermúdez; *Castilla* was owned by one Castillo. In Southern Spain a Basque or Galician ship might be nicknamed *La Vizcaína* or *La Gallega,* and Columbus's second *Santa María* earned the sobriquet *La Galante* by her gallant sailing qualities. *Santa Clara* was always called *Niña* after her master-owner, Juan Niño of Moguer.

Niña is the only one of the fleet of whose burthen we have any record. Michele de Cuneo, who sailed in her to Cuba and back in 1494, said she was of "about 60 tons," and on her unauthorized voyage to Rome in 1497 she carried a cargo of 51 tons. As the reason for chartering her on that voyage was the shipping shortage, she presumably was loaded nearly to capacity. We may therefore be certain that her tonnage was around 60; and 55 tons was a very common size for a caravel.

What did tonnage mean in 1492? Not weight or displacement of the vessel, or her deadweight capacity; tonnage meant simply her cubic capacity in terms of wine tuns. The Castilian *tonelada,* or the Portuguese *tonel* (both of which I translate "ton"), was really a tun of wine, a large cask equivalent in volume to two *pipas* or pipes, the long, tapering hogsheads in which port wine is still sold. As wine was a common cargo, and both pipe and tun of standard dimensions, a vessel's carrying capacity below decks in terms of *toneladas* became a rough-and-ready index of her size; and so a ship's tonnage in 1492 meant the number of tuns or twice the number of pipes of wine she could stow. The tun, *tonelada* or ton being roughly (very roughly) equivalent to 40 cubic feet, this last figure became in the course of time the unit of burthen (or tonnage or capacity) for English vessels, and was so used in America until the Civil War. From the seventeenth century on, it became

Niña under Original Lateen Rig

Pinta (*Niña* Re-rigged Thus)
From the models after the D'Albertis plans in the
Marine Museum, Pegli, Genoa

customary in every country to fix a vessel's official tonnage by a
formula composed of her length, breadth and depth, which gave a
rough measurement of her capacity. But in 1492 tonnage meant
simply the number of tuns of wine that the ship could stow, as
estimated by the owner or verified by common report. It was not
a constant but a variable.

Niña's tonnage then was around 60, rather less than more. The
difficulty comes in translating the ancient capacity measure into
linear dimensions. If we could only get one, we could deduce the
others; for the classic proportion for caravels seems to have been,
beam: length of keel: overall length = 1: 2: 3. Unfortunately I
have been unable to find a single linear dimension of Niña to start
with, and the formulas given by the marine archeologists for
deducing them from tonnage do not inspire confidence. If my personal guess of what a 55- to 60-ton caravel of 1492 measured is any
use, here it is: overall length (between perpendiculars) about 70
feet, length of keel about 50 feet, beam about 23 feet, depth of hold
amidships about 9 feet. And from my own experience in the waters
of Southern Cuba, I should say that Niña's draught could not have
been over 6 feet.

Niña, like her two consorts, was a one-decker. The preposterous
notion that the two caravels were open or half-decked boats was
derived from Eden's bad translation in 1555 of Peter Martyr's
Renaissance Latin. Niña must have had a raised quarter-deck on
which was built a *toldilla* or house for the captain's and master's
cabin. Her forecastle was relatively small and low, accommodating
only the cables and the sail locker; perhaps also the bread room,
and the *fogón* or firebox.

Now for Niña's rig. In the Genoa model and in every popular
picture generally, she is represented as a three-masted lateener of
the Portuguese type, the mainmast with the longest yard being
almost amidships, and the other two aft. She probably was so
masted when she set forth from Palos, although for aught we know
she might have started as a two-sticker. But her rig was certainly
altered to *vela redonda* (square rig) at the Grand Canary, so that
(says Ferdinand) "she might follow the other vessels more quietly
and with less danger." That was good judgment. Running down to
the Canaries with the wind dead aft, Niña must have yawed badly,

exhausting her helmsmen; and every time the wind shifted a little
from port to starboard quarter or vice versa, she had to go through
the complicated maneuver of throwing the great mainsail around
the mast and lowering and hoisting again the other two. In the
meantime, *Santa María* and *Pinta* were placidly scudding along
under their main courses. Thus everyone was "sold" on square rig,
and *Niña's* big lateen sails, efficient as they were for windward work,
had to go.

Exactly how was she altered? When the Portuguese changed a
caravela latina to *caravela redonda* they simply stepped a foremast
right up in her bows, and crossed two yards on which to set course
and topsail for running before the wind, when one or more of the
lateen sails would be furled. This made an ugly but serviceable
rig for the Cape passage. But there is no evidence that the Portuguese invented this rig before 1500, and Columbus's Journal proves
that *Niña* had squaresails on two masts. In the storms of February
and March, 1493, he several times mentions the *papahigo* or square
main course, with its bonnet, and once mentions her *trinquete,*
which always means a square fore course. That sort of re-rigging
required considerable resparring as well; old No. 2 lateen-rigged
mast was probably stepped well forward to serve as the new foremast, and the old mainmast probably had to be moved a few feet
aft. The two discarded lateen yards would have been cut down or
replaced by two shorter yards for the courses. Columbus doubtless
obtained assistance from shipyard workers at Las Palmas, and he
had a week's time for the job. It was evidently well done, as the
only other attention *Niña's* spars required was a new mizzenmast
and yard, which the men cut and fitted from native pine in Cuba.

Thus rigged square, *Niña's* sail plan had the same general appearance as *Santa María's,* except that she had no top to her mainmast, carried no topmast or topsail, and no spritsail. Her sailing
qualities even to windward were not seriously impaired, because
square rig had been so improved in recent years that its effective-
ness was approaching that of lateen. And for service downwind, as
Columbus's fleet sailed most of the way across and at least half the
passage home, square rig was infinitely superior. Sailing west before
the trades, which often show a diurnal variation from ENE to ESE,
a lateener would have been forced at least twice a day to perform

the difficult maneuver of wearing; but in square rig, when the wind veers across your stern, all you need to do is trim the main course. Aboard our barkentine *Capitana* when rolling down to Trinidad in 1939, the only thing that gave us any trouble was gybing the fore-and-aft main and mizzen booms; and as the square-sails on the foremast did most of the pulling we eventually saved ourselves by furling both main and mizzen. No doubt Columbus's fleet furled their mizzens and fore courses, for the main course would have blanketed the fore when wind was dead aft, and the mizzen would have made steering difficult. As altered, *Niña* became the smartest sailer in the fleet out or home. Her rig, moreover, became the favorite one for Spanish caravels in transatlantic work; very few lateeners were ever taken out to the Indies.

Pinta is the vessel that we know the least about. She was a *caravela redonda* or square-rigged caravel of Palos, with the same rig that *Niña* received at Las Palmas. There is no reason to doubt that she was locally built, like *Niña*. Her owner, says Columbus, was Cristóbal Quintero of Palos, who sailed with the rating of seaman. What her real name was we do not know, and her nick-name is not derived from Pinzón, the feminine of which was *Pinzona*. There was a Pinto family at Palos, which possibly had owned her before Quintero did; my conjecture is that Quintero, who seems to have been a mean sort of fellow, was married to a masterful Pinto, and the seamen called his ship *Pinta* as a joke on him. There is no certain clue to her tonnage, and she disappears from recorded history after successfully completing the great voyage of discovery. Quintero in 1495 or 1496 chartered to the crown a caravel of 55 tons carrying forty men as part of a naval fleet in the Neapolitan war, and this caravel may have been *Pinta;* but Quintero is known to have owned other vessels, and 55 tons was a very common size for a caravel. Tradition, based largely on the erroneous belief that *Niña* means "tiny," makes *Pinta* larger, and perhaps she was; but Las Casas says not. My guess would be to give her a tonnage of 55 to 60, overall length about 73–75 feet, beam about 25, and depth of hold about 11 feet.

Pinta proved herself a smart sailer, and Columbus became an-noyed at a habit of Captain Pinzón in pressing on ahead when land was expected, in order to gain the reward. One of her men was first to sight the New World; she was the first to reach Hispaniola, and the first home to Spain. When both caravels were sailing on the wind during the return passage, *Niña* put it all over *Pinta,* but Columbus suggests that this was due to a sprung mizzenmast which Martín Alonso Pinzón had been too lazy (or busy looking for gold) to replace. This at least goes to show how important the lateen mizzen was in giving these square-rigged caravels good performance on the wind.

Santa María the flagship has been the subject of much more intensive study and idle speculation than the caravels. Unlike *Niña* and *Pinta,* which were home-town vessels, *Santa María* was built in Galicia, and for that reason was nicknamed *La Gallega.* Galicia was then the principal Spanish province for the building of large vessels, but *Santa María* was a small vessel for that period. We know nothing of her history before May 1492. She happened to be in the Rio Tinto on a trading voyage when Columbus was looking for ships, and as the Paleños could not be induced to furnish more than the two caravels that the Sovereigns had commanded, he chartered *Santa María* from her owner-master, Juan de la Cosa of Santoña. She became *capitana* or flagship because she was the largest of the fleet; but the Admiral disliked her for her dull sailing qualities, and because she drew too much water for his purposes. After she had been wrecked — through no fault of her own — he recorded in his Journal (December 26, 1492), "The ship was very heavy and not suitable for the business of discovery; and for taking such a ship the men of Palos were responsible, because they did not fulfil with the King and Queen what they had promised, to give vessels suitable for that voyage. . . ." If they made any such promise (which is improbable) it was a verbal one, for the most assiduous search of the archives has uncovered no such promise or contract, only the royal command that Palos furnish two caravels.

No record of *Santa María's* tonnage or any other dimension exists, to our knowledge. Somewhat on the principle of restoring the mammoth from a jawbone, Auguste Jal in 1840 proposed to work out *Santa María's* dimensions from the length of her boat, 5 fathoms, as supposedly given in Columbus's Journal; but unfortunately he picked the wrong jawbone. The 5 fathoms in that entry referred to the depth at the mouth of Baracoa harbor which was being sounded

Models of *Santa María*

Above: Model by R. C. Anderson. Addison Gallery of American Art, Phillips Academy, Andover

Below: Model after the D'Albertis plans in the Marine Museum, Pegli, Genoa

from the boat, not to the boat itself! Three out of four of *Santa María's* restorers built her up from that hypothetical 5-fathom boat; yet none seem able to agree. Fernández Duro made her tonnage 120 to 130; Monléon 127; D'Albertis (who did not use the boat) 150 to 200; and Guillén 120. Obviously there is not enough difference between these to fight about; but in my opinion she was smaller than any of these estimates, for the following reasons.

"SANTA MARÍA" AT ANCHOR
From a photograph

Las Casas says that *Santa María* was "somewhat," not "very much," bigger than the others. And there is also a hint that she was of about 100 tons in Columbus's Journal of the Third Voyage, as abstracted by Las Casas. One reason the Admiral went straight from Margarita to Hispaniola in 1498, he says, is "because the vessels he had were large for exploring, as the one was of more than 100 tons and the other more than 70, and only smaller ones are wanted for exploring; and because of the ship which he took on his First Voyage being large, he lost her in the harbor of Navidad." Now, that 1498 flagship (name unknown) of "more than 100 tons" drew approximately 6 feet of water, whilst the plans for Señor Guillén's 120-ton *Santa María III* call for a draught of 7.2 feet. Columbus says that his 100-plus tonner and his 70-plus

tonner of 1498 were both too large for coastal exploration, and that
Santa María was also too large. So what may we infer from his
comparison? It looks to me as if *Santa María* had been a vessel of
less than 100 tons, certainly smaller than *Santa María III,* or any
other "models" or "replicas" of the original. If anyone wishes to
build a fourth *Santa María,* he had better shoot at something that
will carry about 100 tuns or 200 pipes of wine below hatches, and
draw not more than 6½ feet aft when loaded.

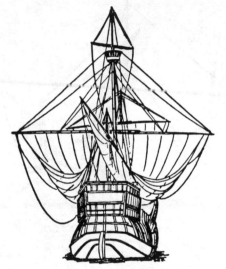

"SANTA MARÍA III" UNDER WAY, WITH YARD HALF HOISTED
From a photograph

Columbus's *Santa María* was a *nao* or ship, not a caravel. That is
perfectly clear from his Journal. Repeatedly he speaks of *la nao*
when he means the flagship, and *la carabela* or *las carabelas* when
he refers to *Niña* or *Pinta* or both. Consequently we are safe in
assuming that her model was round and chunky, like the carracks
of Venice and other *naos* of the period. Perhaps because her
northern builders had not incorporated the experience of African
voyages, she was not so fast or weatherly as *Niña* and *Pinta,* nor
was her general appearance so graceful; the sheer (fore-and-aft
curve) of her deck was broken by the castles. *Santa María III* has a

sheer of 3 feet. Built on the assumption that the original was a caravel, she has no proper castle up forward, merely a half-deck almost level with the sheer of the bulwarks; *Santa María II* and the Genoa and Andover models have high triangular forecastles extending out over the bows, which I believe to be correct.* The designer of *Santa María II* made a bad mistake in giving her a

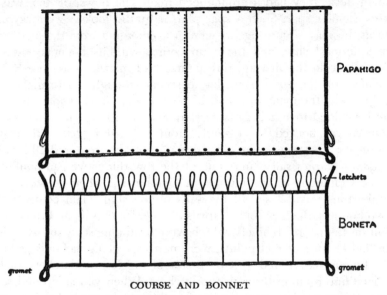

COURSE AND BONNET
From García Palacio, Instrución Náuthica (1587)

square stern; *Santa María III* and the Andover model both have a "round tuck," a neat finish formed by the planks meeting on the sternpost. *Santa María's* greatest breadth was on deck, not between wind and water as on later vessels. "Tumble-home" of topsides was introduced after 1500 in order to enable warships to bear the weight of their guns.

---

* The forecastle originally was just what the name implies, a forward castle for fighting purposes; but maritime conservatism has retained the name for crew's quarters wherever located. *Santa María II* has no more room under her forecastle than *Santa María III,* but the castle itself is quite a platform.

In the spar plan the most striking features of *Santa María* to a modern seaman would be the excessive height of mainmast and length of main yard in comparison with the others. The mainmast, all of one piece and stepped vertically in the middle of the keel, was higher than the ship was long, and the main yard was as long as the keel. Fore and mizzenmasts were only about one-third the height of mainmast, and sufficiently light to be stepped on the main deck; they had a pronounced rake. The bowsprit, too, was a very slender spar. Such a spar plan naturally looks very awkward to us, because square-riggers were just emerging from the medieval one-big-mast ship, and the main course with its bonnets was expected to do the driving; fore course and mizzen were mostly for balance on the wind. In order to spread enough sail to make the ship lively, the main yard had to be made of two big spars scarfed and woolded together. Lifts carried some of its weight when aloft, but it was hoisted by a single stout halyard rigged with triple purchase. Hoisting the main yard was a job that required all hands.

Santa María's sail plan is one of the few things we can bank on; since Columbus in his Journal for October 24, when he wished to make time, says "I set all the sails of the ship, main course with two bonnets, the fore course, spritsail, mizzen, topsail, and the boat's sail on the poop." Bonnets, which were used almost to our own day in lieu of rows of reef points, were narrow rectangular sails as long as the course, secured to it by a row of toggles and latchets, or by a lace line running through the latchets. When you shortened sail, you began by lowering the yard a bit, removing a bonnet, and re-reeving tacks and sheets. The topsail in 1492 was a little square "duster," with no more pull than a topgallant studdingsail of a later era; but trade-wind voyages soon demonstrated the possibilities of the topsail as a driver. It was first lengthened out on the foot like a trapezoid, then the topsail yard was lengthened, and by the seventeenth century Columbus's pocket handkerchief had evolved into the most important sail on a square-rigger. Not until even later did anyone have the wit to substitute a jib for the low-hanging spritsail, which had to be clewed up in rough weather; or to provide triangular staysails to fill the spaces between masts. *Santa María* could have done with a few; *Santa María II* when she crossed in 1893 was provided with jibs and a main staysail "to use in the solitude of the sea" where nobody would remark the anachronism.

We may now consider features that were common to all three vessels, or to any that Columbus sailed across the ocean; for we have very few details on his later ships. The experience of repeated ocean crossings enabled him to make improvements, and before the Fourth Voyage he hoped to have vessels of a new design especially constructed for him. But he was in no position to do that, and had to take what he could get.

Iron bolts were probably used for fastenings at points where the greatest strain was expected, but the 3- to 4-inch planking was fastened to the frames by wooden trunnels; that is why *Santa María* opened up so quickly when she grounded off Hispaniola.* All ships' bottoms were covered with a mixture of tallow and pitch in the hope of discouraging barnacles and teredos, and every few months a vessel had to be hove-down and graved on some convenient beach. This was done by careening her alternately on each side, cleaning off the marine growth, repitching the bottom and paying the seams. In order that the heaving-down process should not strain her, she had to be constructed with heavy wales and wide bilges and floor timbers; vertical skids were secured to the topsides in order to protect the planking. Some kind of dark preservative was applied to the topsides, probably a mixture of whale oil and pine tar, which the Niebla region produced.

Centuries elapsed before shipwrights learned to fasten outside ballast to the keel; and merchant vessels in Columbus's day (as almost to the other day) required no inside ballast if they carried a full cargo of some heavy substance like wine. If not, sufficient sand or shingle or cobblestones was taken in to ensure stability. Columbus's fleet sailed from the Canaries well laden with sea stores, but they must have had some ballast as well, for Columbus writes of a boy knocking down a sea bird with a stone; and where else but in the ballast could he have found a stone aboard ship? On the return passage *Niña*, as her depleted sea stores were consumed, became so crank that the men had to fill empty wine casks

---

* "I have knowne a ship built, hath sailed to and againe over the maine Ocean, which had not so much as a naile of iron in her but onely one bolt in her keele." — Captain John Smith's *Sea Grammar* (1627).

with sea water for ballast; and one of their first objects at the
Azores was to procure stone or shingle before sailing for Spain.

Every wooden vessel will leak more or less under some conditions, and Columbus's vessels generally leaked more rather than
less. A fixed wooden pump, operated by the morning watch until
it sucked, was supposed to take care of the daily leakage; but no
pump of that sort could keep a ship completely dry, and as she
rolled and pitched, bilge water sloshed about the hold among the
bales and barrels and ballast. As the men threw most of their slops
into the bilge, it became a happy refuge for the seaman's inevitable
companion, the *cucaracha* or cockroach: —

> *Ai! que mi piqua*
> *Ai! que mi araña*
> *Con sus patitas*
> *La cucaracha*

as an old song goes. Every landsman who went to sea in the era
of discovery complained of the vermin, and of the horrible stench
that arose from the bilges, especially when the pump was working.
When these "funkes," as Elizabethan seamen called them, became
unbearably foul the ship was "rummaged." She was run into shoal
water, the stores and cargo hoisted out on deck, the ballast (if any)
hove overboard, casks and bilges scraped clean and sprinkled with
vinegar, and new ballast taken in.

On Columbus's ships the white sails were painted with crosses,
and possibly other heraldic or religious devices. Both running and
standing rigging was of hemp rope; wire would not make its appearance aboard ship for 350 years. The blocks (pulleys to landsmen) were blocks indeed; chunks of hardwood carved to an oval
or almond shape, hollowed out to admit the sheave, and pierced
at one end for the pendant, but not stropped. Double- and triple-
purchase blocks were used on halyards. It is a matter of dispute
whether block-and-tackle or deadeye-and-lanyard was used to
secure and set up the shrouds that stayed the masts. Ratlines were
possible only on the latter rig; on the former, as shown in the
Andover model, a Jacob's ladder on the after side of the mast, such
as pilots use to come over a vessel's side today, was the means of
going aloft.

Details of running rigging are so difficult to describe in anything but technical language that anyone really interested had better inspect the models at Andover or Cambridge, or examine the clear drawings in Señor Guillén's book. Sufficient here to say that almost all the lines of a modern square-rigger were already employed: halyards, lifts and braces to hoist, support and adjust the yards; tacks and sheets to trim the sails; clewlines, buntlines and martnets to spill the wind and prepare them for furling; bowlines to stretch their leaches (vertical edges) taut when sailing on the

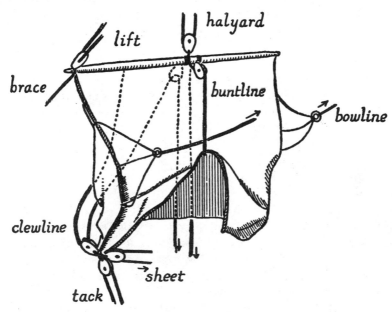

RIGGING OF YARD AND SQUARESAIL ON CARAVELS OF 1492

From Julio Guillén, La Carabela Santa María

wind. *Santa María III* has a stout pinrail at the foot of the great mast to make fast all the main running rigging; the Andover model uses belaying pins spaced along the bulwarks for everything but the main halyard.

In Columbus's day the great majority of anchorages in the Atlantic islands and on the West Coast of Africa were open roadsteads exposed to considerable swell and only partially protected from winds. Vessels commonly moored with two bowers and a stern anchor, and expected to lose one or more in the course of a long voyage. Usually seven anchors were carried: four bowers, two of which were kept constantly ready on the bows, a stream anchor to keep her headed into the swell, a kedge anchor for hauling her ahead in shoal water, and a big sheet anchor (called by the Spaniards *la esperanza* or *ancla de salvación*) which was stowed with its cable in the hold and only let go as a last resort. The two bowers were lashed to catheads forward when at sea. Their cables led through hawse-holes in the bows to a horizontal Spanish windlass, located either under the forecastle or in the waist forward of the main hatch.

All vessels of that period were steered by an outboard rudder and a great wooden tiller, to the forward end of which relieving tackles were attached. The after end was mortised directly to the rudderpost. This junction required a large open port aft, which could not be closed, since there had to be room for the tiller to work. Consequently when the ship was running before a heavy sea, every following wave must have sloshed water into the steerage. On the caravels, with their comparatively short poop decks, the helmsman might have been able to watch the weather clew of the main course, but on *Santa María III* the quarter- or poop-deck over his head (and he had to be a short man not to stoop) completely obscured his view of sea or sails. Captain Concas of *Santa María II* insisted on rigging a steering wheel on the poop deck before he made the ocean crossing. The Andover model affords her miniature helmsman a sight of sails and sky by cutting away a portion of the poop deck; but this consideration was unnecessary, for until the eighteenth century, when the steering wheel was invented, helmsmen were not supposed to see anything. They steered by compass and the feel of the ship, and by instructions shouted down to them by the officer of the watch.

The more you learn about vessels of the Columbian period, the more you have to admire their seaworthiness, and what is now called their "functional" features; but the living arrangements were so primitive that one would suppose shipbuilders were still assuming everyone would go ashore for the night, as in ancient Greece.

The only means of cooking was an open firebox provided with a back to screen it from the wind; on the floor of the box sand was spread, and a wood fire built on that. The builder of *Santa María III* could provide no sleeping accommodations above deck for anyone but the Admiral. The *toldilla* (what we should call a "dog house") on the poop deck afforded him a roomy cabin; but there was no space below the forecastle for anything but the cables, firebox and spare gear. A forward space in the hold below is partitioned off on *Santa María III* and called "Juan de la Cosa's cabin," but it seems incredible that the master would have slept in the stinking hold among the rats and cockroaches. There must have been bunks somewhere for the pilot, master, marshal, comptroller, interpreter and other swells of the afterguard; even *Niña* provided bunks for her Portuguese visitors at the Azores. Probably on the actual vessels the *toldilla* was larger than those of the reconstructions, giving the captain a snug stateroom and a general cabin for the other officers. Or else the steerage was higher, and cabins were installed around its sides. No sleeping place was provided on ships of that era for able seamen, gromets, and soldiers. They simply lay down anywhere — in the forecastle, the steerage, or on deck in fair weather.

Like all vessels of the day, *Santa María's* deck beams were arched, so that the decks had considerable camber,* and the only flat place on deck was the main hatch amidships. That this was a favorite sleeping place appears in an incident of the Fourth Voyage. When *Capitana* was anchored off the Rio Belén some Indian captives, confined below, pried the hatch off, tumbled its sleeping occupants into the scuppers, and jumped overboard. Eventually the Indians' hammocks, first observed in 1492, solved the shipboard sleeping problem for seamen of all nations. The crew of *Santa María II* slung hammocks in the hold, which must have been kept sweeter and cleaner than that of the original.

The low place on the profile of these vessels between mainmast and foremast was called the *combes* or waist. This space was closed in time of battle by waistcloths to protect the men from arrows, and on gala days a ship spread these waistcloths and hung outboard a row of shields bearing the arms of the *caballeros* in her company. On such occasions, too, the royal ensign of Castile and León was

* Latitudinal convexity.

hoisted at the main truck. Columbus had a special banner for his fleet, consisting of a green cross on a white field, with a crown on each arm of the cross, one over an *F* for Fernando and the other over a *Y* for Ysabel; on later voyages he doubtless displayed his own arms on a jackstaff forward. A variety of gaily colored pendants, bannerols and flags was carried to be run up on mastheads and yardarms on great church festivals if the vessel were in port; and these banners were much larger in comparison with the ship's length than is considered proper today. At sea (popular illustrations to the contrary notwithstanding) no flags were flown, because they soon wore out.

All vessels of that era were provided with a number of long ash sweeps, whioh were worked through ports in the bulwarks and used to give the vessels steerageway in a calm, or to keep them from drifting ashore with a current in light airs. We tried one of those on *Santa María III*, were impressed with its excellent balance and surprised how easily one could shove along so beamy and heavy a vessel. If the ship's boat were used in addition to tow her, Columbus's *Santa María* could probably have made 2 knots in smooth water with an "ash breeze." Each vessel carried but one boat, which took up the entire port or starboard gangway in the waist. It was a stout, heavy yawl boat, so difficult to hoist aboard that when once in the water they towed it as long as wind and sea were moderate.

Artillery was carried by all three vessels: iron "lombards" of about 9-cm. caliber which threw a stone cannon ball, mounted in carriages on deck; and small breech-loading swivel guns called "falconets," of about 4.5-cm. caliber, which were charged with odd bits of ironmongery to repel boarders, and were mounted on the bulwarks. The only small arms mentioned by Columbus on the First Voyage are crossbows and *espingardas,* primitive muskets made of a tube of bronze or iron secured to a wooden stock.

After *Niña II, Pinta II* and *Santa María II* were built in Spain in 1892, the first two at the cost of the United States and the last by the Spanish government, the two caravels were towed across. But the Spanish navy, to its great honor and credit, took *Santa María II* from the Canaries to Cuba under her own sail. She departed from Santa Cruz de Tenerife on February 22, 1893. Trade winds were unsteady that year and *Santa María II* had a much tougher passage than her original. For several days, while the wind blew from the W of N, she "rolled badly" and "pitched furiously," records her commander; even articles lashed down broke loose, while hull and masts worked and groaned so that nobody could sleep.* Squally days came in mid-March around latitude 21° N, oilbags were set to windward, and for a time the mainsail was furled. The trades never seemed to last on this voyage for more than two days at a time, and when they blew on the stern it was very difficult to steer, even with a modern wheel. In a fairly high sea *Santa María II* yawed as much as 7 and 8 points. Setting jibs and stay-sails which her captain had smuggled aboard in defiance of marine archeology, and raising the weather clew of the mainsail, helped steady her a bit; but throughout the voyage steering gave the most trouble. To the great relief of all hands, Virgin Gorda was sighted on March 28, thirty-four days out. This was just one day less than Columbus's ocean crossing, but his route was several hundred miles longer. On March 30 *Santa María* entered the harbor of San Juan de Puerto Rico. The best day's run of the passage was 139 miles; the worst 11. It is evident that *Santa María II* was neither so fast nor so well-balanced as the original of 1492. The constructional features that made her pitch and roll so badly were her short keel and round bilges, which were characteristic of seagoing sailing vessels in the fifteenth century.

Santa María III was also designed to be sailed across the Atlantic, but political conditions prevented. She made five short voyages under sail, attained a speed of 8 knots, and with wind abaft the beam steered easily and answered her helm readily. She rolled abominably, though not dangerously, behaving "like a barrel in a surf." The great length of her main yard and lack of ballast probably enhanced the tendency of any vessel with round bilges to roll.

These vicissitudes of the models are suggestive, but by no means conclusive as to the actual performance of the original *Niña, Pinta* and *Santa María.* They, constructed by shipwrights who had centuries of experience behind them, under the supervision of men who

* An American seaman who sailed north in her from Havana when she was being towed is said to have reported that "she jumped about like a Bowery 'hoor.'"

had been on African voyages, were probably better ships in all essential respects than the so-called replicas and reconstructions made by archeologists on the basis of such scanty data as they could cull from the records of the past. The one essential defect in *Santa María II* and *III*, their tendency to pitch and roll, was due to the shortness of their keels in relation to overall length, and to the roundness of their bilges. Columbus complained of the original *Santa María* pitching and taking in water forward the first day out from the Canaries, but that was probably remedied by restowing her stores, as there were no further complaints of that sort. From all that we can learn about the caravels, *Niña* and *Pinta* were sweet little vessels, seaworthy and sea-kindly, the sort that seamen become attached to. Columbus, when he had the pick of the whole merchant marine, took *Niña* on his Second Voyage, and selected her as his flagship on the Cuban reconnaissance.

Anyone could design better seagoing vessels and rig them better today; but the gain would be largely in comfort, labor saving and safety, not in speed. *Niña, Pinta* and *Santa María* were well built, well rigged, well equipped and well manned; *muy aptos para semejante fecho,* "well suited for such an enterprise," as the Admiral himself wrote in the prologue to his Journal. They were fine ships, competent for their allotted tasks. So let us hear no more chatter about Columbus setting forth in "tubs," "crates," or "cockleshells."

NOTES ON SAILING

Although the principles of sailing are the same now as in 1492, I propose to give here a short explanation of them for the benefit of non-nautical readers.

The appended diagram will help to explain the *points of sailing.* Here is a compass rose containing the 32 points of the compass. The wind is Northeast. A ship in Columbus's day could not sail nearer to the wind than five compass points (56°), even with a smooth sea. That is what the two ships headed N by W and E by S are doing; the one on the *starboard tack* (because the wind is blowing on her starboard side), the other on the port tack. The whole shaded quadrant is closed to them by the NE wind. If their destination lies in a northeasterly direction they must *come about* (either by luffing through the eye of the wind, or by *wearing,* i.e., turning away from the wind and then heading up), and sail a zigzag course. That is called *tacking,* or beating to windward. In a high sea, or with a current running in the same direction as the wind, it is impossible to gain anything beating to windward.

The ships in the diagram headed NW and SE have the wind *abeam*, i.e., at right angles to their hull. Those sailing W and S have the wind *on the quarter*. During most of his first outward voyage, Columbus was sailing W with a NE wind, like the ship in the diagram. That is generally a ship's fastest point of sailing. He would not have considered the wind *fair* for any course between WNW around by N to SSE. The ship headed SW is *running* (or *scudding*) *before the wind*. In such a position her foresail was blanketed and her mizzen furled; the mainsail (or main course) and main topsail, if any, did all the work.

Windward means toward the wind; i.e., on the present diagram, with the wind NE, any direction from NW to SE, clockwise. *Leeward* means away from the wind, i.e., any direction from SE to NW, clockwise.

A *lee shore* is a coastline upon which the wind is blowing. If a ship suddenly finds herself on a lee shore, as happened to Columbus when approaching the coast of Portugal in 1493, her only means of saving herself is to *claw off*, i.e., to trim her yards and alter her direction to windward. You cannot anchor in safety off a lee shore. You must anchor in a spot where the wind blows off the land.

Suppose night overtakes a sailing vessel in strange waters off soundings, and she fears to proceed further. She then has a choice between *heaving-to* and *jogging off-and-on*. In heaving-to the vessel is headed fairly close to the wind, and her sails adjusted so that she drifts slowly sideways, also surging ahead a little. In such a position she is said to be *hove-to*, or, as seamen say, *laying-to*. Columbus frequently used this maneuver when he was in unknown waters near the land and did not think it safe to sail at night. The same thing happened to us in *Capitana* off the Gulf of Darien on New Year's Eve, 1939. Approaching the coast with a head wind, we sighted land at 4 P.M. but lost it again in a black squall that came over the mountains, and were unable to verify our position. The dipsey lead yielded no bottom, so we lay her to for the night under main and fore staysails, a night black with heavy clouds through which lightning shot, and saw the New Year in with 16 bells. Laying-to is a peculiar sensation after a long voyage. Everything is unnaturally quiet; there is no sound of waters rushing by the ship or of wind whistling in the rigging. You roll and pitch a little but the motion is different, and the hull makes curious creaks and groans that you do not hear when sailing. Without the familiar noises and routine (for there is nothing to do, not even to steer) your ship seems curiously lonely and cut off from the world; it is a relief to make sail in the morning and fill away on your course again.

Jogging off-and-on means taking short tacks with sail reduced and wind abeam, so that the vessel sails up and down about over the same course. Columbus did that after his first landfall, until day broke.

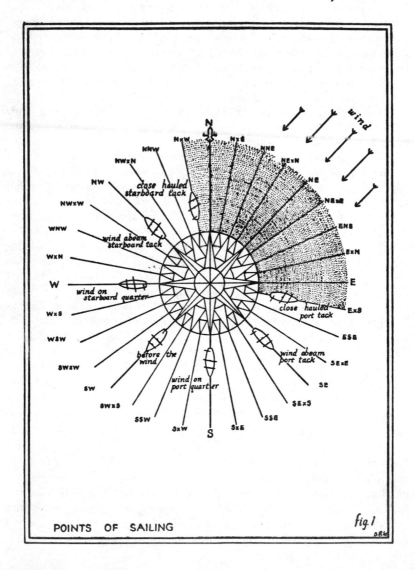

POINTS OF SAILING

fig. 1

CHAPTER X

Officers and Men

149?–1493

Habitatores Sidonis et Aradij fuerunt remiges tui: sapientes tui, Tyre, facti sunt gubernatores tui. Senes Giblij, et prudentes eius, habuerunt nautas ad ministerium variae supellectilis tuae.

The inhabitants of Sidon and Ärvad were thy mariners; thy wise men O Tyrus . . . were thy pilots. The ancients of Gebal and the wise men thereof were in thee thy calkers.

— EZEKIEL xxvii 8, 9

THE business of recruiting officers and men for the Great Enterprise was fully as important as the ships themselves. Fortunately, owing to the fact that everyone's wages were paid by the crown, we have almost a complete payroll and crew list of the First Voyage. Unfortunately the voyage gave rise to a controversy between Columbus and the Pinzón family which has broken all count of chancery records; for it dragged along for fifty years, and is still being debated (with more heat than light) by historians.

The object of these *pleitos* (pleadings) *de Colón* was to defend or annul the hereditary privileges of Columbus's descendants. His family summoned witnesses to sustain the common report that the First Voyage was the conception of Columbus, carried out under his leadership, and against the advice and wishes of most people; the crown tried to prove by another set of witnesses that Columbus was only the nominal head of an enterprise which was set on foot and brought to a successful conclusion by the energy, courage and maritime skill of Martín Alonso Pinzón. Survivors of the First and subsequent voyages and people present when the fleet was being fitted out or when the two caravels returned home were located in various parts of the Spanish empire, doubtless well coached, asked a series of leading questions, and their answers taken down by a notary without cross-examination; so each separate inquest was either pro-Columbus or anti-Columbus.

Common sense tells us that evidence taken under such circumstances and so long after the event should be used only to support or fill out contemporary evidence, and that much of it must be worthless. But a number of writers, eager to defame Columbus, rely on the pro-Pinzón *pleitos* while they ignore the pro-Columbus ones and reject other documents of his time as prejudiced and falsified. Yet we may not discount these *pleitos* completely; and there is much even in the pro-Pinzón testimony that fits in with and supplements the evidence in Columbus's own Journal.

Martín Alonso Pinzón, the head of a middle-class seafaring family of Palos, was between forty-six and fifty years old in 1492. García Fernández, steward of *Pinta*, declared, "Martín Alonso was a very valiant man, and of great courage, and he knows that without his giving the two ships to the Admiral he would not have been where he was, nor would he have found people, because nobody [in Palos] knew the said Admiral, and that by reason of the said Martín Alonso and through giving him the said ships, the said Admiral made the said voyage."

A very judicious statement. Columbus, a comparatively unknown man in Palos and a foreigner to boot, could hardly have induced mariners (proverbially suspicious of any new enterprise) to embark with him on a voyage of dubious safety and improbable success, unless some person of local standing came forward and showed his own faith in it. Martín Alonso took command of *Pinta*, with his younger brother Francisco Martín as her master, while Vicente Yáñez Pinzón, younger than Martín Alonso but older than Francisco, took command of *Niña*, and Diego Pinzón, a cousin of theirs called *el viejo* ("the old boy"), shipped as mariner on *Pinta*. The Pinzons owned neither *Pinta* nor *Niña*; but it must have reconciled somewhat the owners of these expropriated caravels to have prominent Paleños take over their command.

At the inquest held at Seville in 1515, two leading questions were asked by the *fiscal,* who corresponded more or less to our district attorney: "(1). Whether you know that when the Admiral went to discover those regions, Martín Alonso Pinzón of Palos was about to seek them out at his own charge with two of his own vessels, and had certain knowledge and writings of the land, which he had seen in Rome in the library of Pope Innocent VIII in the year that he came from Rome, and had begun to talk of going to discover them, and encouraged him, etc.?" "(2). Whether you know that the said Martín Alonso Pinzón gave information to the said Admiral D. Cristóbal Colón about the land and discussed with him the aforesaid writing, in which it was said it was an opinion of the time of Solomon that the Queen of Sheba had sailed by the Mediterranean Sea to the end of Spain and that there, 95° to the westward, by an easy passage, he would find between north and south a land of *sypanso* (Japan) which is so fertile and abundant and whose extent surpasses Africa and Europe?"

Whatever the truth of this story, it was evidently current in Andalusia in 1515. Several of the hand-picked witnesses, one of whom claimed he had sailed with Martín Alonso on the Roman voyage, simply said yes, they had heard the tale, or knew it to be true; but Martín Alonso's son Arias Pérez, who declared that he had been with his father on that Roman voyage, said a good deal more. One of Martín Alonso's friends, it seems, was a cosmographer employed in the Vatican Library, whom he visited at Rome. One day this man lent him a document from the papal library describing a Sheban transatlantic voyage to Japan, and the story of this mythical marine enterprise so impressed Martín Alonso that he determined to try such a voyage himself. When he was casting about for ways and means, Columbus called at La Rábida for the purpose of removing his son, and intending to leave for France. Martín Alonso encouraged him by reading the document, and persuaded him to visit the court once more. But, after returning to Palos with his royal authority and his contract, Columbus tried for two months to engage men and procure caravels before joining forces with Pinzón, who put the enterprise on its feet.

Can one dismiss Arias Pérez' tale as a cock-and-bull story, created by family pride, jealousy and resentment? I think not. The "docu-

ment" on the Queen of Sheba's marvelous voyage has never been
found or identified, but there may well have been such a legend of
the seagoing queen in some Hebrew codex in the Vatican Library.
What gives the tale verisimilitude is the evidence in Columbus's
own Journal of Pinzón's particular interest in discovering Japan,
and in finding other islands in the Atlantic. But among the numerous false leads that encouraged Columbus, no such heartening story
as a westward voyage by the Queen of Sheba to Japan is mentioned
by Ferdinand and Las Casas.

The substratum of truth in the Pinzón story seems to be that
Martín Alonso picked up a yarn of some mythical transatlantic
voyage which led him to suppose that Marco Polo's Cipangu could
be reached that way, and consequently lent his support to Columbus. No doubt his example and influence were useful in recruiting
men, but his conduct on the voyage was such that Columbus failed
to make what the Pinzón family regarded as suitable acknowledg-
ment.

A Pinzón myth began to take shape aboard *Pinta* on the homeward passage, and after the death of Martín Alonso his friends
and family inflated it to the point where the captain of *Pinta* appeared to be the real source and leader of the First Voyage, while
Columbus was relegated to the role of a mere window dresser who
had influence at court. Jean Charcot, who had plenty of experience
of that sort of thing, noted the tendency "common to Latin countries" to depreciate a great leader who wins popular applause.
"Subordinates often feel this jealousy; if they do not attack openly,
their still more eloquent insinuations and reticences are quickly
picked up and interpreted by those who hope to inflate themselves
by diminishing others." By no means confined to Latin countries!

Whatever one may think of Martín Alonso, his younger brother
Vicente Yáñez, captain of *Niña* and about thirty years old in 1492,
proved to be a first-class seaman, and unlike his brother obeyed
orders. Vicente's discovery of the Amazon on an independent
voyage in 1499–1500 entitles him to the first rank among discoverers
native to Spain. Of Francisco Martín, the youngest brother, nothing
is known after the First Voyage; but their cousin Diego, "the old
boy," accompanied Columbus to Paria in 1498, and made the
Amazon voyage with Vicente Yáñez the following year.

No contemporary record gives the Pinzons of Palos any special position in the Great Enterprise, or proves that they lent it more influence and gave it more aid than another seafaring family of the Niebla region, the Niños, whose social and economic status in the near-by town of Moguer was equivalent to that of the Pinzón family in Palos. At least three Niños went on the First Voyage. Juan, eldest of four brothers, owned *Niña* and sailed on her as master. Peralonso, the second brother, who was about twenty-four years old in 1492, sailed as pilot of *Santa María*, took some supply ships to Hispaniola and back in 1496, was appointed the first *piloto mayor* of Castile, made an independent voyage to the Pearl Coast in 1499–1500, and died soon after. Francisco, the next brother, about nineteen years old, shipped as gromet on the First Voyage, became *Niña's* pilot on the Second, and also made the Fourth Voyage with the Admiral. Several other members of the family went with him on his last three voyages; and their testimony in the *pleitos* was uniformly loyal to the Admiral. In these Niños one recognizes that competent and loyal type of seaman and officer whose work is essential to the success of any voyage; men who never lay claim to more than their deserts, or talk against their captain behind his back. Juan Niño was Columbus's favorite shipmate, whom he took with him to his triumph at Barcelona. As the Niños neither attempted to chisel away Columbus's fame, nor became the favorite sons of a local or patriotic build-up, they are less known than the Pinzons; but I suspect that they did quite as much as anyone to obtain seamen and put the voyage through.

Related to the Niños were the Quinteros of Moguer, two of whom shipped with Columbus. Cristóbal Quintero, owner of *Pinta*, relinquished her command to Pinzón, but became master of Columbus's flagship on the Third Voyage. Juan Quintero, *Pinta's* boatswain, is the only man besides the Admiral who is known to have sailed on all four voyages.

According to the testimony in the *pleitos*, the local seamen were held back less by fear than by skepticism. "All thought that the enterprise was vain" is the phrase constantly repeated, and at least two of the witnesses gave a very interesting reason why they thought so — because many Portuguese had "gone to discover" in the Western Ocean, and found nothing. A Portuguese who accompanied Columbus on the Second Voyage but not the First admitted that he had considered the enterprise "to be a vain thing, and thought that they would not have fallen in with land," because he "knew that the king of Portugal had fitted out once or twice and they returned without finding land."

That being so, it was lucky for Columbus that there happened to be living in Palos an ancient mariner called Pedro Vasques de la Frontera who in 1452 had made a voyage of discovery with a Madeiran named Diogo de Teive, under orders from the Infante D. Henrique. Sailing southwesterly from Fayal in the Azores, Vasques had run into the Sargasso Sea (which, incidentally, he warned Columbus not to fear), then turned northeastward, discovered the two westernmost Azores, Flores and Corvo, continued on that course in search of the mythical island of Brazil and reached the latitude of Cape Clear, Ireland. Although morally certain that they were near an undiscovered island, they turned back. Forty years later Pedro Vasques came forward and told Columbus and Pinzón "that he had information of the land of the Indies," and (says another witness in 1535) "encouraged the people and told them publicly that all should go on that voyage, and they would find a very rich land, . . . and said it publicly in the plazas."

How vivid it all is! The grizzled pilot, who believed he had just missed something big forty years before, becomes greatly excited at Columbus's preparations, confers with him and with Pinzón, and, warmly approving their enterprise, undertakes to beat up recruits for them in the plaza of Palos, where the unemployed hung about just as they do now. One can imagine the talk: Sign on with Master Christopher, you swabs, and he will make you rich for life, I know there's something big out there! Voice from the crowd: Did you ever *see* anything, skipper? — Sure thing, and if I was twenty years younger, I'd sail with you. Why, when I piloted Don Diogo we saw one day a big island with gold shining on the rocks . . . — So what? — Well, the fog closed in, and when it lifted we couldn't find the island, and it got cold, and Don Diogo wanted to go home to his wife (you know how it is), and so we lost it; but if I was twenty years younger and had half the chance of you mugs . . .

Unfortunately Pedro Vasques did not live to learn that his enthusiasm was justified. He was murdered before Columbus returned to Palos.

Now let us see who took his advice. The thoroughgoing researches of Miss Alice Bache Gould have made it possible to give the names of 87 out of 90 men and boys who sailed on this first voyage of discovery to the New World, with most of their wages and ratings and a few biographical details. A few of the names are in Columbus's own Journal, others were obtained from the later *pleitos,* but most of them are found on payrolls in the Spanish archives and elsewhere, owing to their wages being paid by the crown.

The number of men left behind at Navidad, 39, presumably represents very nearly the crew of the wrecked *Santa María,* although some of the garrison were from *Niña,* and some of the *Santa María's* men took their places. Of the remaining 51 more than half can be assigned to *Pinta.* Of the 87 whose names we know, only four besides Columbus were not Spaniards: Juan Arias of Tavira in Portugal, Jácome el Rico of Genoa, Antón Calabrés (presumably a Calabrian), and Juan Veçano (probably a Venetian). English and Irish national pride have been flattered by the idea that a man of each nation accompanied the fleet; but there was no Englishman or Irishman or other North European aboard.

The royal order suspending all civil and criminal processes against men who signed on with Columbus gave rise to the notion, repeated *ad nauseam,* that the Admiral's crews were composed of desperate characters, criminals and jailbirds. The grain of truth is this. Not long before Columbus came to Palos, one Bartolomé de Torres of that town had been found guilty of killing a man in a quarrel, and sentenced to death. When awaiting execution he was rescued from jail by three of his friends, Alonso Clavijo, Juan de Moguer, and Pedro Yzquierdo. In accordance with a curious law of Castile these three also were condemned to death. All four, when still at large, took advantage of the royal offer to enlist under Columbus, and at their return each received a pardon "because to serve us you ventured your person and underwent much danger with D. Cristóbal Colón our Admiral of the Ocean Sea to discover the Islands of the Indies." Even these four were not in the ordinary sense jailbirds, and at least three of them made good. Bartolomé de Torres shipped on the Second Voyage as a crossbowman; Columbus took Juan de Moguer as able seaman aboard his flagship on the Second Voyage, and Juan later became a pilot under Aguado.

Apart from the few foreigners, one man from Murcia, and ten northerners (who were probably of *Santa María's* original crew), all Columbus's men hailed either from some town or village in the Niebla (Palos, Moguer, Huelva, Lepe) or from other towns in Andalusia such as Cadiz, Seville, Cordova, Jerez, Puerto Santa María. There were at least three family groups besides the Niños, Quinteros and Pinzons: Gil Pérez and his nephew Alvaro on *Pinta;* Pedro Arráez and his son Juan on *Niña,* and the Medel brothers aboard *Pinta.* Far from being manned by criminals, cutthroats and desperadoes, Columbus's vessels were what we used to call in New England "home-town ships," manned by the local boys and their neighbors and friends from near-by seaports. They doubtless represented the pick of the seafaring population, active young seamen whose sporting sense was aroused by the novelty of the enterprise, and the hope of gain. Apart from their pardonable apprehension at the length of the outward voyage, these men behaved well while under the Admiral's command; and the bad actions of those left behind at Navidad, which aroused the natives' hostility and caused their death, were probably no worse than what any group of sailors would have done under the circumstances. All in all, it seems to me that Columbus's shipmates were "good guys," hardy, competent and loyal to their commander. No one but real seamen could have sailed *Niña* and *Pinta* home safely; and a considerable number of them are known to have accompanied Columbus on his later voyages.

The total monthly payroll of the expedition was 250,180 maravedis; but except for the advance pay, this was allowed to accumulate and the men were paid off when they returned. Masters and pilots received 2000 maravedis a month; *marineros* (the able seamen), 1000; *grumetes* (gromets, ordinary seamen or ship's boys), 666 maravedis a month or 22 a day. This was the usual pay for long voyages, as the royal order of April 30 specified; Columbus paid exactly the same wages on his Fourth Voyage in 1502–1504.

What these sums were equivalent to in modern terms is difficult to say. A thousand maravedis, if paid in gold (as these men seem to have been paid), were equivalent to $6.95 in gold dollars of before 1934. If paid in silver, they were worth only half. Whatever way you figure it, a maravedi was less than a cent in specie value, but its purchasing power was much greater. Twelve maravedis a day were allowed by the crown for feeding each seaman in the navy. A bushel of wheat in 1493 cost 73 maravedis. Sancho Panza's wages from Don Quixote were 26 maravedis a day and found, a little better than that of Columbus's gromets.

The men were not provided with clothing, and when paid off after the voyage there were no deductions from their wages for "slops." Seamen in those days generally wore what they had. The only distinctive sailor's garments were a hooded smock or parka, and the *gorro,* a red woolen stocking-cap, similar to those worn by Portuguese fishermen today. Everyone went barefoot, and let his beard grow, for there were no shaving facilities aboard ship.

Turning from the forecastle to the afterguard, the officers of Columbus's vessels (as in all Spanish ships in the age of discovery) were the captain, master and pilot. The captain was the commanding officer, responsible for everything and everybody on board; and Columbus, beside being captain of *Santa María,* was captain general of the fleet. García Palacio, who published the first Spanish seafaring manual in 1587, says that the captain should be a good Christian, "very fearful of God," possessed of all manly virtues, of a cheerful disposition to keep his people happy and contented, zealous to see that everyone did his duty, and above all things vigilant. He did not necessarily have to be a seaman, because the master had immediate command of all the mariners, and full responsibility for getting under way, stowing the cargo, managing the ship under sail, and anchoring. The master "above all things, must be a good seaman."

The owner of a vessel, when chartered to the crown or to others, normally acted as her master. Thus Juan Niño, owner of *Niña,* was her master as well; and Columbus's second in command on *Santa María* was her owner, Juan de la Cosa. But Martín Alonso Pinzón took his younger brother Francisco as master of *Pinta,* whose owner, Cristóbal Quintero, rated as able seaman.

Juan de la Cosa, master of *Santa María,* is commonly supposed to be the man of the same name who made the famous world map and later explored the Spanish Main; but these were two different persons. The confusion is natural, since both were Basques, the one from a ward or parish of Santoña called Santa María del Puerto, and the other shifted his residence to a town on the Bay of Cadiz called Puerto Santa María. Juan de la Cosa of the First Voyage disgraced himself when his ship grounded, and never again was mentioned by the Admiral; Juan de la Cosa the map maker shipped aboard *Niña* in 1493 as able seaman, and made the Cuban voyage with Columbus. While the Second Voyage was under way the first Juan de la Cosa, having procured another ship in Spain, applied to the crown for permission to carry 200 *cahizes* of wheat from Andalusia to Guipuzcoa; and this privilege was granted by Ferdinand and Isabella on February 28, 1494 (when the second Juan de la Cosa was in Hispaniola), on the express ground that he had lost his ship in the Indies.

The pilot on Spanish vessels of that era corresponded to the first mate or first officer of English and American ships. Second to the master in command over the seamen, he also had to take charge of the navigation, keeping the reckoning and pricking off the estimated daily positions on the chart. García Palacio declares that this officer should be a man of considerable age and experience, vigilant and weather-wise, knowing when to take in sail and acquainted with astronomy. Columbus's pilots were good men and true, and on the outward passage Peralonso Niño, pilot of *Santa María,* was more accurate than the Admiral; but none knew celestial navigation, and on the return voyage Columbus kept the better dead-reckoning. Cristóbal García Sarmiento (or Xalmiento) piloted *Pinta;* and Sancho Ruiz de Gama, *Niña.* Bartolomé Roldán also did some "making points" aboard *Niña.* He and Sarmiento sailed on the Second Voyage, and Roldán also on the Third, as well as making voyages with Aguado, Hojeda and Lepe. Eventually he settled down and became a leading citizen of Santo

Domingo. Pilots were paid 2000 maravedis a month, twice the seaman's pay, and the same as masters.

Besides the ships' officers, there were a number of landsmen in the fleet with particular duties. Luis de Torres, a *converso* or converted Jew, was taken along as interpreter because he knew Hebrew and a little Arabic. It was then commonly supposed that Arabic was the mother of all languages, so Torres was expected to make shift at conversing with the Grand Khan and other oriental potentates. Diego de Harana, cousin of Columbus's Cordovan mistress, shipped as *alguacil de la armada,* marshal of the fleet. The same office existed in English ships into the seventeenth century. Captain John Smith says, "The Marshall is to punish offenders, and to see justice executed according to directions; as ducking at the yards arme, haling under the keel, bound to the capsterne or maine-mast with a bucket of shot about his necke, setting in the bilbowes." Diego de Harana sailed on *Santa María; Pinta* and *Niña* each had her own marshal.

Rodrigo de Escobedo was *escribano de toda la armada,* secretary of the fleet. He had nothing to do with keeping the journal, but wrote up proceedings when possession was taken of any island in the name of the Sovereigns. He would probably have been called upon for diplomatic correspondence if the Indians had been able to read and write.

Two royal officials were aboard *Santa María.* Rodrigo Sánchez de Segovia, *veedor real* or comptroller, came to keep track of expenditures, and to see that the crown got its share of gold and precious stones. Pedro Gutiérrez is referred to as *repostero de estrados del rey,* butler of the king's dais. He appears to have been a gentleman volunteer, for Columbus had a personal steward (Pedro de Terreros, who rose to command a caravel on a later voyage) and a page-boy.

Each vessel carried her own surgeon. Maestre Juan Sánchez of *Santa María* belonged to the Haranas' circle of friends in Cordova; Maestre Alonso of Moguer took care of *Niña,* and Maestre Diego of *Pinta.* There was so little for them to do aboard this healthy fleet that the first two were allowed to stay at Navidad; Alonso's heirs were paid 11,688 maravedis for his services.

Among the petty officers and men of *Santa María* were nine northerners, Basques and Galicians, probably the only members of her original ship's company who could be induced to remain. They formed a clique under Juan de la Cosa, and five of them, greatly to the relief of the Andalusians, elected to remain at Navidad. Chachu (Basque for Juanito), boatswain of *Santa María,* was the leader of this gang. The boatswain then as now had special charge of the gear. It was his duty to lead the seamen in carrying out the master's or pilot's orders, to direct the stowage of cargo, to watch the spars for weakness and the rigging for chafe, to see that the cables were kept dry at sea, that the coils of the running rigging were properly made up, that the pump was kept clear, that the galley fire was extinguished every night, that the ship's boat was kept clean and properly fitted, and that the rats were prevented from eating the sails in port. He must have been the busiest man aboard. Juan Quintero, the one who accompanied Columbus on all four voyages, was Chachu's opposite number on *Pinta,* and Bartolomé García was boatswain of *Niña.* These two were paid 1500 maravedis a month, and Chachu somewhat more — a bonus perhaps to induce him to stay with the ship. Even today it is easier to procure a good captain than a good boatswain.

The *despensero* or steward was another important petty officer. He had entire charge of the water, wine and food, of firewood, and of some of the chandlery; he trimmed the lamps and fed the fire on the galley hearth; and he also saw that the boys learned to box the compass and say the proper ditties when the glass was turned and the watch relieved. García Fernández was steward of *Pinta;* we do not know the names of the other two.

Below the boatswains and stewards were a group of petty officers known as *oficiales* who received able seaman's pay, but had special duties, such as carpenter, cooper and caulker. "Chips" had the same duties as today, except that *calafate* the caulker took charge of the pump, as well as seeing that the decks, topsides, and bottom (when she was hove-down) were kept properly caulked and payed with pitch and tallow. He also saw to it that the gromets employed their spare time making up caulking stuff instead of skylarking. *Tonelero* the cooper "is to looke to the caske, hoopes and twigs, to stave or repaire the buckets, baricos, cans, steepe tubs, runlets, hogsheads, pipes, buts, etc. for wine . . . fresh water, or any liquor." *Pinta* carried a painter, and one gromet aboard *Santa María* had the resounding title of "silversmith, assayer of minerals and washer of gold."

The total complement was about 24 men aboard *Niña;* 26 aboard *Pinta;* 40 aboard *Santa María.*

According to contemporary standards, this was an unusually well-organized fleet for discovery and exploration. There were no "idlers" except the royal butler, secretary and interpreter, and these might have been useful if Columbus had had occasion to entertain the governor of a Chinese province. Popular illustrations usually show men-at-arms complete with pike and morion stalking about *Santa María's* deck, apparently as a marine guard; but Columbus shipped no men-at-arms on this voyage, not even cannoneers or crossbowmen. He was not equipped for fighting or conquering but for just one thing, discovery. The three caravels were provisioned for at least a year, which suggests that Columbus expected to be home in much less time than that. He was not planning so long a voyage as Bartholomew Dias had already made to South Africa.

Columbus did not once mention in his writings a tragic movement that was under way at the same time as his preparations, one which must in some measure have hampered his efforts and delayed his departure. This was the expulsion of the Jews from Spain. On March 30, 1492, one month before concluding their agreements with Columbus, Ferdinand and Isabella signed the fateful decree giving the Jews four months to accept baptism or leave a country where many thousands of them had made their home for centuries, and to whose intellectual life they had contributed in a degree far beyond their numbers. As Columbus journeyed from Granada to Palos he must have been witness to heart-rending scenes similar to those which modern fanaticism has revived in the Europe of today. Swarms of refugees, who had sold for a trifle property accumulated over years of toil, crowded the roads that led seaward, on foot and leading donkeys and carts piled high with such household goods as could be transported. Rabbis read the sacred scrolls and others played the traditional chants on pipe and tabor to keep their spirits up; but it was a melancholy procession at best, what with weeping and lamenting, and the old and sick crawling into the fields to die. When they arrived at Puerto Santa María and for the first time beheld the ocean, the Jews raised loud cries and invocations, hoping that Jehovah would part the waters and lead them dry-shod to some new promised land. Camping where they could find room or crowded aboard vessels that the richer Jews chartered, they forlornly awaited the order to leave; finally word came from the Sovereigns that every Jew-bearing ship must leave port on August 2, 1492, the day before Columbus set sail from Palos. Perhaps that is why he waited until the following day; but even then he did not avoid sailing in unwanted company. Sixty years later an old man deposed in Guatemala that he had been gromet on a ship of the great migration that dropped down the Rio Saltés on the same tide with the Columbian fleet; and by a curious coincidence, when his ship was sailing back to Northern Spain after discharging her cargo of human misery in the Levant, she spoke *Pinta* returning from the great discovery, and heard news that in due time would give fresh life to this persecuted race.

Of the many difficulties that Columbus and the Pinzons had to surmount in order to get their people aboard and the vessels ready for sea, no details have survived; all have been swallowed up in the surpassing interest of the voyage itself. Tradition designates a fountain near the Church of St. George at Palos, connected by a Roman aqueduct with a spring of sweet water in the hills, where the water casks of the fleet were filled. Last thing of all, every man and boy had to confess his sins, receive absolution, and make his communion. Columbus, after making his confession (writes the first historian of the Indies), "received the very holy sacrament of the Eucharist on the very day that he entered upon the sea; and in the name of Jesus ordered the sails to be set and left the harbor of Palos for the river of Saltés and the Ocean Sea with three equipped caravels, giving the commencement to the First Voyage and Discovery of the Indies."

THE FIRST VOYAGE TO AMERICA

CHAPTER XI

Bound Away

AUGUST 3–SEPTEMBER 9, 1492

Et turbabuntur insulae in mari, eo quod nullus egredia-
tur ex te.

Yea, the isles that are in the sea shall be troubled at thy
departure.

— EZEKIEL xxvi 18

C OLUMBUS began his Book of the First Navigation and Discovery
of the Indies, commonly called the Journal of his First Voyage, with a preamble characteristic both of the Admiral and of his
times: —

IN THE NAME OF OUR LORD JESUS CHRIST

BECAUSE, most Christian and very exalted excellent and mighty
Princes, King and Queen of the Spains and of the islands in the Sea,
our Lord and Lady, in this present year 1492, after Your Highnesses
had made an end to the war with the Moors who ruled in Europe, and
had concluded the war in the very great city of Granada, where in
the present year, on the second day of the month of January, by force
of arms I saw the royal standards of Your Highnesses placed on the
towers of Alhambra (which is the citadel of the said city), and I saw
the Moorish King come forth to the gates of the city and kiss the
royal hands of Your Highnesses and of the Prince my lord, and soon
after in that same month, through the information that I had given to
Your Highnesses concerning the lands of India, and of a prince who
is called "Grand Khan" which is to say in our vernacular "King of
Kings," how many times he and his ancestors had sent to Rome to seek
doctors in our Holy Faith to instruct him therein,* and that never had
the Holy Father provided them, and thus were lost so many people
through lapsing into idolatries and receiving doctrines of perdition;

---

* Note similarity of language to that of the Toscanelli letter.

AND Your Highnesses, as Catholic Christians and Princes devoted to the Holy Christian Faith and the propagators thereof, and enemies of the sect of Mahomet and of all idolatries and heresies, resolved to send me Christopher Columbus to the said regions of India, to see the said princes and peoples and lands and [to observe] the disposition of them and of all, and the manner in which may be undertaken their conversion to our Holy Faith, and ordained that I should not go by land (the usual way) to the Orient, but by the route of the Occident, by which no one to this day knows for sure that anyone has gone; —

THEREFORE, after all the Jews had been exiled from your realms and dominions, in the same month of January Your Highnesses commanded me that with a sufficient fleet I should go to the said regions of India, and for this granted me many rewards, and ennobled me so that henceforth I might call myself by a noble title and be Admiral-in-Chief of the Ocean Sea and Viceroy and Perpetual Governor of all the islands and mainlands that I should discover and win, or that henceforth might be discovered and won in the Ocean Sea, and that my eldest son should succeed me, and thus from rank to rank for ever.

AND I departed from the city of Granada on the 12th day of the month of May of the same year 1492, on a Saturday, and came to the town of Palos, which is a seaport, where I fitted for sea three ships well suited for such an undertaking, and I departed from the said harbor well furnished with much provision and many seamen, on the third day of the month of August of the said year, on a Friday, at half an hour before sunrise, and took the route for the Canary Islands of Your Highnesses, which are in the said Ocean, that I might thence take my course and sail until I should reach the Indies, and give the letters of Your Highnesses to those princes, and thus comply with what you had commanded.

AND for this I thought to write down upon this voyage in great detail from day to day all that I should do and see, and encounter, as hereinafter shall be seen. In addition, Lord Princes, to noting down each night what that day had brought forth, and each day what was sailed by night, I have the intention to make a new chart of navigation, upon which I shall place the whole sea and lands of the Ocean Sea in their proper positions under their bearings, and further to compose a book, and set down everything as in a real picture, by latitude north of the equator and longitude west; and above all it is very important that I forget sleep and labor much at navigation because it is necessary. All of which will be great labor.

So begins the most detailed, the most interesting and the most entrancing sea journal of any voyage in history. And it is, furthermore, the source of about 98 per cent of our information about the actual discovery of America. Columbus's Journal, as I shall call it in deference to long usage, although it is much more than an ordinary sea journal, contains not only the navigator's "day's work" of courses steered, and distances covered, objects sighted at sea and lands discovered, but long descriptions of people, places, fauna and flora, and the Admiral's reflections and conclusions on cosmography, on future colonial policy and on many other subjects.

The original manuscript of the Journal has long since disappeared. It was sent or presented in person by Columbus to the Sovereigns at Barcelona, where it doubtless found its way into the ever-perambulating royal archives, and so was lost or thrown away before one of the frequent moving days. Fortunately, one or more fair copies were made shortly after the Journal was received at Barcelona. One was in the possession of Las Casas, who made an abstract for his own use, quoting long passages of the original. The same or another was used by Ferdinand Columbus in writing the *Historie*, wherein he preserved in direct quotation some parts that Las Casas merely abstracted, and which prove that the bishop did his work honestly and well. Las Casas's abstract of the Journal, in his own hand, is still preserved in the National Library at Madrid; and that is the text we have today.

This Journal, as Las Casas abstracted it, has been the target of every writer with a peculiar theory. Those who pretend that Columbus was never seeking "The Indies," the advocates of someone else having discovered them first, or of his having been there before under another name; those who insist that Colón the discoverer was a different person from Colombo the Genoese, patriotic Spaniards who wish to give Martín Alonso Pinzón the credit; Scandinavians who assert that Columbus deliberately concealed important information gleaned in Iceland — all these and others with even wilder theories which the text of the Journal proves to be preposterous must do their best to discredit the document. Vignaud and Carbia in particular have built up a case for the abstract Journal having been truncated, garbled, falsified, and rewritten by Las Casas or Ferdinand or others in order to prove

what they call the exploded tradition that one Christopher Columbus, a Genoese, discovered America on October 12, 1492, when
searching for a western route to the Indies.

The scribe who copied the Journal made common errors such
as writing "east" for "west," which are shown up when you plot
the fleet's course. Las Casas doubtless omitted some nautical detail
that we should wish to have, and interpolated some stupid remarks
of his own that are easily detected. But the charge that he or anyone else garbled the Journal is false. My shipmates and I, who have
probably given the Journal the most intensive study to which it
has ever been subjected, will go even further. We say that nobody
not a seaman, and no seaman who did not follow Columbus's route,
could possibly have faked this document, so accurate are the bearings, the courses and the observations; and any such navigator
would have needed the aid of the cleverest of literary forgers to
complete the work, so closely are woven into it Columbus's ardent
quest for the Indies, and the wonder and surprise at completely new
experiences. Columbus did not even take the trouble to expunge
the numerous mistakes that he made in navigation, and which he
knew to be mistakes a few days later.

The Preamble that we quoted at the head of this chapter has
been the particular target of the critics, because of its mention of
the "lands of India" and the Grand Khan. All the "debunkers"
insist that this was written after the voyage was over, and Columbus was making the best of a bad failure. It is indeed probable that
the Preamble was not written on the opening day of the voyage,
when Columbus was busy with other things, but at the Canaries.
That it could not have been written much later is shown by the
promise in the last paragraph that was not performed: to set down
all the "sea and lands of the Ocean Sea in their proper positions
under their bearings," with latitude and longitude. This Columbus
did not do because he had not the science. Like other navigators, he
probably thought he could "work it up at sea"; but we have only
three latitudes (all wrong) and no longitude for the entire voyage.
This gap between promise and performance did not escape the
eyes of the Sovereigns, who invited him rather pointedly to supply
the missing data before his Second Voyage began. They would
hardly have asked him to do what no navigator of that period had

sufficient skill to do, had they not noted his rash promise in the Preamble.

Columbus's plan for the voyage was to sail first to the Canaries, and thence due west to the Indies. And about this simple plan have been spun fancy webs of theory. It seems clear enough why he chose that route. A direct westerly course from Spain was ruled out by the experience of the Portuguese, who so many times had bucked the westerlies of the North Atlantic in vain. But the Canaries were within the zone of the northeast trade winds, and to reach the Canaries there was assurance, at that season, of favorable northerlies. There is no hint in the Journal or elsewhere that Columbus knew that the northeast trade wind would carry him across; but he must have observed on his African voyage that a westward course from the Canaries would enjoy a fair wind as soon as you pass out of the Canary calms. It was merely his good fortune that the same wind carried his fleet all the way to America.

There was another and compelling reason for choosing the Canaries as the point of departure. They lay on the same parallel of latitude as Cipangu or Japan. Turn back to glance at our sketch of Martin Behaim's Globe, completed the year that Columbus sailed, and note how the route that he chose was the simplest and shortest to the Indies, in the light of the geographical misinformation then current. It has always been the plan of simple dead-reckoning navigators to get on the presumed latitude of their destination, and run their easting or westing down until they reach it. The Orient most nearly approached the Occident on the parallel of the Canaries, in Columbus's estimation. The winds at the Canaries generally blew from the eastward. So what could be more sensible than to make these islands his point of departure? Moreover, a break in the voyage made the first leg of it a sort of "shake-down cruise," highly useful to test the quality of his ships and the temper of his men.

The Captain General, as we should style Columbus on the outward-bound passage, made his communion at St. George's, Palos, in the small hours of the morning Friday, August 3, went aboard his flagship before dawn, and "in the name of Jesus" gave the command to get under way. Cheerful chanteys accompanied the creak of the windlasses, and at half an hour before sunrise (which at that date and latitude came about a quarter past five) the anchors were aboard *Santa María, Pinta* and *Niña.* It was one of those gray, calm days that herald the coming of autumn, when the sea is like a mirror of burnished steel, and the spectacular cloud masses of Castile (such as El Greco alone could paint) seem to pause in their endless change; a halcyon day, when not a leaf stirs ashore, and but for the outward flow of tide one could imagine that time stood still. Lack of wind mattered not to the fleet, for their departure was timed at the beginning of the ebb, which had sufficient strength to take them over the bar before the water fell too low for *Santa María's* draught. The sweeps were manned to give steerageway, and with sails hanging limp and no sound but the slow plash of the long oars and their rattle and creak in the ports, the fleet dropped downriver. A mile and a half from Palos on the port hand they passed the buildings of La Rábida close aboard; it was the hour of prime, and the friars were chanting their ancient liturgical hymn for that office: —

> *Iam lucis orto sidere*
> *Deum precemur supplices,*
> *ut in diurnis artibus*
> *nos servet a nocentibus.*

The Captain General, who often had joined in that hymn during his stay at La Rábida, removes his hat; seamen who are not working follow his example; all cross themselves and many kneel as the last stanza comes out over the water: —

> *Deo Patri sit gloria,*
> *eiusque soli Filio,*
> *cum Spiritu Paraclito*
> *et nunc et in perpetuum.*

"Evermore and evermore." This modest armada was setting forth on a conquest for the Cross that would outlast all worldly empires.

A few hundred yards beyond La Rábida the course was altered to port and the fleet entered the Río Odiel, then called the Saltés. With ebb current and the lightest of airs they floated between pine-

clad sand dunes of the mainland and the isle of Saltés, then turned
50 degrees to starboard, and at eight in the morning crossed the bar.
There the sails caught a "strong sea breeze" which would not
permit them to steer nearer the wind than due south, or to make
better speed than four knots. Until sunset they were within sight
of land. The wind then backed to the north and they steered southwest to get a good offing. Sometime during the night, when he was
sufficiently offshore, the Admiral set the course for the Canaries:
Sur cuarta del sudoeste – South and by West.

Although nothing is said about it in the Journal, Columbus
must have devised or adopted from his Portuguese instructors
a system of signals to keep the fleet together. In the iron cresset
or brazier which hung over the stern, it was possible to make a
fire by night or smoke by day, and to smother it with a swatch of
wet canvas. Thus two, three or even four *fuegos* or *fumos* could
be made in succession, as orders to change course, make or strike
sail, or draw up to the flagship for instructions. A *farol* or torch
of pitch pine could be used in combination with the brazier. For
weighty occasions such as a landfall, the Journal informs us that a
gun was fired. The natural course for any fleet of sailing vessels
is to draw apart, as we see in ocean yacht races today; but the
object of Columbus was to keep his fleet together. That was no
easy task, as the flagship was a slower sailer than *Pinta* and *Niña*.
So the two caravels had constantly to restrict their speed by reduc-
ing sail, in order not to drop the flagship astern.

The ocean between Spain and the Canaries is a rough bit of
water, which the Spaniards generally required eight or ten days
to cover. They called it *el Golfo de las Yeguas* (the Sea of the
Mares) because so many brood mares being shipped to the Canaries
died on board; "and might as well have called it *el Golfo de las
Vacas*," says Oviedo, "because no fewer cows than mares died in the
same manner." Columbus's fleet was lucky to raise the Grand
Canary only six days out, but he did not make it without accident.
On August 6 the big outboard rudder of *Pinta* jumped its gudgeons.
She made the usual distress signal, the flagship drew near and
Columbus went aboard. Martín Alonso Pinzón confided to Colum-
bus that in his opinion this was the result of dirty work by the
caravel's owner, Cristóbal Quintero, who hated having his ship

commandeered for this voyage, and had been grousing and grumbling ever since the start. The sea was too heavy for *Santa María* to go alongside and lend her tackle to ship the heavy rudder, but Columbus "reflected that Martín Alonso Pinzón was a man of energy and ingenuity," and could manage alone.

This was the first and last compliment to Pinzón recorded in the Admiral's Journal. But I have special reasons for not being favorably impressed by Pinzón's hint of foul play, knowing by personal experience that these waters are hard on steering gear. *Mary Otis's*

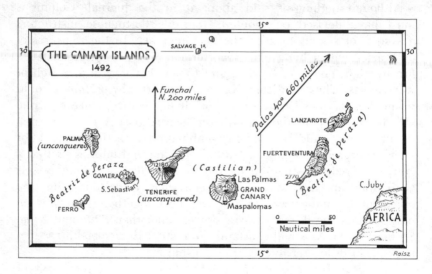

rudder worked loose from the post as we were beating to windward from Cadiz toward Madeira on November 4, 1939; and when we put in at Casablanca for repairs, there was an English cutter with a big outboard rudder like *Pinta's* which had become unshipped off the African coast. Moreover, if Quintero had wished to put *Pinta* out of commission in order to escape the dangers of the deep, the place for such trickery was in the Canaries. Deliberately to tamper with steering gear on the high seas would endanger his life as well as his vessel.

By the next day, August 7, *Pinta's* rudder was secured for the time being, and the fleet filled away for Lanzarote. This drifting about spoiled the reckoning, and on the eighth the pilots could not agree as to their position; Columbus's reckoning proved the nearest to the truth, he admits. (The commanding officer is always right.) *Pinta's* rudder gave trouble again, and she began to leak. So Columbus changed course for the Grand Canary, with the idea of exchanging *Pinta* there fore some other vessel; or, if that were impossible, repairing her at a place where there were facilities for forging iron. At dawn on August 9 the Grand Canary was in sight, but the fleet ran into a flat calm. Neither that day nor the two following could they reach the island. Consequently, in order to save time, and to have a double chance of encountering a suitable vessel that could be bought or chartered, Columbus, when a breeze sprang up on the third night, left Martín Alonso to take *Pinta* into Las Palmas, while he with *Santa María* and *Niña* proceeded to Gomera.

As yet the Canaries were only in part conquered by Spain from their warlike and vigorous native inhabitants the Guanches; the story of their conquest, as Roger Merriman points out, was a microcosm of the early history of America. Columbus might have read a prophecy of his own fate, and that of the Indians, in current events that he must have heard discussed. Two Spanish conquistadors had been falsely accused, seized and sent home in chains. The Guanches had been overcome by a combination of cruelty and treachery, forcibly converted to the Catholic faith, and reduced to slavery. The conquest of the island of Palma was being pursued that very summer, and Tenerife was still completely in the hands of the natives.

Columbus, passing the northern coast of the Grand Canary and the south coast of Tenerife, islands so lofty and beautiful that we sometimes wonder at his enthusiasm for the Bahamas, anchored in the roadstead of San Sebastián, Gomera, on the evening of August 12.

That island, one of the first of the Canaries to be conquered, was an hereditary captaincy held by the Herrera y Peraza family under the crown of Castile. In 1492 the virtual captain was a young, energetic and beautiful widow, Doña Beatriz de Peraza y Bobadilla, who was governing the island as guardian of her minor son Guillén, later the first Count of Gomera. It was perhaps fortunate for the success of the enterprise that she was then absent, although daily expected from Lanzarote in a vessel of 40 tons, which Columbus hoped might prove a fit substitute for *Pinta*.

San Sebastián, a small town fronting the best roadstead in Gomera, at the mouth of a river that flows down from the mountainous interior through a deep *barranca* (ravine), preserves its fifteenth-century aspect better than any other Old World town associated with Columbus. The stone castle where Columbus was entertained is still standing, a house is shown where he is said to have lodged, and the Church of the Assumption, where he certainly worshiped, has remained virtually unchanged. Gomera afforded the best of meats, breadstuffs and cheeses, a river of excellent water flowed past San Sebastián, and the heights were well forested. So Columbus sent gangs of men to procure more wood and water, and purchased more provisions. The caravels carried a number of knocked-down water butts which the coopers set up and the men filled; and if they had no salt for preserving meat, jerked beef could be made in a few days under the hot Canary sun. On August 14 Columbus sent one of his best men aboard a small island coaster bound for Las Palmas in order to tell Martín Alonso where he was, and to help him repair *Pinta's* rudder.

Nine days slipped by, and no ship bearing Doña Beatriz appeared. Finally Columbus felt he could wait no longer, and decided to join Martín Alonso at Las Palmas. On the way he overtook the coaster that had sailed nine days earlier, and took his man aboard again. That night he sailed close under Tenerife, whose superb volcano, rising 12,000 feet above sea level, was belching forth fire and smoke. On August 25 Columbus arrived at Las Palmas to find that *Pinta* had arrived only the previous day, after drifting about for two weeks. Her steering gear must indeed have been in a bad way. And Doña Beatriz had sailed five days earlier for Gomera. So Columbus decided not to play hide-and-seek with her any longer, and to make the best job he could of repairing *Pinta*.

The Grand Canary had been "pacified" in 1483, and by the time of Columbus's visit the chief settlement of Las Palmas had already become, as it still is, the metropolis of the Canaries; a brisk and busy little settlement of merchants and planters who were prospering from the incredibly rich soil and marvelous climate. Sugar cane had been brought over from Morocco, grape-vines from Spain, and slaves from Africa; as many as four crops a year of grass or grain could be reaped in some favored localities. Las Palmas was the best place to have *Pinta's* rudder rebuilt; near the waterfront is the *Herrería* or blacksmiths' quarter, where her new pintles and gudgeons and bolts and straps were forged under the eye of Martín Alonso.

At the same time, "that she might follow the other vessels with more tranquility and less danger" *Niña's* lateen rig was altered to square by crossing yards on main and foremast and recutting the great triangular sails. Columbus and the Pinzons evidently agreed that the big, unwieldy lateen mainsail of the Portuguese-style caravel was a hazard on the high seas, especially in a following wind. One careless gybe, and your mast and gear would be gone. The great virtue of the lateen rig, its ability to take a vessel close to the wind, would have been little use, since there was no point in having *Niña* outfoot the fleet on a beat to windward; the change of rig more nearly equated her speed and performance with her larger consorts.

From the list of personnel in Columbus's fleet, which is fairly complete, it is clear that there were no desertions in the Canaries, although one new hand may have been shipped there. Knowing the propensity of seamen to become dissatisfied and take a "pier-head jump" at the first port of call, this fact speaks well for the confidence that Columbus and the Pinzons inspired in their men.

On Friday, September 1, in the afternoon the fleet sailed from Las Palmas, and on the following day made San Sebastián. There at last Columbus met the fair if somewhat formidable ruler of Gomera, Doña Beatriz de Peraza. Born Beatriz de Bobadilla, and first cousin once removed of the Marquesa de Moya, when a beautiful young girl she was appointed maid of honor to Queen Isabella, and attracted the amorous attentions of King Ferdinand. At the time when Isabella noticed this and was wondering what to do about it, Hernán Peraza the Captain of Gomera appeared at court, to answer charges of having murdered a rival conquistador in the Canaries. He was pardoned in return for marrying Beatriz and taking her back to Gomera, an arrangement that pleased every-one but the King. Hernán was so arbitrary, despotic and cruel that his seduction of a native girl touched off an uprising in which he was killed. Beatriz, beseiged with her two children in the castle of San Sebastián, managed to get word to Pedro de Vera, Governor of the Grand Canary, who came to her rescue. That act of gallantry did not save Pedro's son, Hernando, from later being captured by Beatriz in the hope of regaining Isabella's favor, there being a price on his head for having written libelous verses against the Queen. Fortunately he made good his escape.

At the time of Columbus's visit this energetic widow was still under thirty, and very beautiful; and we have it on good authority that he fell in love with her. Why not? His own Beatriz was far away, and Doña Beatriz, belonging to one of the first families of Castile, would have made a very suitable match for him. That she returned his admiration, if not his love, is evident by the splendid reception she gave him on his next visit, in 1493; but this nascent romance did not delay the Great Enterprise.

Doña Beatriz must have entertained Columbus in the old stone castle at San Sebastián, a part of which, the Torre del Conde, still stands. And we read in his Journal, "many honorable Spanish gentlemen who were at Gomera with Doña Inés [sic] Peraza, mother of Guillén Peraza, who was afterwards the first Count of Gomera, and who were natives of the island of Ferro, declared that every year they saw land to the west of the Canaries; and others, native of Gomera, affirmed the same on oath."

This land was the mythical St. Brendan's Isle, or *San Borondon*, the most persistent phantom island of the Atlantic. Martin Behaim's Globe of 1492 depicts it just above the equator, and the Canary Islanders were still searching for it in the eighteenth century. Probably you could find aged fishermen in Ferro or Gomera today who would claim they had seen San Borondon, just as old fishermen of Galway still believe that they catch sight of O'Brasil now and then.

Columbus did not take much time out for dalliance with Doña Beatriz; he did not even wait for the night of the full moon (September 6). His men who were left behind in the previous call had not been idle, and within four days' time the caravels were loaded to the gunwales with additional ships' stores, water casks secured on deck, and piles of firewood lashed down on every bit of vacant space. In the early hours of September 6, Columbus heard his last Mass in the Church of the Assumption, where we of the Harvard Columbus Expedition attended an impressive memorial service in 1939. Then, saying farewell (a tender one, we hope) to Doña Beatriz, the future Admiral of the Ocean Sea went aboard, and anchors were weighed for the last time in the Old World.

All that day and night the winds came faint and variable, and on the morning of September 7 the fleet found itself between Gomera and Tenerife. At 3 A.M. Saturday, September 8, "the NE wind began to blow, and he made his way and course to the West," leaving Gomera well to starboard. *Santa María* plunged heavily, taking in water over her bows and so retarding the fleet's progress that for the next twenty-seven hours they made an average speed of less than one knot. By sunrise on Sunday the ninth this fault, due probably to stowing the last of the provisions and water too far forward, had been remedied, and for the next twenty-four hours the fleet made a good run of 130 miles.

Before leaving San Sebastián Columbus had been warned by a caravel that arrived from Ferro that three Portuguese vessels were cruising off that island "with the object of taking him." Probably they had been sent by D. João II merely to observe the Castilian fleet, and to warn them from making discoveries south of the Canaries and west of Africa, a section of the ocean which the king of Portugal regarded as his own sphere of influence. Whether or not the report was true, Columbus saw nothing of this Portuguese squadron; it might however have been lying under the island's lee as he passed some 12 miles to windward of Ferro.

During the morning and early afternoon of September 9 the coast of Ferro lay abeam and the peak of Tenerife was still visible astern. By nightfall every trace of land had disappeared, and the three ships had an uncharted ocean to themselves.

CHAPTER XII

A Day at Sea

Qui nauigant mare enarrent pericula eius, et audientes
auribus nostris admirabimur.

They that sail on the sea tell of the danger thereof, and
when we hear it with our ears, we marvel thereat.
— ECCLESIASTICUS xliii 26

A DECENT formality has always been observed aboard ships at
sea, even to our own day. The wheel is relieved in a certain
manner, the watches are changed according to formula, solar and
stellar observations are made at fixed hours; and any departure
from the settled custom is resented by mariners. In Columbus's ships
these formalities were observed with a quasi-religious ritual, which
lent them a certain beauty, and reminded the seamen every half
hour of the day and night that their ship depended for safety not
only on her staunchness and their own skill, but on the grace of God.

In Columbus's day, and until the late sixteenth century, the
only ship's clock available was the *ampolleta* or *reloj de arena*
(sand clock), a half-hour glass containing enough sand to run
from the upper to the lower section in exactly thirty minutes.*
Made in Venice, these glasses were so fragile that a large number
of spares were carried — Magellan had eighteen on his flagship.
It was the duty of a gromet or ship's boy in each watch to mind
the *ampolleta,* and reverse it promptly when the sand ran out.
A very rough sea might retard the running of the sand, or the
gromet might go to sleep; Columbus on one occasion expresses in

---

* Cf. Shakespeare's *Tempest,* V i 265: "Our Ship, which but three glasses since, we
gave out split . . . " The British navy kept time by glasses of half an hour each until
1839.

his Journal the fear that the boys were slack about it. As a ship
gains time sailing east and loses it sailing west, even the most
modern ship's clock has to be corrected daily by wireless. The
only way Columbus could do this with his hour-glass clock was
to erect a pin or gnomon on the center of his compass card, and
watch for the exact moment of noon when the sun's shadow
touched the fleur de lis that marked the north, and then turn the
glass. But that could hardly be counted on to give him true noon
nearer than 15 or 20 minutes, and he did not do it very often;
for it is evident from some of his log entries that his "ship's time"
was as much as half an hour slow by the sun.

The *marineros, grumetes* and *oficiales* of the ship's company —
the able seamen, gromets (ordinary seamen and boys) and ratings
such as caulker and cooper — were divided into two watches
(called by Columbus *cuartos* or *guardias*) of four hours each.
Each watch was headed by an officer. Aboard *Santa María*, Master
Juan de la Cosa, having the greater dignity, would have taken starboard watch, and pilot Peralonso the port watch. From sundry
entries in Columbus's Journal, it is clear that watches were set at
3, 7, and 11 o'clock. These hours seem odd to a modern seaman,
who by immemorial usage expects watches to change at 4, 8, and 12.
Possibly changing watch at 3, 7, 11 was the usual practice in
Columbus's day. Perhaps it was left to the captain's discretion,
and Columbus set the night watch on his first day out at 7 P.M.,
the approximate hour of sunset, and kept up the four-hour intervals on that basis. Presumably the afternoon watch was "dogged"
as we still do today in order that the men may change their hours
nightly. Suppose, for instance, the port watch comes on at 3 P.M.
It goes off at 5, and is on again from 7 to 11. The men then have
four hours' sleep, until 3 A.M. They go below again at 7 A.M.,
and take the noon watch from 11 A.M. to 3 P.M. They then come
on deck for the second dogwatch, 5 to 7 P.M., which gives them
from 7 to 11 P.M. below on the second night. Aboard many modern steamships the watches are no longer "dogged," only the
hours are changed at each fresh departure; for in short runs there
is little inconvenience in having the same hours on and off every
day and night. But on a sailing vessel that might be many weeks
or even months at sea, it was fairer all around to "dog" the watches

daily, so that each man would have the unpopular "graveyard watch" from midnight to 4 A.M. (or from 11 to 3) on alternate nights.

Seamen did not think of time in terms of hours, but of *ampolletas* and *guardias,* glasses and watches, eight glasses to a watch. The system of half-hourly ship's bells that we are familiar with was simply a means of accenting the turning of the glass. No ship's bell is mentioned in any of the sea journals of the sixteenth century that I have seen, and García Palacio's *Instrución Náuthica* (Mexico 1587), the Spanish seamen's first Bowditch, says nothing of them.

At night, whenever the weather was clear and the latitude not too low, Columbus could tell approximate clock time from the Guards of the North Star. The Little Bear or Little Dipper swings around Polaris once every 24 hours sidereal time. The two brightest stars of that constellation, β (Kochab) and γ, which mark the edge of the dipper farthest from the North Star, were called the Guards; and if you knew where Kochab the principal Guard was stationed at midnight every two weeks of the year, you could tell time from it as from a clock hand. The early navigators constructed a diagram of a little man with Polaris in his middle, his forearms pointing E and W, and his shoulders NE and NW. That gave eight positions for Kochab: Head, West Shoulder, West Arm, Line under West Arm, Feet, Line under East Arm, East Arm, and East Shoulder. As Kochab moved from one position to another in three hours, you could tell time at night if you knew the relative position of Kochab at midnight on that date. Around 1500, Kochab was at "Head" at midnight April 15, at "West Arm" at midnight July 15, at "Feet" at midnight October 15, and at "East Arm" at midnight January 15. Thus, if you found this natural clock hand to be at the "East Shoulder" position on January 15, you knew it was 3 A.M. and time to call the watch.

Columbus shows his familiarity with this method by an entry in his Journal for September 30, 1492. He probably had a simple instrument, the nocturnal, with which you sighted Polaris through a hole in the center, and then turned a movable arm representing the constellation until it hit Kochab. That gave you the exact position, and so the time. With a little practice, anyone on a long voyage can learn to tell time by this method within a quarter-hour.

Occasionally in his Journal Columbus mentions clock time in such terms as "the first hour of the night" (1 A.M.); but more often he times events by the changing of the watch, or by tierce, vespers and compline, three of the canonical hours of prayer. As a pious Christian, faithful in his religious duties, Columbus kept a book of

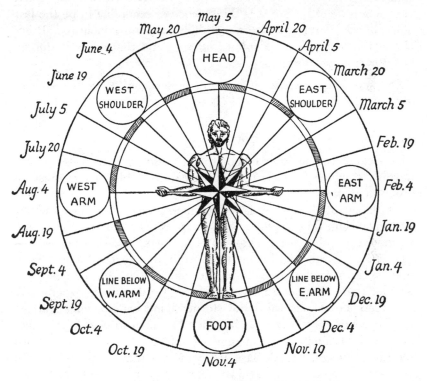

DIAGRAM FOR TELLING TIME FROM POLARIS, 1942
Kochab (β Ursae Minoris) moves counter-clockwise one line per hour. Its position relative to Polaris at midnight is indicated for each date.

hours in his cabin, and whenever possible said his prayers in private at the appointed hours, as he had learned to do when staying at La Rábida. But what hours in clock time did he mean by tierce, vespers and compline? That is a difficult question, for there was then no uniformity in usage. Tierce might be said anywhere between 8 and 9 A.M., vespers anywhere from 2 P.M. to dark, and compline between 6 and 9 P.M. A careful comparison of the liturgical authorities with Columbus's journals indicates that he said the office of tierce at 9 A.M. midway in the morning watch; vespers at 2 or 3 P.M., and compline immediately after the *Salve Regina* was sung, at 7 or a little after. For it is the essence of compline to be the last office of the day — *completas,* a fulfillment and conclusion. It includes the hymn *Te lucis ante terminum,* and that noble Psalm xci of faith and confidence: —

Qui habitat in adiutorio Altissimi, in protectione Dei caeli commorabitur.

Whoso dwelleth under the defense of the Most High, shall abide under the shadow of the Almighty.

These canonical hours or offices that Columbus read were private devotions, which he said in his own cabin. Public prayers were a different matter.

In the great days of sail, before man's inventions and gadgets had given him false confidence in his power to conquer the ocean, seamen were the most religious of all workers on land or sea. The mariner's philosophy he took from the 107th Psalm: "They that go down to the sea in ships and occupy their business in great waters; these men see the works of the Lord, and his wonders in the deep. For at his word the stormy·wind ariseth, which lifteth up the winds thereof . . ." It behooved seamen to obey the injunction of the psalmist, "O that men would therefore praise the Lord for his goodness, and declare the wonders that he doeth for the children of men!" That is just what they did, after their own fashion. Even the Protestant Reformation did not change the old customs of shipboard piety: as Captain John Smith wrote in 1627, "they may first goe to prayer, then to supper, and at six a-clocke sing a Psalme, say a Prayer, and the Master with his side begins the watch, then all the rest may doe what they will till midnight; and then his Mate with his Larboord men with a Psalm and a prayer releeves them until foure in the morning."

These religious observances which marked almost every half-hour of the day were led or performed by the youngest lads aboard, the *pajes de escober* ("pages of the broom") if any there were. This I suppose was on the same principle as having family grace said by the youngest child; God would be better pleased by the voice of innocence. On Columbus's first fleet there was no rating of page, but this duty was performed by the youngest gromets, probably those who were also called *criados* (servants), and who received slightly better pay than their mates.

Of the public prayers or hymns, Columbus's Journal mentions only the most important, when at sunset the Blessed Virgin was saluted with her ancient canticle, *Salve Regina*. But we have an account of a voyage from Spain to Santo Domingo in 1573 by a humorous Spanish official named Eugenio de Salazar, which gives every detail. Assuming that a pious commander like Columbus, venturing on unknown seas where the divine protection was imperatively needed, would have omitted nothing of these traditional observances, I have repeated them just as Salazar reports them, with a translation.

Daybreak was saluted by a young gromet of the dawn watch with this ditty: —

Bendita sea la luz,	Blessed be the light of day
y la Santa Veracruz	and the Holy Cross, we say;
y el Señor de la Verdad,	and the Lord of Veritie
y la Santa Trinidad;	and the Holy Trinity.
bendita sea el alma,	Blessed be th'immortal soul
y el Señor que nos la manda;	and the Lord who keeps it whole,
bendito sea el día	blessed be the light of day
y el Señor que nos lo envía.	and He who sends the night away.

The gromet then recites *Pater Noster* and *Ave Maria*, and adds: —

Dios nos dé buenos días; buen viaje; buen pasaje haga la nao, señor Capitán y maestre y buena compaña, amén; así faza buen viaje, faza: muy buenos días dé Dios a vuestras mercedes, señores de popa y proa.

God give us good days, good voyage, good passage to the ship, sir captain and master and good company, so let there be, let there be a good voyage; many good days may God grant your graces, gentlemen of the afterguard and gentlemen forward.

Before being relieved the dawn watch was supposed to have the decks well scrubbed down with salt water hauled up in buckets, and stiff besoms made of twigs. At 6:30 the *ampolleta* is turned up for the seventh and last time on that watch, and the gromet who has charge of it sings out:—

Buena es la que va,	Good is that which passeth,
mejor es la que viene;	better that which cometh,
siete es pasada y en ocho muele,	seven is past and eight floweth,
mas molerá si Dios quisiere,	more shall flow if God willeth,
cuenta y pasa, que buen viaje faza.	count and pass makes voyage fast.

As soon as the sands of the eighth successive glass run out, at 7 o'clock, the gromet in turning it up says, instead of his usual ditty: —

Al cuarto, al cuarto, señores marineros de buena parte, al cuarto, al cuarto en buena hora de la guardia del señor piloto, que ya es hora; leva, leva, leva.

On deck, on deck, Mr. mariners of the right side,* on deck in good time, you of Mr. Pilot's watch, for it's already time; shake a leg!

There is no need to give the new watch time to dress, for nobody has undressed; when they "went below" at 3 A.M. each man simply sought out his favorite soft plank, anywhere that he could brace himself against the rolling and pitching. They are soon awake, rubbing their eyes and grumbling, and each man grabs a ship biscuit, with some garlic cloves, a bit of cheese, a pickled sardine or what-have-you for breakfast and shuffles aft to the break in the poop. The helmsman gives the course to the master who is captain of his watch, Juan de la Cosa repeats it to the pilot who is captain of the new watch, he repeats it and gives it to the new helmsman, and he repeats it again. No chance for error! And most of the time on this outward passage the course is simply

Oeste: nada del noroeste, nada del sudoeste.

West: nothing to the northward, nothing to the southward.

A lookout is posted forward, another in the round-top, the off-going master transfers his reckoning from slate to logbook and a

---

* Meaning the watch, port or starboard, that is due on deck.

gromet wipes the slate clean for the pilot, Chips the carpenter (or *calafate* the caulker if it is his watch) primes the pump, and if the ship has made water during the night two or three hands pump her dry. The off-going watch eat whatever is on for breakfast, and curl up somewhere out of the sun to sleep.

Now the decks are dry, the sun is yardarm high, and the caravel is dancing along before the trades with a bone in her teeth. Columbus, whose servant has brought him a bucket of sea water, a cup of fresh water and a bit of breakfast in his cabin, comes on deck, looks all around the horizon, ejaculates a pious *gracias á Dios* for good weather, and chats with the pilot.

Each watch is responsible for the entire work of the ship during its hours of duty, except in case of tempest or accident, when all hands are called. The usual duties are keeping the decks both clear and clean, making and setting sail as required, trimming sheets and braces; and when there is nothing else to do, scrubbing the rails, making spun yarn and chafing gear out of old rope, and overhauling the gear. In this morning watch, as soon as the running rigging has dried from the night dews, it has to be swayed up, and every few days the lanyards or tackles that hold the shrouds must be taken up taut.

On large ships the master's or pilot's orders were transmitted to the men through the *contramestre* or boatswain, who carried a pipe or whistle on a lanyard around his neck and on it played a variety of piping signals. But there is no mention of one on Columbus's ships. The captain of the watch gives all orders himself, as on the ship of Salazar, who said he had never seen an officer so well and promptly obeyed by his soldiers as the pilot by his watch. Let him but cry *Ah! de proa* (Hey! up forward), they all come aft on the run "like conjured demons" awaiting his pleasure. Here are some samples of the orders: —

dejad las chafaldetas	well the clewlines
alzá aquel briol	heave on that buntline
empalomadle la boneta	lace on the bonnet
tomad aquel puño	lay hold of that clew
entren esas badasas aprisa por esos ollaos	pass them toggles through the latchets quick
levá el papahigo	hoist the main course

izá el trinquete	raise the foresail
dad vuelta	put your back into it
enmará un poco la cebadera	give the spritsail a little sheet
desencapillá la mesana	unbend the mizzen
ligá la tricia al guindaste	belay the halyard on the bitts
tirá de los escotines de gabia	haul in on the topsail sheets
suban dos á los penoles	two of you up on the yardarm
untá los vertellos	grease the parral trucks
amarrá aquellas burdas	belay them backstays
zafá los embornales	clear the scuppers
juegue el guimbalete para que la bomba achique	work that pump brake till she sucks

Nautical Castilian, like nautical English of the last century, had a word for everything in a ship's gear and a verb for every action; good strong expressive words that could not be misunderstood when bawled out in a gale.

For any lengthy operation like winding in the anchor cable or hoisting a yard, the seamen had an appropriate *saloma* or chantey, and of these Salazar gives an example which it is useless to translate. The chanteyman sung or shouted the first half of each line, the men hauled away on the "o" and joined in on the second half, while they got a new hold on the halyard: —

> *Bu izá*
> *o dio — ayuta noy*
> *o que somo — servi soy*
> *o voleamo — ben servir*
> *o la fede — mantenir*
> *o la fede — de cristiano*
> *o malmeta — lo pagano*
> *sconfondi — y sarrahin*
> *torchi y mori — gran mastín*
> *o fillioli — dabrahin*
> *o non credono — que ben sia*
> *o non credono — la fe santa*
> *en la santa — fe di Roma*
> *o di Roma — está el perdón*
> *o San Pedro — gran varón*
> *o San Pablo — son compañón*
> *o que ruegue — a Dio por nos*

> *o por nosotros — navegantes*
> *en este mundo — somo tantes*
> *o ponente — digo levante*
> *o levante — se leva el sol*
> *o ponente — resplandor*
> *fantineta — viva lli amor*
> *o joven home — gauditor*

And so on, improvising, until the halyard is "two-blocks," when the captain of the watch commands *dejad la driza, amarrá* (well the halyard, belay!).

When he was not ordering the men about, the captain of the watch kept his station on the poop, conning the helmsman through a hatch in the deck just forward of the binnacle. The helmsman had a compass to steer by, but he could not see the sails, and consequently had to be an expert at the feel of the ship to keep her on her course. Salazar gives us some specimens of the pilot's orders to the helmsman: —

botá a babor	port your helm
no boteis	steady
arriba	up helm *
goberná la ueste cuarta al sueste	steer W by S

Besides a nautical language, a nautical slang had developed. Just as modern seamen with mock contempt speak of "this wagon" or "the old crate," a Spaniard called his ship *rocín de madera* (wooden jade) or *pájaro puerco* (flying pig). The nickname for the firebox meant "pot island." People on board got in the habit of using nautical phrases for other things; Salazar for instance says, "When I want a pot of jam I say *saca la cebadera*, break out the spritsail; if I want a table-napkin I say *daca el pañol*, lead me to the sail-locker. If I wish to eat or drink in form I say *pon la mesana*, set the mizzen. When a mariner upsets a jug he says *¡oh! cómo achicais*, oh how she sucks. When one breaks wind, as often happens, some-one is sure to cry *¡ah! de popa*, hey there, aft!"

Naturally there was a good deal of joking about the seats that were hung over the rail forward and aft, for the seamen and after-guard to ease themselves. These were called *jardines*, perhaps in

---

* Or, as we should say nowadays, "keep her off."

memory of the usual location of the family privy. Salazar writes in
mock sentiment of the lovely views they afforded of moon and
planets, and of the impromptu washings that he there obtained
from the waves. A later voyager, Antonio de Guevara, complained
of the indecency of thus exposing a Very Reverend Lord Bishop
to the full view of the ship's company, and adverts bitterly to the
tarred rope end which performed a function assigned by American
folklore to the corncob.

Apparently the seamen on Columbus's ships had only one hot
meal a day. This would naturally have come around 11 A.M., so
that the watch below could get theirs before coming on deck, and
the watch relieved could eat after them.

Who did the cooking? I do not know. There was no rating of
cook on any of Columbus's ships, or on Magellan's. The *Instruoión
Náuthica* of 1587, which gives all ratings and tells everyone's duties,
has neither cook nor cooker, although the steward, it says, has
charge of the fire. Probably the hard-worked gromets did the
cooking, except that the captain's servant would naturally have
taken care of him and perhaps of any gentlemen volunteers who
made up the afterguard. Columbus when visited by the cacique
at Port de Paix, Haiti, was dining in his cabin, apparently alone.
Aboard the big galleons described by García Palacio a table was
set for the men forward, the boatswain presided and the pages
served and cleared away. Aboard *Santa María, Pinta* and *Niña* it is
more likely that foremast hands took their share in a wooden bowl,
and ate it with their fingers wherever they could find room. How
the little *fogón* or open firebox could take care of food for 125
people on a small caravel, as it must have on *Niña's* voyage home
in 1496, staggers the imagination.

The only drinks mentioned in Columbus's Journal and in his
orders for supplies are water and wine, both of which were kept
in casks; for Vasco da Gama first learned from the Arabs to construct wooden watertanks below decks. It was the cooper's job
to see that these casks kept tight and were stowed or lashed so
that they would not roll. Coffee and tea had not been introduced,
and Spaniards did not care for beer.

The staff of life for Spanish seamen was wine, olive oil and
bread in the form of sea biscuit or hardtack, baked ashore from

wheat flour and stowed in the dryest part of the ship. Columbus's
ideas of the proper provisioning of vessels on an American voyage
are given in a letter to the Sovereigns of about 1498–1500: "Vic-
tualling them should be done in this manner: the third part of
[the breadstuff to be] good biscuit, well seasoned and not old, or
the major portion will be wasted; a third part of salted flour, salted
at the time of milling; and a third part of wheat. Further there
will be wanted wine, salt meat, oil, vinegar, cheese, chickpeas,
lentils, beans, salt fish and fishing tackle, honey, rice, almonds and
raisins." Olive oil, carried in huge earthenware jars, was used
for cooking the fish, meat and legumes. Salted flour could be made
into unleavened bread and cooked in the ashes, as the Arab seamen do today. Barreled salt sardines and anchovies are frequently
mentioned among ships' stores of the time, and garlic would certainly not have been forgotten. It is probable that Columbus's seamen fared quite as well as peasants or workers ashore, except during
a storm, or weather so rough that a fire could not be kept.

Dinner for the afterguard was announced by a gromet in this
wise: —

*Tabla, tabla, señor capitán y maestre y buena compaña, tabla puesta;
vianda presta; agua usada para el señor capitán y maestre y buena
compaña. ¡Viva, viva el Rey de Castilla por mar y por tierra! Quien
le diere guerra que le corten la cabeza; quien no dijere amén, que no
le den á beber. Tabla en buena hora, quien no viniere que no coma.*

Table, table, sir captain and master and good company, table ready;
meat ready; water as usual for sir captain and master and good company. Long live the King of Castile by land and sea! Who says to him
war, off with his head; who won't say amen, gets nothing to drink.
Table is set, who don't come won't eat.

Salazar describes how the pages would slam on the table a great
wooden dish of ill-cooked stringy salt meat, when everyone would
grab his share and attack it with a sheath knife as if he were a
practitioner of anatomy; and how every bone was left "clean as
ivory." The table conversation, he says, was mostly sighing for
what you couldn't have — "O how I'd like a bunch of white grapes
of Guadalajara — I could eat a few turnips of Somo Sierra — If we
only had aboard a plate of Ilescas berries!"

Dinner over, we may assume that Columbus retires to his cabin and indulges in a little shut-eye until it is time to say vespers.

At 3 the first dogwatch is set. The day's work of scrubbing, splicing, seizing and making repairs is now over; and if the wind is such that the gear needs no handling, as was almost always the case on this outward passage, the men sit about talking and spinning yarns, tending a fishline, washing as well as they could in salt water. These Spanish seamen were a cleanly lot; at least twice on the First Voyage Columbus mentions their going swimming, and they never missed a chance to wash themselves and their clothes upon landing near a river.

In the second dogwatch, just after sunset and before the first night watch is set, all hands are called to evening prayers. The ceremony begins by a gromet trimming the binnacle lamp: and as he brings it aft along the deck he sings out: —

Amén y Dios nos dé buenas noches, buen viaje, buen pasaje haga la nao, señor capitán y maestre y buena compaña.

Amen and God give us a good night and good sailing; may the ship make a good passage, sir captain and master and good company.

The gromets then lead the ship's company in what was technically called *la doctrina cristiana.* All hands say the *Pater Noster, Ave Maria* and *Credo,* and sing the *Salve Regina.* This beautiful hymn, one of the oldest Benedictine chants, was a fitting close to the day. The music of it has come down to us, so that we can in some measure re-create that ancient hymn of praise to the Queen of Heaven that floated over uncharted waters every evening, as the caravels slipped along.

We are not to suppose that the seamen kept very close to this music. Columbus once refers to the "*Salve Regina,* which seamen sing or say after their own fashion," and Salazar wrote his friend: "Presently begins the *Salve,* and we are all singers, for we all have a throat . . . For as mariners are great friends of divisions, and divide the four winds into thirty-two, so the eight tones of music they distribute into thirty-two other and different tones, perverse, resonant and very dissonant, as if we had today in the singing of the *Salve* and Litany a tempest of hurricanes of music, so that if God and his glorious Mother and the Saints to whom we pray

SALVE REGINA

Sal - ve Re - gi - na Ma - ter Mi - se - ri - cor - di - æ,

Vi - ta, Dul - ce - do, et spes no - stra sal - ve.

Ad Te cla - ma - mus ex - su - les Fi - li - i E - væ.

Ad Te sus - pi - ra - mus Ge - men - tes et flen - tes

In hac la - cri - ma - rum val - le. E - ia er - go

Ad - vo - ca - ta no - stra, il - los tu - os

Mi - se - ri - cor - des o - cu - los ad nos con - ver - te.

Et Je - sum Be - ne - di - ctum fru - ctum ven - tris tu - i,

No - bis post hoc ex - si - li - um o - sten - de. O cle - mens,

O Pi - a, O Dul - cis Vir - go Ma - ri - a.

should look down upon our tones and voices and not on our hearts and spirits, it would not do to beseech mercy with such a confusion of bawlings!"

The boatswain or boatswain's mate, whichever is on watch, extinguishes the galley fire before the first night watch is set at seven o'clock. As the *ampolleta* is turned up, the gromet chorister sings: —

Bendita la hora en que Dios nació,	Blessed be the hour in which God was born
Santa María que le parió,	Saint Mary who bore Him
San Juan que le bautizó.	Saint John who baptized Him.
La guarda es tomada,	The watch is called,
La ampolleta muele,	the glass floweth;
buen viaje haremos	we shall make a good voyage
si Dios quisiere.	if God willeth.

On sail the caravels through the soft tropic night. Every half hour the gromet turns his *ampolleta* and sings his little ditty: —

Una va pasada	One glass is gone
y en dos muele;	and now the second floweth;
más molerá	more shall run down
si mi Dios querrá,	if my God willeth.
á mi Dios pidamos,	To my God let's pray
que bien viaje hagamos;	to give us a good voyage;
y á la que es Madre de Dios y abogada nuestra,	and through His blessed Mother our advocate on high,
que nos libre de agua de bomba y tormenta.	protect us from the waterspout and send no tempest nigh.

Then he calls to the lookout forward: —

¡Ah! de proa, alerta, buena guardia.

Hey you! forward, look alive, keep good watch.

At which the lookout was supposed to make a shout or grunt to prove that he was awake (like our "Lights burning brightly, sir!"). Every hour the helm and the lookout are relieved, but the captain of the watch keeps the quarter-deck for the whole watch, pacing up and down and peering into the binnacle to see if the helmsman is keeping his course. If the night is quiet, all members of the watch not on lookout or at the helm lean over the forecastle rail, watching entranced the phosphorescent sea, dreaming of epic morrows.

CHAPTER XIII

How Columbus Navigated

1492–1504

Tria sunt difficilia mihi . . . Viam aquilae in caelo, viam colubri super petram, viam navis in medio mari . . .

There be three things which are too wonderful for me . . . the way of an eagle in the air; the way of a serpent upon a rock; the way of a ship in the midst of the sea . . .

— PROVERBS XXX 18, 19

MANY have applied this to Columbus. Granted that he had to hit land if he kept on going, how did he get back to Spain, and what's more, how did he find "The Indies" again? In other words, how did Columbus know where he was on the surface of the globe?

There are two main methods of keeping track of "the way of a ship in the midst of the sea": celestial navigation and dead-reckoning. Celestial navigation means plotting your position on the earth's surface by observing the motions of the heavenly bodies, which (fortunately for mariners) can be predicted to a split hair. When practised with instruments of precision (which Columbus did not have), celestial navigation is most accurate, and every ship's officer must now learn it. But in Columbus's day the art was in its infancy, and neither he nor his shipmates knew very much about it.

The Admiral liked to pose as an expert in celestial navigation, which (he well said) was a mystery to the uninitiated, like prophetic vision. In forty years at sea, off and on (so he wrote in 1501), he had acquired sufficient "astrology" (that is, astronomy), geometry and arithmetic, as well as practical knowledge, for the purposes of maritime discovery. In a postil of uncertain date he talks of "taking the sun" on his Guinea voyage. Yet the testimony of his own journals proves that the simple method of finding latitude from a meridional observation of the sun, long used by Arabs in "camel navigation" of the desert, was unknown to Columbus. Polaris observations for latitude he made not infrequently on his last two voyages, but these observations, though "not too bad," were of no use to his navigation, because he never knew the proper corrections to apply. It has been stated that the invention of the astrolabe

MARINER'S ASTROLABE
*From García Palacio. The Altitude is
read from the upper pointer of the Alidade*

enabled Columbus to discover America; but his Journal proves that he was unable to use the astrolabe on his First Voyage, and there is no evidence of his taking such an instrument on any other. The picture books also show Columbus taking solar or stellar altitudes with a cross staff. That simple instrument would have been more useful to him than a quadrant for shooting Polaris in low latitudes; but he never had one, and probably never saw one.

The common quadrant (not to be confused with Hadley's quadrant or any other reflecting instrument) was the only instrument of celestial navigation that Columbus ever employed. This was a simple quarter-circle of hardwood, with sights along one edge through which the heavenly body could be lined up, a plummet attached to the apex by a silk cord, and a scale of 90° on the arc, from which the altitude could be read as cut by the cord at the moment when sun or star was lined up through the sights. On a rolling and pitching ship it was very difficult to keep the plane of

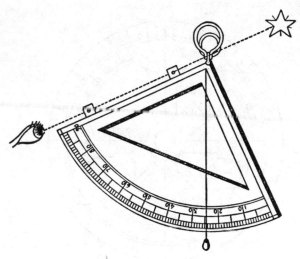

MARINE QUADRANT OF 1492

Altitude is read from the point where thread cuts Arc

the quadrant perpendicular and at the same time catch your star through the pin holes. When you did, you hallooed to the other fellow to mark the degree on the arc cut by the cord; but the cord just then might be doing a big swing. Columbus never managed to do any accurate work with his quadrant until he had a whole year ashore at Jamaica.

The only known method of ascertaining longitude in Columbus's day was by timing an eclipse. Regiomontanus's *Ephemerides* and Zacuto's *Almanach Perpetuum* gave the predicted hours of total eclipses at Nuremberg and Salamanca respectively, and if you compared those with the observed hour of the eclipse by local sun time, wherever you were, and multiplied by fifteen to convert time into arc,* there was your longitude west of the almanac maker's meridian. Sounds simple enough, but Columbus with two opportunities (1494 and 1503) muffed both, as did almost everyone else for a century. At Mexico City in 1541 a mighty effort was made by the intelligentsia to determine the longitude of that place by timing two eclipses of the moon. The imposing result was 8h 2m 32s (= 120° 38′) W of Toledo; but the correct difference of longitude between the two places is 95° 12′; so the Mexican savants made an error of about 25½ degrees, or 1450 miles! Even in the eighteenth century, Père Labat, the earliest writer (to my knowledge) who gives the position of Hispaniola correctly, adds this caveat: "I only report the longitude to warn the reader that nothing is more uncertain, and that no method used up to the present to find longitude has produced anything fixed and certain."

So many indoor geographers and armchair admirals have adduced Columbus's ignorance of celestial navigation as evidence that he was no seaman that I must rub in two points.

1. Celestial navigation formed no part of the professional pilot's or master's training in Columbus's day, or for long after his death. It was practised only by men of learning such as mathematicians, astrologers and physicians, or by gentlemen of education like Antonio Pigafetta who accompanied Magellan, or D. João de Castro, who on India voyages in the 1530's and '40's had everyone down to the ship's caulker taking meridional altitudes of the sun. Mathematics was so little taught in common schools of that era, and the existing ephemerides (compiled largely for astrologers) were so complicated, that even the best professional seamen could do nothing with them. So simple an operation as applying declination to altitude and subtracting the result from 90° was quite beyond their powers. The great Portuguese-Jewish mathematician Pero Nunes (Nonnius), who discovered the vernier, wrote some forty-five years after Columbus's discovery, "Why do we put up with these pilots, with their bad language and barbarous manners; they know neither sun, moon nor stars, nor their courses, movements or declinations; or how they rise, how they set and to what part of the horizon they are inclined; neither latitude nor longitude of the

* One hour of time is equivalent to 15 degrees of longitude.

places on the globe, nor astrolabes, quadrants, cross staffs or
watches, nor years common or bissextile, equinoxes or solstices?"

2. Celestial observations were not used in Columbus's day, even
by the Portuguese, to find one's way about the ocean; but to determine latitudes of newly discovered coasts and islands in order
to chart them correctly. Vasco da Gama on his great voyage of
1497–1499 to India was far better equipped than Columbus for
celestial navigation, but he always disembarked and hung his astrolabe on a tree or a tripod to take the altitude of the sun, as the poet
Camoëns describes him doing.

So, in order to determine his daily positions at sea, and trace his
course across the unknown stretches of the Western Ocean, Columbus was dependent on *dead-reckoning* (D.R.), which means simply
laying down your compass courses and estimated distances on a
chart. That is not so easy as it sounds. In the previous chapter we
have seen how he kept track of time with the *ampolleta* or half-hour
glass. How did he know his course, and estimate distance?

Columbus took the course off his mariner's compass, which was
the most reliable and the one indispensable instrument of navigation aboard. We do not know when the magnetic needle was first
used for purposes of navigation, but it had been so used for at least
three centuries before Columbus, and practical improvements in the
mounting of the needle must have been worked out by the Portuguese for their African voyages. Columbus's instrument was similar to the dry-card dory compasses that could be purchased in ship
chandlers' shops until the other day. A circular card, on which
diamonds, lozenges and lines marked the 32 compass points, was
mounted on a pivot in a circular bowl, so that it could turn freely
in any direction with the motion of the ship.* Its virtue was derived
from a magnetized needle or wire fixed on the underside, between
the north and south marks. Whenever this needle showed any
disinclination to "seek the north" it was remagnetized with a bit
of lodestone that the captain guarded as his life; and plenty of
spare needles were taken — Magellan had thirty-five on his flagship. At the forward edge of the bowl a black vertical line (the

---

* Gimbals had been invented by 1545, and possibly were used by Columbus. Without
a gimbal mounting of the bowl, the card must have jammed on every steep pitch or heavy
roll of the ship.

"lubber line") was drawn. As the needle always sought magnetic north, the point on the floating card that touched the lubber line indicated the direction in which the ship was heading, provided the diameter of the bowl that passed through the lubber line was kept parallel to the ship's keel. That was done by keeping the compass in a fixed position in the *bitácora* or binnacle, a rectangular box fastened with wooden pins and secured to the deck, provided with a hood to protect the compass from the weather and with a little copper oil lamp to illuminate the card at night. This binnacle, containing what we should call the "standard" compass, was on the quarter-deck where the captain or officer of the watch could keep an eye on it; on the main deck close to the great tiller was another for the helmsman to steer by. The officer of the watch gave the course to the helmsman, and checked him by keeping an eye on the standard compass. He communicated with the helmsman through an open hatch in the quarter-deck.

COMPASS CARD OF
THE SIXTEENTH CENTURY
(*García Palacio*)

MODERN COMPASS CARD
Courtesy Kelvin & Wilfrid O.
White Company

Modern compass cards have abbreviations for the points or degrees, or both, printed on them, but those that Columbus used had neither; nor would letters have done any good, as few seamen could read. They simply distinguished between points by the length, shape or color of the diamonds and lozenges; except that

North was marked by the fleur-de-lis then as now. In 1939 we
shipped aboard *Capitana* at São Miguel an illiterate Azorean who
proved to be the best helmsman among us. Those who spoke English only had to indicate with their finger the point on the card by
which he must steer; but when I said *Leste cuarta del Sudeste* (E
by S) he understood perfectly, and held her close to that point.
Literacy has helped seamanship very little indeed.

Spaniards, like other seafarers at the time, did not think of direction in terms of degrees as we do, or of compass points as our immediate forbears did, but in terms of winds, *los vientos.** Although
the ancients recognized twelve winds, and wind roses on medieval
maps followed this system, by Columbus's time the winds had been
reduced to eight· N, NE, E, SE, S, SW, W, NW. The intermediate
points (NNE, ENE, ESE, SSE, SSW, WSW, WNW, NNW) were
called *los medios vientos,* the half-winds; and what we call the
"by" points (N by E, NE by N, and so on) they called *las cuartas,*
the quarter-winds; consequently *una cuarta* was their name for a
compass point (11¼°). Thus, if Columbus wished to give the course
that we should call West by South, he would call it *Oeste cuarta del
Sudoeste,* literally "West, one quarter of the Southwest wind."

How about compass variation, the difference between a magnetic
and a true course? We shall find Columbus wrestling with that
problem on his first three voyages, and, if not solving it, at least
recognizing its existence. Fortunately his routes seldom crossed a
region where the compass variation was more than 6° or half a
point, and a good part of the time in the West Indies he was in
the zone of no variation. Deviation, the variation caused by local
attraction, did not bother him because his vessels contained only
negligible quantities of iron.

It was an easy matter for the captain of the watch to keep reckoning. He simply wrote the course steered on a slate that hung against
a bulkhead on the poop deck, and indicated by a stroke every half
hour that she sailed on that course. But he also had to estimate the
third factor in dead-reckoning, the rate of speed.

In the sixteenth century there was invented the chip log, a billet
of wood weighted and flanged so it would float without moving in
the water, attached by a light line in which knots were so spaced

---

* The Portuguese still call the compass card *a rosa dos ventos,* the wind rose.

that the number of knots paid out over the rail in half a minute, which was measured by a special log glass, equaled the number of nautical miles per hour the ship was making. Hence our term "knots" for speed at sea. You "hove the log" every watch, or whenever the ship picked up or lost speed, and recorded the rate. That, multiplied by time, gave distance. But this simple device for finding speed was unknown to Columbus. He or the officer of the watch simply estimated by eye the speed that *Santa María* was making, in Roman miles per hour, by watching the bubbles or the gulfweed float by.

Any seaman of good judgment and experience can estimate the speed of a vessel by this primitive method within a knot, or even a half-knot if he is used to her. But, just as modern dead-reckoning at sea can be checked by daily sights, so a modern estimate of speed can be checked by patent log, or a measured mile. Columbus had no such check, yardstick or other fixed standard. He estimated speed in Roman miles per hour, and distance in leagues of 4 Roman miles each, his league being equivalent to 3.18 nautical miles. But with no standard save experience, and no check, Columbus was not accurate. A careful plotting of his ocean crossing in 1492 proves that he overestimated the distance run at sea on the average 9 per cent, and he came very close to that overestimate on crossings such as Crooked Island Passage and the Windward Passage. In other words, by crediting *Santa María* with too much speed, the league that he actually used measured only 2.89 nautical miles. Moreover, when sailing within sight of land, Columbus either used a different league, or, by fixing his eyes on objects ashore instead of on flotsam, made an even greater overestimate; for when you check the alongshore distances recorded in his Journal by actual distances, it appears that his alongshore league was roughly equivalent to but 1.5 nautical miles. This error was so constant that I am inclined to believe he was consciously using a different "land" league. He never knew exactly how fast his vessel was sailing, because he had no fixed standard and no check.

The one thing everyone knows about Columbus's navigation of the First Voyage is that he kept the "accurate" reckoning to himself, and made a reduced or "phony" one for the crew, so that they would not complain of being taken so far from home. But, owing to his overestimate of distance, the "phony" reckoning was nearer the truth than the "accurate" day's work!

So much for computation of time, speed and distance. The next indispensable aid to navigation that Columbus used was a collection of sea charts. These were big sheepskins on which the coasts of Spain, Portugal and North Africa, and the Azores, Madeira and the Canaries were sketched in fairly accurately, hypothetical islands such as Antillia were laid down by guess, Cipangu and Cathay drawn in where Columbus thought they should be according to Marinus of Tyre and Marco Polo. The surface of the chart was crisscrossed by rhumb (that is, straight) lines, which radiated from a number of wind roses placed at convenient intervals out in the ocean. Every chart had a scale of leagues, but no latitude and longitude grid. Columbus did not think in terms of latitude, but of the Ptolemaic "climates," arbitrary parallel belts laid down by the Alexandrian geographer; he had copied a table of them into his *Imago Mundi*. Instead of longitude, he thought in terms of "hours" west of Cadiz, 15° of longitude to one hour.

Columbus began "making points" for the big jump by taking a simple departure from the place where he lay becalmed between Gomera and Tenerife on the night of September 7–8, 1492. It was only two or three days after full moon, so he could see both islands, take their bearings by squinting across the compass card, and estimate their distance. He pricked the corresponding point on his chart, and that was his point of departure. He then set the course due W for the Indies. On Sunday, September 9, at sunrise he reckoned that they had made 9 leagues from the point of departure. So he took his ruler, laid its edge on that point and parallel to the nearest W rhumb line on the chart, laid off 9 leagues with his divider, and pricked a new point. This process was called by the Spaniards *fazer* or *echar punto* (to make, or apply the point), or simply *cartear* (do the chart); and in English it used to be called "pricking the chart," or "pricking her off." One's progress on the chart was traced by a series of small holes punched by the points of the dividers.

Columbus did not do this all himself; on one occasion he mentions the pilots and mariners looking on and giving advice while he pricked off the course. It seems odd to us that Columbus should

let in mariners even on his "phony" navigation; but apparently
that was the rule in his day. García Palacio says (1587) that able
seamen should be able to "make point," and he advises the pilot,
if he gets into difficulties with his navigation, to consult with the
captain and master and some good able seamen, giving and taking
counsel, and to be gracious about it. I feel sure, however, that
Columbus allowed no discussion about the speed, and that he came
on deck frequently to see that the officer of the watch used his
standard and no other for logging speed.

"Making points" on the chart was simple enough when you did
not often change course, as on most of Columbus's outward passage; but when you had to beat to windward, as in the first month
of the homeward passage, the error involved in laying down a
multitude of very short courses on an ocean chart would be serious.
Under such conditions a dead-reckoning navigator resorts to a
traverse table; and there is evidence in Columbus's Journal that he
had one and knew how to work it. The principle of the traverse
table is to transform any number of diagonal courses into one big
right angle: so many miles east or west (departure), and so many
miles north or south (difference of latitude). The principle may
be compared with finding your way about in New York City.
Suppose you wish to walk from 53rd Street and First Avenue to
58th Street and Fifth Avenue. You may make it by a series of
north and west "tacks," according as the traffic lights make you
"come about," occasionally catching a "fair wind" to cross diagonally a block that is an open park. But if you can manage to find
a native New Yorker and ask him the way, he will say "five blocks
north and six west." He has transformed the short tacks by his
mental traverse table into "diff. lat." and departure. So by a very
simple computation Columbus could transform any number of
tacks or changes of course into one big right angle. This he applied
to the chart and made a point for the resulting position. He then
measured on the chart the course and distance between the two
points, and noted in his Journal, "we made good 13 leagues NE,"
or whatever the result was.

As a former map maker Columbus was well equipped to chart
his own discoveries, and undoubtedly he entered every new island
and sketched in every coastline on a blank chart as he sailed along.

Twice on the Second Voyage we find references to his entering even the smallest islands on a chart that he was preparing; Hojeda's voyage of 1499 was admittedly based on a chart of the mainland that the Admiral had sent home; a witness in the *pleitos* of 1514 said that all later discoverers of the mainland "went by the charts that the Admiral had made, because he alone made charts of all that he discovered." As the new lands were more minutely explored, new charts were made and the Admiral's destroyed, all save one rough sketch of Northern Haiti. This has a sureness of touch that fully sustains his reputation as a cartographer, and gives us a keen sense of our loss in having none of the larger charts that he presented to the Sovereigns.

Like all good practical navigators Columbus made frequent use of the sounding lead when approaching the coast, or when he thought he was near land. The standard length of lead line for small vessels in those days, and for centuries after, was 40 fathoms; but each of Columbus's fleet carried a dipsey (deep sea) lead line of 100 fathoms, and on one occasion he bent two together to make a 200-fathom sounding. We may smile at his trying to sound in mid-ocean, where the modern chart reports a depth of some 2400 fathoms; but the leadsman reporting "No bottom, sir," after repeated casts through heavy mats of gulfweed was far more reassuring as to the safety of the Sargasso Sea than any amount of speculation. Sounding in a breeze is troublesome, as a vessel has to back some of her sails in order to check her way and give the lead a chance to reach bottom. For that reason this elementary precaution when approaching a coast is often forgotten, and more vessels go ashore through neglect to heave the lead than from any other cause.* Columbus was very punctilious about sounding until he found by experience that the outer Bahamas were so steep and the water so clear that you could find no bottom until it was visible. Then he too grew careless, and so lost his flagship on Christmas eve.

Columbus's only aids to navigation, then, were the mariner's compass and dividers, quadrant and lead line, sea chart and ruler, traverse table and ordinary multiplication table, and one of the

---

* Several groundings of large steamships in recent years have been caused by too confident reliance on electrical sounding devices. Yachtsmen are just as bad.

recent Ephemerides of Johannes Müller (Regiomontanus) designed more for astrologers than for navigators. There is no evidence that he added to this equipment on any later voyage; indeed the astrolabe that he had on the First Voyage and was unable to use seems to have been left behind. Two mariners who were with him on the Third Voyage later testified that he carried "charts, quadrants, tables, sphere, and other things." So, to all intents and purposes, he was a dead-reckoning navigator pure and simple.

This is not to say that Columbus was a poor navigator; far from it. Dead-reckoning was about 99 per cent of the navigator's art in 1492, and in high latitudes there are long periods of overcast or stormy weather when celestial observations are impossible. Dead-reckoning is still the foundation of navigation. On the navigating table of every ocean liner or battleship today you will find the ship's "D.R." laid down on a chart, and the most modern systems of celestial navigation are worked out by assuming your D.R. position and correcting it by celestial observation. Columbus's few recorded celestial observations before 1504 were of the most cock-eyed description — as we shall see when we come to them; but like every good dead-reckoning navigator he had the common sense to throw them out. That is done nowadays more often than you think. What navigator has not heard a shipmate say, after a prolonged bout of figuring, "Well, that can't be right; my D.R. shows . . ."? A New London–Bermuda race in recent years was lost because the navigator trusted a celestial observation rather than his D.R. and altered course accordingly — excusing himself because it was an observation of Venus's lower limb!

It must be remembered, however, that the modern navigator checks his D.R. daily (if weather permits) by latitude or longitude sights or both, which Columbus never learned to do. And, as an error of half a point in your course will mean an error of about 250 miles in landfall on an ocean crossing, it is evident that Columbus's D.R. was extraordinarily careful and accurate. Possibly he was not much more skillful than his better contemporaries, although the bad guesses of the pilots on the First Voyage home, and their surprise at Columbus's excellent landfall in 1496, would seem to show the contrary. Andrés Bernáldez, who had his information directly from the Admiral after that event, wrote, "No one considers himself a good pilot and master who, although he has to pass from one land to another very distant without sighting any other land, makes an error of 10 leagues, even in a crossing of 1000 leagues, unless the force of the tempest forces him and deprives him of the use of his skill." No such dead-reckoning navigators exist today; no man alive, limited to the instruments and means at Columbus's disposal, could obtain anything near the accuracy of his results.

Judged therefore not simply by what he did, but by how he did it, Columbus was a great navigator. He took his fleet to sea not as an amateur possessed of one big idea, but as a captain experienced in *el arte de marear*. He was well, though not superlatively well, equipped with such navigational aids and instruments as the age had produced. Modestly conscious of his own imperfections, he wrote to the Sovereigns before his last voyage predicting that "with the perfecting of instruments and the equipment of vessels, those who are to traffic and trade with the discovered islands will have better knowledge" than was vouchsafed to him. Over and above his amazing competence as a dead-reckoning navigator, he had what a great French seaman, Jean Charcot, recognized and named *le sens marin*, that intangible and unteachable God-given gift of knowing how to direct and plot "the way of a ship in the midst of the sea."

CHAPTER XIV

Atlantic Crossing

SEPTEMBER 9–30, 1492

Cumque extendisset Moyses manum contra mare, reuersum est primo diluculo ad priorem locum. . . .

And Moses stretched forth his hand over the sea, and the sea returned to his strength when the morning appeared.

— EXODUS xiv 27

T HIS most momentous voyage in modern history was also one of the easiest, from the nautical point of view. Columbus's greatest difficulty, that of obtaining ships and men and securing royal authorization, was over when he sailed from Palos. The vessels were in fine shape after their "shake-down cruise" to the Canaries and the repairing and re-rigging at Las Palmas; they had water, wine, provisions and stores enough to last a year; the officers and men had had five weeks to get used to each other and to their ships. Now that the Canaries had dropped below the eastern horizon, no Portuguese warships had materialized, and "wind come fair," Columbus was serene and confident of success. He knew, for he had read it in great works on geography, that the sea was narrow between Spain and the Indies and could be traversed easily *paucis diebus,* in a few days. And, if we insert "West" before "Indies," was he not right? Thirty-three days from departure to landfall was a few days, as traveling was counted in that era; it was less time than a Roman needed to reach Britain, or than a pilgrim from Northern France required for a sea voyage to the Holy Land. The only question was, whether these "few days" would not be too many for the men, whether their fears would not force Columbus to turn back when the goal was just over the horizon, as had happened to Bartholomew Dias, and doubtless to other brave captains.

In other words, the difficulties ahead of Columbus on this voyage were entirely of a moral or (if you will) psychological nature. Practical difficulties there were none; no storms or prolonged calms, no foul winds or heavy seas, no shortage of victual or drink, nothing to bother a well-built, properly equipped and well-found ocean-going fleet, as this was. If Columbus had died in the West Indies before the fleet returned to Spain, there might be some reason to suspect that he was merely a competent mariner with an idea, but no great navigator. His opportunities to prove seamanship of the highest order occurred on the homeward passage in 1493, and on the other three voyages.

Lord Dunraven, the English yachtsman who made a study of Columbus's navigation of this First Voyage, declared that if a modern sailing vessel wished to make a voyage from Palos to the Bahamas and back, she "could not follow a better course out and home than that adopted by Columbus." And George Nunn, in his study of the First Voyage, concluded that Columbus knew everything essential about ocean winds and currents, "and understood them so thoroughly that he did not make a single false move in the entire voyage." Both these judgments need considerable qualification. A westerly course from the Canaries runs out of the trade-wind belt into the "horse latitudes" of calms and variables. Moreover the northern limit of the northeast trades for October (and September 22 in the Julian Calendar is October 1 in ours) dips south of his course after he was a few days out, and runs approximately along latitude 26° N, so that he only re-entered the trade-wind zone on the last few days of the passage. This northern limit of the trades is variable, and the variations are unpredictable. Some years you catch them further north, as Columbus did, and in others further south; our *Mary Otis* did not find them until she was below latitude 20° N in November 1937, and averaged less than 2 knots in waters where Columbus's fleet did better than 5. Any sailing vessel proceeding from Spain to the West Indies today, whether or not calling at the Canaries, would be well advised to drop down almost to latitude 15°, 500 miles south of Tenerife, before straightening out on a westerly course. Even the recommended trade-wind sailing route for September from Northern Europe to New York swings away down below latitude 24° N, some 250 miles south of the parallel of Ferro. So Columbus did not take the best route, even for the position — 750 leagues west of the Canaries — where he supposed

Cipangu to be; and his course was not the correct one for making such a voyage. He had what we Yankees call "a mighty good chance," skirting as he did the horse latitudes in the hurricane season. Not a single day of storm, not one day of flat calm, only a few days of variables did he experience. He had all the "breaks" you may say; but fortune always favors the brave.

September 9, the day that Columbus passed Ferro, "he decided to reckon less than he made, so that if the voyage were long the people would not be frightened and dismayed." It was easy enough for him to practise this deception, because nobody ever ventures to check up on a commanding officer's arithmetic. The stratagem was entirely proper and ethical, considering the sort of people with whom he had to deal. Mariners are an odd tribe, little understood by landsmen. The same man who is capable of the highest courage in going aloft in a gale, or manning a boat to save a shipmate, will be frightened as a high-strung horse at anything outside his experience. And if his code of superstition has been violated by something like sailing on Friday, he will be uneasy the entire voyage. It has always been difficult to recruit common seamen for exploring expeditions, at least down to this age of publicized sea dogs. Columbus knew very well that the time would come when his men would clamor to return; and he wished to be in a position to quiet them by telling the boys they weren't so very far from home, they had sailed further than that on voyages to Africa, hadn't they? But the amusing thing is that Columbus overestimated speed and distance in his own mind by almost the same amount that he underestimated it for the ignorant seamen; so that his "phony" reckoning was nearer the truth than his "true" one! The pilots kept independent reckonings as well; and on the one occasion when the four reckonings were compared, Peralonso Niño of *Santa María* came nearest the truth.

Those whose knowledge of the sea is confined to modern high-powered vessels, which constantly tend to fall off their courses, may question the accuracy of Columbus's courses as given in the Journal. But it is usually easier to keep a square-rigger on her course than a steamship. In a steady wind the helmsman soon gets the feel of a well-balanced sailing vessel, and only glances at the compass now and then to check himself. Columbus's helmsmen

were carefully conned by the officer of the watch, who had his eye
on the standard compass in the binnacle. In the Journal for September 9, Columbus says, "The seamen steered badly, letting her
run up to the W by N, and even WNW, for which the Admiral
scolded them many times." (One can imagine sarcastic inquiries
if they thought they were steering a ferryboat across the River of
Seville, whether they had a girl in the Azores, and so on.) It would
not be considered a serious offense today on a sailing vessel the
size of the *Santa María* if the helmsman let her run up a point or
two scudding before a brisk trade and a rising sea, provided that
he compensated for it by letting her fall off a corresponding amount
to leeward. The steering of *Santa María* and her consorts must have
been watched with very great care. And there are no further
complaints of bad helmsmanship in the Journal.

During the first ten days (September 9–18 inclusive) the trade
wind blew as steadily as it ever does, the westerly course was
constantly followed, and the fleet made 1163 nautical miles. The
least twenty-four hours' run was 60 miles, and the best 174, which
for sailing vessels of their burthen was very good sailing indeed.*
That was the honeymoon period of the voyage, the sort of sailing
that old salts dream of. Wind and sea on the stern gave the caravels
a regular lift and roll that sea legs take in their stride; no making
and setting of sail or hauling on sheets and braces; seascape of
surpassing beauty (and don't imagine, you esthetic snobs, that
common seamen don't appreciate it), brightest of blue seas, fat
puffy trade-wind clouds constantly rising up from astern, deliberately passing overhead, and setting under the western horizon;
weather warm and balmy but always fresh from the blessed trades.
Nothing to do but keep the vessels clean, observe ship routine,
watch for birds and flying fishes, and spend the gold you are going
to pick up in Cipangu.

"The Admiral says here," abstracts Las Casas for September 16,
que era plazer grande el gusto de las mañanas, "that the savor of
the mornings was a great delight." What memories that phrase
evokes! A fragrant cool freshness of daybreak in the trades, the
false dawn shooting up a pyramid of grayish-white light, the paling

---

* All distances quoted are net, after deducting the 9 per cent average overestimate
from the distances logged by Columbus.

stars, the navigators bustling about to shoot their favorites in the brief morning twilight of the tropics, rosy lights on the clouds as sunrise approaches, sudden transformation of the squaresails from dark gray to ruddy gold, smell of dew drying from the deck, the general feeling of God's in his Heaven and all's right with the world. "The weather was like April in Andalusia," said Columbus; "the only thing wanting was to hear nightingales." Well, you landsmen can have the nightingales, I'll take the flashing boatswain-birds screaming overhead, and the downy little petrels skimming the seas in wide circles about the ship, softly chirping as they dabble for plankton in the vessel's wash or wake.

There was no lack of these or of the tropic birds, *rabo de juncos,* "reed-tails," as Columbus called them; old-time seamen call them boatswain-birds "because they carry a marlinspike in their tails." Two came aboard our *Capitana* in mid-ocean. Columbus and his men, who were no ornithologists, thought that the appearance of these and of some birds that he calls *garaxaos* (probably the small Arctic tern, or a young boatswain-bird) indicated land; but the nearest land that day (September 14) was Santa Maria in the Azores, some 570 miles to the NNE.

On Sunday, September 16, when they crossed 33° west longitude, they saw their first sargassum, or gulfweed — "many bunches of very green weed, which had a short time (as it seemed) been torn from land; whereby all judged that they were near some island, but not the mainland according to the Admiral, who says 'because I make the mainland to be further on.'" Next day they picked up more of it, and found therein a live crab, the little green *Nautilus grapsus minutus,* about as big as a thumbnail. They were entering the Sargasso Sea, that great oval-shaped area of the Western Ocean that extends roughly from longitude 32° W to the Bahamas, and from the Gulf Stream down to latitude 18° N. It is probable that nobody aboard had noticed gulfweed before, because one seldom encounters it within a day's run west of the Azores, and almost never on a voyage between Spain or Portugal and Africa. But Columbus had been warned about it by our old friend Pedro de Velasco, and advised to keep on a straight course when he struck the weed. Ferdinand relates that the men were alarmed on September 21–22 when the ocean was one great meadow of the green and yellow weed, and the caravels wasted time trying to find open water, fearing lest they be "frozen" in sargassum. Actually, gulfweed is no hindrance to navigation; for even when it forms an almost continuous mat on the surface it is never more than half an inch thick, and parts readily to admit a vessel's prow. Within a few days everyone was used to the gulfweed, and *vieron muchas yerbas*, "saw plenty weed," became an almost daily notation in Columbus's Journal. But the superstition of getting stuck in the Sargasso Sea is still alive.

Columbus's serene plunge into the Sargasso Sea, about which only vague, contradictory and alarming data were hitherto known, was sufficient to make this voyage one of the most important in maritime history. His theory that the weed grew on rocks or submarine ledges not far from the Azores, from which it was wrenched by storms, died very hard; for similar weed does grow on rocks along the tropical shores of America. Columbus's theory was still held by scientists such as the great Von Humboldt a century ago, and has even been seriously maintained in the present century. The *Challenger* expedition of 1873, by disproving the existence of any such oceanic banks, gave this idea a blow; and the report of the Danish scientist Winge on the Danish Oceanographical Expedition of 1908–1910 leaves no doubt that gulfweed is a pelagic perennial, the descendant of algae torn loose in prehistoric times. It propagates itself by partition, the plants constantly growing the fresh greenish shoots (that Columbus noted) at one end, and withering to a brown color at the other. The *como fruta* ("sort of fruit") that Columbus noted are the little berrylike globules filled with air that keep the weed afloat.

The only phenomenon that caused any dismay during these ten days of ideal sailing was an apparent variation of the compass needles. On September 13 Columbus reported that at the beginning of night the needles varied to the NW of the polestar, and in the morning to the NE. Again, on the seventeenth the pilots "took the north, in order to mark it." That ancient custom, the traditional gesture which used to be called the "pilot's blessing," consisted in raising the arm with flattened palm between the eyes, pointing at the North Star, and bringing the palm straight down on the compass card, to see if the needle varied from true north. On this occasion they found that the needles "varied to the NW a full point, and the mariners took fright and were troubled and did not say why." They were familiar with easterly variation, but none of them had ever been in the zone of westerly variation, into which the fleet had crossed on the fourteenth. "The Admiral knew," continues the Journal for September 17, "and ordered that the North be marked again at dawn, and found that the needles were true. The cause was that the star appeared to move and not the needles."

Columbus was right. Polaris in 1492 described a radius of about 3° 27′ about the celestial pole, as against a 1° radius or polar distance today. At nightfall in mid-September 1492 Polaris lay at this full distance east of the pole. Consequently, on the thirteenth, when there was no variation, the needle pointed about 3½° west of the star just after dusk, and about the same small angle east of the star just before dawn. It is astonishing that this small variation should have been observed on compass cards graduated only to full points of 11¼° each. On September 17, when the fleet had entered the zone of 2° westerly variation, the needle varied about 5½° at dusk, less than half a full point, but the "pilot's blessing" method was hardly accurate; whilst just before dawn, Polaris having moved over, star and needles were only a little over one degree apart. To anticipate a bit, on September 30, when the fleet had reached the isogonic line of 7° westerly variation, Columbus observed that at nightfall the needles varied a full point to the westward. Polaris then lay some 3° 20′ east of the celestial pole, and that angle plus the real variation of 7° falls little short of a compass point (11¼°). At dawn, says Columbus, they were "right on the Star." Polaris having moved over, the actual 7° westerly variation was cut down to about 3½°, as observed by the compass needle, and on this occasion the small difference was not observed. Eventually Columbus realized that he had observed a westerly variation of the compass, and no doubt he was the first to report it. But during the voyage he was at some pains to deny a phenomenon so novel and disturbing to the mariners. What he then discovered for himself was the diurnal rotation of Polaris, a fact which many late medieval and renaissance astronomers had denied. Practical seamen had assumed for centuries that the North Star marked true north.

September 18, when the fleet made a twenty-four-hour run of

159 miles, was the last good sailing day that month. Columbus's course was taking him out of the trades; he was very lucky to have carried them to longitude 40°, sailing as he did along the 28th parallel of latitude. On the nineteenth "it fell calm," and they made only 72 miles' westing. The gradually flattening sea, a more or less stationary cloudbank, a drizzle of rain, visits from boobies and other sea fowl such as the small Arctic tern (which Columbus did not recognize and supposed to be land birds), a westward flight of petrels, a tuna fish that was caught from *Niña*, even the crab in the gulfweed, were so many signs of land to these innocent mariners on their first ocean crossing. The chart that Columbus had aboard, "compiled from the most reliable sources" as all the worst modern charts claim, showed islands on both sides of them at this position. Everyone was very cheerful, and the caravels sailed gaily ahead of the flagship, hoping to win the prize for first landfall. Columbus, however, ordered the bonnet unlaced from *Santa María's* main course, as the wind at that moment was freshening.

On the nineteenth the three pilots totted up their position. Peralonso Niño of *Santa María* made it 400 leagues west of the Canaries, which was according to the "phony" reckoning handed out by Columbus — and was very nearly correct! Cristóbal García Sarmiento of *Pinta* made it 420, and Sancho Ruiz of *Niña*, 440, which was very near Columbus's own reckoning from the place where the wind came up on September 8. The actual distance was about 396 leagues or 1261 nautical miles. Columbus observed that he "did not wish to delay matters by beating to windward to ascertain if there was land," although he felt certain that they were "going through between" islands, "because his desire was to follow right along to the Indies. 'And the weather is favorable; wherefore on the return passage, please God, all will be seen.' These are his words." Actually the nearest land at that time was Flores in the Azores, some 850 miles to the northeastward. They were not yet halfway across to America.

Next day, September 20, they ran out of the trades and had to change course: "sailed this day to the W by N and WNW because the winds were very variable." Several birds came aboard — some of them mistaken for warblers — and hopes ran high of an early landfall. In a flat calm Columbus ordered the dipsey lead hove.

No bottom at 200 fathoms. (The nearest sounding to that point on the modern ocean chart is 2292 fathoms!) The fleet made 57 miles in the next two days, for they were in that section of the North Atlantic that has the largest percentage of calms, light airs and variables in September, and were lucky to have any wind whatsoever. At dawn on the twenty-first the sea was covered with weed, "very smooth like a river, and the air the best in the world." That night at sundown they saw the new moon.

Columbus was sorry to lose the trades, but he always found consolation in contrarieties. In his Journal for September 22, when the fleet could do no better than WNW, he noted, "This contrary wind was of much use to me, because my people were all worked up, thinking that no winds blew in these waters for returning to Spain." They had had too much of a good thing. But seamen can always find something to beef about. Next day, when the wind dropped, "the people grumbled, saying that since there was no heavy sea, that proved it would never blow hard enough to return to Spain." All right boys, just wait a few hours, the Old Man knows his stuff. "Afterwards the sea made up considerably, and without wind, which astonished them." There must have been a hurricane far to the southwestward, for it was now the season for a Line gale. Columbus's stock went up several points: "Thus very useful to me was the high sea, a sign such as had not appeared save in the time of the Jews when they came up out of Egypt and grumbled against Moses who had delivered them out of captivity."

Columbus always loved to apply the Sacred Scriptures to his own life and adventures; it is ridiculous to read into this passage a secret admission of Jewish blood, or an ambition to provide a new home for a persecuted race. The really significant thing about these entries for September 22–23, as Charcot pointed out, was the men's uneasiness over scudding free for so many days on end, which proves that they had no previous experience of the trade winds. Columbus knew little if anything more than they; his serenity came from an inward assurance and confidence in God, not from superior knowledge. And the "very useful to me" passage is one in which a seaman speaks to seamen. No mariner in a small sailing vessel welcomes rough water, which renders navigation more difficult and dangerous. He accepts foul weather or heavy sea, but never likes it, and is not afraid to say so. Columbus explains that he welcomes the high sea merely because it enhances his reputation among the men. And when he has smooth water, he ejaculates "Thanks be to God!" It is the nautical bluffers who pretend to glory in stormy weather and rough water, and affect to find smooth-water sailing dull.

It was dull enough to be sure that week of the autumnal equinox — 234 miles in five days. The men even went in swimming. During these calms and light airs, it was easy for the crews to exchange banter and for their officers to consult. In the smooth sea the caravels could be shoved along with their sweeps whenever the Captain General gave the signal; and in the absence of whistling wind and rushing waves, conversations from ship to ship were not difficult. On September 25 *Pinta* came close alongside the flagship in order to discuss with Columbus a chart containing mythical islands, which he had lent Martín Alonso three days before. Pinzón, whose particular interest in discovering islands is evident, wished to spend more time looking for them, because he said they must be somewhere about. Columbus "replied that so it appeared to him; but since they had not fallen in with them, the currents must have . . . set the ships all the while to the NE, and they had not gone so far as the pilots said." Martín Alonso sent the chart over to the flagship on a line, and Columbus "began to plot their position on it with his pilot and mariners."

While the plotting was going on, just at sunset on the twenty-fifth, Martín Alonso suddenly rushed up on *Pinta's* poop and joyfully shouted, *"Tierra! tierra! señor, albricias!"* — Land, land, sir! I claim the reward! There was a general scramble up the rigging on all three vessels, and everyone declared he saw land, about 25 leagues to the southwestward. Columbus fell on his knees to thank God, *Gloria in excelsis Deo* was sung by all hands, the course was altered to SW, and "all continued during the night declaring it to be land." They supposed it to be a high mountain like Tenerife, which is visible over 100 miles in clear weather.

At dawn no land was visible. Columbus continued the same course until the afternoon, when he decided "that what had been supposed to be land was not, but sky." False landfalls are a common sea phenomenon. A cloud on the horizon at sunset, as this seems to have been, is often mistaken for land, especially when people on board are eagerly searching for it; and man is so suggestible that if one sees it all see it. Such was the origin of the phantom islands of the Atlantic, which Columbus thought would make good ports of call on the passage to India.

Columbus was not greatly disturbed by this false alarm, because at the time he reckoned they had sailed only 533 leagues, a little over two thirds of the way to "The Indies." Twice he states that since the main object of this voyage is to reach the Indies, he does not care to delay by looking up odd islands. His Journal reflects nothing but confidence, serenity, and joy at the beauty of the ocean. "The sea was like a river," he noted on September 26, "the air sweet and very soft." The wind was so light, and so near were they to the northern edge of the trades, that no sea made up; one often sees such summer days in the North Atlantic. But the people, says Ferdinand, saw the westerly course resumed with heaviness of heart. Day after day they had "wind on the stern," but little of it, and the ships sailed slowly west. In six days (September 26–October 1) they made only 382 miles. There was nothing to keep the men busy, nothing to do but keep the vessels clean and the gear in good shape, troll for fish (and they caught some savory *dorado* or dolphin, that tastes like salmon) and watch the birds.

Under these circumstances the usual grumbling began to assume the proportions of incipient mutiny. This Genoese, in his mad fantasy, is trying to make himself a great lord at the expense of our lives, someone suggested. To follow this westerly course much longer will be our ruin. Food and water will give out, for it never rains in this desert waste of salt water. (It seldom does rain on the northern edge of the northeast trades.) After all, he is a foreigner, wouldn't it be a sound plan to heave him overboard, and to pretend that when observing the stars he had fallen in by accident? Isn't that the only means for our safe return?

Columbus must have known what was going on. No Spanish seaman can hold a poker face very long; and the sour looks, the violent gestures (with sidelong glances at himself) when a group of mariners got together for a gam, told him that something very evil was stewing. Indeed he showed that he knew it, for when some of the officers remonstrated and said he should turn back, Columbus remarked they might kill him if they would, he and his

servants were too few to resist; but it would do them no good, the
Sovereigns would have the whole lot hanged if they returned without him. His usual policy, however, was to use *palabras dulces,*
"soft words," as Oviedo says. As anxiety increased among the
common seamen, the more serene and confident appeared their
Captain General, the more he flattered them with prospects of
oriental wealth, and of the favors that they would receive from
their Sovereigns after a successful voyage.

It became more and more difficult to maintain morale. The
fleet had now been three weeks without sight of land; probably no
man aboard had ever equaled that record. Only those who have
experienced it, know what wear and tear shipmates inflict on each
other's tempers during a long sea voyage. Ashore you may hate
your boss or despise your fellow workers, but you are with them
only from nine to five. Even in a boys' school or military training
camp, there are some means to gain privacy for short intervals. But
on a vessel like these caravels, where men even had to ease themselves in public, it is impossible to get away from your mates
except by sleep; and even then they fall over you or wake you up
to ask silly questions, such as, where did you leave that marlinspike last watch? In a really long voyage such as this, which is full
of anxiety and disappointment, especially if there is no stiff weather
to keep them busy, the men invariably form gangs and cliques,
work up hatreds against each other and their officers, brood over
imaginary wrongs and unintended slights, and fancy that they are
shipmates with some of the world's worst scoundrels. Warm friend-
ships are formed as well, and the finest loyalty and sacrifice are
brought out at sea; but simply seeing the same faces and hearing the
same voices day after day and week after week, with no chance to
shake it off even for an hour, wears many a man ragged. There is
no reason to suppose that these human relationships were any
worse aboard *Santa María*, *Pinta* and *Niña* than on other ships of
the time; these people, to judge by the record, were pretty good
fellows: but by the time September changed to October they were
not only working up a mighty fear of the unknown, but getting in
each other's hair. Columbus and the Pinzons needed all their moral
force and prestige to prevent outbreaks or even mutiny.

CHAPTER XV

Adelante! Adelante!

Tonet mare, et plenitudo eius.

Let the sea roar, and the fulness thereof.
— I CHRONICLES xvi 32

A T DAWN October 1, last day of the stretch of variable winds, pilot Peralonso Niño of *Santa María* figured out the distance they had sailed from Ferro as 578 leagues. "The lesser reckoning that the Admiral showed to the people was 584 leagues; but the true one that the Admiral found and kept back, was 707." According to Captain McElroy's reckoning, Peralonso was right again, for the correct figure was 575 leagues. But the actual westing made, what really counted, was only 1794 miles or 564 leagues. Consequently Columbus's "phony" reckoning was much nearer the truth than his real one. Since he had predicted land at 750 leagues west of the Canaries, he must have been getting anxious at this point; but in order to make time and reach land before anything boiled up among the men forward, and because the moon was nearing full, he continued to carry on day and night.

And how they did sail, that first week of October! An average of 142 miles every twenty-four hours for five days (October 2–6), including the best day's run, 182 miles, of the outward passage; almost 8 knots. The magnetic course was still due west, but owing to the unsuspected variation of the compass the fleet was slowly (and fortunately as it turned out) trending southward. Rumblings of revolt were again heard forward, but flocks of petrels and other birds came to the rescue of authority on October 3 and 4, raising new hopes of land. The seamen still had much to learn about the habits of petrels; but Columbus by this time had decided that petrels were pelagic. For on October 3 he believed that they had left astern the islands depicted on his chart. "The Admiral here says that he did not care to delay by beating to windward last week and on those days when they had so many signs of land, although he had information of certain islands in this region, so as not to delay; because his object was to reach the Indies, and if he had delayed, he says, it would not have been good sense." His repetition of this remark is interesting, and not only as additional proof of his oriental objective. Columbus evidently feared that on his return he would be accused of having missed something; and he wished to make it clear to the Sovereigns why he pressed on.

Martín Alonso Pinzón put in a plea for altering the course to SW by W on October 6, when the fleet had passed the 65th meridian of longitude and lay directly north of Puerto Rico. Columbus observed that it seemed to him "that Martín Alonso did not say (that is, mean) this for the island of Japan, and the Admiral saw that if they were going wrong, they would be unable to reach land so soon, and that it was better to go at once to the mainland, and later to the Islands."

This, as to Columbus's route and intentions, is one of the most significant entries in his Journal. It proves by a circumstantial and somewhat involved statement that no faker could possibly have invented, that Columbus's plan was to make due west for Japan. Reading between the lines of the sea journal, one can guess what happened. By dawn October 6 the fleet has sailed so much further than the expected 750 leagues that everyone who has kept a reckoning is asking the question, supposing we have missed Japan? *Pinta* shoots under the flagship's stern, and Martín Alonso shouts something like *sudoeste cuarta del oeste, señor; sudoeste cuarta del oeste . . . Cipango* — "SW by W, sir, SW by W, . . . Japan." His explanation of why he wants this change of course, and the connection of it with Japan, is lost in the sound of rushing waters; but Columbus, who is anxious enough himself, assumes that Martín Alonso believes that they have passed Japan hull-down, and advises a SW by W course in order to reach China. Or, may be the captain of *Pinta* thinks Japan lies SW by W. In any case, Columbus decides that even if they have missed Japan, a due west course will take them to land quicker than a more southerly rhumb, which might miss the southeast cape of China, where Martin Behaim located Zaitun. It would be best to make sure of land first, and visit Japan on the way home.

At sunrise on Sunday, October 7, when the fleet was about 370 miles from the nearest land (Turks Island), came the second false landfall. *Niña*, ranging ahead of her consorts contrary to Columbus's orders, in the hope of winning the reward, broke out a flag at her masthead and fired a gun, the signal for land dead ahead. People aboard the flagship had seen this "land" earlier, but dared not sing out; for the Captain General was so fed up with false landfalls that he gave orders to the effect that anyone who raised another false cry of *tierra* would be disqualified for the reward, even though he should sight the true land later. (By the same token, Columbus should later have disqualified himself!)

By sunset, when they had run 67 miles and no land had materialized, Columbus ordered the course to be changed to WSW (one point more westerly than Martín Alonso had recommended) because great flocks of birds were passing overhead to the southwestward. He remembered that the Portuguese had discovered the outermost Azores by attending to the flight of birds. This judgment was good, for the fall migration of North American birds to the West Indies via Bermuda was in full flight, and Columbus's decision to follow these feathered pilots rather than his inaccurate man-made chart was vital for the whole future of Spanish colonization. For when Columbus determined to follow the birds, his fleet was on latitude 25° 40′ and fast approaching the area of zero compass variation. Had the due west course been maintained from that point, the voyage would have taken at least a day longer, and the landfall, provided Columbus had managed to keep down mutiny another day, would have been Eleuthera Island or Hole-in-the-Wall on Great Abaco. What then? Except for the unlikely contingency of the local Indians piloting Columbus south through Tongue of the Ocean, the fleet would have sailed through Providence Channel slap into the Gulf Stream; and once involved in that mighty current, the caravels could never have made any southing. The fleet would have touched (and perhaps more than touched — gone ashore) on the coast of Florida somewhere between Jupiter Inlet and Cape

Canaveral; and then, provided they survived that ocean graveyard, have been swept along the coast of Georgia and the Carolinas, returning to Spain (if they managed to return) by the westerlies north of Hatteras and Bermuda.

Obviously the results of any such voyage, considering what Columbus was after and what his Sovereigns wanted, would have been highly disappointing to everyone, and it is questionable how soon if ever he would have been allowed to try again. For it was the gold of Hispaniola, and nothing else, that attracted Spaniards to the New World. A great deal was made of this change of course in post-mortems on the voyage, and rightly so; but most of the witnesses attributed it to Pinzón's advice. The Journal shows that the birds of North America deserve the credit.

During the eighth day of October, when " 'Thanks be to God' says the Admiral 'the air is soft as in April in Seville, and it's a pleasure to be in it, so fragrant it is,' " the WSW course was maintained. On the ninth a shift of wind forced them W by N for 43 miles, but on the tenth a fine run of 171 miles was made to the WSW. Moon came full on the fifth, consequently there was no risk of overrunning the land. And all night October 9–10 the men could hear flocks of birds flying overhead to the southwestward, and sometimes could see them against the moon. Martín Alonso Pinzón remarked to his men, "Those birds know their business."

Notwithstanding this encouraging sign, October 10 was the most critical day of the entire voyage, when the enterprise came nearest to failure through the stubborn conservatism of the men. It is unfair to present the issue between Columbus and his crew as one between a brave man and cowards. Nor was it one between knowledge and ignorance, education and superstition: for if Columbus had had a university education, or listened attentively to the best opinions of his day, he would never have expected Japan to lie 750 leagues west of the Canaries. It was, rather, the inevitable conflict between a man of one great, compelling idea and those who did not share it in anything like the same degree. Look back at the events of the voyage, think of the two false landfalls, the innumerable "signs of land" that failed to make good; glance at the fleet's position October 10, on a modern chart with America blotted out,

and reflect that thirty days out, they had doubled all previous records for ocean navigation, that they had long passed the position
where Columbus predicted land would be found, and that the
men knew it; no "phony" reckoning could conceal that fact from
the pilots, who were as keen as any to turn back, and communicated
their fears to the people. So can we fairly blame the men? Their
issue with their commander was the eternal one between imagination and doubt, between the spirit that creates and the spirit that
denies. Oftentimes the doubters are right, for mankind has a hundred foolish notions for every sound one; it is at times of crisis,
when unpredictable forces are dissolving society, that the do-noth-
ings are tragically wrong. There are tides in the affairs of men, and
this was one of them.

And so, on October 10, when the fleet was steering straight for
the Bahamas, and the nearest land was less than 200 miles ahead,
all the smoldering discontent of the men flared up into open
mutiny. They had done enough and more than enough; the ships
should and must turn back. This mutiny, so far as we have any
record, was confined to the flagship, although the crews of *Niña*
and *Pinta* were as eager to return. Aboard *Santa María* there was
a clique of stubborn, know-it-all Basques and Galicians, and to all
her crew the Captain General was a foreigner. What Columbus
noted down (and Las Casas abstracted) is short and to the point,
and not ungenerous to the men: —

"Here the people could stand it no longer, complained of the
long voyage; but the Admiral cheered them as best he could, holding out good hope of the advantages they might have; and he added
that it was useless to complain, since he had come to go to the
Indies, and so had to continue until he found them, with the help
of Our Lord."

Perhaps what the Captain General said was not quite so dramatic;
for it was later stated, as a matter of common report, that he promised the men to turn back if they did not sight land within two or
three days. He would certainly have pointed out that, with a fresh
easterly trade wind and rising sea, the ships could do nothing
anyway on a course for home, and so might as well carry on until
the next soft spot in the weather. In any case, the mutiny was
quelled.

Although we may dismiss as incredible the Pinzón yarn about Columbus being frightened at the gulfweed early in the voyage, we cannot ignore the damaging testimony brought out in the protracted lawsuit of 1514–1536 to the effect that at some time during this second week of October the Admiral either lost confidence or, frightened by the attitude of his men, proposed to turn back; and that the Pinzons dissuaded him.

Although all this testimony was taken down at least twenty-two years after, and some of it forty-four years after the event, illiterate men in simple social surroundings, where they are not continually assailed by newspapers, loud-speakers and the like, have good memories; and the First Voyage of Columbus was one that a man would not readily forget. On the other hand, Martín Alonso was a man with a grievance, and for almost four months (November–March) *Pinta* was sailing alone, or without any communication with the flagship. Pinzón, then, had plenty of time to create a sort of *Pinta* myth of the discovery, and inculcate it among his relatives and other men of Palos aboard his ship.

This testimony was evoked by a leading question propounded by the *fiscal* or crown attorney to picked witnesses in various Andalusian seaports, in 1515: —

"Whether you know that . . . they had run 800 leagues westward from the island of Ferro, and that during this time, 200 leagues before the Admiral sighted land, and when he did not know where to go and thought he would make no discovery, he went aboard the ship of Martín Alonso and asked what he thought they should do, for they had already gone 200 leagues beyond what he expected and should by now have reached land?

"Also whether you know that the said Martín Alonso said, 'Adelante! Adelante! this is a fleet and mission of such great princes as the Sovereigns our lords of Spain, . . . but if you, sir, wish to turn back I am determined to go on until land is found or never return to Spain,' and that because of his efforts and counsel they went forward?"

A number of the witnesses said what was expected of them, and played up to these leading questions, with suitable trimmings. For instance, Francisco García Vallejo, seaman aboard *Pinta*, declared that on October 6, with 800 leagues gone and 200 to go, Columbus held a conference of all the captains, and said, " 'What shall we do, captains; my people are complaining; what, sirs, do you think we should do?' And then said Vicente Yáñez, 'Let's proceed, sir, up to 2000 leagues, and if there we don't find what we set out to find we'll turn back'; and then replied Martín Alonso Pinzón, who was the senior captain, 'Come, sir, when we have scarcely left Palos, your honor is displeased; go forward, sir, for God will give us success in discovering land, for God would not wish us to turn back so shamefully.' Then replied the said Admiral Don Cristóbal Colón, 'Good luck to you,' and so because of Martín Alonso Pinzón they went on. . . ." And Martín Alonso advised him to steer a course SW for land, and Columbus replied "so be it."

The legend of the timid landsman Colombo being bucked up by the hearty seafaring Pinzons improved and enlarged with age as this sixteenth-century case of Jarndyce *v.* Jarndyce dragged on its weary way. In 1536 an octogenarian cousin of the Pinzons who pretended to have been on the voyage (which was not true) declared that seven days before they made land, Columbus called a conference, disclosed the mutinous state of his crew, and asked his captains' advice; and Martín Alonso replied, " 'Sir, let your honor string up half a dozen of 'em or heave 'em overboard, and if you don't dare to, I and my brothers will board you and do it; a fleet like this under the orders of such high princes can't return without good news.' And with this, all cheered up. Don Cristóbal Colón said, 'Martín Alonso, let's fix these fellows and carry on for some days, and if we don't find land we shall consult further what we ought to do.' And so they sailed seven more days. . . ."

On the other hand, the greater part of the witnesses simply gave a formal "yes" to the leading questions, or said *no sé;* and some came out unexpectedly with a very different version. Manuel de Valdovinos, who sailed with Vicente Yáñez Pinzón on his Amazon voyage, heard from him and the other Palenos aboard Vicente's flagship that it was the Pinzón brothers who wanted to turn back. They represented to Columbus, "Sir, where are we going now that we have run 800 leagues and not found land, and these people say that they are going to be lost?" And Columbus replied, "Martín Alonso, do me this favor, to stay with me this day and night, and if I don't bring you to land before day, . . . cut off my head and you

shall return." The Pinzons then gave in, and next morning land
was sighted.

The heirs of Columbus asked just as leading questions in the
hearings held under their auspices. For instance, "Whether it is
known, believed and is public and notorious that . . . many people
and mariners wished to turn back without finding land, saying
that they would be lost?" Neither Columbus nor his heirs (so far
as we have record) accused the Pinzons of being in this cabal,
but Francisco Morales, who had made the Second Voyage on the
Niña under her former master Juan Niño, reported him as having
said that "in mid-ocean or somewhat further, the masters of the
three ships which composed the First Voyage joined forces and proceeded to request the Admiral to return to Castile, because, on
account of the easterly winds prevailing in the ocean, they did not
believe that if they went any further they could return to Spain,
and that the Admiral replied that he cared not for that, for God
who gave them this weather would give them other to return, . . .
and that they would not gain their end, because in killing him and
his servants, who were few, they would not accomplish much,
. . . but that they might do one thing: they might set him a limit
of three or four days and hold to the course they were following
and if they did not sight land within that time, they might turn
back, as they wished; and that with this agreement they went ahead
on their voyage, and within that limit saw land."

The only thing common to all these depositions is that at some
date very close to the landfall a conference of captains was held,
that Columbus (or the Pinzons) wanted to turn back, and that the
Pinzons (or Columbus) agreed to go on a few days more. Now,
it is no easy matter to hold such a conference at sea; impossible to
do so when a high sea is running, and a strong wind blowing.
Unlashing and lowering with crude tackle a heavy boat, and rowing
men from two of the ships and boarding a third, is both difficult
and dangerous. And you cannot hold conversations such as these
deponents describe by bellowing back and forth from ship to ship,
at sufficient distance to avoid collision. If a shipboard conference
occurred shortly before the landfall, it must have been on October 9
when the wind was variable and the fleet made only 58 miles, or

the previous day when they made only 33 miles. It could not possibly have been on October 10, which both Columbus and Oviedo declare to be the day of greatest danger of mutiny, because that day a run of 171 miles was made, and the sea was making up fast. To insist in 1941 on a new interpretation of documents that were known four hundred years ago, and known in their original setting with all the attendant circumstances that enabled some tales to be discounted and others accepted, seems to me highly presumptuous. Yet historians like Fernández Duro, Vignaud, and Carbia have not hesitated to declare that Columbus's Journal is false, that Las Casas and Ferdinand are liars, and the "real truth" is told by pro-Pinzón *pleitos* taken down between sixteen and forty-five years after the event.

Ferdinand's version (and he makes no accusations against the Pinzons, but declares his father handled the mutiny himself) we may perhaps discount as overloyal. There is less reason to do this with Las Casas; but let us pass him over. A really impartial authority on the First Voyage is Fernández de Oviedo, the first official historian of the Indies, who had every temptation to adopt the crown's official theory, but did not; and who knew and talked with Vicente Yáñez Pinzón and Hernán Pérez Mateos, the author of the "throw 'em overboard" story. Oviedo says categorically that by tactful and cheering words Columbus "moved the courage of the weakened minds of those who were about to resort to something shameful, *especially the three brother captains I have mentioned*, and they agreed to do what he commanded and sail three days and no more," within which space of time land was discovered. Oviedo pays his respect to the Pinzón theory in these words: "Some say the contrary of what has been said here of the steadfastness of Columbus, they even declare he would have turned back voluntarily from the course and would not have finished it, if the brothers Pinzón had not made him go forward; and they say more, that because of them the discovery was made, and that Columbus already weakened and wanted to come about. This would be better referred to a long suit between the Admiral and the royal *fiscal*, where many things are alleged pro and con, and in which I do not intervene, for since they are matters of *justicia* and by it are to be determined they should take the course that they will. . . . The reader may take that which his judgment dictates." There is no doubt, then, that Oviedo was well apprised of the Pinzón version, and that he discarded it as false.

Here is what I believe happened. On October 9, when the course was altered to W by N by reason of a southerly shift in the wind, a wind so moderate that the average speed was only a trifle over 2 knots, Martín Alonso and Vicente Yáñez came aboard the flagship, held a more or less stormy conference with Columbus in his cabin, demanded that the search for land be abandoned, and that advantage be taken of the southerly breeze to start home. But Columbus (supported by the birds) succeeded in persuading the brothers to carry on three more days, and they returned to their respective vessels. Then, at sunrise October 10, the trade wind made up fresh, sending the fleet along at a speed of 7 knots, which reawakened the fears of Santa María's crew that they would never be able to return. Hence the flare-up of mutiny that day. Columbus made the same promise to his men that he had to the Pinzons, and by nightfall the last danger of abandoning the Great Enterprise on the brink of success, was over.

All day Thursday, October 11, the trade wind still blew a gale, the sea rose higher than at any time on the voyage, and the fleet ran 78 miles between sunrise and sunset, an average speed of 6.7

knots. But signs of land were so many and so frequent that "everyone breathed more freely and grew cheerful." *Niña* picked up a green branch with a little flower that resembled the dog roses on hedges in Castile. *Pinta* gathered quite a collection: a cane and a stick, a piece of board, a land plant, and "another little stick fashioned, as it appeared, with iron," doubtless carved by an Indian with a stone chisel. These objects must have floated up from the Lesser Antilles or even South America; but they served their purpose of stopping complaints, and preparing every man aboard for a speedy end to this first Atlantic crossing.*

* Summary of the First Voyage Outward: —

	Columbus		McElroy
	leagues	n. miles	n. miles
Distance logged from Ferro September 9 to landfall October 12	1072	3409	3066
Add distance from departure 3 A.M. September 8 to Ferro	18	57	51
Total	1090	3466	3117

Capt. John W. McElroy, chief navigating officer of the Harvard Columbus Expedition, made the detailed study of the navigation of Columbus's First Voyage that appeared in *American Neptune* I (1941) 209-40.

CHAPTER XVI

Landfall

OCTOBER 11–14, 1492

Et potestas eius a mari usque ad mare, et a fluminibus usque ad fines terrae.

And his dominion shall be from sea even to sea, and from the rivers even to the ends of the earth.

— ZECHARIAH ix 10

Sun set under a clear horizon about 5.30, every man in the fleet watching for a silhouette of land against its red disk; but no land was there. All hands were summoned as usual, and after they had said their evening prayers and sung the *Salve Regina* "which all seamen are accustomed to say and sing in their own fashion," Columbus from the sterncastle made his men a little speech, reminding them of the grace Our Lord had shown them in conducting them so safely and prosperously with fair winds and a clear course, and in comforting them with signs of better things to come; and he urged the night watch to keep a particularly sharp lookout on the forecastle, reminding them that although he had given orders to do no night sailing after reaching a point 700 leagues from the Canaries, the great desire of all to see land had decided him to carry on that night. Hence all must make amends for this temerity by keeping a particularly good watch, and looking sharp for land; and to him who first sighted it he would then and there give a silk doublet, in addition to the annuity of 10,000 maravedis that the Sovereigns had promised. The gromet then sang his little ditty for changing the watch and turned the *ampolleta*, boatswain Chachu bellowed out the Castilian equivalent to "Watch below lay belo-o-w!" and the men took their stations with eyes well peeled.

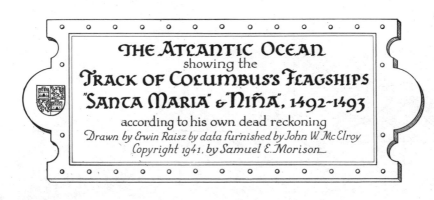

THE ATLANTIC OCEAN
showing the
TRACK OF COLUMBUS'S FLAGSHIPS
"SANTA MARIA" & "NIÑA", 1492-1493
according to his own dead reckoning
Drawn by Erwin Raisz by data furnished by John W. McElroy
Copyright 1941, by Samuel E. Morison

Overleaf

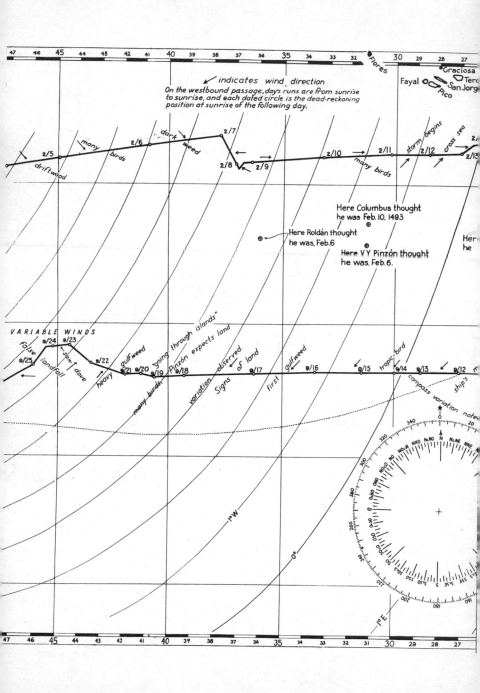

Top scale: 47 46 45 44 43 42 41 40 39 38 37 36 35 34 33 32 · 30 29 28 27

Flores

Graciosa
Fayal · San Jorge · Terc
Pico

← indicates wind direction

On the westbound passage, days runs are from sunrise
to sunrise, and each dated circle is the dead-reckoning
position at sunrise of the following day.

2/5 many birds 2/6 dark weed 2/7 2/8 2/9 2/10 2/11 many birds 2/12 cross sea 2/1
driftwood storm begins 2/1

Here Columbus thought
he was Feb. 10, 1493

Here Roldán thought
he was, Feb. 6

Here VY Pinzón thought
he was. Feb. 6.

Her
he

VARIABLE WINDS

false landfall 9/24 9/23 9/22 gulfweed "going through islands" Pinzón expects land
9/25 storm dove heavy 9/21 9/20 9/19 9/18 variation observed 9/17 first gulfweed 9/16 9/15 tropic bird 9/14 9/13 9/12
many birds Signs of land ship's
compass variation noted

P W

P E

Bottom scale: 47 46 45 44 43 42 41 40 39 38 37 36 35 34 33 32 31 30 29 28 27

Compass rose markings: 340 320 NNW NNO N NxNE NNE ...

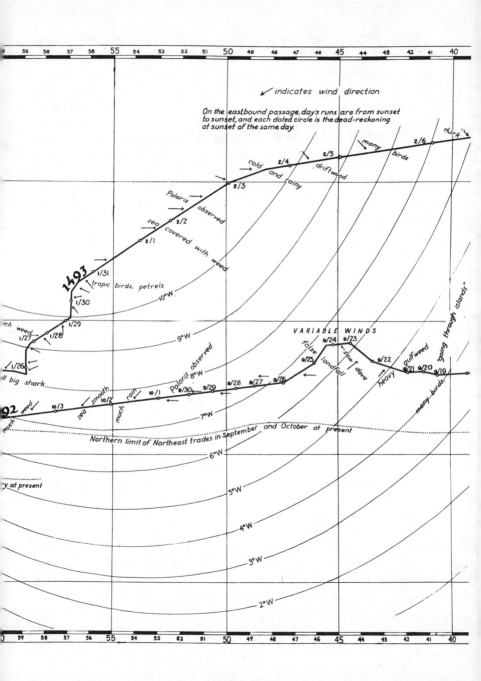

During the eleven and a half hours since sunrise, with a brisk trade wind and the heaviest following sea of the entire voyage, the fleet had made 78 miles, an average of almost 7 knots. At sunset it breezed up to gale force, until the vessels were tearing along at 9 knots. At the same time Columbus ordered the course changed from WSW back to the original West. Why he did this, nobody has explained. I suspect that it was simply a desire to prove that he was right. He had begun the voyage by steering a course due west for Japan, and so he wished to pick up land on a due west course. I have known commanders, good seamen too, who are like that. Or the change may have been just a hunch. If so, it was a good one, for the WSW course would have missed Guanahaní, and put the fleet next day in a dangerous position with the long shelterless shore of Long Island under its lee. Common prudence would have made Columbus heave-to for the night, since shoals and rocks invisible by moonlight might lie ahead. *María's* pilot, Peralonso Niño, is said to have so advised him; but the Captain General felt that this was no time for common prudence. He had promised the men to turn back if land were not made within three days, and he intended to make all possible westing in this gale of wind. So the signal was made for *oeste!*

Anyone who has come onto the land under sail at night from an uncertain position knows how tense the atmosphere aboard ship can be. And this night of October 11–12 was one big with destiny for the human race, the most momentous ever experienced aboard any ship in any sea. Some of the boys doubtless slept, but nobody else. Juan de la Cosa and the Pinzons are pacing the high poops of their respective vessels, frequently calling down to the men at the tiller a testy order — keep her off damn your eyes must I go below and take the stick myself? — pausing at the break to peer under the main course and sweep the western horizon, then resting their eyes by looking up at the stars. Consultation as to whether or not to shorten sail; Martín Alonso perhaps confiding to pilot Cristóbal García that he doesn't like carrying sail this way in a gale of wind with possible shoals ahead, but if that crazy Genoese can carry sail we can carry sail; *Pinta* can stand it better than that Galician tub, and heave-to quicker if anything shows up, and I want one of you men of Palos to win that *albricias,* d'ye see?

Lookouts on the forecastles and in the round-tops talking low to each other — Hear anything? Sounds like breakers to me — nothing but the bow wave you fool — I tell you we won't sight land till Saturday, I dreamt it, and my dreams — you and your dreams, here's a hundred maravedis says we raise it by daylight. . . . They tell each other how they would have conducted the fleet — The Old Man should never have set that spritsail, she'll run her bow under — if he'd asked my advice, and I was making my third voyage when he was playing in the streets of Genoa, I'd have told him. . . . Under such circumstances, with everyone's nerves taut as the weather braces, there was almost certain to be a false alarm of land.

An hour before moonrise, at 10 P.M., it came. Columbus, standing on the sterncastle, thought he saw a light, "so uncertain a thing that he did not wish to declare that it was land," but called Pedro Gutiérrez to have a look, and he thought he saw it too. Rodrigo Sánchez was then appealed to, "but he saw nothing because he was not in a position where he could see anything." One guesses that Rodrigo was fed up with false alarms, and merely stuck his head out of the companionway to remark discouragingly that he didn't see nothing; no, not a thing. The light, Columbus said, "was like a little wax candle rising and falling," and he saw it only once or twice after speaking to Gutiérrez.

At this juncture one of the seamen named Pedro Yzquierdo, a native of Lepe, thought he saw a light and sang out, "*¡Lumbre! ¡Tierra!*" Pedro de Salcedo, Columbus's page-boy, piped up with "It's already been seen by my master," and Columbus, who heard the cry, snubbed the man with, "I saw and spoke of that light, which is on land, some time ago."

What was this feeble light resembling a wax candle rising and falling, which Columbus admits that only a few besides himself ever saw? It cannot have been a fire or other light on San Salvador, or any other island; for, as the real landfall four hours later proves, the fleet at 10 P.M. was at least 35 miles offshore. The 400,000 candlepower light now on San Salvador, 170 feet above sea level, is not visible nearly so far. One writer has advanced the theory that the light was made by Indians torching for fish — why not lighting a cigar? — but Indians do not go fishing in 3000 fathoms

of water 35 miles offshore at night in a gale of wind. The sentimental school of thought would have this light supernatural, sent
by the Almighty to guide and encourage Columbus; but of all
moments in the voyage, this is the one when he least needed encouragement, and he had laid his course straight for the nearest
land. I agree heartily with Admiral Murdock, "the light was due
to the imagination of Columbus, wrought up to a high pitch by
the numerous signs of land encountered that day." Columbus
admitted that only a few even thought they saw it. Anyone who
has had much experience trying to make night landfalls with a
sea running knows how easy it is to be deceived, especially when
you are very anxious to pick up a light. Often two or three shipmates will agree that they see "it," then "it" disappears, and you
realize that it was just another illusion. There is no need to criticize
Columbus's seamanship because he sighted an imaginary light; but
it is not easy to defend the fact that for this false landfall, which
he must have known the next day to have been imaginary, he demanded and obtained the annuity of 10,000 maravedis promised by
the Sovereigns to the man who first sighted land. The best we
can say in extenuation is to point out that glory rather than greed
prompted this act of injustice to a seaman; Columbus could not
bear to think that anyone but himself sighted land first. That form
of male vanity is by no means absent from the seafaring tribe today.

At 2 A.M. October 12 the moon, past full, was riding about 70°
high over Orion on the port quarter, just the position to illuminate
anything ahead of the ships. Jupiter was rising in the east; Saturn
had just set, and Deneb was nearing the western horizon, toward
which all waking eyes were directed. There hung the Square of
Pegasus, and a little higher and to the northward Cassiopeia's Chair.
The Guards of Polaris, at 15° beyond "feet," told the pilots that
it was two hours after midnight. On speed the three ships, *Pinta*
in the lead, their sails silver in the moonlight. A brave trade wind
is blowing and the caravels are rolling, plunging and throwing spray
as they cut down the last invisible barrier between the Old World
and the New. Only a few moments now, and an era that began in
remotest antiquity will end.

Rodrigo de Triana, lookout on *Pinta's* forecastle, sees something like a white sand cliff gleaming in the moonlight on the western horizon, then another, and a dark line of land connecting them. "*¡Tierra! ¡tierra!*" he shouts, and this time land it is.

Martín Alonso Pinzón, after a quick verification, causes a lombard already loaded and primed to be fired as the agreed signal, and shortens sail in order to wait for the flagship. As soon as *Santa María* approached (remembered *Pinta's* steward many years later) Columbus called out, "Señor Martín Alonso, you have found land!" and Pinzón replied, "Sir, my reward is not lost," and Columbus called back, "I give you five thousand maravedis as a present!"

By Columbus's reckoning the land was distant about 6 miles. The fleet had made 65 miles in the eight and a half hours since sunset, an average better than 7½ knots; according to our reckoning they were very near latitude 24° N, longitude 74° 20' W when Rodrigo sang out.

As the fleet was heading straight for a lee shore, Columbus wisely ordered all sail to be lowered except the *papahigo,* which as Las Casas explains was the main course without bonnets; and with the main yard braced sharp and port tacks aboard, *Santa María, Pinta* and *Niña* jogged off-and-on until daylight. When they appeared to be losing the land they wore around to the starboard tack, so the net result was a southerly drift at a safe distance from the breakers, during the remaining two and a half hours of moonlit night. The windward side of the island today is strewn with the wrecks of vessels that neglected this precaution.

This first land of the Western Hemisphere sighted by Columbus, or by any European since the voyages of the Northmen, was the eastern coast of one of the Bahamas now officially named "San Salvador or Watlings Island." Other candidates there have been for this honor: the Grand Turk, Cat Island, Rum Cay, Samana Cay and Mayaguana. But there is no longer any doubt that the island called Guanahaní, which Columbus renamed after Our Lord and Saviour, was the present San Salvador or Watlings. That alone of any island in the Bahamas, Turks or Caicos groups, fits Columbus's description. The position of San Salvador and of no other island fits the course laid down in his Journal, if we work it backward from Cuba.

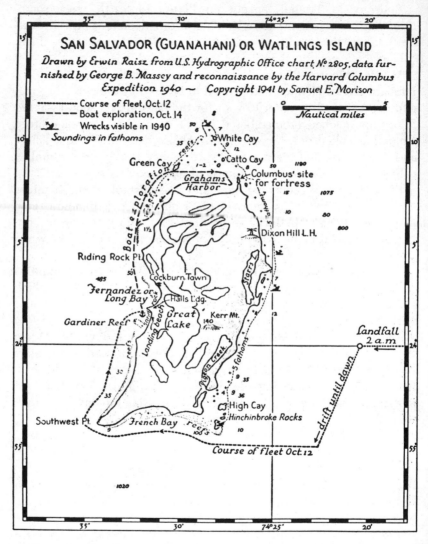

SAN SALVADOR (GUANAHANI) OR WATLINGS ISLAND

Drawn by Erwin Raisz from U.S. Hydrographic Office chart Nº 2805, data furnished by George B. Massey and reconnaissance by the Harvard Columbus Expedition 1940 ~ Copyright 1941 by Samuel E. Morison

```
············ Course of fleet, Oct. 12
────── Boat exploration, Oct. 14                Nautical miles
    Wrecks visible in 1940
Soundings in fathoms
```

San Salvador is a coral island about 13 miles long by 6 wide; the 24th parallel of latitude and the meridian of 74° 30′ West of Greenwich cross near its center. The entire island, except for a space of about 1¾ miles on the west or leeward side, is surrounded by dangerous reefs. By daylight Columbus's fleet must have drifted to a point near the Hinchinbrooke Rocks off the southeastern point. Making sail and filling away, they sought an opening through the reef barrier where they might safely anchor and send boats ashore. And the first gap that they could have discovered, one easy to pick out with a heavy sea running, was on the western shore about 5 miles north of Southwest Point. Here, rounding a prominent breaking ledge now called Gardiner Reef, the caravels braced their yards sharp and entered a shallow bay (Long or Fernandez), protected from winds between N by E around to S by W. Off a curving beach of gleaming coral sand, they found sheltered anchorage in 5 fathoms of water.

Somewhere on this beach of Long or Fernandez Bay took place the famous Landing of Columbus, often depicted by artists, but never with any respect for the actual topography. Las Casas's abstract of the Journal, and Ferdinand Columbus, who had the Journal before him when he wrote the biography of his father, are the unique sources for this incident. Fitting together the two, we have this description: —

Presently they saw naked people, and the Admiral went ashore in the armed ship's boat with the royal standard displayed. So did the captains of *Pinta* and *Niña*, Martín Alonso Pinzón and Vicente Yáñez his brother, in their boats, with the banners of the Expedition, on which were depicted a green cross with an F on one arm and a Y on the other, and over each his or her crown. And, all having rendered thanks to Our Lord kneeling on the ground, embracing it with tears of joy for the immeasurable mercy of having reached it, the Admiral arose and gave this island the name *San Salvador*. Thereupon he summoned to him the two captains, Rodrigo de Escobedo secretary of the armada and Rodrigo Sánchez of Segovia, and all others who came ashore, as witnesses; and in the presence of many natives of that land assembled together, took possession of that island in the name of the Catholic Sovereigns with appropriate words and ceremony. And all this is set forth at large in the testimonies there set down in writing. Forthwith the Christians hailed him as Admiral and Viceroy and swore to obey him as one who represented Their Highnesses, with as much joy and pleasure as if the victory had been all theirs, all begging his pardon for the injuries that through fear and inconstancy they had done him. Many Indians having come together for that ceremony and rejoicing, the Admiral, seeing that they were a gentle and peaceful people and of great simplicity, gave them some little red caps and glass beads which they hung around their necks, and other things of slight worth, which they all valued at the highest price.

At this point Las Casas begins to quote the *palabras formales* (exact words) of the Admiral, as we may now fairly style Columbus. So we may gather, as well as words can convey, the impression made by this branch of the American Indians on the vanguard of the race that would shortly reduce them to slavery, and exterminate them: —

In order that we might win good friendship, because I knew that they were a people who could better be freed and converted to our Holy Faith by love than by force, I gave to some of them red caps and to some glass beads, which they hung on their necks, and many other things of slight value, in which they took much pleasure; they remained so much our friends that it was a marvel; and later they came swimming to the ships' boats in which we were, and brought us parrots and cotton thread in skeins and darts and many other things, and we swopped them for other things that we gave them, such as little glass beads and hawks' bells. Finally they swopped and gave everything they had, with good will; but it appeared to us that these people were very poor in everything. They go quite naked as their mothers bore them; and also the women, although I didn't see more than one really young girl. All that I saw were young men, none of them more than 30 years old, very well made, of very handsome bodies and very good faces; the hair coarse almost as the hair of a horse's tail and short; the hair they wear over their eyebrows, except for a hank behind that they wear long and never cut. Some of them paint themselves black (and they are of the color of the Canary Islanders, neither black nor white), and some paint themselves white, and others red, and others with what they have. Some paint their faces, others the whole body, others the eyes only, others only the nose. They bear no arms, nor know thereof; for I showed them swords and they grasped them by the blade and cut themselves through ignorance; they have no iron. Their darts are a kind of rod without iron, and some have at the end a fish's tooth and others, other things. They are generally fairly tall and good looking, well made. I saw some who had marks of wounds on their bodies, and made signs to them to ask what it was, and they showed me how people of other islands which are near came there and wished to capture them, and they defended themselves. And I believed and now believe that people do come here from the mainland to take them as slaves. They ought to be good servants and of good skill, for I see that they repeat very quickly all that is said to them; and I believe that they would easily be made Christians, because it seemed to me that they belonged to no religion. I, please Our Lord, will carry off six of them at my departure to Your Highnesses, so that they may learn to speak. I saw no beast of any kind except parrots in this island.

Saturday October 13: At daybreak there came to the beach many of these men, all young men as I have said, and all of good stature, very handsome people. Their hair is not kinky but loose and coarse like horsehair; and the whole forehead and head is very broad, more so than any other race that I have seen, and the eyes very handsome and not small, and themselves not at all black, but of the color of the Canary Islanders; nor should anything else be expected, because this is on the same latitude with the island of Ferro in the Canaries. Their legs are very straight, all in a line; and no belly, but very well built. They came to the ship in dugouts which are fashioned like a long boat from the hole of a tree, and all in one piece, and wonderfully made (considering the country), and so big that in some came 40 or 45 men, and others smaller, down to the size that held but a single man. They row with a thing like a baker's peel and go wonderfully [fast], and if they capsize all begin to swim and right it and bail it out with calabashes that they carry. They brought skeins of spun cotton, and parrots and darts and other trifles that would be tedious to describe, and gave all for whatever was given to them.

In his Letter to the Sovereigns, which was promptly printed at Barcelona and widely distributed throughout Europe in a Latin translation, Columbus lays stress on the gentleness and generosity of the natives: —

They are so ingenuous and free with all they have, that no one would believe it who has not seen it; of anything that they possess, if it be asked of them, they never say no; on the contrary, they invite you to share it and show as much love as if their hearts went with it, and they are content with whatever trifle be given them, whether it be a thing of value or of petty worth. I forbade that they be given things so worthless as bits of broken crockery and of green glass and lace-points, although when they could get them, they thought they had the best jewel in the world.

Unfortunately this guilelessness and generosity of the simple savage aroused the worst traits of cupidity and brutality in the average European. Even the Admiral's humanity seems to have been merely political, as a means to eventual enslavement and exploitation. But to the intellectuals of Europe it seemed that Columbus had stepped back several millennia, and encountered people living in the Golden Age, that bright morning of humanity which existed only in the imagination of poets. Columbus's discovery enabled Europeans to see their own ancestors, as it were, in a "state of nature," before Pandora's box was opened. The "virtuous savage" myth, which reached its height in the eighteenth century began at Guanahaní on October 12, 1492. As Peter Martyr, who first gave it currency, wrote of these Indians, and as Richard Eden translated him in 1555: —

And surely if they had receaued owre religion, I wolde thinke their life moste happye of all men, if they might therwith enioye their aunciente libertie. A fewe thinges contente them, hauinge no delite in such superfluites, for the which in other places men take infinite paynes and commit manie vnlawfull actes, and yet are neuer satisfied, whereas many haue to muche, and none inowgh. But emonge these simple sowles, a fewe clothes serue the naked: weightes and measures are not needefull to such as can not skyll of crafte and deceyte and haue not the vse of pestiferous monye, the seede of innumerable myscheues. So that if we shall not be ashamed to confesse the truthe, they seeme to lyue in that goulden worlde of the whiche owlde wryters speake so much: wherin men lyued simplye and innocentlye without inforcement of lawes, without quarrellinge Iudges and libelles, contente onely to satisfie nature, without further vexation for knowlege of thinges to come.

These Indians of the Bahamas, and indeed all whom Columbus encountered on his First Voyage, belonged to the so-called Taino culture of the Arawak language group. Their ancestors had emigrated to the Antilles from the mainland of South America, and within a century of Columbus's voyage had branched out from Haiti, overrunning Cuba, Jamaica, and the Bahamas, pushing back or enslaving an earlier and more primitive tribe known as the Siboney. The Tainos were fairly advanced in civilization, growing corn, yams and other roots, making cassava bread from yucca, spinning and weaving cotton, making a fine brown pottery adorned with grotesque heads, and various ornaments and utensils of shell, living in huts made of a wooden frame and palm thatch. The broad, low forehead that Columbus remarked was due to a process of artificially flattening the skulls of infants, by pressing them between boards.

Columbus's frame of reference, it is interesting to note, was partly African and partly classical. He expected to find kinky-haired blacks such as he had encountered on the coast of Guinea, because Aristotle taught that people and products on the same latitude were similar; but he reflected that being on the same latitude as Ferro — a mistake of 3° 41' — it was not surprising to find them of the same brown color as the Guanches, the primitive inhabitants of the Canaries. The word that he used for their canoes, *almadias,* was what the Portuguese used for the dugouts of West Africa; and the trading goods that he brought, Venetian glass beads, brass rings, red caps, and the small round bronze bells used in falconry, were exactly what the Portuguese had found to be in most demand among the Negroes.

Although the Tainos had driven back the primitive hunter folk, their only weapon, a short spear or dart with a fish-tooth or fire-hardened wooden point, was insufficient to cope with the Caribs, who occasionally raided them from the Caribbee Islands. Much less were they prepared to resist domination by the Spaniards. And it is clear from the concluding sentences of Columbus's Journal for October 12 that on the very day of discovery the dark thought crossed his mind that these people could very easily be enslaved. On October 14 he noted, "These people are very unskilled in arms, . . . with fifty men they could all be subjected and made to do all that one wished." It is sad but significant that the only Indians of the Caribbean who have survived are those who proved both willing and able to defend themselves. The Tainos, whom Columbus found so gentle and handsome and hospitable, are long since extinct.

Guanahaní, the native name of this island, means the *iguana,* a reptile now extinct there. Columbus described it as "very big and very level and the trees very green, and many bodies of water, and a very big lake in the middle, but no mountain, and the whole of it so green that it is a pleasure to gaze upon." The island is honeycombed with salt lagoons, the largest of which is only a few hundred yards from the beach where Columbus landed; and the highest hill on the island is only 140 feet above sea level. Later, after exploring the northern part, Columbus noted groves of trees, the most beautiful he had ever seen, "and as green and leafy as those of Castile in the months of April and May." Visitors to San Salvador and the other Bahamian Islands find Columbus's descriptions of nature extravagant, and are inclined to accuse him of laying it on thick to impress the Sovereigns.

Any land looks good to seamen after a long and perilous voyage and every woman fair; but Columbus's description of the Bahamas was not extravagant for 1492. At that time they were highly fertile and covered with a dense growth of tropical hardwood which the Indians had cleared but slightly to plant gardens. In the late eighteenth century, the English colonists (many of them loyalist refugees from the United States) caused a large part of the forest to be cut down in order to grow sea-island cotton. This exhausted the soil, and hurricanes stripped the island at not infrequent intervals. When cotton culture ceased to pay, the fields were abandoned, and today such parts of the islands as the Negroes do not use for their potato patches and pasturage are covered with a scrubby second growth and ruins of old plantation houses. Large trees for making dugout canoes of the size that Columbus described no longer exist. Near an inland lagoon of San Salvador we were shown a surviving grove of primeval forest which for lushness and beauty merits Columbus's praise, and this grove harbors a variety of tropical woodpecker that must once have had a wider forest range. Skeletal remains of other birds which could only have lived among dense foliage have been discovered on the island by naturalists.

All day Saturday, October 13, the caravels lay at anchor in Long Bay with a swarm of canoes passing back and forth, while the Spaniards in turn took shore leave, wandered into the natives' huts, did a little private trading for the curios that all seamen love, and doubtless ascertained that the girls of Guanahaní were much like others they had known. Columbus, who ever had an eye for "improvements," reported that he found "a quarry of stones naturally shaped, very fair for church edifices or other public uses." Three centuries elapsed before anyone thought to build a church at San Salvador, and then it was found easier to fashion the soft coral rock into rectangular blocks; the outcrop that Columbus saw at Hall's Landing just north of his landing place, partly under water and curiously split into squares like flagstones, is still unquarried.

The Admiral was busy gathering such information as he could from signs and gestures; his Arabic interpreter was of no use in this neck of the Indies. On Saturday night he decided that no time must be lost, he must press on to Japan. But first San Salvador must be explored. On Sunday morning the three ships' boats took the Admiral north along the leeward coast "to see the other side, which was the eastern side, what was there, and also to see the villages; and soon I saw two or three, and the people all came to the beach, shouting and giving thanks to God. Some brought us water; others, things to eat. Others, when they saw that I did not care to go ashore, plunged into the sea swimming and came aboard, and we understood that they asked us if we had come from Heaven. And one old man got into the boat, and others shouted in loud voices to all, men and women, 'Come and see the men who come from Heaven, bring them food and drink.' Many came and many women, each with something, giving thanks to God, throwing themselves flat and raising their hands to Heaven, and then shouting to us to come ashore; but I was afraid to, from seeing a great reef of rocks which surrounded the whole of this island, but inside it was deep and a harbor to hold all the ships in Christendom, and the entrance of it very narrow."

This was the place now known as Grahams Harbor, formed by the reefs that surround the island coming together in an inverted V. At three or four places the reefs rise high enough to form cays, and beside one of these on the western side, Green Cay, is a good boat channel with 7 feet of water. Here, rather than the alternate High Reef channel, which is difficult for a stranger to find, was probably where the boats entered. "Inside there are some shoal spots," Columbus correctly observed, "but the sea moves no more than within a well." The smooth water inside these coral-reef harbors is always a pleasant surprise to mariners.

Glenn Stewart's yacht lay quietly and safely in Grahams Harbor during a heavy norther in January 1930.

Columbus's boats rowed across the harbor, about two miles to the eastward, where they found a rocky peninsula that thrusts out from the northern side of San Salvador, half of it almost an island, and "which in two days could be made an island," suitable for a fortress. Since Columbus's visit the sea has here broken a narrow channel that one can wade across at low water. Someone, probably the English, took up Columbus's suggestion that the place was a natural fortress, for Dr. Cronau found an iron cannon there in 1891. After inspecting the harbor the boats returned to the vessels at their anchorage in Long Bay, a row of some twenty miles going and coming; and in the early afternoon the fleet made sail for Cipangu.

So ended forty-eight hours of the most wonderful experience that perhaps any seamen have ever had. Other discoveries there have been more spectacular than that of this small, flat sandy island that rides out ahead of the American continent, breasting the trade winds. But it was there that the Ocean for the first time "loosed the chains of things" as Seneca had prophesied, gave up the secret that had baffled Europeans since they began to inquire what lay beyond the western horizon's rim. Stranger people than the gentle Tainos, more exotic plants than the green verdure of Guanahaní have been discovered, even by the Portuguese before Columbus; but the discovery of Africa was but an unfolding of a continent already glimpsed, whilst San Salvador, rising from the sea at the end of a thirty-three-day westward sail, was a clean break with past experience. Every tree, every plant that the Spaniards saw was strange to them, and the natives were not only strange but completely unexpected, speaking an unknown tongue and resembling no race of which even the most educated of the explorers had read in the tales of travelers from Herodotus to Marco Polo. Never again may mortal men hope to recapture the amazement, the wonder, the delight of those October days in 1492 when the New World gracefully yielded her virginity to the conquering Castilians.

CHAPTER XVII

The Quest for Japan

Rex insule palacium magnum habet auro optimo supra-
tectum sicut apud nos ecclesie operiuntur plumbo. Fenestre
ipsius palacij omnes auro ornate sunt; pauimentum aularum
atque camerarum multarum aureis tabulis est coopertum,
que quidem auree tabule duorum digitorum mensuram
in grossitudine pertinent. Ibi sunt margarite in copia
maxima. . . .

The king of the Island [Japan] hath a mighty palace
all roofed with finest gold, just as our churches are roofed
with lead. The windows of that palace are all decorated
with gold; the floors of the halls and of many chambers are
paved with golden plates, each plate a good two fingers
thick. There are pearls in the greatest abundance. . . .
— COLUMBUS'S OWN COPY OF *Marco Polo* fol. 57

W AS this island really of the Indies? That must have been the
first question Columbus asked himself on reaching Guanahaní, and the last question that he asked himself about all his discoveries, when sailing for home. Or was it but an island in the
Atlantic like Antillia? One may say that all the Admiral's voyaging
for the next six years was a search for evidence that would enable
him to answer that second, teasing question with a thumping "No!"
San Salvador must be of the Indies, for it was where the Indies
should be; and the definite clue that fairly shouted "Indies!" at
every man in the fleet was gold. Not much of it to be sure, only
little pieces of gold "hanging from a thing like a needle-case which
they wear in the nose," but certainly gold, and so of the Indies. —
Do you not remember, my Lord Admiral, that the Portuguese who
reported Antillia to Prince Henry brought back gold? — Ah no, this
cannot be Antillia, it is too far away, and the people are not Portu-

guese; it must not be Antillia. — Yet this Guanahaní cannot be Japan, great golden Cipangu, inhabited by white and civilized people, Cipangu of the royal palaces roofed, paved, and pierced with gold? — Granted, but who said that Cipangu was the only island in the Indies?

On two world maps of the fifteenth century that show Cipangu, the Genoese of 1457 and the Behaim Globe of 1492, it lies (for so Marco Polo had reported) some 1500 miles off the coast of China. North of it is an archipelago of islands large and small. Columbus wished to believe and did believe that he had reached the edge of this archipelago, through which his fleet might sail in a southwesterly direction to strike Cipangu; if Japan were missed, they must fetch up on the coast of China. It was clear that the little gold ornaments displayed by the natives of Guanahaní came from somewhere else. The names *Cipangu, Cathay, Gran Can* rang no bell in the simple minds of the savages, eager as they were to please; but by signs they gave the Admiral to understand that other islands, perhaps a continent, lay all around the horizon arc between northwest and south. Somewhere in that direction must be Cipangu. So Columbus concluded his Journal for October 13, "I intend to go and see if I can find the Island of Japan." All the rest of his First Voyage was, in fact, a search for gold and Cipangu, Cathay and the Grand Khan; but gold in any event. In all else he might fail, but gold he must bring home in order to prove *la empresa* a success.

So it was in quest of Japan that the fleet sailed SW from San Salvador on the afternoon of October 14. Columbus was a bit puzzled what course to take, for the six Indians whom he had detained as guides and future interpreters swept their arms in a wide arc around the western and southern horizon, "and called by their names more than a hundred" islands. Southwest was evidently the average course that Columbus selected from these swivel-like indications. Under easy sail the fleet jogged along before a moderate trade. In the later afternoon, when about 15 miles from San Salvador, they sighted what appeared to be a string of six islands, and the Admiral gave orders to steer for the biggest. As they approached nearer, the six parts seemed to join, for they were all hillocks of a single island. Unable to reach this six-in-one island before dark, the fleet lay-to that night, filled away at dawn, and at noon made land. Columbus named this second island of his discovery *Santa María de la Concepción* after a doctrine to which he was devoted, the Immaculate Conception of the Virgin. The modern name is Rum Cay.

Columbus describes this island as ten leagues long and five leagues wide. This is the first instance of what we shall find numerous examples of his using, when sailing alongshore, a different league from the sea league of 3.18 nautical miles. Whenever Columbus estimated distances run at sea, he was usually accurate within 10 per cent. But when he was estimating the length of a coastline, he used, consciously or unconsciously, a league of about 1½ nautical miles.

Monday, October 15, must have been an unusually clear day since from off the southeast point of Rum Cay Columbus "saw another bigger one to the west." That was Long Island, distant 22 miles. Columbus coasted along the south shore of Rum Cay, and about sunset anchored under Sandy Point, at the southwest end. It certainly did not look much like Cipangu; but as Columbus had gathered from his unwilling guides that the people ashore sported heavy gold armlets and anklets, the island had to be investigated. On Tuesday morning at daybreak the Admiral went ashore with the boats, and ascertainted that the natives were numerous, naked, and in all respects like those of San Salvador. They "let us go over the island and gave us what we asked for." Gold armlets and anklets there were none; that story was evidently "all humbug"; the San Salvadoreans merely wished him to anchor at Rum Cay "in order to escape." One of them had swum ashore the previous night; and while the Admiral was ashore another Guanahaní boy jumped into a Rum Cay canoe that came alongside. Her crew paddled away much too fast for the Spaniards to catch them in their heavy ship's boat. The pursuit continued ashore, but "they all ran away like chickens" says Columbus. While this exciting chase was under way, a small canoe from another cape of the island came alongside *Niña*, with a single native who wished to sell a skein of cotton. The sailors seized him as a substitute for the escaped Salvadorean; but the Admiral, observing this from the poop of *Santa María*, ordered him to be brought aboard the flag-

ship, presented him with the standard red cap, glass beads and
hawks' bells, and sent him ashore happy. "For this reason I used
him thus," wrote Columbus, "in order that they might hold us in
such esteem that on another occasion when your Highnesses send
men back here again, they [the natives] may not make bad company." Unfortunately the Admiral's kindly acts to the Indians
only rendered them less prepared to cope with the kidnapers who
followed him. The next Spaniard that came to these parts was
Alonso de Hojeda on a slaving raid.

These alarums and excursions came fairly early in the morning of October 16. The Indian guides, in no wise discomfited because their previous information was incorrect, now cheerfully
assured Columbus that in the island already sighted to the westward "there is a lot of gold, and they wear it in the form of
bracelets on the arms, legs, ears, nose and neck." In the forenoon
the wind shifted to the SE and veered southerly, making the Rum
Cay anchorage untenable, so Columbus ordered anchors aweigh.
All day the fleet ghosted westward in light southerly airs. In mid-
channel the flagship picked up a native in a single canoe, who evidently came from San Salvador, as he had a string of glass beads
and two small coins in a native basket; he also carried "a lump of
bright red earth powdered and then kneaded," doubtless body
paint, "and some dry leaves which must be something much valued
by them, since they offered me some at San Salvador as a gift."
Tobacco leaves, almost certainly; but the Spaniards did not observe
anyone smoking until they reached Cuba. This native was fed
and given a free ride to the next island, where he was released.

Columbus named this island *Fernandina* after the King of Castile
and Aragon. That regal derivative has long since disappeared in
favor of the common appellation Long Island, which fits this island
better than most of that name, for it is 60 miles long and in no place
more than 4 miles wide. Columbus reported Fernandina to be
"very level, without any mountains like those of San Salvador and
Santa María"; but to us, approaching it from the same angle, it
presented the same appearance of a disconnected chain of small,
hilly islands. The Admiral accurately described the windward
shore as "all beach without boulders" except for "some rocks under
water near the shore, for which you must keep your eyes peeled

when you wish to anchor, and not anchor very near the shore, although the water is always very clear and you see the bottom . . . for here it is necessary to take great care in order not to lose the anchors." Columbus was making the acquaintance of that bane of Bahamian navigators, the pinnacle of coral rock that rises unexpectedly from a clean bottom. These "nigger heads" shear off any anchor cable that fouls them, and punch holes in any wooden vessel so unfortunate as to run upon them. "And among all these islands," he justly adds, "at a distance of two lombard shots* off shore there is so much depth that you can't find bottom." His dipsey lead line, as we have seen, measured 100 fathoms, but the windward shore of Long Island drops off so sharply that the hydrographers have not bothered to sound along it, and the channel between Long Island and Rum Cay runs to 1400 fathoms, over a mile and a half deep.

Off a village somewhere near the present Burnt Ground the fleet closed with the Long Island shore, but was unable to come to an anchorage by daylight, and lay-to for the night. Columbus sent ashore the wayfarer, who gave Long Island natives such a good account of these "men from Heaven" that a fleet of canoes at once came out with "water and what they had." Water is an article of value in the Bahamas because there is not a single river or stream in the entire archipelago — not even Ponce de León's fountain of youth; fresh water can only be had by collecting rain water or digging wells. The volunteer water carriers were given beads, brass tambourine jingles and lace points (the metal tips of the laces then used instead of buttons on men's clothing); and those who came aboard were treated to molasses. It is difficult now to imagine that there ever was a time when molasses was a curiosity in the West Indies; but many years elapsed before the Spaniards brought the sugar cane from Africa, and the only sweetening that the Tainos had was wild honey.

At nine the next morning (October 17) the flagship's boat was sent ashore for water, and the natives led the seamen to the wells and obligingly carried the full casks to the boats. These helpful acts on the part of the Indians, which occurred in most places where the

---

* Comparing Columbus's frequent measurements by lombard shots, the distance that his larger cannon could fire, this unit seems to have varied between 500 and 1000 yards.

Spaniards landed, were unfortunate for the Indians. Columbus himself remarked before the end of the voyage, "Nothing was lacking but to know the language and to give them orders, because every order that was given to them they would obey without opposition." Every man in the fleet from servant boy to Admiral was convinced that no Christian need do a hand's turn of work in the Indies; and before them opened the delightful vision of growing rich by exploiting the labor of docile natives.

Columbus noted the absence on Long Island of sheep, goats, or any animal life except birds; and the absence of mammals is one of the features of West Indian fauna. He viewed for the first time a patch of Indian corn, which he supposed to be a kind of panic grass; and marveled at the brightly colored fishes that swam about the flagship, easily visible in the clear water. He observed that the natives wore short cloaks of woven cotton, and that unlike those of San Salvador, they had some idea of driving a bargain. Perhaps the released canoeman had given them the tip that "men from Heaven" were more cheerful receivers than givers. The anticipated gold armlets and anklets did not appear. They were always at the next island.

As a result of his shore visit, Columbus reported an extraordinary sort of tree that had "branches of different kinds, all on one trunk, and one twig is of one kind and another of another, and so unlike that it is the greatest wonder in the world. . . . For instance, one branch has leaves like a cane, other like mastic; and thus on one tree five or six kinds, and all so different." Of course no plant even approaches this polymorphy; Columbus must have observed a tree full of the different parasites that are common in the West Indies. Apart from this tall story, his reports of natural phenomena are objective and accurate. And that they were so is to be commended; for Marco Polo, Sir John Mandeville and their imitators had made Europeans expect any traveler returning from unknown parts to report marvels and monsters, such as fish growing on trees, tailed men, and headless people with eyes in their bellies. Columbus knew perfectly well what was expected, indeed hoped to see such things; but he invented nothing, and only rarely was tempted to twist or exaggerate a bit in order to satisfy his Sovereigns' thirst for the marvelous.

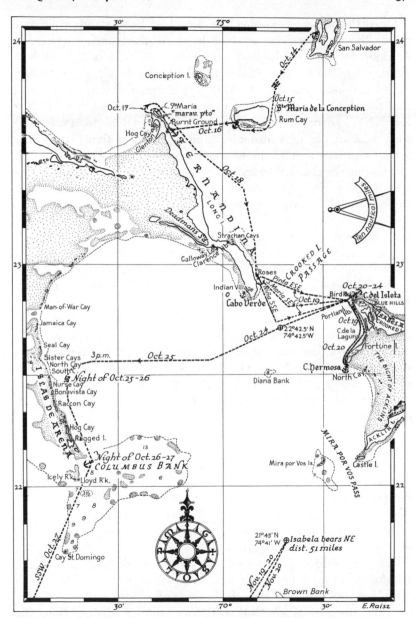

COURSE OF COLUMBUS'S FLEET THROUGH THE BAHAMAS

Since the previous evening the fleet had been standing off-and-on, as the lee shore was so steep-to as to make anchoring unsafe. At noon October 17 the fleet got under way with a light offshore wind, intending to steer SE for Crooked Island, which the Indians called *Saomete*. But Martín Alonso boarded the flagship insisting that the shortest way to Saomete was to sail around Long Island to the NNW, so one of the captives had given him to understand. Very bad advice, or a misunderstanding, since nothing larger than a boat can pass around the leeward side of Long Island. Nevertheless Columbus decided to try it, as the wind was fair for this course and foul for the other. "And when I was distant from the island cape [Cape St. Maria] 2 leagues, I discovered a very wonderful harbor with . . . two mouths, for it has an islet in the middle, and both are very narrow, and within it is wide enough for a hundred ships, if it were deep" — which unfortunately it was not. But "there seemed good reason to look it over well and take soundings, so I anchored outside and went in with all the ships' boats, and saw that there was no depth."

This *maravilloso puerto* is not shown on modern charts, but is easily identified by those who have sailed there. It is a harbor with two entrances, one each side of an island called Newtor Cay, and with a maximum depth of about a fathom. Columbus rather stupidly assumed this shallow harbor to be the mouth of a great river, and sent the boats within for more water, which they obtained at a village well.

The watering party visited in several natives' houses, and reported that "their beds and furnishings were like nets of cotton." "These," comments Las Casas, "are here in Hispaniola called *hamacas,* which are in the form of slings, not woven like nets with the threads going zigzag, but the lengthwise threads are so loose that you can insert the hand and fingers, and at a hand's breadth more or less they are crossed with other close-woven threads like well made lace-trimmings, in the manner of the sieves which in Seville are made of esparto-grass. These hammocks are a good *estado** in fullness or length, and the two ends are finished off in many loops of the same threads, in each of which are inserted some delicate threads of another substance stouter than cotton, like

* Five and a half feet.

hemp; and each of these is a fathom long. And at the head all these loops are joined together as in a sword hilt, which at each end is attached to the posts of the houses, and thus the hammocks are off the ground and swing in the air; and as the good ones are three and four *varas** and more in width one opens them when they swing as we should open a very big sling, putting oneself in diagonally as in an angle; and thus there is the rest of the hammock with which to cover oneself, and that is sufficient because it is never cold. It is very restful to sleep in."

Every successive navigator in the West Indies noted and admired the hammock. The Spaniards, first to experience its convenience in a hot climate, were the first to introduce it aboard ship; the hammock is just going out in the United States navy. Big family hammocks woven in several colors as Las Casas describes are still used by the natives of Yucatán and elsewhere in Central America.

While the watering party was away Columbus wandered about the shores of this marvelous harbor (which no Spaniard to our knowledge ever revisited) and made some observations of his own. The native dwellings he compared in shape to Moorish tents "very high and with good chimneys," these being a sort of open cupola to let the smoke out. His men reported them to be "very simple and clean inside," a reflection of the contrary quality in Castilian hovels. The natives were much the same as those already encountered; "the married women wore clouts of cotton, the wenches nothing." They kept pet dogs — the barkless kind, of which more anon — and one man wore a big gold nose-plug which Columbus was eager to possess because it seemed to have letters which he suspected to be the inscription on a Japanese or Chinese coin. But the fellow would not part with it, and Columbus was too scrupulous to take it by force. The vegetation of Fernandina aroused the Admiral's enthusiasm; he assured the Sovereigns that it was "the best and most fertile and temperate and level and goodly land that there is in the world." Poor Long Island! Nobody has praised you like that since 1492; most of your visitors nowadays are glad to leave your shallow harbors, arid soil, impoverished pastures and scrubby vegetation.

* Eight to eleven feet.

"After taking on water," says Columbus, "I returned to the ship and made sail, and sailed to the NW until I had explored all that part of the island along the coast which runs east-west." In other words, he rounded the Aeolian limestone cliffs of Cape St. Maria, and sailed far enough to see the coast of Long Island falling away to the southwestward. The wind now veered to WNW, and the fickle or misunderstood Indian guides now insisted that the shortest route to Saomete lay in the contrary direction, which was correct. So the fleet came about at nightfall, and all that night, an oppressive and rainy one, steered E, ESE and SE in order to keep clear of the land. "There was little wind, and it did not permit me to approach the land to anchor." "And all these days since I've been in the Indies it has rained more or less," says the Admiral. This little sentence is significant on two counts. It is the first place in his Journal since the landfall that Columbus uses the term "Indies" for the Bahamas; and it is the first meteorological report of the New World. The rainy season had set in.

Daybreak October 18 found the fleet "at the SE cape of the island, where I hope to anchor until it clears off, to see the other islands to which I have to go." By the southeast cape he must have meant the southerly third of Long Island, from the Strachan Cays onward. "After it cleared up I followed the wind and went around the island as far as I could, and anchored in weather such that I could no longer sail; but I did not go ashore." This anchorage must have been off or very near the village of Roses.

At daybreak on the nineteenth, about 5 A.M., Columbus ordered the anchors broken out, and dispatched his fleet fanwise in search of Saomete: *Pinta* to the ESE, *Niña* to the SSE, and *Santa María* between them to the SE. The caravels had orders to proceed on their respective courses until noon, when they should converge on the flagship, unless land were sighted earlier. Wind came fresh out of the north. At about 8 A.M. *Pinta,* having made 14 or 15 miles from the Long Island anchorage, sighted the Blue Hills of Crooked Island (elevation 200 feet) bearing about E by S, distant 20 miles. *Santa María* was about 5 miles to leeward, and *Niña* as far again; but Columbus had a system of signaling by gunfire, so they were able to communicate. All three altered course for Saomete, which Columbus named *Isabela* after his royal patroness. Before noon the fleet made rendezvous off the islet now called Bird Rock, and which now supports a high and powerful lighthouse to guide vessels through Crooked Island Passage.

This passage, which Columbus had just crossed, is now one of the world's most frequented waterways, through which steamers from North Atlantic ports of the United States pass on their way to Eastern Cuba, Southern Hispaniola, Jamaica, and the mainland from Costa Rica to Venezuela. While we in the *Mary Otis* were hove-to in the passage on the night of June 10–11, 1940, within the orbit of Bird Rock Light's split-second flash (for we failed to time our departure as Columbus did), the running lights of steamers kept our watch on the alert. But we shared one delight with the men of 1492. The wind that night was offshore, and "there came so fair and sweet a smell of flowers or trees from the land, that it was the sweetest thing in the world," as Columbus observed.

Santa María and *Pinta* paused off Bird Rock only long enough for *Niña* to catch up; fortunately the wind held north, so she was able to fetch. The fleet then squared their yards and coasted along the curve of Crooked and Fortune Islands, a distance of about 18 miles, to the southern point of Fortune, which to Columbus seemed so exceptionally beautiful that he named it Cabo Hermoso. "And it is indeed handsome," says the Admiral, "round and low-lying, with no shoals offshore . . . and here I anchored this night Friday until morning." The south end of Fortune Island is bold, and the anchorage there is still recommended for its excellent holding ground — it is amazing how often Columbus found the best anchorages. But nobody would call that end of Fortune Island *hermoso* today. Low cliffs of dark, weathered Aeolian limestone, which is far from a beautiful rock, interspersed with a few small sand beaches, support a plateau that is covered with scrubby trees and bushes. The hill on Fortune Island, which Columbus praised as "a thing that beautifies the rest — not that it can be called a mountain," is green and shapely; but both island and cape must have been covered with an exceptionally fine growth of tropical hardwood in 1492 to have aroused such enthusiasm on the part of Columbus. Fortune Island "is the most beautiful thing that I have seen," he wrote, "nor can I tire my eyes looking at such handsome verdure, so very different from ours. And I believe that there are in it many plants and many trees which are worth a lot in Spain for dyes, and for medicines of spicery; but I do not recognize them, which gives me great grief." Columbus often wished that he had shipped a botanist instead of a Hebrew interpreter on this voyage. But his guess about the dye wood was correct. The Bahamas were once rich in logwood; a shipload of it from Eleuthera in 1641 paid for a house and lot in the Harvard College Yard.

From his anchorage off the south cape of Fortune Island (which he did not name although he noted that it was separated from Crooked Island) Columbus looked into the great protected sound now known as the Bight of Acklins, but could find no channel to enter. The Bight is very shoal. So at sunrise on Saturday, October 20, the fleet weighed and proceeded to the anchorage (still recommended in official Sailing Directions) off the gap between Crooked and Fortune Islands. Columbus hoped to enter the Bight of Acklins at this point, which he named *Cabo de la Laguna,* and to proceed across the lagoon to Acklin Island, where his pressed guides said he would find the king who owned so many golden vessels. But there was even less water here than at Cabo Hermoso, so the Admiral decided to try and sail around Crooked Island by its outer coast. Before dark the fleet put to sea again. The wind flattened out, and *Santa María* lay-to that night; the caravels misunderstood the Admiral's signals and anchored close to the shore. Sunday morning the twenty-first at 10 o'clock the whole fleet arrived at the Cape of the Islet, as Columbus named the northwestern cape of Crooked Island, and anchored in Portland Harbor, the small and well-protected anchorage between the cape and Bird Rock. Wind had veered to the eastward, so there was no use trying to proceed further in that direction.

Here the Admiral and his captains made a shore excursion. They saw marvelous verdure, grass like springtime in Andalusia, air full of birdsong, flocks of parrots that "obscured the sun," and a great salt lagoon, on the edge of which they hunted and killed a large iguana. The only plant that Columbus thought he recognized was aloes; but as aloes was not introduced into America until the following century he must have seen one of the agaves, such as the Bahama Century Plant. All natives fled from the only village that the explorers encountered. One native, bolder than the rest, approached to receive the usual handout of beads and bells, and then showed the Christians where to fill their ever-empty water casks.

After a good day's work this Sunday, Columbus sat down and wrote exactly what he intended to do next.

"I here propose to leave to circumnavigate this island until I may have speech with this king and see if I can obtain from him the gold that I heard he has, and afterwards to depart for another much larger island which I believe must be Japan according to the descriptions of these Indians whom I carry, and which they call *Colba,* in which they say that there are ships and sailors both many and great; and beyond this is another island which they call *Bofio,* which also they say is very big; and the others which are between we shall see as we pass, and according as I shall find a collection of gold or spicery, I shall decide what I have to do. But in any case I am determined to go to the mainland and to the city of Quinsay, and to present your Highnesses' letters to the Grand Khan, and to beg a reply and come home with it."

It is clear that by now the captive guides had grasped that gold was what the men from Heaven were after. Very likely their former false directions had been due to a misunderstanding. Having observed the Christians taking specimens of plants and going over everything in the native houses in search of gold, the simple savages perhaps thought that they were collecting leaves, earthenware and hammocks, of which there were plenty everywhere. Now the Indians decided to take their inexplicable captors to "Colba" (Cuba) by the regular canoe route; and from Cuba they could visit Haiti, where there really was gold, plenty of it. The word *bofío* or *bohío,* which Columbus later identified with Haiti, was really, as Las Casas explains, the Arawak word for "house" or "home"; the palm-thatched huts of the peasantry are still called *bohíos* in Cuba. Columbus's guide-interpreters were either trying to say that in Haiti there were big *bohíos,* or were endeavoring to convey the idea that Haiti was their mother country. Columbus, from their gestures and misunderstood phrases, believed Colba to be Japan, and Bohío to be another big island unknown to Marco Polo. He proposed, after visiting them both, to go on to Quinsay (Hangchow), the "City of Heaven" that Marco Polo described in such glowing terms that for Europe it had become a symbol of the fabulous wealth of the Indies. Quinsay, located on Martin Behaim's Globe just around the corner from Zaitun, would be easy to hit if the fleet missed Cipangu. Unfortunately they had wested only 56° of longitude since leaving Ferro, and had 186° to go before making Quinsay, with America between.

Having decided on this course, Columbus made no attempt to buck the trades and circumnavigate the Crooked-Acklin group. The fleet lay in Portland Harbor over Sunday and Monday, October 21 and 22, "waiting to see if the king here or other people would bring gold or anything substantial." A crowd of natives paddled out, and a few gold nose-plugs were swopped for a hawk's bell or a handful of beads; "but there's so little that it amounts to nothing at all," wrote Columbus. Martín Alonso killed another big iguana, and the men cut a load of useless agave under the impression that it was valuable lignum aloes.

Columbus was ready to sail Tuesday the twenty-third, but there was a dead calm with rain. At midnight a breeze sprang up, and "I weighed anchors from the island of Isabela, Cape of the Islet, which is on the northern side where I was lying, to go to the island of Cuba, which I heard from this people is of very great extent and trade, and has gold, spices, big ships and merchants, and they showed me that to the WSW would lead to it. And to my course I held, for I believe that . . . it is the island of Japan, of which are related marvellous things; and on the globes that I saw,* and in the delineations on the world-map it is in this region. And so I sailed until day to the WSW."

It was now October 24, and again he was crossing Crooked Island Passage. At daybreak the wind dropped flat, and only revived at noon, very feebly. As *Santa María* in a light breeze was at a disadvantage compared with the caravels, Columbus like a true seaman set every sail he had: main course with two bonnets, maintopsail, fore course, spritsail under the bowsprit, lateen mizzen, and even a bonaventure mizzen on the poop, contrived out of the boat's mast and sail. But by nightfall, when Columbus reported "Cabo Verde of the island of Fernandina, which is at the

---

* An interesting admission that Columbus had seen a globe which must have resembled Martin Behaim's.

western point of the southern end," bearing NW distant 7 leagues, the fleet had made only 21 miles from Bird Rock.

Columbus then signaled the fleet to strike all sail except the fore courses; and later, when the wind freshened, stripped down to bare poles. He explained for the Sovereigns' benefit what all good seamen knew, that it would have been imprudent to carry sail at night "because all these islands are very steep-to, with no bottom around them except within two lombard shots, and this all patchy, a bit of rock and another of sand, for which reason it is not possible to anchor safely except by eyesight." The hunters' moon was only four days old, affording little light and setting early. That night "we did not make two leagues," he says.

At sunrise October 25 the fleet made sail and resumed the WSW course. At 9 A.M., presumably on the advice of his Indian guides who were anxious to pick up the line of cays that marked their canoe route to Cuba, the Admiral changed course to West. The trade wind blew fresh that day, so that at 3 P.M., after logging 32 miles, "they sighted land, and there were seven or eight islands strung out north to south." These were the line of cays (Seal, Sister, North, South, Nurse) that mark the eastern edge of the Great Bahama Bank. Columbus named them *Las Islas de Arena,* the Sandy Isles, which is just what they are. Approaching the nearest, he either hove-to or jogged along during the night, and on the twenty-sixth sailed slowly along the line of islands until he found himself in shoal water to the southward of the last of them, Little Ragged Island. At this point the Great Bahama Bank makes a fluke-like salient to the south and east, which has appropriately been named Columbus Bank after the Discoverer. It was now the afternoon of Friday, October 26. The Indians aboard said that from there to Cuba was a journey of a day and a half in their canoes; Columbus figured that his fleet could do it in less, but as he wished to cross the bank in daylight he decided to anchor there and make a fresh start at sunrise. "Departed thence for Cuba," reads the Journal, "because from the signs that the Indians made of its greatness and of its gold and pearls, he thought it was Japan."

If this seems a peculiar course to take for Cuba, the explanation came to us readily enough when we followed it in the *Mary Otis.*

Columbus was in the hands of his pressed Indian guides, who only knew the way from cay to cay, making the shortest possible jump over blue water. At sunrise on Saturday, October 27, the Admiral, following their pointed arms, set the course SSW. By eight o'clock the trade wind freshened, and the fleet fairly tore over Columbus Bank for 16 or 17 miles at 6 knots, leaving Icely and Lloyd's rocks close aboard and passing into deep water by Santo Domingo Cay, most southerly outpost of the Bahamas, a scant 30 miles from the Cuban coast. The wind moderated in the afternoon, and the Admiral was just able to sight the Cuban mountains by nightfall.

That night he jogged off-and-on, taking short tacks to windward in order to hold his position and avoid possible shoals. At sunrise on Sunday the twenty-eighth the fleet resumed the SSW course, which took them "into a river very beautiful and without danger of shoals or other impediments, and the whole coast that he came upon in that direction was very steep-to and clear up to the shore. The mouth of the river has 12 fathoms, and is wide enough to beat in. He anchored inside."

"The Admiral says that he never beheld so fair a thing; trees all along the river, beautiful and green and different from ours, with flowers and fruits each according to their kind, and little birds which sing very sweetly." But no ivory and alabaster cities rose golden-crowned from the strand, no gentlemen of Japan in gold-stiffened brocade awaited the Christians on marble jetties, no lords and ladies advanced in screened palanquins over curved stone bridges, no temple bells clanged, no silver trumpets brayed, no dragon-mouthed bronze cannon roared. Certainly this was not Japan, unless Marco Polo was a liar.

Could it be Cathay, and was the "City of Heaven" around the next cape?

CHAPTER XVIII

Pursuit of the Grand Khan

Beati oculi qui vident quae vos videtis. Dico enim vobis, quod multi prophetae et reges voluerunt videre quae vos videtis, et non viderunt. . . .

Blessed are the eyes which see the things that ye see: for I tell you, that many prophets and kings have desired to see those things which ye see, and have not seen them. . . .

— LUKE X 23, 24

As COLUMBUS had named the two larger islands of the Bahamas after Ferdinand and Isabella, so he christened *Juana* this land that the Indians called Cuba, after the heir to the throne of Castile and Aragon, the Infante Don Juan.

Almost every town and village of the beautiful Oriente Province of Cuba from Baracoa to Puerto Padre, as well as Nuevitas in the Province of Camagüey, claims to be the San Salvador that Columbus entered on October 28, 1492. There is no doubt in our minds, after following his SSW course from the Ragged Islands, that San Salvador was Bahía Bariay. As Columbus says, that harbor is approached "without danger of shoals or other impediments." It is wide enough — three quarters of a mile — to tack in, and the curve of 12 *brazas* (11 of our fathoms), which Columbus gives as the depth, swings well within the two headlands. Mangrove trees cover the beaches inside as Columbus observed, and mountains rise from the country behind. One of these reminded him of the Peña de los Enamorados in the kingdom of Granada, the Lovers' Leap whence Christian Manuel and Moorish Laila leapt to their death when pursued by angry father. Another mountain, unmistakable as a landmark for Bahía Bariay, "has on its summit another little peak like a pretty little mosque" (*una hermosa mezquita*). The Spanish pioneers of Cuba, with more homely realism and less poetry than Columbus, named it *La Teta de Bariay*. There is not another such mountain east of Baracoa.

After the impressed Indian pilots, no doubt unintentionally, had filled the Admiral with high hopes of encountering Chinese junks at anchor off a great stone city of the Grand Khan, the reality of Bahía Bariay was a bit depressing. Columbus went ashore in the first boat, but found no trace of human beings except some fishermen's palm-thatched *bohíos* containing palm-fiber nets, bone fishhooks and harpoons, and "a dog that didn't bark." These small dumb dogs, which the Spaniards observed throughout the Antilles, were not a special breed of canine, but common yellow "hound dogs" that the Tainos domesticated largely for eating purposes. They gave a sort of grunt instead of a proper bark, and were completely useless as guardians of the home. Michele de Cuneo, the Genoese gentleman who accompanied Columbus on his Second Voyage, said that roast barkless dog was "none too good"; but Oviedo declares

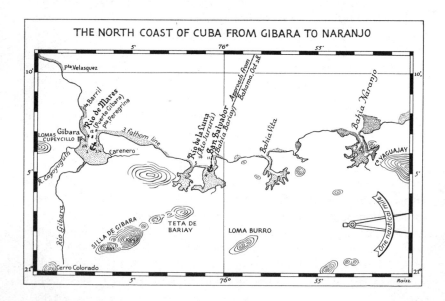

THE NORTH COAST OF CUBA FROM GIBARA TO NARANJO

that the *perros mudos* became extinct because the Spaniards liked their flavor only too well. Some escaped to the forest, reverted to species and became such a nuisance to farmers that they were hunted down in the last century.

Columbus had the men row him up the river where "the grass was as high as in Andalusia in April and May," and he saw purslane and amaranth and palms unlike those of Africa, and it was "a great pleasure to see those green things and groves of trees, and to hear the birds sing," so that he could hardly bear to turn back. But natural beauty was nothing he could take home. So on Monday, October 29, the fleet weighed and sailed westward for the City of Quinsay. It was almost noon when they got under way, and the wind was light. After passing a river "not so wide at the entrance" which the Admiral named Río de la Luna, they reached "at the hour of vespers," "another river much greater than the others," on the shores of which was a large village. Columbus named this bay *Río de Mares*. It was the best harbor he had yet seen in the Indies, and he predicted — this time correctly — that it would become a place of importance for trade. Río de Mares, "River of Seas," was undoubtedly Puerto Gibara.

On the western shore of this harbor was a large Indian village, the huts reminding the Spaniards of tents in a Moorish camp; and these were eagerly searched by the first landing party in quest of gold. None was found. Columbus does not mention finding a single gold object in Cuba, nor have any been excavated; it is a wonder he still believed anything that his Indians said. But they were useful as interpreters, for the same language prevailed in Cuba and Haiti as in the Bahamas. One in particular, who lived to reach Spain (where he was baptized Diego Colón) and who made the whole Second Voyage with the Admiral, became indispensable. As yet Diego had not picked up enough Castilian to be a two-way interpreter; but he could assure the natives that his captors were good people, and had an interesting line of trading goods. That was sufficient.

The westward search for the Grand Khan did not last long. An easy day's sail from Puerto Gibara took the fleet to a cape covered with palms, undoubtedly Punta Uvero which is conspicuous for palms today. The wind then unseasonably backed to the westward. All night October 30–31 the fleet beat to windward, and on the next day, still close-hauled, saw "an inlet or bay where small vessels could lie" and an outjutting cape, either Punta Cobarrubia or Punta Brava. By morning the wind had veered to the northward and the temperature dropped; a typical Caribbean winter norther was making up. And so, because it was impossible with a north wind to sail along a coast trending NNW, and dangerous to attempt it, Columbus ordered the fleet to come about and scud back to the Rio de Mares. A night sail over waters traversed before, especially with a moon past first quarter, offered no difficulty. They arrived at Puerto Gibara about dawn on November 1, and there remained for eleven days.

Columbus's first object was to acquire the confidence of the natives, in the hope of finding out where gold could be had and the Grand Khan located. After Diego the interpreter had reassured the local Tainos, a brisk exchange began of trading truck for food, cotton and hammocks. The natives, eager to please, unwittingly fed Columbus's delusion that he was hot on the trail of the Chinese emperor, not far from the "noble city of Zaitun" and Quinsay, the City of Heaven. Las Casas has a plausible explanation of how the Admiral was misled by his helpful hosts. A district in the interior of Cuba where a limited quantity of gold existed was called by the natives *Cubanacan* (mid-Cuba). Whenever Columbus produced a gold object and asked where more could be found, the natives pronounced this word, which he mistook for *El Gran Can*. Perhaps they simply mistook the Spaniards' dumb-show of imperial majesty for a desire to meet their cacique, who resided near the present town of Holguín, about 25 miles from Gibara up the pretty valley of the Cacoyuguin.

So the Admiral prepared with pathetic punctilio an embassy to visit the Emperor of China at Holguíin. The official interpreter Luis de Torres, a converted Jew "who knew Hebrew and Aramaic and even some Arabic," was made the head of it; and to him were intrusted all the diplomatic paraphernalia: Latin passport, Latin letter of credence from Ferdinand and Isabella, and a royal gift, the nature of which unfortunately we do not know. He was accompanied by Rodrigo de Xeres, who had visited a Negro king in Guinea, by a local Indian and one from Guanahaní; samples of spicery were taken to compare with local products, and strings of Venetian glass beads to exchange for food. The "embassy" was instructed to return within six days.

While the two Spaniards and their eager guides were plodding up the Cacoyuguin valley, the Admiral was not idle — he never was. On the night of November 2, two days before full moon, he endeavored to establish his position by taking the altitude of the North Star with his wooden quadrant. After applying the slight correction he decided that Puerto Gibara, actually in latitude 21° 06′ N, was in 42° N, the latitude of Cape Cod! And by his dead-reckoning he figured that he had wested 1142 leagues, that is, 3630 nautical miles, since his departure from Ferro in the Canaries. In other words, his fleet had made over 90 degrees of westing; ample distance, according to his underestimate of the globe and overestimate of the length of Asia, to place him in China. He therefore decided that Cuba was not Japan, but the Asiatic mainland.

Given Columbus's faulty geographical premises, his conclusion as to his longitude was inevitable. But why the faulty latitude, exactly double the true one? When at sea in about the same latitude on November 21, he tried the old quadrant once more, and obtained the same result. The reasons for this colossal error have much exercised the pundits. Navarrete postulated an imaginary, nonexistent quadrant that read double. Magnaghi argued that Columbus was trying to throw the Portuguese and others off the scent. Las Casas believed that the scribe copied "21" as "42." The real explanation is simple: Columbus picked the wrong star. He was "shooting" Alfirk (β Cephei), which in November bore due north at dusk; mistaking her for Polaris, whose familiar "pointers" were below the horizon. Columbus knew perfectly well that latitude 42° N was fantastically wrong. He had earlier noted in the Journal that Guanahaní was on the same parallel as the Canaries; and in his printed Letter on the First Voyage he gives the mean latitude of his new discoveries as 26° N. But, as he remarked rather plaintively in his Journal, "The North Star" (that is, Alfirk) "looks as high as in Castile."

One day was spent exploring the Rio Gibara in a boat. Martín Alonso Pinzón brought in specimens of the native creole pepper, and something he thought to be cinnamon, which raised hopes of a lucrative trade in spicery. Columbus had his first taste of sweet potatoes — or were they yams? — with "the flavor of chestnuts" and of cultivated American beans; he saw the wild cotton growing, with flowers and open bolls on the same bush. The boatswain of *Niña* brought in resin from the gumbo-limbo, which the Admiral thought he recognized as the mastic he had seen in Chios on one of his early voyages. Some Indians "yessed" the Spaniards when they inquired about the one-eyed and dog-headed men of Sir John Mandeville; others accurately pointed eastward toward Haiti when asked where gold came from.

Until the last day of his stay, Columbus kept the confidence of the natives, because he maintained good discipline among his men, and the natives had no gold to tempt their cupidity. There must have been considerable sporting between the seamen and the Indian girls, for the habits of the Tainos were completely promiscuous. But Columbus says nothing of that, since his Journal was intended for the eyes of a modest queen. Instead, he dwells on the Indians' docility and imitativeness; when they heard their visitors saying the *Ave Maria* and singing *Salve Regina* at sundown they tried to join in, and readily imitated the sign of the cross. His own words about the natives of Puerto Gibara are directly quoted by Las Casas: —

They are a people very guileless and unwarlike, all naked, men and women, as their mothers bore them. It is true that the women wear merely a piece of cotton big enough to cover their genitals but no more, and they are very handsome, not very black, less so than the Canary Islanders. I maintain, Most Serene Princes, that if they had access to devout religious persons knowing the language, they would all turn Christian, and so I hope in Our Lord that Your Highnesses will do something about it with much care, in order to turn to the Church so numerous a people, and to convert them, as you have destroyed those who would not confess the Father, Son, and Holy Ghost. And after your days (for we are all mortal) you will leave your realms in a very tranquil state, and free from heresy and wickedness, and will be well received before the eternal Creator, whom may it please to grant you long life and great increase of greater realms and lordships, and both will and disposition to increase the holy Christian religion, as hitherto you have done. Amen.

On the night of November 5 the embassy returned from Holguín with a most discouraging report. They had walked up the valley, past fields cultivated with sweet potatoes, beans and maize; they observed many kinds of birds, including the Hispaniola mocking-bird that they took for a nightingale; but they had pricked the Grand Khan bubble. Instead of visiting the imperial court of Cathay where Luis de Torres expected to air his Arabic, they received a primitive welcome in a village of fifty palm-thatched huts and a few hundred inhabitants. They had been treated with great dignity, "chaired" into the principal house, and seated on one of the carved seats or *metates* that Taino caciques used, well described by Ferdinand as "made of one piece, in a strange shape, and almost like some animal which had short legs and arms and the tail, which is no less broad than the seat, lifted up for conveniency to lean against; with a head in front and the eyes and ears of gold. These seats are called *duchi*." Rodrigo the mariner doubtless enjoyed it, but Torres felt humiliated in having to call upon the interpreter from Guanahaní to make a speech to the men. After that was over the women and children were allowed in to see the "men from Heaven," whose hand and feet they adoringly kissed. They pressed their visitors to spend a week or two; but the Spaniards, seeing "nothing that resembled a city," returned next day, in company with the cacique and his son. These were entertained aboard one of the caravels, since *Santa María* was then high and dry.

If the embassy missed meeting the King of Kings, they never-theless encountered a more pervasive sovereign, My Lady Nicotine. "The two Christians met on the way many people who were going to their villages, women and men, with a firebrand in the hand, and herbs to drink the smoke thereof as they are accustomed." The tobacco pipe of the North American Indians was unknown to the Tainos, who rolled cigars which (as in Cuba today) they called *tobacos*. Inserting one end in a nostril, they lit the other from a firebrand and inhaled the smoke twice or thrice, after which the cigar was handed to a friend or allowed to go out. When a party of Tainos went on a journey, as Rodrigo and Luis de Torres ob-served them, small boys were charged to keep one or more fire-brands glowing in readiness for anyone who wanted a light; and

by halting every hour or so for a good "drag" all around, Indians
were able to travel great distances. Las Casas, commenting on this
passage some forty years later, says that the Spaniards of Hispaniola were then beginning to take up smoking, "although I know
not what taste or profit they find in it." Apparently the bishop
never got beyond his first cigar. Within a century of his writing
this, the use of tobacco had spread throughout the Western World,
to men and women alike, despite the opposition of kings and clerics.
As a gift from the New World to the Old it proved far more
valuable than gold.

On the morning of November 5, in a bight of Puerto Gibara
that is still used for that purpose, the Admiral had *Santa María*
careened and her bottom cleaned, a seamanlike precaution against
teredos. The next day she floated, and plans were made to sail on
the eighth; but strong easterly trades kept the fleet in harbor four
days more. Possibly this opportunity was taken to careen *Pinta* and
Niña, but there is no mention of it in the Journal. Samples were
taken of the gumbo-limbo resin, which Columbus supposed to be
mastic, and of the agave which he mistook for aloes. As a final
reward to these nonresistant Indians of the Golden Age "without
knowledge of what is evil, . . . and so timid that a hundred of them
flee before one of ours," the Admiral kidnaped five young men who
came aboard for a farewell visit, and then sent his boat ashore to
bag "seven head of women, large and small, and three boys." The
husbands and fathers of some came out and begged to join them,
which was granted. Columbus explained that he wanted the youths
to train as interpreters, and the women to keep them from getting
spoiled; for he had already observed when voyaging for Portugal
that the Negroes brought home from Guinea in order to learn the
language received so much attention in Portugal that they were
no good when returned to Africa. Two of the young men escaped
at Tánamo Bay; none of the rest survived the voyage to Spain.

"At the relieving of the dawn watch" on Monday, November 12,
the fleet left Puerto Gibara "to visit an island which many of the
Indians aboard declare to be called *Babeque* where, the Indians
aboard declare by signs, the people gather gold on the beach by
candles at night, and then make bars of it with a hammer."

"Babeque" undoubtedly was Great Inagua Island; for the Indians gave the correct course for it, and *Pinta* actually went there.

All that day the wind held fair, but very light. Columbus set a straight course, E ½N, for Punta Cañete, noted but did not examine Puerto Naranjo, noted Puerto Sama and named it *Rio del Sol*, River of the Sun. He excused himself for not exploring these inlets because they looked too shoal for his ships (as indeed they were), and because the wind was fair for Babeque. On his next Cuban voyage the Admiral took *Niña* as flagship and two smaller caravels; and even they drew too much water for coastal work. You cannot sail into narrow, uncharted harbors and rivers with a vessel drawing more than 6 feet, except by running undue risks. The lookout can see bottom up to 6 feet, and even deeper in clear weather with the sun abaft.

By sunset the fleet had made a scant 30 miles. It was off Punta Lucrecia, which Columbus named *Cabo de Cuba* because he thought it was the easternmost promontory of the island. One looking south from that point toward Nipe Bay, sees the lowlands of the Mayarí valley below the horizon, and the high mountains to the eastward look as if they belonged to another island. This Columbus supposed to be "Bohío," that is, Haiti. All night he stood off-and-on in order to hold his position, and at daylight November 13 steered toward the land, passing Punta Mulas. But the weather was overcast, and the atmosphere thick, so that even then Columbus could not see that Cuba and Bohío were contiguous. Another norther was making up. So with the object of making Babeque and avoiding the danger of being driven onto a lee shore with a strong north wind, Columbus ordered the course set due east. With the wind abeam, the fleet logged 31 miles by sunset.

After another night during which the fleet cautiously stood off-and-on (moon was in last quarter and sky overcast), wind veered to NE, making the easterly course for Babeque no longer possible. So, after jogging awhile to the E by S, the Admiral decided to make for a harbor somewhere along the coast of Bohío. A southerly course took him to a point somewhat near the eastern entrance to Puerto Cayo Moa, which he dared not enter through the gap in the breakers with a high sea running; so he ran along shore northwesterly, looking for a safe opening. After coasting some 30 or 35 miles, he came upon a bottleneck entrance a little over 200 yards wide. A boat sent forward to sound reported no bottom at 40 fathoms in the fairway, and the fleet sailed boldly in. There was an elbow in the fairway, requiring three changes of course, but a following wind made these possible, and the Admiral's courage was rewarded when this twisty passage opened into a great bay studded with high, picturesque islands. This was the Bahía Tánamo. Columbus named it *La Mar de Nuestra Señora*, the Sea of Our Lady, and the first harbor just inside the entrance (probably Bahía Jucaro), which he did not stop to investigate, he called *Puerto del Príncipe* after the Infante Don Juan. It was now Wednesday evening, November 14.

Along this coast of Oriente the Admiral's descriptions are so accurate that one can identify his harbors even from the air. Following his course in *Mary Otis*, drawing 7½ feet (about the same as *Santa María*), we were impressed with his courage in sailing near enough to the shore to spy out the numerous openings in the many-harbored Oriente, and with his good judgment in the places that he selected for anchoring and detailed exploration.

Martín Alonso Pinzón considered Columbus to be reckless and foolhardy; but unless an explorer is willing to take risks that merchant captains avoid, he does not discover much that is worth while. Thus, Captain Robert Gray of the Boston ship *Columbia*, named after the Great Admiral, was sharply criticized by his officers for standing too close inshore, and occasionally running aground. But it was Captain Gray's willingness to take risks that sent *Columbia* across the breaking bar of the great river that bears her name, where no earlier explorer had dared enter. Columbus, to be sure, had missed Nipe Bay, one of the best harbors in the world; but anyone who has experienced a norther in those waters will not blame him for then seeking sea room.

Tánamo Bay with its cluster of wooded islands running up "like diamond points" and others flat-topped "like tables," as Columbus said, and a lofty sierra arising from all around the scalloped shore, well deserved the Admiral's enthusiasm. There was good soft bottom everywhere, "which the seamen like very much," says Las Casas, "because rocks cut the ships' anchor cables." Columbus was rowed all around the bay in the ship's boat, and on the windward point of the entrance he found two big trees which *Santa María's* carpenter fashioned into a great cross, and there set up. It was the Admiral's custom to leave a cross standing at every place where he anchored. He found Indians fishing for "large snails" (conchs), and made his people dive for oysters in the hope of finding pearls; they caught a curious trunkfish which the Admiral salted down to show the Sovereigns. The seamen found their first *hutía,* the Cuban quadruped resembling a large rat, which still furnishes food to the natives. The most interesting new flora observed about Tánamo Bay were "big nuts of the same kind as those of India." Columbus had read of *nueces de India* (coconuts) in Marco Polo, and supposed that these were they; but they cannot have been, because the coconut palm was introduced to the Caribbean by later Spaniards. Furthermore, Columbus does not say that these *nueces* grew on a palm tree — nor does Marco Polo. What he probably saw was the local nut called *nogal del país* (*Juglans insularis*), which was formerly very abundant in Oriente Province.

Although it was not new moon until November 19, the day after Columbus left Tánamo, he there made a remarkable lunitidal observation. In his day the tidal establishment of each port was determined by the bearing of the moon at low water. "The tide is the reverse of ours in Spain," says he, "because here when the moon bears SW by S, it is low tide in that position." The waning moon bore SW by S at Tánamo about noon November 15, when Columbus could have observed her in a clear sky. Bowditch gives the mean high-water lunitidal interval at Huelva in Spain as 1h 40m and at Tánamo as 7h 51m, a difference of 6h 11m. So, as the mean interval between high and low water is 6h 13m, it was low water at Tánamo *at almost the exact hour and minute* by local time when it would have been high water at Huelva. And, as the mean range of tide on the north coast of Cuba is a trifle under two feet, the Admiral here proved himself to be an observer of almost uncanny accuracy.

There was no gold in this lovely bay, no hint of Asia except the mistaken coconuts, no large village of natives, nothing of profit to the Spaniards. Only Columbus's love of natural beauty, a trait unusual in that era and still uncommon among navigators, kept him there five days. He even excuses himself for not departing on the

fourth day because it was Sunday. But mere scenery was not getting him anywhere; another attempt must be made to reach
Babeque.

Before sunrise November 19 the fleet departed with a light land
breeze. Columbus was learning the technique for leaving these
northern harbors of the greater Antilles under sail; you must catch
the offshore wind at night or in early morning, for the trades that
come up with the sun draw right in as through a funnel. That day
the trade wind came from due E, and the fleet sailed NNE, 6 points
off the wind. At sunset, when the entrance to Tánamo bore SSW,
distant 20 miles, Columbus thought he sighted Babeque bearing
due east. Actually Great Inagua was over 80 miles distant from that
point, and could not possibly have been seen. Probably the Indians,
seeing a cloud making up over the horizon at sunset, pointed to it
and shouted "Babeque!" and Columbus believed them. From sunset
November 19 to 10 o'clock the next morning the fleet made good
52 miles to the NE by N, which took them to the approximate
position of latitude 21° 45' N, longitude 74° 41' W.

This course was fast leading them away from the presumed position of Babeque; so when the wind turned ESE and the sea began
to make up from the eastward, Columbus decided to return to
Tánamo. The alternative, he wrote, was to maintain the northeasterly course to Isabela (Crooked Island) which he believed lay
12 leagues ahead. Sixteen leagues was the correct distance if I have
plotted his course accurately; and it was one month and a day
since he had left Cabo Hermoso of Isabela. Few modern navigators
by dead-reckoning could hope to do better than that.

Columbus turned back toward Cuba, he says, for two reasons.
He feared lest the Indians from Guanahaní escape at Isabela. And,
second, he sighted two islands to the southward that he wished to
investigate. These were clouds, not islands, as he must have ascertained within an hour or two; but that entry in his Journal stood.
It is a great temptation to any shipmaster, when he makes an entry
that proves to be mistaken, to alter or erase it with a stroke of the
pen; but Columbus always let his mistakes stand; and a shipmate on
the Second Voyage observed how careful he was to log any accident. Crackpot critics of Columbus always base their theories on

a presumed going-over of the Journal by Columbus or Las Casas to iron out inconsistencies and play up "The Indies." But Las Casas's abstract reveals plenty of errors by the Admiral, as well as kidnaping episodes of which the editor thoroughly disapproved.

CHAPTER XIX

Oriente

NOVEMBER 20–DECEMBER 5, 1492

Vidimus enim stellam eius in oriente, et venimus adorare eum.

We have seen his star in the east, and are come to worship him

— MATTHEW ii 2

RETURNING to Tánamo was easier decided than done; and the next few days were full of such disappointment and vexations as beset all mariners in sail. Tánamo lay about SSW, 8 points off the wind; but the distance was too great (some 71 miles) for the fleet to cover that day, and the current carried it to leeward. So at nightfall November 20, when within sight of land, Columbus decided to make another try for Babeque. He ordered the fleet about, and for a time sailed NE with a stiff ESE wind. At the third night watch (about 3 A.M. November 21) the wind moderated and became variable between S and SE, so that an easterly course could be sailed. At sunrise November 21 Tánamo bore SW westerly, distant about 35 miles. Although the wind held south during the day, the sea was so heavy as to check the easterly progress of the caravels; and up to vespers (about 3 P.M.) they had made only 15 to 18 miles to the eastward. The wind then backed to the E, forcing the fleet S by E.

As soon as the North Star appeared that evening, and when, according to my plotting of his dead-reckoning he was in latitude 20° 52′ N, Columbus broke out his quadrant and tried a little celestial navigation. He reached the same deplorable result of latitude 42° that he had obtained on November 2, and for the same reason: mistaking Alfirk for Polaris. The Admiral himself was puzzled, and "here says that he has had the quadrant hung up until he reaches land, to repair it, since it seemed to him that he could not be so far distant" from the equator. Many better navigators than he, even in our own century, have given up star sights with disgust, to rely on "good old dead-reckoning." The truth is, Columbus was not conscious of the stars, even from an esthetic point of view. Many times in the course of his four voyages he comments on the beauty of tropical landscapes, sometimes when off soundings he adverts to the glory of the sea; but never does he remark on the splendor of the stars in the tropics. Not once does he mention the Southern Cross, or the enormous constellation of the ship Argo or brilliant Canopus, which he must have seen for the first time since his African voyages. His eyes were not turned upward, at least not above the clouds that carried messages of wind and rain; he had enough to do to watch them, and the compass card and the surface of the ocean, and to keep his reckoning and constantly to run his eyes over sails and gear for signs of weakness or chafe. Almost any old-time shipmaster can construct an accurate model of a vessel for which he has once been responsible, with every spar, block and line in place; but only a trained celestial navigator can identify the stars without consulting a sidereal chart, and between voyages that sort of lore is quickly forgotten. Columbus, we repeat, was a dead-reckoning and not a celestial navigator.

The defection of Martín Alonso Pinzón worried the Admiral much more than did his screwy latitude sights. During the dawn watch (3 to 7 A.M.) November 22 the wind backed to NNE, and the Admiral kept on to the southward in the hope of reaching land. *Niña* dutifully followed, but Martín Alonso "without the permission or desire of the Admiral" took advantage of the change of wind to alter *Pinta's* course to the eastward. It was not until the second week of the New Year that Columbus saw him again, at Monte Cristi. The one reason for Martín Alonso's insubordination, says Columbus, was his cupidity; an Indian guide aboard *Pinta* had filled him up with tales of the gold at Babeque, and he wished to get there first.

Although this is the earliest indication in the Journal of unpleasantness between the Admiral and his senior captain, clearly it was not the first. "Many other things he had done and said to me," concludes the day's work for November 21. Martín Alonso died

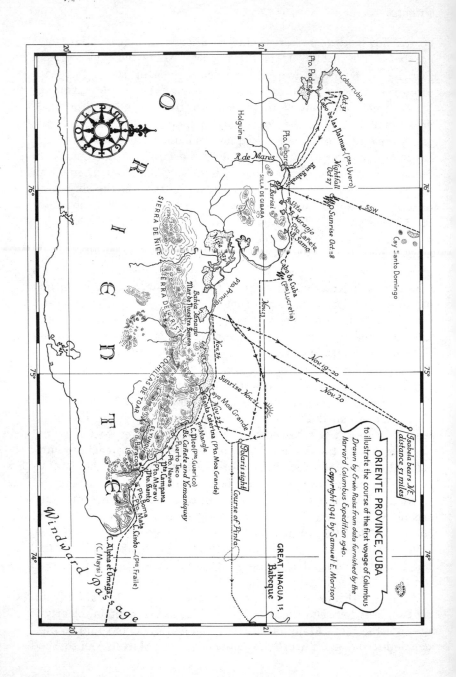

ORIENTE PROVINCE, CUBA
to illustrate the course of the first voyage of Columbus
Drawn by Erwin Raisz from data furnished by the
Harvard Columbus Expedition 1940.
Copyright 1941 by Samuel E. Morison

shortly after the voyage ended, and in the long *pleitos* that began in 1512, the only explanation of this gross breach of discipline offered by his friends and partisans was the feeble one that the Admiral got lost, while Pinzón went on. One therefore assumes that he had no case, and that the greedy motive assigned to him by Columbus was correct. Yet one may imagine other motives as well. *Pinta* was a smarter sailer than *Santa María,* especially in the conditions of light wind and heavy head swell that prevailed on November 21; and very likely Pinzón was exasperated at continually having to shorten sail in order not to outdistance the flagship. When the wind turned fair for Babeque on November 22, and the Admiral continued on his course for Cuba instead of turning east, it was too much for Martín Alonso. He'd be damned if he'd follow that Genoese upstart any longer! The proper thing to do, in his way of thinking, was to go after the gold. And although he found not a grain of it at Great Inagua, he did discover Haiti and had first whack at the gold of the Cibao.

Columbus's "many other things he had done and said to me" suggests a good deal. Friction between these two strong men was inevitable. Martín Alonso's local influence had been essential for manning the expedition. Possibly Columbus failed to give him due credit for these practical details. There had been, as we have seen, dissension just before the Bahamian landfall, and Columbus, by rubbing in the fact that he was right, may have irritated Martín Alonso into saying and doing those unmentioned things. Men of genius are not always easy on their subordinates. But in contrast to the insubordination of Martín Alonso, note the loyalty of his brother Vicente Yáñez, who had the same temptation to put off for Babeque, but dutifully steered *Niña* where his Admiral commanded.

The wind was so light on November 22 that *Pinta* was in sight of the others all day, and they made little progress. Friday the twenty-third was about the same, the westerly-setting current taking *Santa María* and *Niña* to leeward faster than they could sail south. The Indian guides were terrified because they thought that the land ahead belonged to the people "called *Canibales,*" the Caribs who were accustomed to make slave raids on the Tainos. Finally at 9 A.M. on the twenty-fourth the reduced fleet of two made land at "the flat island," Cayo Moa Grande. When they passed it ten days before, the sea was breaking so heavily that the Admiral dared not enter the harbor. We do not blame him; the entrance to Puerto Cayo Moa through a gap in the breakers looks pretty tough, even when you have a chart.

After three days of light wind, the sea had calmed down so that the entrance now did not seem so bad. *Santa María's* boat, sent in ahead to sound, reported 20 fathoms in the fairway and 6 fathoms with good clean sand bottom inside, as today. In sailed the caravels "turning the bow to the SW and then to the W, keeping the flat island to the northward close aboard" (directions which we found useful in June 1940, all buoys then being absent), and found themselves within "a lagoon in which all the ships of Spain could lie and be safe without cables from all winds." It was the morning of November 24, and the most unprofitable leg of the First Voyage was over. In five days *Santa María* and *Niña* had logged about 200 miles and made good 25.

Puerto Cayo Moa is unlike any other harbor in the Oriente province of Cuba. About 8½ miles long by 1½ wide, it runs along the base of a mountain range, protection from the north being given by the "flat island" (Cayo Moa Grande) and "a reef the length of the mountain, like a bar." Through this reef there are two entrances, sailing directions for both of which Columbus noted in his Journal. Several streams flow down the sierra, forming short deltas and a bar where they empty into the harbor; but, as Columbus observed, the salt water does not back up into their lower courses, as into the Rio Gibara. The Admiral had the men row him up the Rio Moa, in whose bed and on whose banks he detected signs of valuable minerals — stones the color of iron, others that someone associated with silver, iron pyrites which glittered for so many explorers, but were never gold; "and he recollected that gold is found at the mouth of the Tagus." While Columbus and the officers were prospecting, "the gromets sung out that they saw pine trees; he looked toward the sierra and saw many great and such marvelous ones that he could not exaggerate their height and straightness, like spindles, thick and elongated, whence he realized that ships could be had, and planks without number, and masts for the best ships of Spain." Today the descendants of these *pinus cubenses* are being sawed into boards and planks by a mill run by the mountain stream whose distant roar the Admiral heard on that far-off Sunday in 1492. He caused a new mizzenmast and a yard to be cut and shaped for *Niña;* but the great shipbuilding industry that he planned for this place, and described "in great style to the Sovereigns," has never materialized. Except for a few fishermen's cabins on the shore, and a few lumbermen's clearings among the pine groves on the sierra, the aspect of the harbor is still clean of human touch.

Columbus the poet appreciated Puerto Cayo Moa as well as Columbus the seaman. "The land and the air are milder than hitherto, owing to the height and beauty of the sierra." Words failed him, as they do us, to describe the peculiar beauty of this harbor, resting so placidly between austere mountains and the arc of hissing reefs. "Finally, he says," reports Las Casas, "that if he who sees it is so full of wonder, how much more will it be for him who hears of it, and that nobody can believe it without seeing."

At sunrise November 26 they reluctantly weighed anchors from Puerto Cayo Moa, and sailed slowly along with a light SW wind to Punta Guarico, which the Admiral called *Cabo del Pico.* There the coast makes a turn to the southward. Soon he sighted the most prominent headland in this part of Oriente, and named it *Cabo Campana,* "Cape Bell." It has a smooth, curved surface, which was probably cultivated by the Indians in 1492. Between these two capes "he noted and marked nine very remarkable harbors which all the seamen considered wonderful, and five great rivers; because he always sailed close along shore, in order to see everything well." He certainly sailed closer than we cared to do in a vessel of like draught, for we could make out only seven harbors and rivers, including Bahías Cañete and Yamanigue, which the Admiral particularly described. But we were near enough to agree with him that "all this country has very high and beautiful mountains, not dry and rocky but all accessible, and most beautiful valleys; and the valleys like the mountains were thick with high and leafy trees, which 'twas glorious to see."

As the wind left him that evening when off Cabo Campana, and the weather was clear, Columbus decided not to attempt entering any one of these numerous harbors, but hove-to and drifted. When day broke on the twenty-seventh he was so far offshore, and the clouds hung so low, that the country behind Baracoa seemed to be an inlet of the sea, with "a mountain lofty and square, that looked like an island" standing out in the middle. This was El Yunque, the anvil-shaped mountain that can be seen 50 miles away, a landmark known to everyone who navigates these waters. With a land breeze from the SW blowing on the port side, the fleet returned to Cape Campana in order to resume exploring the coast. The wind then veered to the N, and the caravels sailed gaily along close inshore, noting eight little basin-shaped harbors and V-shaped river mouths. Foothills bright green with guinea grass and bristling with royal palms rise from a rim of white surf; above them high, wooded mountains in tumbled irregular shapes thrust up into the trade-wind clouds which are constantly piling up in nubilous traffic jams, and then dissolving into showers. By the time he reached a point off Puerto Maraví at the end of this string of little harbors, the Admiral found that the supposed inlet "was only a great bay."

Throughout this scenic cruise along the north shore of Oriente, Columbus's Taino passengers were shaking with terror at the thought of landing on the so-called Island of Bohío, which they supposed to be the land whence their Carib enemies came. "After they saw that he was shaping a course for that land, they couldn't speak for fear lest they (the Caribs) make a meal of them, nor could he quiet their fears; and they said that these people had but one eye and dogs' faces. The Admiral believed that they were lying" — why, when he himself had suggested these monsters out of Mandeville? — and thought that the Caribs "must really be subjects of the Grand Khan" — in other words, Chinese soldiers! The Admiral was further off than the simple natives.

These had a very pronounced attack of Caribphobia when the fleet sighted a big village beyond Puerto Maraví, "and saw countless people come to the seashore making great shouts, all naked and with darts in hand." At this horrid sight, all Indians aboard promptly retired below hatches, and became so useless from sheer funk that no effort was made to take them ashore as interpreters. The fleet came to an anchor, and Columbus sent both boats ashore with orders to placate the yelling natives with trading truck. The boats' crews landed on the Playa de Duaba (just west of Baracoa), crying out some appeasing phrase that they had picked up from their Taino shipmates; but the entire native population took to flight.

At noon on November 27 the two vessels made sail from their anchorage off this now deserted beach, and steered eastward for Cape Maisi. They had not gone two miles when there opened up, a short distance to the southward, "a most singular harbor" (Puerto Baracoa), surrounded by open country and big villages, and Columbus decided to call. Entering by the 300-yard-wide fairway, avoiding the rock just off the windward point, *Santa María* and *Niña* found themselves in a harbor round "like a little porringer," and separated by a narrow beach from a river "of such depth that a galley could enter." Columbus promptly decided that this harbor, which he named *Puerto Santo*, was the best he had yet seen for building a city and fortress — "good water, good land, good surroundings, and much wood"; and on the strength of his recommendation it was pitched upon for the first Spanish settlement in Cuba, in 1512. Baracoa today is the largest town located on the route of Columbus's First Voyage, a lively little city with a thriving export trade of bananas and coconuts. Native sloops and lighters still unload in the river "that a galley could enter," which flows around the harbor's rim, behind the beach.

Bad weather kept *Santa María* and *Niña* at Baracoa for a week. The people went ashore and washed their clothes in the river, as seamen love to do. Other parties wandered about the interior, found the land well cultivated with yams, maize and pumpkins, visited many Taino villages from which all natives fled on their approach, and reported finding "a man's head in a basket, covered with another basket and hanging to a post" in a house. "The Admiral believed the heads must have been those of some ancestors of the family." An old Guinea custom, perhaps? The Tainos are not known to have preserved their ancestors' skulls, nor were they head-hunters; one suspects that the seamen enjoyed pulling their Admiral's leg. Several immense dugout canoes were seen, neatly moored under palm-thatched boathouses; one was over 70 feet in length and big enough to hold 150 people. The men raised a great cross on the windward point of Baracoa Harbor, where now there is a ruined fort.

Unfavorable winds gave Columbus an excuse to tarry, and opportunity to explore by boat the next bay east of Baracoa. There he entered the mouth of the Rio Miel with a fathom's depth over the bar, and found inside a lagoon where the whole Spanish navy might ride. Rowing upstream, he found five large canoes in a backwater, with a thatched boathouse to protect them, and, leaving his boats, climbed the hillside until he rached a plain with cultivated fields of pumpkins, and many huts. Here he managed at last to make contact with the natives of Baracoa by sending "Diego" ahead with a supply of brass rings, glass beads and hawks' bells. They proved willing to do business, but had nothing to exchange except their wooden darts with fire-hardened points. Returning to his boats, Columbus sent another party of seamen up the hillside to investigate a collection of huts that he mistook for beehives; and while they were gone, large numbers of natives flocked around the Spaniards, and "one of them went into the river next the stern of the boat and made a great speech, which the Admiral didn't understand, except that from time to time the other Indians raised their hands to Heaven and gave a great shout. The Admiral thought that they were reassuring him and that his coming pleased them; but he saw the face of the Indian whom he took with him change color and become yellow as wax, and he trembled much, saying by signs that the Admiral had better leave the river, that they sought to kill them. And he went up to a Christian who held a loaded crossbow and showed it to the Indians, and the Admiral understood that he told them that they would all be killed, because that crossbow shot far and to kill. Also he took a sword and drew it from its scabbard, brandishing it, saying the same; the which when they heard, all took to flight, the said Indian trembling from cowardice and slight courage, and he was a man of good stature and strong."

In the meantime other Tainos had gathered on the opposite bank of the Rio Miel, to which the Admiral crossed. "They were very many, all painted red and naked as their mothers bore them, and some with feathers on the head and others plumes, all with their bundles of darts." These darts, too, were handed over in return for the usual trading truck, and for bits of the shell of a turtle that the gromets had killed. Columbus came away filled with admiration for the workmanship of the canoes and the native huts, but disappointed at the total absence of "gold and spicery," and contemptuous of the natives' courage. "Ten men could put to flight ten thousand, so cowardly and timid are they." If a relatively humane Columbus reacted thus, it is no wonder that the common seamen regarded the Tainos as despicable, fit only to be slaves.

On December 4 *Santa María* and *Niña* left Baracoa with a light but favorable wind, skirting the coast and looking in at Puerto Boma, a narrow V-shaped harbor with high banks, and at Puerto Mata, one of the round bottlenecked harbors common on that coast. By sunset they were off the Punta del Fraile (which Columbus named *Cabo Lindo*, "Pretty Cape") of Cape Maisí, and within sight of the Windward Passage between Cuba and Hispaniola. Having twice been fooled by bays that he mistook for passages, the Admiral at first thought this was merely another bay, and did not discover his error until the morning after a night spent hove-to off Punta del Fraile. At sunrise December 5 he sighted the tip of Cape Maisí, from which the land trended south, and then southwest; and in that direction he saw a dark, high cape, Punta Negra. So he decided that this was a passage after all, and named the easternmost extremity of Cuba "Cape Alpha and Omega," to indicate that it was the beginning or end of the Eurasian continent, corresponding to Cape St. Vincent in Europe.

Up to the morning of December 5 Columbus planned to make Great Inagua (Babeque) his next stop after finishing with Cuba; for it was high time that he should be collecting some gold before Martín Alonso got it all into the hold of *Pinta*. But that morning the trade wind came up from the northeast, which the Indian guides, quite correctly, indicated as the course for Babeque. And when *Santa María* was steering close-hauled on the port tack, headed about ESE, the Admiral sighted land on the starboard bow, "and it was a very great island, of which he already had information from the Indians, that they called it 'Bohío.'" This was Haiti; a sight welcome to the Spaniards as it was a disappointment to the Guanahaní and Gibara guides, who, having successfully escaped being killed and eaten at Baracoa, were trying to divert the Admiral to the Great Inagua, inhabited by their own kind. If, as seems probable from their calling Haiti by the name for "home," they had retained the tradition of its being their mother country, they

also believed that the Caribs had since moved in, and were hungry
for Taino meat.

Columbus now made a quick change of plan, which was uncommon for him, and decided to use the favorable wind for Haiti,
instead of beating up to Great Inagua. Steering SE by E, in order
to keep a little to windward of the course (for he had noted the
diurnal variation of the trade wind from NE to SE), he crossed
the Windward Passage that day and arrived off the mouth of a
great harbor "like the Bay of Cadiz" at nightfall December 5, vigil
of the feast of Saint Nicholas. *Port Saint Nicolas* it still is; the first
of Columbus's New World names that has never been altered.

As he left Cuba and crossed the Windward Passage, Columbus
must have wondered how he, in his fumbling Castilian and with
such poor evidence as he had picked up, could convince the Sovereigns that this beautiful coastline along which he had been sailing
for five weeks really belonged to the semi-fabulous Cathay. No
Grand Khan, no potentates or mandarins in silk brocade had he
encountered, but naked savages with cotton clouts; no towering
Chinese junks, but dugout canoes; no teeming cities of a thousand
bridges, but villages of palm-thatched huts; not one grain of gold
or other precious metal, but artifacts of wood, bone and shell; no
merchantable spicery, but poor substitutes for cinnamon and pepper; no monsters of humankind or marvels of the vegetable kingdom, but a few odd nuts and a trunkfish in pickle. We who have
benefited from Columbus's voyage can hardly imagine what a disappointment it had been, after the first wonder and delight at San
Salvador had worn off. But for the visit to Haiti, where gold was
discovered, this voyage would undoubtedly have been written off
by the Sovereigns as a curious adventure but a costly failure. That,
obviously, is what the Pinzons and most of Columbus's shipmates
thought it to be, on December 5, 1492. But the Admiral's faith
that God had sent him forth for His glory and for the benefit of
mankind made him see the bright side of things; and, in a significant
passage entered in his Journal during the delay at Baracoa, point
out that even if he had not found a western route to Asia, he had
lifted the veil from a New World of opportunity.

I do not write how great will be the benefit to be derived hence. It's certain, Lord Princes, that where there are such lands there should be profitable things without number; but I tarried not in any harbor, because I sought to see as many countries as I could, to give the story of them to Your Highnesses, and also I knew not the language, and the people of these lands did not understand me nor I them, nor anyone aboard. And these Indians aboard I often misunderstood taking one thing for the opposite, and I don't trust them much, for many times they have tried to escape. But now, please Our Lord, I will see the most that I can, and little by little I shall come to understand and know, and I will have this language learned by people of my household, because I see that all so far have one language. And afterwards the benefits will be known, and it will be attempted to make all these folk Christians, for that will easily be done, since they have no religion; nor are they idolaters.

And Your Highnesses will command a city and fortress to be built in these parts, and these countries converted; and I certify to Your Highnesses that it seems to me that there could never be under the sun [lands] superior in fertility, in mildness of cold and heat, in abundance of good and pure water; and the rivers are not like those of Guinea, which are all pestilential. For, praise be to Our Lord, up to the present among all my people nobody has even had a headache or taken to his bed through sickness; except one old man with pain of gravel, from which he has suffered all his life, and he was well at the end of two days. This applies to all three vessels. So may it please God that Your Highnesses send here . . . learned men, who will ascertain the truth of all. . . . And I say that Your Highnesses ought not to consent that any foreigner do business or set foot here, except Christian Catholics, since this was the end and the beginning of the enterprise, that it should be for the enhancement and glory of the Christian religion, nor should anyone who is not a good Christian come to these parts.

Thus, before he had been seven weeks in the New World, Columbus sketched in outline the colonial policy of Spain that has left a permanent impress on America, foretold "the profitable things without number" that Europeans would find therein, and predicted the vast extension of Christianity that his discovery made possible.

CHAPTER XX

La Isla Española

DECEMBER 6–24, 1492

A son arrivée "dans un nouveau monde et sous un
nouveau ciel," il observe attentivement la configuration des
contrées, la physionomie des formes végétales, les mœurs
des animaux, la distribution de la chaleur et les variations
du magnétisme terrestre. Tout en s'efforçant de découvrir
les épiceries de l'Inde et la rhubarbe, rendue déjà si célèbre
par les médecins arabes et juifs, par Rubruquis et les voya-
geurs italiens, il observait avec un soin scrupuleux les ra-
cines, les fruits et les feuilles des plantes.
                                    — VON HUMBOLDT Cosmos II 320

DURING the night of December 5, while *Niña* was comfortably
anchored in Port St. Nicolas, and beacon fires of the Indians
flared from the surrounding hills, *Santa María* sailed to the NNE
with the land breeze, in order to be in a good position to coast
down-wind to her first Haitian harbor next morning.

At daylight Columbus took a set of bearings so accurate that we
can confidently place *Santa María* 12 miles N by E from Cape St.
Nicolas Môle, which is the exact distance given by the Admiral
himself. Anyone who has tried to take bearings without pelorus or
other sighting apparatus, merely by squinting across a small compass card, will share my surprise that four out of five of Columbus's bearings actually converge at a point on the modern chart.
From that position, latitude 20° 03′ N, longitude 73° 24′ W, he
sighted and named from its resemblance to a turtle the famous buc-
caneer island of Tortuga; the northwestern point of Haiti, which
he called the *Cape of the Star;* Pointe Jean Rabel, which he named
Cabo Cinquín; and the Haut Piton mountain with its northern
slope, which he called *Cabo del Elefante.* Haut Piton does suggest

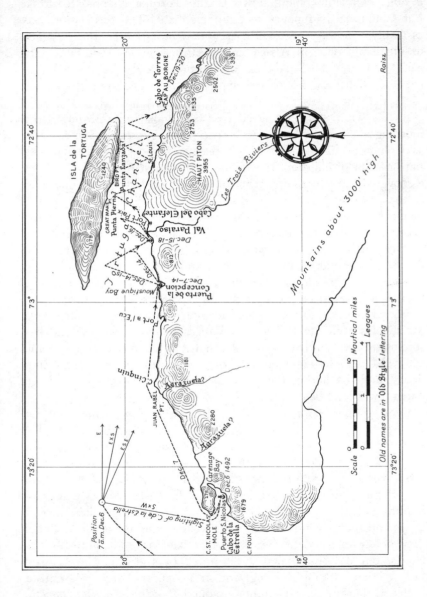

ISLA de la TORTUGA

Cabo de Torres
CAP AU BORGNE
Dec.19-20

393
2502
2753 15.35
St Louis
HAUT PITON
3955
Cabo del Elefante?
Val Paraiso
Dec.15-18
619
Puerto de la Concepcion
Dec.7-14
Moustique Boy
Dec.14-15 iso
Port a l'Ecu
Cinquin?
1181
Agrazuela?
JUAN RABEL PT.
2280
Agrazuela ?
Dec 7
C. ST. NICOLAS
MOLE
Puerto S. Nicolas Dec.6 1492
Cabo de la Estrella
1679
C. FOUX
Carenage Bay
1732
Sighting of C. de la Estrella
Position 7 a.m. Dec.6
E
ExS
ESE
SxW

GREAT MAN Pt.
Punta Pierna?
Punta Angel
Port Flaix
BIRD I
2240
1179

Les Trois Riviers

Mountains about 3000' high

Roiz.

Scale
10 Nautical miles
2 Leagues
4

Old names are in "Old Style" lettering

Portugal Channel

a huge elephant coming down to the Tortuga channel to drink, but Columbus had never seen an elephant. The association was probably a literary one, with Aristotle's remark that the presence of elephants both in Africa and in India proves that fauna are similar on the same parallels of latitude. Doubtless the Admiral expected that very day to see elephants sporting among the forests of Hispaniola.

As the wind was light December 6, it took *Santa María* all the morning and part of the afternoon to reach *Puerto de San Nicolás,* as Columbus named the harbor because it was the feast of the patron saint of children. It was much the finest seaport he had yet discovered; deep with clean bottom and good holding ground, and at the head of it an inner and completely landlocked harbor (the modern Carénage) where a ship could moor close enough to the shore to lay her gangplank on the grass. He noted a fine beach and a river, and trees "of a thousand kinds, all laden with fruit which the Admiral believed to be spiceries and nutmegs — but they were not ripe and he did not recognize them." He proposed that the narrow isthmus at the head of the inner harbor be pierced to make a second channel, and predicted a great future for the place. Port St. Nicolas Môle, as we call it today, is so fine a harbor, and lies so close to the Windward Passage, that it seems destined to become a naval base. The eighteenth-century fortifications have fallen into decay, and the harbor today is deserted except for a poor village and a few fishing boats.

Every Indian fled at the fleet's approach, so the Admiral did not see fit to tarry. "At the relieving of the dawn watch" on Friday morning, December 7, *Santa María* and *Niña* got under way with the land breeze. Outside the harbor they were fortunate to catch a SW wind that whipped them around Cape St. Nicolas Môle and sent them scudding along the coast to the eastward. At what Columbus calls *un' agrezuela* (a craggy spot), a fertile valley opened up inland, but no inhabitants were visible. Off Pointe Jean Rabel they noted an isolated rock that is marked on eighteenth-century charts, but has since been undermined by the sea. They passed Port à l'Écu without entering, and at 1 P.M. anchored in a harbor between the hills that Columbus named *Puerto de la Concepción,* because it was the vigil of the Conception of the Virgin. For more practical reasons, the Spaniards soon renamed it *Bahía de los Mos-quitos*, now Moustique Bay.

Here, although the anchorage was only fair, he was detained five days by rain and easterly winds; and here, according to Las Casas, "seeing the grandeur and beauty of this island, and its resemblance to the land of Spain, although much superior, and that they caught fish similar to . . . those of Castile, and for other and similar reasons, the Admiral decided on Sunday, December 9, being in this Puerto de la Concepción, to name and call this island *La Isla Española*, as it is called today." *Hispaniola* (as Peter Martyr latinized it) is still the name of this great and beautiful island, the scene of the first European colony in the New World, of Colum-bus's trials and of his bitterest humiliation, and the final resting place of his ashes.

The Indian guides whom "every day we understand better, and they us," convinced Columbus that this land was insular, and that beyond it lay a continent called *Caribata*, the land of the *Caniba* or Caribs. Eager as ever to establish an oriental connection, Columbus jumped to the conclusion that these *Caniba* must be sub-jects of *El Gran Can*, and that the miscreants who made slave raids on his gentle Tainos were Chinese pirates or sea raiders.

On December 12 Columbus raised a great cross on the western cape of Moustique Bay, and took formal possession of Hispaniola for Ferdinand and Isabella. On the same day his men made their first contact with the people of Haiti. Three seamen who were ex-ploring the fertile valley at the head of the harbor pursued a crowd of fleeing natives, and captured a "very young and beautiful woman" clad only in a gold nose-plug. They brought her aboard *Santa María*, where she conversed with the captives from Cuba. They must have given her a good account of their usage by the Spaniards, for when the Admiral "sent her ashore very honorably," decently covered with some of the sailors' cast-offs and bedecked with jingly trading truck, she declared that she would rather stay with the "men from Heaven," whose godlike attributes evidently impressed her. It was deemed more useful, however, that she serve as a sort of decoy.

On the following day the Admiral sent nine men with an Indian interpreter upcountry in the hope that the restored damsel would have allayed the people's fears. The seamen followed a well-beaten trail which took them to the valley of Trois Rivières, where they came upon an immense village of a thousand huts, from which all the inhabitants fled. The Spaniards gave chase, their Indian guides calling out reassuringly that these "were not from Caniba but from Heaven," and to such good purpose that the delegation was soon surrounded by a curious though fearful crowd of some two thousand natives, who conducted them in triumph to the village. There the natives offered their guests cassava bread and fish, and satisfied their other wants. Understanding that seamen liked parrots, they presented them with a whole flock of the birds, which doubtless began their education in nautical Castilian forthwith. The Spaniards reported these natives to be handsomer than those of Cuba, "and among them they saw two wenches as white as they can be in Spain." The land, too, was fertile and beautiful, better than the plains of Cordova; there was a wide path up the valley; the Hispaniola mockingbird sang by day like the nightingales of Spain, crickets chirped and frogs croaked in a homelike manner at night, "the fishes were as in Spain," and "it was the greatest delight in the world" to be there. Columbus's only disappointment was their failure to find gold. Even the beautiful girl's nose-plug appeared to be exceptional, as she was a cacique's daughter.

At Moustique Bay Columbus made another celestial observation, the only one recorded in Haiti. He found the latitude to be 34° N, which is about that of Wilmington, N. C.; Moustique Bay is on latitude 19° 55'. He had mistaken for Polaris a star (Er Rai) of the constellation Cepheus.

Columbus still intended to visit Babeque, not knowing that Martín Alonso had already taken *Pinta* there and found no gold whatsoever. The Indian guides believed that it lay to the northeastward of Tortuga. So on December 14 with the wind due E, *Santa María* and *Niña* sailed NNE for Tortuga. They approached near enough to ascertain that it was a high and well-cultivated tableland "like the plain of Cordova," and to name three promontories. But as the wind was contrary for the presumed course to Babeque, they returned to Moustique Bay that night. Making a fresh start on December 15, they beat up the Tortuga Channel to the mouth of Trois Rivières, a clear river that flows over a pebbly bottom to the

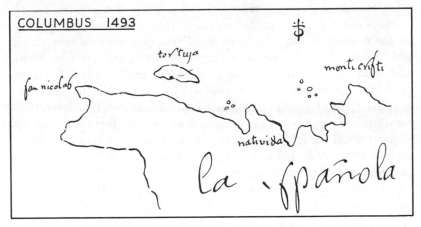

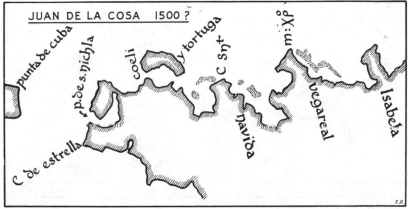

COLUMBUS'S SKETCH OF NORTHERN HAITI
COMPARED WITH LA COSA'S MAP

sea. Columbus, proposing to visit the great village that his men had
seen on the thirteenth, had the people row him in *Santa María's*
boat over the bar, and then, finding the current swift, had them
haul the boat upstream by a hawser. That did not take him very far,
for Trois Rivières is a mountain stream, quite unlike the drowned
river valleys of Northern Cuba. It was far enough, however, for
him to see "lands fit for crops and cattle of all sorts (of which
they have none), for orchards, and for everything in the world
that man can want."

On January 15, 1939, I visited the spot where the Admiral's boat journey ended, and can testify that this river valley, opening up the country for miles inland, and lined with wooded mountains and banana groves, is one of the loveliest of the Antilles. Columbus well named it *Valle del Paraiso* (Valley of Paradise), and the river the Guadalquivir, because it reminded him of that famous Andalusian river at Cordova. "This island throughout is a terrestrial paradise," commented Las Casas, "and as for Tortuga, near to which I lived some years, its beauty is a thing incredible." They say that no one who has not had a wild-boar hunt on Tortuga knows the ultimate joys of good hunting.

Columbus on his voyages seldom made protracted land excursions himself; he usually sent some of the men, while he stayed near or

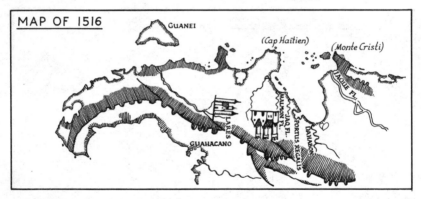

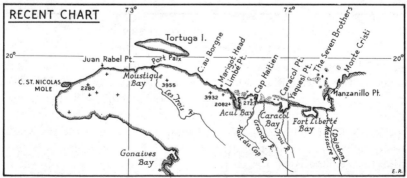

BOLOGNA MAP AND MODERN CHART OF HAITI

aboard the ships. I do not know whether this was owing to some constitutional defect that made walking difficult and painful to him, or whether he felt that an admiral should remain afloat. When it appeared that the great village on this new Guadalquivir could not be reached by boat, he gave up the attempt and remained aboard that night, wondering at the Indians' beacon fires that gleamed from the mountains, and from the heights of Tortuga. "This folk must be hunted hard by someone" he correctly inferred.

Progress in the Tortuga Channel had proved so difficult against head wind, sea and current that Columbus made sail from the Valle del Paraiso at midnight with the land breeze, hoping to get clear of Tortuga before the trade wind sprang up. "At the hour of tierce," about 9 A.M., "the wind came east." In mid-channel where the sea was roughest they encountered a solitary Indian in so small a canoe that the men wondered how he could keep it afloat in that rough sea. They hoisted him and canoe aboard, presented him with beads, bells and rings, and set him ashore at a village of newly built huts on a beach of the Hispaniola coast. This settlement was probably on the site of Port de Paix, a pretty little town founded by the French in 1664.

The solitary Indian made an excellent ambassador, and at this place the Spaniards made their first satisfactory contact with the Tainos of Haiti. About five hundred people came down to the beach accompanied by their "king," a youth of about twenty-one years to whom they showed much reverence. "This king and all the others went naked as their mothers bore them, and so the women without any shame; and they are the most handsome men and women he had found hitherto; so white that if they went clothed and protected themselves from the sun and air they would be as white as in Spain." Nowadays, we who sail Caribbean waters dress as near to the Indians as decency will permit and acquire all the sunburn we can; but the Spaniards were strongly of the opinion that too much sun was unhealthy, and a tanned body undignified.

Several of the common people came out to the ships, and Columbus sent ashore his marshal Diego de Harana accompanied by an interpreter, to present the king with a gift, and inquire about gold and Babeque. The monarch supplied the desired sailing directions and came aboard that evening (December 16). Columbus

"showed him due honor" and offered him Castilian food, of which
he ate a mouthful, and passed the rest along to some aged men of
his suite whom Columbus took to be his tutors and counselors.

What cheered Columbus more than anything else was a relative
abundance of gold ornaments worn by the natives of this village.
The next day, when men were sent ashore to trade, they encountered a cacique (the first time that Columbus uses this word)
whom they took to be a "governor of a province," and who showed
a remarkably acute trading sense with a piece of gold leaf that he
owned, as big as a man's hand. Instead of handing it over and ac-
cepting whatever was offered in exchange, the cacique kept this
piece of gold in his hut so that the Spaniards could not see how
much he had, and peddled it out in little bits, one at a time. Naturally the men bid against each other in eagerness to get their share.
He declared that there was plenty of gold in Tortuga, but evidently
did not welcome competition from that quarter; for when a canoe
with forty men came over from that island, the cacique threw
pebbles in the water until they sheered off. Columbus tarried at this
anchorage two days, hoping that the promised gold would arrive.

On December 18, the feast of the Annunciation, "Santa María de
la O" as the Spaniards called it because the proper anthems of the
day began with an invocation, Santa María and Niña dressed ship.
Every banner aboard was displayed, armorial escutcheons were
hung along bulwarks and waist, and salutes were fired with the
lombards. Gunpowder evidently failed to frighten the natives, for
at the hour of tierce the youthful cacique appeared on the beach,
and not long after came aboard Santa María with his attendants.
Las Casas has preserved for us the Admiral's own vivid account of
this state visit: —

Without doubt his dignity and the respect in which all hold him
would appear well to Your Highnesses, although they are all naked.
He, when he came aboard, found that I was dining at the table below
the stern castle, and at a quick walk he came to sit down beside me,
nor would he let me rise to meet him or get up from the table, but
begged that I should eat. I thought that he would like to eat our viands
and gave orders that he should straightway be brought some. And when
he entered below the castle, he made signs with the hand that all his
suite should stay outside, and so they did with the greatest readiness

and respect in the world, and they all seated themselves on the deck, except two men of mature age, whom I took to be his counselors and tutor, who came and seated themselves at his feet. And of the viands which were placed before him he took of each as much as one would take for a pregustation, and then sent the most part to his suite, and all ate of it; and so he did with the drink, which he simply raised to his lips and then gave to the others, and all with a wonderful dignity and very few words, and those that he said, according to what I could understand, were well arranged and sensible. . . . After dinner a squire brought a belt which is like those of Castile in shape but of different workmanship, which he took and gave me, and two pieces of worked gold which were very thin, so that I believe that here they obtain little of it, although I hold that they are very near to where it comes from and much exists. I saw that a tester which I had over my bed pleased him; I gave it to him, and some very good amber beads which I wore at my neck, and some red shoes, and a bottle of orange water, with which he took such satisfaction that it was marvellous. And he and his tutor and counselors were much troubled because they understood not me nor I them. Withal I recognized that he said that if anything here pleased me, the whole island was mine to command. I sent for some more beads, among which for a symbol I had a gold *excelente* on which are portrayed Your Highnesses, and showed it to him, and told him again as yesterday that Your Highnesses ruled and were lords over the best part of the world, and that there were none such great princes; and showed him the royal banners and the others with the cross. With this he was much impressed and said before his counselors what great lords Your Highnesses must be, since they had sent me without fear from so far and from Heaven. And many other things were said, but I understood not, except that I saw well that he held everything in great admiration.

It will be recalled that Columbus had already received aboard a cacique from the village near Holguín, Cuba; but the port and state of this young Haitian king, who was only a subordinate chief to the cacique Guacanagarí, impressed him as indicating a state of culture far superior to that of the sister island. He had the naked but dignified young savage piped over the side in proper naval style, and gave him "numerous lombard shots," the equivalent of our twenty-one guns, as he was being rowed ashore. There the cacique mounted a litter and was carried off by retainers to his residence, which lay some miles inland.

Although Columbus might treat a visiting cacique with dignity and even honor, his real thoughts, as he recorded them in his Journal for the eyes of his Sovereigns, indicate that he meant to take full advantage of the Tainos' weakness and good nature. "Your Highnesses may believe . . . that this island and all the others are as much yours as Castile, that here is wanting nothing save a settlement, and to command them to do what you will. For I with these people aboard, who are not many, could overrun all these islands without opposition; for already I have seen but three of these mariners go ashore where there was a multitude of these Indians, and all fled without their seeking to do them ill. They bear no arms, and are all unprotected and so very cowardly that a thousand would not face three; so they are fit to be ordered about and made to work, to sow and do aught else that may be needed, and you may build towns and teach them to go clothed and to adopt our customs."

There never crossed the mind of Columbus, or his fellow discoverers and conquistadors, any other notion of relations between Spaniard and American Indian save that of master and slave. It was a conception founded on the Spanish enslavement of Guanches in the Canaries, and on the Portuguese enslavement of Negroes in Africa, which Columbus had observed and taken for granted, and which the Church condoned. It never occurred to him that there was anything wrong in this pattern of race relations, begun and sanctioned by that devout Christian prince, D. Henrique of Portugal. But Las Casas, who spent the better part of a noble life vainly invoking the words and example of Jesus against the cruel and inordinate greed of Castilian Christians, comments on these words of the Admiral in stern and measured words: —

"Note here, that the natural, simple and kind gentleness and humble condition of the Indians, and want of arms or protection, gave the Spaniards the insolence to hold them of little account, and to impose on them the harshest tasks that they could, and to become glutted with oppression and destruction. And sure it is that here the Admiral enlarged himself in speech more than he should, and that what he here conceived and set forth from his lips, was the beginning of the ill usage he afterwards inflicted upon them."

If gold or something else of great and immediate value had not been discovered, the conquest of the New World might have been a brighter page in the history of Christianity. But Columbus was now nearing the gold-bearing regions of Hispaniola. On Monday, he was still talking of Babeque; on Tuesday "the Admiral learned from an old man that there were many neighboring islands within a hundred leagues or more . . . in which much gold was produced; he even told him of an island that was all gold, and in the others so great a quantity that they gather it and sift it as in a sieve, and smelt it and make bars and a thousand works of art; he showed the work by signs. This old man indicated to the Admiral the route and the position where it was; the Admiral determined to go there, and said that if the old man had not been so important a subject of that king, he would have detained him and taken him along, or, if he had known the language, he would have invited him; . . . but there was no sense in irritating them, so he decided to let him go." Without any sense of incongruity, Columbus follows this revelation of his covetousness by an account of raising a cross in the Indian village, at which ceremony the Indians exhibited such proper respect that "he hopes in Our Lord that all these islands will be converted."

Whether the old man had some knowledge of far-off Costa Rica where the Indians really did smelt gold and copper, or whether Columbus misunderstood his gestures, does not matter; the point is that the Admiral was now convinced that the gold-bearing regions lay toward the east; and to the eastward he got under way with the land breeze that very night.

"With the coming of day the wind turned east, with which all this day he could not get clear of the channel between those two islands, and at night he could not make a harbor that showed up there." But from mid-channel he could look far to the eastward, where cape after cape jutted out, a new mountain range showed up, and a high island (as it first appeared) which he called *Monte Caribata,* for he thought that this was the land of the Caribs. It was the mountainous Cape Haitien. That evening the new moon first appeared and soon set; but in the bright tropical starlight Columbus ventured to use the land breeze to make easting.

Sunrise December 20 discovered to the south of them a bay so beautiful that Columbus completely ran out of adjectives, and wished he had not used them all up on earlier harbors and bays. "He excuses himself," abstracts Las Casas, "saying that he has praised the former ones so much that he knows not how to extol this one, and that he fears that he will be supposed to have exaggerated it excessively; but . . . ancient mariners say and will say the same." In twenty-three years' following the sea, and sailing from the Levant to England and south to Guinea, he had seen nothing like it.

La Mar de Sancto Thomé (or *Santo Tomás*) as Columbus called this bay, because it was the vigil of Saint Thomas the Apostle, Acul Bay, as it is now called after a lady once loved by many sailors, is indeed one of the world's loveliest harbors. It offers such perfect protection in all weathers as to wring admiration from the most hard-boiled mariners. The mountains "which appear to reach the sky," wrote Columbus, "so that the Peak of Tenerife is nothing in comparison," compose like a landscape of Claude Lorrain, about the conical "Bonnet de l'Evêque" that King Henri Christophe crowned with a great stone citadel. But the entrance to Acul Bay is forbidding by reason of the outlying reefs, and Columbus had to feel his way in by lead line and the sharp eyes of boys posted aloft. He left exact directions which are still good today; you line up a little wooded island with the head of the harbor and steer straight for it, favoring the eastward side of the channel, and passing within a lombard shot of the island, which Columbus named *La Amiga*.

That day the wind was very light, the shoaler and more lively *Niña* sailed ahead; and while waiting for *Santa María* to catch up, Vicente Yáñez sent a boat ashore on the friendly little island, where the men dug up some roots that he and the Admiral took to be medicinal rhubarb, the Chinese drug that was imported into Spain over the caravan routes. So excited was Columbus at this evidence of being in Cathay that he later sent a boat 30 miles to obtain more of the plants, which turned out to be only a false rhubarb after all.

At sunset the vessels anchored in the inner harbor, which the Spaniards later called Lombardo Cove, doubtless because it is about half a mile, a "lombard shot," across the mouth. It is so protected, the Admiral says, "that one could moor with the ship's most ancient cable." The American yacht *Alice* proved the truth of this a few years ago, when she rode out a heavy norther in Lombardo Cove without even straightening her anchor chain.

Next morning, December 21, Columbus explored the harbor in the boats and landed and sent two men up a mountain to look for signs of a village. He knew that there must be one near by, from a canoe that had visited the flagship the night before. The men reported a village not far from the sea (the Tainos seldom built right on the seashore for fear of Carib raids), and the boats rowed to the nearest landing, where "so many came, men, women and children, that they covered the shore." As the visitors the previous night had been treated well, these Indians brought cassava bread and water in calabashes and earthenware vessels, and everything that they had. " 'And it should not be said that they gave it freely because it was worth little,' says the Admiral, 'for those who had pieces of gold gave them just as freely as those who gave a calabash of water; and it is easy to recognize,' says the Admiral, 'when something is given with a real heart to give.' "

These Acul Bay people were in an even more pristine state of innocence than elsewhere, for the women did not even wear the customary cotton clout; and whilst "in the other places all the men try to conceal their women from the Christians out of jealousy, here they do not, and the women have very pretty bodies, and they were the first to give thanks to Heaven and to bring what they had, especially things to eat, bread made of yams, and shrivelled quinces, and five or six kinds of fruit," which Columbus tried to preserve in order to exhibit them to the Queen. It is feared that none of his specimens reached Barcelona.

The Admiral remained with the boats, as was his custom, while six men were sent to view the Indian settlement. During their absence some canoes came from the "lords" of other villages on the bay, pressing the Admiral to visit them. This he did later in the day, and the same scenes of cheerful giving and profitable barter were repeated.

At daybreak on the twenty-second the fleet made sail with the land breeze, but found so strong an easterly wind outside that they returned to an anchorage near the mouth of the bay. There Columbus received messengers from Guacanagarí, the cacique who held sway over all northwestern Haiti, and whose seat was on the other side of Cape Haitien. The cacique's messenger brought as a gift the finest work of art that Columbus had yet seen in "The Indies." Las Casas describes it as a cotton girdle embroidered with white and red fishbones interspersed "in the same manner that the embroiderers make the orphreys on the chasubles in Castile." It was four fingers wide, and so stiff and strong that a shot from an arquebus could not penetrate it. In the center was a mask with the ears, tongue and nose of hammered gold.

It was late that day before the messengers managed to convey their invitation, for the Indian interpreters did not understand them very well. Columbus then decided to accept, but to send a boat piloted by the native canoe, to report on the route. In the afternoon he sent six men to another village upcountry, accompanied by Rodrigo de Escobedo the secretary, in order to see that the Indians were not imposed upon; the entire population escorted this embassy back to the ship, carrying the Spaniards pick-a-back across rivers and through swamps, and bearing fat tree ducks, skeins of cotton, and some little pieces of gold. That night and the next the Spaniards were kept awake entertaining visitors; Columbus reckoned that a thousand natives boarded *Santa María* in canoes, each bringing some gift, and that five hundred more came out swimming for want of canoes, although she was anchored almost a league from the shore. Everyone who appeared to enjoy some authority was questioned through the interpreters about gold, and the Admiral wrote, "Our Lord in his goodness guide me that I may find this gold, I mean their mine, for many here say they have knowledge of it." Columbus had high hopes of finding a rich gold-bearing region, like La Mina which he had visited on the coast of Guinea.

Sunday evening, December 23, the boat returned from Guacanagarí's village, reporting multitudes of people so eager to see the Admiral that "if the feast of the Nativity could be held in that harbor, all the people of that island, which he now guessed to be bigger than England, would come to see them." They brought basketfuls of presents for the Admiral, including pieces of gold and live parrots, as well as promises of lavish hospitality. The men who manned the boat reported that the course was clear to the royal residence, and recommended it as the perfect place to keep Christmas.

A merry enough Christmas might have been spent in Acul Bay; the real pull of Guacanagarí's invitation was the report of one of his subjects who came back with the boat, "concerning *Cipango,* which they called *Cybao.*" Cipangu, it will be recalled, was Marco Polo's name for Japan; and although he intended the initial "Ci" to be pronounced in the Italian manner *chi,* the Spaniards pronounced it after their manner, *Sipango.* So, when the Indians spoke of the *Cibao,* as central Hispaniola is still called to this day, and "declared that there was a great quantity of gold there," which was in a measure true, "and that the cacique bore banners of beaten gold," which was not, Columbus concluded that at last he was on the road to the fabulous Cipangu of the gold-roofed palaces.

So, after inditing another tribute to the kindness, generosity and "singularly loving behavior" of the Indians whom he was planning to enslave, Columbus took his departure from Acul Bay before sunrise on December 24, planning to spend a merry Christmas with Guacanagarí in Japan. He was heading for his first serious accident.

CHAPTER XXI

La Navidad

DECEMBER 24, 1492–JANUARY 16, 1493

Qui autem in praesidiis et speluncis sunt, peste morientur.

And they that be in the forts and in the caves shall die.

— EZEKIEL XXXIII 27

IN DUE course the trade wind blew up from the eastward — in Northern Hispaniola it generally runs parallel to the coast — and the two vessels had a tiresome day beating to windward, taking long tacks off shore, and making little progress because the wind was light and the current set westerly. Columbus took the opportunity to note down sailing directions for Acul Bay, and to write the words in praise of the natives that we have already quoted. Nightfall Christmas eve found *Santa María* and *Niña* off a high, rocky headland that he named *Punta Santa* in reference to the approaching festival, and which is now called Cape Haitien. At 11 P.M. when the watch was changed, *Santa María* had progressed only a league beyond the cape. The wind had died away until only occasional light airs ruffled the calm surface of the bay, and no sound was heard but a far-off swish of surf on the coral ledges of Cape Haitien harbor and the barrier reef that encloses Caracol Bay from the ocean. It was just such a night as Milton tells preceded the day of Christ's Nativity, when

> The winds, with wonder whist
> Smoothly the waters kist,
> Whispering new joys to the mild ocean,
> Who now hath quite forgot to rave,
> While birds of calm sit brooding on the charmed wave.

The middle watch was very loath to be routed out, for it had been impossible to sleep aboard on the two previous nights with curious savages swarming all over the flagship. The course to their destination seemed perfectly clear, for it had already been studied by the men who made the journey in the ship's boat; this was in fact the first night's sail on the entire voyage whose course had in some measure been charted before. *Niña* as usual was showing the way, and in the faint light of a setting five-day-old moon her spars and limp sails could be dimly seen. Yet the moon was too young and low to reveal any ruffle of white water where the ground swell was breaking lazily on three coral reefs, almost dead ahead. A feeling of complete security, the most fatal delusion that a seaman can entertain, stole like an opiate over the sleepy men aboard *Santa María*. The great majority of accidents at sea are not due to violence of the elements or defects in the ship, but to ignorance and over-confidence as to the ship's position.

Eleven o'clock, one hour before Christmas. The gromet on duty turns the *ampolleta* and sings his ditty,

> *Siete va pasada*
> *y en ocho muele;*
> *más molería*
> *si mi Dios quería,*
> *a mi Dios pidamos,*
> *que bien viaje hagamos . . .*

The pilot scratches on his slate the few miles he reckoned *Santa María* had made during the last four hours, the helm is relieved, and everyone off duty curls up in the steerage or along the bulwarks, and soon falls fast asleep. Columbus paces the quarter-deck for a few minutes, exchanges a few inconsequential remarks with Juan de la Cosa, the new officer of the watch, and retires to his cabin. He thanks God for another day's safe sailing, and for sending His only begotten Son to redeem the world. For a few moments he ponders on that scene in the stable at Bethlehem, then says an *Ave Maria* and falls into a deep sleep, his first in over forty-eight hours.

As soon as the Old Man is out of sight, the lookouts, boys and other members of the middle watch select soft spots on the deck

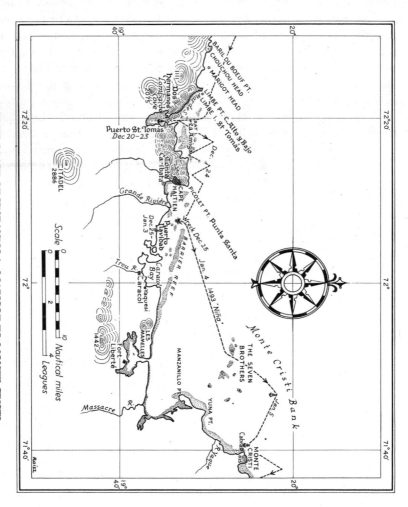

NORTH COAST OF HISPANIOLA, MARIGOT TO MONTE CRISTI

to indulge in a bit of "shut-eye" themselves. Juan de la Cosa paces
the quarter-deck a few times, yawning heavily, looks all around
the horizon and sees no sign of wind, notes *Niña* leading the way,
orders the helmsman (whom it was his duty to con) to steer by a
star and call him if there is any change in wind or weather, and lies
below to resume his own sleep. And pretty soon the helmsman, who
had dozed off once or twice already, decides he can bear it no
longer, kicks awake the gromet whose duty it is to turn the *ampolleta,* gives him charge of the huge, unwieldy tiller (which Columbus had forbidden under all circumstances) and curls up to sleep
in the steerage. So of forty men and boys (not counting Indian captives) aboard the flagship, nobody was awake but one little gromet.
Niña was invisible to him. He could see nothing out of the dark,
low steerage. The creaking of the great rudder on its gudgeons,
and the groans and squeaks and slats and rattles that any sailing
ship makes in a calm, shut out the sound of surf from his ears.

Just as the sand in the *ampolleta* ran out for the second time that
watch, indicating that Christmas Day had begun, *Santa María* slid
onto a shelving coral reef in Caracol Bay, so gently that nobody was
awakened. The sleepy boy was brought to attention by feeling the
rudder ground, then he heard the ground swell breaking close
aboard, and "gave tongue," says Columbus. The Admiral was first
on deck, then Juan de la Cosa ran out of his cabin, and before many
moments elapsed the deck was full of men and the calm night was
broken with shouts, orders, curses and imprecations.

Columbus promptly sized up the situation. *Santa María* had
grounded gently, bow on; and as she drew more water aft than
forward, the best chance to float her was to warp an anchor out into
deep water, lead the cable through the tiller-port to the big windlass
forward, and kedge her off stern first.

He ordered the master to haul in the ship's boat that was towing
astern, take the anchor and cable aboard, and go to it. Instead of
executing this proper seamanlike order, Juan de la Cosa with some
of his Basque pals piled into the boat and pulled away to *Niña* in
order to save their own skins. And *Santa María* had but the one
boat. Vicente Yáñez very properly refused to allow these cowardly refugees aboard, and ordered them back, having previously

sent over *Niña's* boat well manned to do what they could to help the Admiral.

In the meantime, *Santa María* was being driven higher and higher on the reef by the long swells that came in from seaward, her stern swung around so that she lay athwart the seas, each surge lifted her up and let her down with a thump on the rock; and coral rock can punch holes in a wooden ship faster than any other kind. So Columbus ordered the heavy mainmast cut away in order to lighten her. By the time *Niña's* boat came alongside it was too late to kedge her off and presently the seams had opened with the pounding, and the hull was filling with water. Seeing he could do no more, Columbus allowed himself and his crew to be ferried to *Niña,* and stood by until daylight.

Since this was one of the notable shipwrecks of history, we may pause a moment to comment. There is no allusion to it in the prolonged lawsuit between the heirs of Columbus and the crown, in which every effort was made to cast dirt on the departed Admiral. Hence it is natural to conclude that his own account of it is correct. The major blame attaches to Juan de la Cosa, who was not only master and part owner of *Santa María,* but officer of the middle watch that night. It was his responsibility to see that proper discipline was maintained, and he had no business to turn in and leave the deck in charge of a gromet. When the ship struck he showed gross insubordination and want of common seamanship in disobeying the Admiral's orders; pulling away to *Niña* and leaving *Santa María* to her fate was mutinous. Was it cowardice? Columbus himself calls the action of the master and his pals *traición* — treachery, making no charge of *cobardía* or poltroonery; and pure treachery I think it was. For men who had made the first ocean crossing, a gentle grounding on a calm night a few miles from shore was no occasion for funk. Reading between the lines, it seems that Juan de la Cosa was one of that contemptible breed of mariners who are jealous of their superior officer, and who make factions among the crew. Perhaps he thought himself a better seaman than Columbus, and his pride had been hurt by frequent overriding of his orders; for men of genius, imbued with one idea, are not always considerate of their inferiors. Perhaps there had been some wrangle between them about the very course they were sailing that night. Hence, I imagine, Juan de la Cosa's first thought on waking up and finding his ship aground was "damn him, he got her on and he can get her off," and he obeyed a disloyal impulse to save his particular cronies and leave the Castilians to get off as best they could. So singular an action on the part of a shipmaster and shipowner can hardly be explained except by some grave defect in his character.

The first Christmas to be celebrated in the New World was marked not by Masses and carols or feasting and sports, but by unremitting hard labor to float *Santa María* and salvage her stores, cargo and equipment. At daybreak Columbus sent ashore Diego de Harana and Pedro Gutiérrez to ask Guacanagarí's assistance, while he in the other boat made directly for the ship from behind the line of reef. By the time the sun was high Guacanagarí had sent out all his canoes and many of his people to discharge the ship, and that heavy task was almost completed on Christmas day. The cacique and his brothers kept careful watch both aboard and ashore to see that none of the cargo or the gear was stolen; and Columbus records that not so much as a lace point, a board or a nail was pilfered, although holes had to be chopped in the deck and topsides in order to get at some of the cargo. "From time to time," the cacique "sent one of his relatives to the weeping Admiral to console him, telling him that he must not be troubled or annoyed; that he would give him whatever he had." At sunrise December 26 Guacanagarí came aboard *Niña,* to which the Admiral had transferred his flag, "and almost weeping said that he must not show grief, that he would give him all he had, and that he had given the Christians who were ashore two very big houses, and would give more if necessary. . . . 'To such extent,' says the Admiral, 'are they loyal and without greed for the property of others, and that king was virtuous above all.'"

Gold dried more tears than sympathy. Even as he was receiving this early morning consolation from Guacanagarí a canoe from another place came alongside, the paddlers so eager for hawks' bells that they stood up, showing bits of gold and shouting *"Chuque! chuque!"* to imitate the sound of the little tinkly bells which they were mád to possess. Guacanagarí stood by in dignified silence until this unseemly barter was concluded, and then let fall that if the

Admiral would keep one hawk's bell for him, he would pay for it "four pieces of gold as big as the hand. The Admiral rejoiced to hear this, and later a seaman who came from shore said to the Admiral that it was marvellous the pieces of gold that the Christians ashore bartered for nothing; for a lace-point they gave pieces of gold worth more than two castellanos, and that this was nothing in respect to what it would be after a month. The king rejoiced to see the Admiral merry, and understood that he desired much gold, and said by signs that he knew a place near at hand where there was plenty of it in great abundance, and that he should be of good cheer, that he would give him as much gold as he wanted, . . . and especially that in *Cipango,* which they call *Cybao,* there was such a lot of it that they hold it for naught."

After giving this welcome information the cacique was presented with a shirt and a pair of gloves which pleased him immensely; thus clothed he was invited to dinner aboard *Niña,* which was probably not so pleasant. After that was over Guacanagarí treated the Admiral to what he considered a real dinner ashore. Columbus partook of "two or three kinds of *ajes*" (yams or sweet potatoes), of roast hutía and lobsters, and "their bread that they call *caçabí,*" cassava bread. The cacique ate so cleanly and decently, even washing his hands and rubbing them with herbs after the meal, that Columbus regarded him as one of nature's gentlemen. After dinner Guacanagarí led his guest to the *playa,* the strip of level white sand between his village and the mangrove swamps that fringe Caracol Bay; and when he began to talk of the dreadful Caribs and their bows and arrows which so terrified the Tainos, Columbus said, "I'll show you," and had one of his men put on an archery exhibit with a Turkish bow and arrows saved from the wreck. This was followed up by some lombard and musket shots, which terrified the natives and convinced Guacanagarí that his visitors were allies worth having. He presented to the Admiral, apparently without ironical intent, a great mask that had golden ears and eyes.

In no entry of Columbus's Journal are the workings of his mind so clear as on this day after his first Christmas in the New World. He now concluded that the shipwreck was the predestined will of God, in order to enable him to discover the Cibao gold mine and make a settlement. As Las Casas quotes his exact words, "So many things came to hand that in truth it was no disaster but great luck; for it is certain that if I had not run aground I should have kept to sea without anchoring in this place, because it is situated within a great bay, . . . nor on this voyage could I have left people here, or, had I desired to leave them, could I have given them good equipment, or so many weapons or supplies." Even poor mishandled *Santa María* is now written off the Admiral's books, because she was "very heavy and not suitable for the business of discovery." He concludes this day's work with the pious hope that the men he is leaving behind will obtain a barrel of gold by barter and also find "the mine of gold and the spicery," from whose products the Sovereigns will be able "to go and conquer the Holy Sepulchre" within three years. For, says he, "I declared to Your Highnesses that all the gain of this my Enterprise should be spent in the conquest of Jerusalem, and Your Highnesses smiled and said that it pleased you, and that even without this you had that strong desire." Smile if you will; but there can be no doubt of Columbus's sincerity in this matter. Even in such a crisis of the voyage his thoughts ran to Jerusalem regained.

Before the shipwreck Columbus had no intention of founding a settlement on this voyage of discovery, for he had only enough men to work his vessels. Now, making a settlement answered the question what to do with *Santa María's* people. There was no knowing what had become of *Pinta*, and the forty men from *Santa María* overcrowded little *Niña* with her crew of twenty-two. Guacanagarí was friendly, even affectionate; Cipangu-Cibao lay near, and the Spaniards were begging their Admiral for permission to remain behind, in order to get first whack at the gold, before all Castile came flocking over to buy castellanos at two a penny. So Columbus gave orders that a "tower and fortress" be erected ashore, and named it *La Navidad* in honor of the day of disaster that had so unexpectedly been turned to advantage — as he thought.

The shallow bay where fate decreed that this first, ill-fated European settlement in the New World should be attempted still remains nameless, although in the eighteenth century it was one of the richest localities in all America. About twelve miles long by three wide, it is bounded by the rocky peninsula of Cape Haitien

(Columbus's Punta Santa), where the French later built their gay
"Paris of the Antilles," by a rich alluvial plain, a tangle of mangrove swamp, and a barrier reef pierced by the broad channel
where *Santa María* sailed her last sail. This reef protects the bay
from the sea. A little behind the shore of the eastern section of
this bay, which the Spaniards named *Caracol* because of the snail-
like boat channels through the mangrove swamp, was Guacanagarí's village.

Facing the reef where *Santa María* was wrecked, near the middle of the bay and about two miles to the southward, is a long sand
beach; and somewhere near its eastern end Columbus selected the
site for Navidad.

Here the French founded an *embarcadère* for the wealthy alluvial parish of Limonade, which on the eve of the Revolution
had thirty-seven sugar mills with an annual production of eight
million pounds, and numerous coffee plantations, indigo works, and
rum distilleries. All that is now ruined; but there is a small Haitian
fishing village, Limonade Bord-de-Mer, very near the point on
the beach where Columbus founded his fort; and in the Admiral's
Puerto de la Navidad the fishermen moor their small craft today,
except when a norther compels them to haul out. Columbus would
have done better to have pitched this first American colony on Cape
Haitien Harbor; but the convenience of having it near the wreck
was obvious, and the misconduct of the garrison would have
brought the same result, wherever located.

Navidad fort was built largely of *Santa María's* planks, timbers
and fastenings, and provided with a "great cellar" for storage of
wine, biscuit and other stores salvaged from the flagship. Seeds
for sowing crops and a supply of trading truck to barter for gold
were also left. Thirty-nine men picked from the two caravels were
placed under the command of Diego de Harana, the marshal of
the fleet, and cousin to the Admiral's mistress. Juan de Medina the
tailor, Lope the ship-caulker, Alonso Morales, "chips" of *Niña*,
Domingo Vizcaino the cooper, Chachu the Basque boatswain,
Diego Pérez the ship's painter, "a gunner who was a man of good
skill," Luis de Torres the converted Jewish interpreter, Rodrigo de
Escobedo the secretary, Maestre Juan and Maestre Alonso the
two ships' surgeons, and Pedro Gutiérrez the former butler of

the king's dais, were among the volunteers who deemed themselves lucky to be chosen to man the fort. Columbus left *Santa María's* boat with the garrison, so that they could explore the coast, discover the gold mine, and find a better harbor than Navidad for a permanent settlement.

Several days elapsed while the men worked on the fort, with helpful Indians doing the lighterage and heavy lifting. Columbus exchanged daily visits, banquets and presents with Guacanagarí and his subject caciques. On the twenty-seventh some Indians arrived with news that *Pinta* was lying in a river two days' sail to the eastward. Guacanagarí furnished a canoe to bear a messenger and a "loving letter" from Columbus, who tactfully concealed his displeasure at the desertion, and begged Martín Alonso to return, "since Our Lord had shown them all so much favor." For Columbus did not wish to explore that unknown coast without a consort; one more grounding might be fatal. The canoe turned back without delivering the letter, but the messenger reported having seen a "king" with two great plates of gold on his head. On the thirtieth another Indian from the eastward declared that he had seen *Pinta;* and although some believed he was lying, the Admiral thought it best to make haste in that direction.

A choice item in the collection of mendacious stories that were circulated about Columbus after his death is this. Columbus lost himself on the way to Hispaniola, and only by virtue of letters and pilots sent by Martín Alonso did he manage to find the island and join *Pinta.*

On January 2, 1493, Guacanagarí and Columbus had a farewell party. The Admiral staged a sham fight and had *Niña* fire lombard shots through the grounded hull of *Santa María* in order to impress the natives. "The cacique showed the Admiral much love and great grief at his parting, especially when he saw him embark." After final embraces, and protestations of mutual love and esteem, Columbus was rowed aboard his new flagship *Niña*, intending to weigh anchors at once; but the wind in the meantime had turned east, and the sea was reported rough outside. So he remained in harbor that night and all next day, and also a second night because some of the Indians were still missing, and he wished to give them another chance to come aboard. How typical of exploring voyages was this delay to await the pleasure of dilatory, drunk or unwilling shipmates! Finally on the morning of Friday, January 4, "at sunrise he weighed anchors with a light wind, and the boat led the caravel out on a NW course, to get clear of the reef."

Columbus intended to shape a course directly for Spain, fearing lest Martín Alonso beat him home with the news and escape "the punishment that he deserved for having done so ill by parting company without permission." Once outside the reefs he sighted to the eastward what appeared to be an island "in the shape of a very fine tent, to which he gave the name Monte Cristi," a name it bears to this day. The peninsula, as it proved to be, looks exactly like a great yellow tent with a ridgepole, when one sights it at sea. You do not see its connection with the shore until about halfway from Cape Haitien.

Owing to light wind, *Niña* could not make Monte Cristi that day. She passed among the islets called the Seven Brothers and anchored on the edge of the bank, well out to sea. On the fifth she made the natural harbor between Monte Cristi and Isla Cabra, a harbor "sheltered from all winds except the N and NW, and he says that they seldom blow in that country." Oh! don't they? Las Casas, who knew better, interpolates here, "The Admiral had never experienced the fury of these two winds."

On the morning of January 6, sailing on a Sunday as he was so eager to get along, the Admiral did a good stretch eastward with the land breeze. At noon the trade wind blew up fresh, forcing *Niña* to take a leg offshore, near some shoals where the Comte de Grasse's great flagship *Ville de Paris* touched in 1781 when she was hastening to Chesapeake Bay. Columbus sent a seaman aloft to spy out the deep spots, when whom should he see but *Pinta* scudding down-wind towards them. And as there was no anchorage near, *Niña* put about and sailed back to the Isla Cabra anchorage in her company.

Martín Alonso came aboard the flagship that evening "to excuse himself, alleging that he had left him against his will, giving reasons for it. But the Admiral says that they were all false, and that with much insolence and greed he had separated that night that he parted from him, and that he knew not (says the Admiral) whence came the insolence and disloyalty that he had shown him on that voyage, which the Admiral wished to forget, in order not to help the evil works of Satan, who sought to hinder that voyage." It appeared that *Pinta* had called at Babeque (Great Inagua) and found no gold, thence proceeded eastward to Monte Cristi, and for three weeks had been in a harbor to the eastward — probably Puerto Blanco — where she had found plenty. According to his son Arias Pérez, who joined *Pinta* at Bayona and heard the story of this voyage from his father's lips, Martín Alonso made an excursion upcountry from the harbor, reached the territory of the powerful Caonabó, and brought back much gold. If this be true, and not merely part of the Pinzón "build-up," Martín Alonso was first to reach the Cibao, the gold-bearing region which had been Columbus's objective in Hispaniola.

Martín Alonso, it seems, had heard from the Indians of *Santa María's* shipwreck, and was sailing down-wind to join the others when he met *Niña*. Both Admiral and captain must have been relieved at finding a consort for the homeward passage, and Columbus decided that he could now afford to explore the rest of Northern Hispaniola before taking off for Spain. But, owing to the manner in which they had parted, the meeting must have been unpleasant. Vicente Yáñez showed a tendency to gang up with the rest of the Pinzón family against Columbus, "and did not obey his orders, but did and said many improper things against him . . . and they were very undisciplined people," and "a mutinous lot." So the Admiral determined "to make the greatest possible haste" home. "I will not suffer," he says, "the deeds of lewd fellows devoid of virtue, who contrary to him who conferred honor upon them, presume to do their own will with slight respect."

Two days wind-bound at Monte Cristi were employed in caulking *Niña*, taking on wood and water, and exploring the lower course of the Rio Yaque del Norte. Columbus reported it to be so full of gold that grains of the fine metal adhered to the barrel hoops when they filled the casks with river water, and some of these grains were as large as lentils. Las Casas comments marginally, "I think that most of it would have been fool's gold, because there's much of it in that place, and the Admiral was much too inclined to think that all's gold that glitters." Perhaps so; but this Rio Yaque drains the Cibao, principal source of gold in Hispaniola, and on its upper waters in 1494 Columbus built his first interior fort. Even today there is gold in the valley of the Yaque; the country women pan it out and collect the grains in quills of turkey feathers, which they take to the market towns as currency. So I think that here the Spaniards found their first virgin gold in the New World.

On the way to this Rio del Oro, as Columbus called the Yaque del Norte, "he saw three *serenas* (mermaids) who rose very high from the sea, but they were not as beautiful as they are painted, although to some extent they have a human appearance in the face. He said that he had seen some in Guinea on the coast of Malagueta." These last were the West African dugong; the Haitian "mermaids" were the Caribbean manatee or sea cow whose articulated head and armlike fore limbs have an uncanny human appearance. They are certainly not beautiful, but stuffed manatee used to be a staple of our country fairs as "gen-u-wine mermaids." Columbus's habit of accurate and honest observation is proved by resisting the temptation to engraft these sea cows onto the classical myth. What a good story it would have made for the Sovereigns, to have the Spaniards conducted to their first River of Gold by lovely and seductive mermaids!

Eager to get on with the voyage, and break up the Pinzón cabal, Columbus ordered sail to be made at midnight January 8 despite a SE wind, and took an ENE leg out to sea. Coming about during the day, the two vessels made anchorage that night in the shelter of a cape that Columbus named *Punta Roja;* it was probably the modern Punta Rucía. The rich hinterland and wooded mountains tempted him to stay, but he pressed on. On January 10 the caravels made Puerto Blanco, where *Pinta* had traded so profitably on her own. Martín Alonso had named it after himself; but Columbus, annoyed at this presumption on the part of his disloyal subordinate, changed the name to Rio de Gracia, River of Grace. This indicated that Martín Alonso was pardoned, but had better behave himself in future. "His wickedness was notorious," notes Columbus, "for he had kept half the gold obtained for himself, and had taken by force four Indian men and two wenches," whom the Admiral caused to be set ashore. Apparently it was immoral for anyone but himself to kidnap Indians.

Next day, the fleet sighted the Loma Isabela de Torres, which Columbus named *Monte Plata*, because of the silver clouds that covered its summit; he looked into the harbor at its foot (Puerto Plata), but did not tarry. Many capes and harbors were discovered that day, and the night was spent jogging off-and-on outside Escocesa Bay, for fear of shoals to the eastward. At dawn January 12 the two caravels made sail and went boiling along before a fresh westerly, skipping several tempting bays and harbors because of the good chance to make easting. That evening they rounded Cape Samaná, which Columbus well said looked like Cape St. Vincent, but he romantically named it *Cabo del Enamorado* (of the Lover), probably because it suggested some "lovers' leap" that he had seen in Spain. They continued along the coast southwesterly around Punta Balandra, and came to an anchor in 12 fathoms near the mouth of Samaná Bay, between Cayo Levantado (which Columbus described as *una isleta pequeñuela*, "a tiny little island") and the northern shore.

Here, on a pretty beach just east of a point that is still called Las Flechas (The Arrows), Columbus came as close as he ever did on this voyage to a dangerous encounter with the Indians. Samaná Bay, according to Las Casas, was inhabited by a tribe called the Ciguayos, Arawaks who had either received an infiltration of Caribs, or who in self-defense adopted Carib weapons. When the boat went ashore to obtain a few yams — for Columbus had been overgenerous with supplies for Navidad, and wished to stock up for the homeward passage — his people encountered some very ugly natives whose faces were stained with charcoal instead of painted in bright Taino colors, and whose long coarse hair was gathered behind into nets of parrots' feathers. And, what was more significant, they were carrying bows and arrows, the first that the Spaniards had seen in the Indies. Columbus had passed Escocesa Bay so far offshore that he could see no land at the head of it, consequently he believed that Cape Samaná and Balandra Head belonged to a separate island, and that these ill-favored fellows were the dreaded Caribs. He questioned one of them through an interpreter, who, as Las Casas comments, did not understand the language; for when inquiry was made about gold the interpreter picked up the word *guanin*. This was an alloy of gold and copper that the Indians smelted on the mainland, but the Spaniards took it to be the name of an island where gold was to be found. After this quiz the Indian was brought aboard to be suitably entertained as a decoy for the others, and later sent ashore with an assortment of trinkets and bits of colored cloth; but the usual impression made by these free samples was not produced.

When *Niña's* boat landed over fifty naked Indians armed with bows and arrows and palm-tree cudgels were encountered. At the instance of the shore-going native they laid aside their weapons, which the Spaniards endeavored to buy; but after two bows had been sold, the Indians ran back to their deposit of weapons as if to pick them up and attack. "The Christians being prepared, as always the Admiral advised them to be, fell upon them, and gave an Indian a great slash on the buttocks and wounded another in the breast with an arrow. Seeing that they could gain little, although the Christians were not more than seven and they fifty and more, they turned in flight, until not one remained, one leaving his arms here, and another his bows there." Plenty of souvenirs were obtained by the landing party.

ANCHORAGE OF "NINA" AND "PINTA" IN SAMANA BAY

Next day, January 14, a cacique came down to the beach without weapons and was entertained aboard and sent away "content," biscuits and honey inside, and a red cap and beads outside. He promised a gold crown in return; and the crown was duly sent aboard on the fifteenth, together with some skeins of cotton.

Both caravels were leaking badly (owing, says the Admiral, to scamped work by the Palos shipyards), and he and Pinzón were eager to find a suitable beach for careening and caulking them before the long voyage home. But there was something so odd and sinister about these Ciguayos that the men were uneasy and eager to be off. Columbus had planned, he says, to stay over the seventeenth, in order to observe a conjunction of Mars with Mercury, and an opposition of Jupiter with the sun that was predicted in his Regiomontanus *Ephemerides*. But he dared not risk a longer stay; and when the wind came west on Wednesday, January 16, he decided to leave this "Bay of the Arrows." It was the last anchorage of *Pinta* and *Niña* in the New World.

CHAPTER XXII

Homeward Passage

JANUARY 16–FEBRUARY 11, 1493

Et cum anchoras sustulissent, committebant se mari, . . .
et leuato artemone secuendum aurae flatum . . .

And when they had taken up the anchors, they committed themselves unto the sea . . . and hoisted up the mainsail to the wind. . . .

— ACTS xxvii 40

I N THE dark of the moon, three hours before daybreak on Wednesday, January 16, 1493, the Admiral "departed from the gulf
which he called *el Golfo de las Flechas* (of the Arrows) with the
land breeze, afterwards with the wind West, turning the prow East
and by North." So begins his Journal of the first homeward passage
from America to Europe. It proved to be a far more difficult feat of
navigation than the outward passage of discovery, for no soft trade
winds would serve to blow the two caravels gently back to Spain.
Columbus must get them out of the trade-wind area and into the
zone of westerlies; and it was the winter season when westerlies in
the North Atlantic are strong and boisterous, accompanied by heavy
rain and high seas. The Admiral would need all his resources of
seamanship to cope with the weather, and all his native wit to deal
with the Portuguese, before he could report his discovery to the
Sovereigns of Spain. And he must accomplish this without *Santa
María*. The homeward passage is a fascinating story of a man of
genius, with the greatest geographical secret of all time locked in
his breast, fighting against human depravity and winter weather
for the privilege of making known his glad tidings.

When *Niña* and *Pinta* passed Balandra Head, Bay of Samaná,
before daybreak on January 16, it was not supposed that the voyage
of discovery was over. From the Indians of Hispaniola, particularly

four youths who boarded *Niña* at Samaná and were promptly impressed, Columbus learned of an *Isla de Carib* (probably Puerto Rico), visible "from there." The Admiral was curious to see those dreadful man-eating Caribs, of whose incredible exploits he had been told by the timid Tainos; and he was even more eager to check their tale of an island named *Matinino*, "wholly inhabited by women without men." Later conquistadores connected this with the classical myth of the Amazons, and so named the world's greatest river; but Columbus was looking for oriental evidence. He had read in Marco Polo of the Islands Masculina and Feminea in the Indian Ocean, the one exclusively inhabited by men and the other only by women. Every year the men visited the female island and stayed three months, after which the women threw them out, along with the small boys who were growing up. This tale seemed such an amusing and practical solution to the eternal war between the sexes that it became one of the most popular of Marco Polo's yarns.

Now, curiously enough, the Arawaks had a very similar myth. Their culture-hero Guagugiona set forth with a chosen band of shipmates and women passengers from the cave Cacibagiagua in which all mankind hitherto had lived, in order to discover new lands for *Lebensraum*. He left all the women on an island called Matinino, where they had lived an Amazon-like existence ever since, receiving the annual male visitation and all that, just as Marco Polo had described on the Female Island in the Indian Ocean. Columbus's eagerness to see this Isle of Women came not only from a natural male curiosity, and the desire to relate a genuine marvel, but because it would furnish that incontrovertible evidence of being in the Indies which he still lacked. And he wished, as he wrote, "to bring five or six" of the women "to the Sovereigns." So the Admiral's plan was to touch at the Carib Isle, visit Matinino, and then head for Spain.

Niña and *Pinta* passed out of Samaná Bay on January 16, 1493, with a westerly wind (which was exceptional for that season), and steered E by N, which the impressed Indians indicated to be the course for the Isle of Women. Actually that course took the fleet out to sea. Before they had sailed 40 miles the Indians began to make signs that the Amazon Isle lay to the southeastward. Assuming that they meant the actual island of Martinique, this was correct.

Columbus changed course accordingly, and very shortly changed his plan too. As the Journal says: —

"After he had gone two leagues the wind freshened, very good to go to Spain. He observed among the people that they began to be downhearted because they were deviating from the direct course, because of the considerable water that both caravels were making, and they had no remedy save in God. He had to abandon the course that he thought led to the island, and turned to the direct course for Spain, NE by E, and proceeded thus until sunset 48 Roman miles which are 12 leagues."

This is one of the few quick changes of plan that Columbus made, and certainly it was wise. On the return passage of his Second Voyage, in the winter season of 1496, it took *Niña* a month to beat from Isabola in Northern Hispaniola to Guadeloupe, which is nearer than Martinique. The chance of collecting a few women, some oriental evidence and a tall tale, was not worth the delay.

The key to Columbus's plan for the homeward passage is that sentence in his Journal for January 16 on the change of course: *bolvió al derecho de España, nordeste quarta del leste,* "he turned to the direct course for Spain, Northeast and by East." He was grossly mistaken if he supposed this to be the direct course for Spain. It would have missed even the British Isles, and fetched up somewhere in the Arctic. Yet, just as his colossal underestimate of the width of the Ocean led him to discover America, so this equally gross error in the course for home enabled him to get there. For, as the experience of later voyages proved, the fastest route for a sailing vessel from Hispaniola to Europe was to work northward, close-hauled on the trade wind, to the latitude of Bermuda, and there catch the prevailing westerlies for Spain. Columbus, of course, did not know this. He apparently expected a convenient westerly turn of wind, in the latitude where he then was. Actually the trade wind never did allow him to steer NE by E; yet, by clinging as close as he could to that course, sailing anywhere from N by E to NE by N on the starboard tack, coming about and heading from E to SE on the port tack when the wind headed him, he made northing pretty steadily, toward the latitude of Bermuda where the brave winter westerlies would send the caravels rolling home before the wind.

Columbus had a very good chance for his homeward as for his outward passage, and the caravels did very well on this long beat to windward; their performance inspires respect for their weatherly qualities. Although most of the twenty-four-hour runs were less than 100 miles, *Niña* (with *Pinta* holding her back) logged 127 on January 21 and 138 on January 19, this last being an average of 5.7 knots, and on four different courses; very nice sailing indeed.* As yet the trade wind had not raised enough head sea to bother them. " 'The air,' says the Admiral, 'very soft and sweet as in Seville during April and May,' and 'the sea,' says he, 'many thanks be to God, always very smooth.' " Next day, having reached latitude 25°, the air was notably cooler. After you become used to the tropics, a drop of five degrees Fahrenheit seems terrible.

On the first day out they entered the Sargasso Sea, on the evening of the third they saw the new moon, and every day boatswain-birds, boobies and petrels were about; the man-o'-war birds followed them for 200 miles from the islands. Columbus, observing one of these that circled the caravel "and later made off to the SSE," inferred "that in that quarter there were some islands," which gave him an idea for the Second Voyage. A welcome sight was a school of tunny fish, with which Spaniards were familiar at home. As they sped away northeasterly the Admiral joked with the men, saying that the tunnies must be bound for the Duke of Cadiz's tuna-meat factory at Conil near Cape Trafalgar; too bad we can't throw them a line!

Shortly before midnight of January 22, *Niña* and *Pinta* crossed the route of the outward passage, and entered a wide stretch of the North Atlantic where no ship had sailed before. Seamen used to call this zone the "horse latitudes" from the long calms fatal to livestock, but Columbus fortunately knew nothing about that. On January 25, when he crossed latitude 28° and sailed but 49 miles, "the seamen killed a porpoise and a tremendous shark; and he says that they had good need of them, because they had nothing left to eat but bread and wine and *ajes* of the Indies." A pretty grim prospect for grub, to be sure.

---

* Distances quoted are all net, after deducting the 15 per cent average over-estimate in the Journal for the homeward passage.

From noon January 27 to sunrise January 30 the fleet ran ENE
with a light southerly breeze, and in sixty-six hours footed only 112
miles. They were lucky to do so well. Fish were caught and birds
and gulfweed were sighted every day. During the last two days of
January the wind picked up a little, and by sunset January 31,
according to Captain McElroy's plotting of the Admiral's dead-
reckoning, they had reached latitude 31° 46′ N, very near that of
Bermuda (32° 15′), which lay about 450 miles to the westward.
This was the point where, as the Spaniards learned a few years
later, one might expect to catch the westerlies, and straighten out
for the run home; and that is what happened to Columbus. From
sunrise January 31 until sunset February 3, "with the same wind
aft" and "the sea very smooth, thank God," the caravels made 358
miles to the ENE. "sea so covered with weed that if they hadn't
seen it before they would have been afraid of shoals." They were
right in the midst of the Sargasso Sea. February 1 was the night of
full moon, and the effect of moonlight on a sargassum-covered
ocean with a fresh and favoring wind impelling your ships through
the undulating meadow at a high rate of speed, the weed making
a peculiar soft swishing sound as it brushes by, has a strange and
magical beauty.

Undoubtedly Columbus had set the new course ENE, one point
south of his "direct" course for Spain, because he deemed it necessary to compensate for the many days that he had been forced to
sail to the northward. But how far north of that direct course was
he? With changes of course almost every day it had been difficult
to plot the dead-reckoning, and Columbus was none too sure that
this ENE course would lead to Spain. Actually it would have led
him somewhere between Scotland and Iceland. Accordingly on
the night of February 2–3, the much-abused quadrant and a
hitherto unmentioned astrolabe were brought on deck for the
Admiral to try another shot at Polaris. But he was out of practice
and had waited too long. Three days of westerlies had raised
quite a swell, and Niña was rolling and pitching too heavily for
these crude instruments to catch a luminous pinpoint in the heavens.
Too bad, for this time Columbus made no mistake in the identity
of Polaris. He remarked "the North Star appeared very high, as
on Cape St. Vincent," which is on latitude 37° N. According to

our interpretation of Columbus's dead-reckoning, at sunset February 2 he was crossing latitude 33° 36', and at sunrise the third had reached 34° 15'. Consequently his calculation was not less than 165 and not more than 200 miles out; not bad for a naked-eye star shot.

Columbus's belief that he was approaching latitude 37° N was confirmed by a change of weather on the night of February 3: "The sky was very overcast and rainy, and it was rather cold, because of which he knew he had not reached the height of the Azores." This statement seems a *non sequitur,* for the Azores are notably cold and rainy in winter. But he evidently believed that *Niña* had made sufficient northing, for at sunrise on February 4 he set his course due East.

Niña and *Pinta,* according to our plotting of Columbus's dead-reckoning, were now in latitude 35° 30' N, and so about 100 miles south of the parallel of Santa Maria, most southerly of the Azores. A 90° (true) course from this point would have missed the Azores and fetched up on Cape Spartel, but for two circumstances. The caravels were crossing the isogonic lines of 7° and 10° westerly variation of the compass, and consequently a magnetic E course worked out at 80° to 83° true, which constantly took them a little further north. The other was a storm that drove *Niña* northeasterly just in time to fetch up at Santa Maria.

A winter northwest gale was now blowing the two caravels home at steamboat speed. During the four days February 4–7 they did the fastest sailing of the entire voyage out or home, making 598 miles, an average of almost 150 a day. From sunset February 5 to sunset on the sixth, *Niña* and *Pinta* made the magnificent run of 198 miles, and at times approached a speed of 11 knots.

Suppose we luff up a minute and consider what this means. With the wind on their port quarters, fore and main courses set, in a rough, breaking sea of cobalt blue under a brilliant winter sky, these caravels of 1493 were making a speed that any ocean-going sailing yacht of today might envy. Whenever a modern schooner or ketch of the approximate length of *Niña* makes a 200-mile run, her owner's friends hear about it. In ocean races, yachts built only for speed, equipped with wire rigging and a cloud of light sails, tuned up to a high pitch and driven by a crew of tough young

Corinthians, often surpass the performance of *Pinta* and *Niña;* but old-fashioned gaff-headed schooners and brigs do not often equal it.

Speed under sail, because of the beauty of the ship herself, the music of wind and water, and also because of some deep, unfathomable sentiment in the soul of a seaman, yields even today an acute sensation of speed, comparable only to skiing or riding a fast horse in a steeplechase. Motorized travel afloat or ashore, or even in the air (unless in the latest fighting planes of which I have no experience), is slow and tame in comparison. Imagine then if you can what a glorious experience those seamen were having aboard *Niña* and *Pinta.* Unless any of them had ridden a racehorse, 11 knots was a greater absolute speed than they had ever known. They were homeward bound after the greatest sea adventure in the history of mankind, bursting with stories of a world unknown even to the boldest sea rovers of antiquity, a world untouched by a Rome in the days of her greatest glory, undivined by the subtle Arabs. Their Admiral knew the way, and all the saints in Heaven were conspiring to send him fair winds, clear weather and following seas. But this was the domain of the pagan gods Neptune and Aeolus, who were getting ready to uncork something very nasty.

On February 6, in the midst of this gorgeous and long-sustained burst of speed, there was an interesting discussion aboard *Niña* about her position; the wind was blowing too hard to take the opinion of navigators aboard *Pinta.* Captain Vicente Yáñez Pinzón declared that on the morning of February 6 Flores in the Azores bore due N, and Madeira due East. Bartolomé Roldán, who had been studying pilotage on the voyage, said that Fayal bore NE and Porto Santo, East. Both were very wrong indeed, but the amateur less so than the professional. Roldán's position was about 375 miles SE by E, and Pinzón's about 600 miles ESE of the true position, as plotted from Columbus's dead-reckoning.

On February 7 another pilot, Peralonso Niño, declared that *Niña* was already between the meridians of Terceira and of Santa Maria and would pass 38 miles north of Madeira; he was only 200 miles out in latitude and 600 miles in longitude! Columbus himself placed the fleet 75 leagues south of the parallel of Flores, an overestimate of about 65 miles. He wisely did not commit himself about longitude at this point.

Disagreements of this sort among navigators were to be expected in days of primitive instruments and rule-of-thumb plotting; and they are by no means absent today when we have instruments of precision and scientific methods. Eugenio de Salazar, who crossed from the Canaries to Hispaniola in 1573, exclaimed in one of his letters home, "O! how God in his omnipotence can have placed this subtle and so important art of navigation in wit so dull and hands so clumsy as those of these pilots! And to see them inquire, one of the other, 'how many degrees hath your honor found?' One says 'sixteen,' another 'a scant twenty,' and another, 'thirteen and a half.' Presently they ask, 'how doth your honor find himself with respect to the land?' One says 'I find myself 40 leagues from land,' another 'I say 150,' another says 'I find myself this morning 92 leagues away.' And be it three or three hundred, nobody agrees with anyone else, or with the truth."

By nightfall February 7 the fresh northwesterly gale was spent, and during the next two days the fleet experienced "soft and variable winds," according to Las Casas. In an E wind they made 75 miles to the SSE, which pulled them further from an Azorean landfall, but before dawn of the ninth the wind veered to ESE, so starboard tacks were boarded and the caravels steered NE. Columbus did not intend to call at the Azores, but he was probably now hoping to pick up one of them in order to check his position. At ten in the morning of February 9 the fleet straightened out again on an easterly course, but made only 24 miles by sunset. The brave west winds then returned; and during the next twenty-four hours *Niña* and *Pinta* made a fine run of 154 miles.

That day, February 10, there was more anxious plotting of the reckoning. Vicente Yáñez, Peralonso Niño, Sancho Ruiz and the amateur Roldán agreed that they had reached a meridian 5 leagues east of Santa Maria in the Azores, and were about on the latitude of Madeira and Porto Santo. This was about 500 miles E by S ½S of their true position. Columbus reckoned that at the end of this day's run, when the fleet according to our calculation was in latitude 35° 58′ N, longitude 33° 15′ W, the island of Flores bore due north. He also figured out that Nafe (Casablanca in Morocco) bore

due east. In other words, he put the fleet 175 miles SE ¾S of its
true position—supposing he knew the correct positions of Flores and
of Casablanca.

Yet in comparison with the pilots' reckoning, and assuming that
they all agreed on the relative positions of the Azores, Madeira and
Casablanca, Columbus was about 30 miles nearer the true latitude
and 340 miles nearer the true longitude than anyone else.

It must have been during these three weeks of good weather
and serviceable if not always fair winds that Columbus composed
the famous Letter on his First Voyage, often called the Letter to
Santangel or to Sánchez. This letter, not addressed to any particular person, but intended as a public announcement of his voyage,
was enclosed in one to the Sovereigns that has been lost. They
had a number of manuscript copies made for different court officials, and one of these, endorsed to Luis de Santangel, was printed
(very badly) at Barcelona in the summer of 1493 as a four-page
folio pamphlet, the unique surviving example of which is in the
New York Public Library. From a better copy than the Barcelona
printer used, a Latin translation was made by Leandro de Cosco,
which passed through nine editions (Rome, Paris, Basle, Antwerp)
in 1493–1494; this was promptly turned into Italian verse, of which
three editions were printed before the end of 1493. Some editions
of *De Insulis inuentis* (the earliest Latin title) were liberally illustrated by woodcuts taken from other books, having no relation
whatsoever to Columbus, his ships, or the West Indies. The letter
is dated February 15 *en la caravela, sobre las yslas de Canaria*,
"aboard the caravel, off the Canaries," but it must have been composed before February 12, not in the storm that followed; and for
"Canaries" read "Azores," within sight of which Columbus was on
the fifteenth. He probably completed and signed the letter a few
days later aboard *Niña* when at anchor off Santa Maria, hoping to
forward it thence by way of Portugal in case anything should
happen to him on the last leg of the voyage; but the attitude of
the Azorean authorities, as we shall see, was such that the Admiral
decided to be his own postman.

Everything important or calculated to interest the Sovereigns and
invite support for a second voyage is cited in the Letter; but courses

and distances are omitted, lest interlopers gather forbidden fruit. The loss of *Santa María* is not told; Columbus deceptively remarks that he left one of the vessels with his men at Navidad. On the whole, the Letter is an excellent précis of the Journal, and proves that Columbus had developed considerable skill in exposition.

CHAPTER XXIII

Azorean Agony

*Turbati sunt, et moti sunt sicut ebrius: et omnis sapientia
eorum deuorata est. Et clamaurunt ad Dominum cum tri-
bularentur, et de necessitatibus eorum eduxit eos.*

They reel to and fro, and stagger like a drunken man,
and are at their wit's end. Then they cry unto the Lord in
their trouble, and he bringeth them out of their distress.
— PSALM cvi 27–28

THE winter of 1492–1493 was unusually cold and tempestuous
in Southern Europe. Even the harbor of Genoa was frozen
over on Christmas day, so that small vessels could not enter or clear,
and ships lay wind-bound at Lisbon for months. *Niña* and *Pinta* had
been lucky so far, but they were headed right into one of the
stormiest regions of the North Atlantic.

On Monday, February 12, after another fine day's run of 150
miles to the eastward, the fleet ran into dirty weather, the first
experienced this voyage. Columbus's account of the next few days
is exceedingly interesting, for it is one of the earliest, if not the
first detailed description of an actual storm at sea. The data in his
Journal when examined in the light of modern meteorology show
that this was no ordinary cyclonic storm, but a disturbance marked
by well-developed "fronts," dividing radial areas where a cold air
mass moving south from the Arctic comes up against a warm air
mass moving north from the tropics.

Storms of this character are not uncommon in the region of the
Azores, and their importance for shipping and flying is so great

that in recent years they have been intensively studied. Among existing descriptions of such storms during the last five years there are at least two which fit in almost every detail those that Columbus experienced. We can see that the disturbance which brought so much agony to *Pinta* and *Niña* was caused by an intense low-pressure area the center of which was passing north of the Azores, with SW to W winds of "strong" or "full gale" strength (9 or 10 on Beaufort scale) in its southern and southwestern sectors. The isobaric system was probably elongated in a WSW to ENE direction, which by bringing different winds near one another was responsible for the terrible cross seas that almost overwhelmed *Niña*. Three distinct air masses, separated by one warm and two cold fronts, seem to have been involved in the circulation; and the passage from one air mass to another through the front separating them gave the caravels their worst beating.

At daylight February 12 Columbus "began to have heavy seas and tempest, and, says he, if the caravel had not been very staunch and well found, he would have been afraid of being lost." From sunrise to sunset, wind SW and force 7 to 8, she ran about 35 miles "with much toil and peril" under bare poles — "dry tree" the Spaniards called it. That night *Niña* labored heavily. Lightning flashed thrice to the NNE, direction of the low center. In the morning of February 13 the wind moderated a little, since they were skirting the southern edge of the disturbance; and *Niña* made a little sail. In the afternoon the wind increased again, "the ocean made up something terrible," with a cross sea that caused the caravels to labor heavily. They rolled and pitched in an alarming manner, and everything that was not lashed down went tumbling about the decks and cabins. A westerly swell kicked up by another sector of the storm was coming through and crossing the wave crests raised by the strong SW wind.

At nightfall February 13 the wind blew yet harder, and the cross seas formed dangerous pyramidical waves that stopped the caravels' headway with a menacing shiver, and then broke on their decks in torrents of green water and white foam. These seas were all the more dangerous to *Niña* because she was under-ballasted. Columbus explains that she sailed from Hispaniola in that condition because so much of her heavy stores and provisions had been consumed, and he had intended to replace them with water and native edibles at the Isle of Women, but the change of plan prevented. During the voyage the men had done their best to restore her stability by filling empty wine casks with salt water; but these were a poor substitute for good rock ballast, well secured, covering the bottom of the hold.

All attempts to steer a compass course were now abandoned. The helmsmen were ordered to let her scud before it in a general northeasterly direction, while the officer of the watch scanned each oncoming wave and gave quick orders that the caravel might take it at the best angle. Without extreme watchfulness and expert handling, *Niña* would have broached-to and filled, which would have been fatal to all; *Pinta* had no means of picking up survivors. For sail *Niña* carried only her *papahigo*, a small main course with the bonnet off, on a yard slung as low as possible in order to take the strain off the mast. A modern vessel, provided with a "North Atlantic Directory," a Bowditch, and hydrographic office charts, would have hove-to on the starboard tack, in order to drift as far as possible from the storm center; but Columbus knew nothing of the law of storms. Even if he had, scudding before the wind was the only proper course, for in that heavy, breaking cross sea any attempt to heave-to might have swamped a vessel so low in the water as *Niña*. These high-pooped caravels did pretty well scudding in heavy sea, since there was small chance of their being pooped by a following wave. But every big one swashed in through the rudder port, drenching the helmsmen, and it was all they could do to keep her before it and prevent a fatal broaching-to.

Pinta, with whom no hails had been exchanged during the strong wind of the previous week, paid off and scudded before the tempest at the same time as *Niña*. In the night of February 13–14 the Admiral "made flares and the other replied," until they were too far apart to exchange signals, and by morning they had lost sight of each other. *Pinta* missed the Azores, and the two caravels did not meet again until a month later, in the harbor of Palos.

The same conditions continued all day February 14, when the first of the two successive cold fronts overtook *Niña*. She was still scudding with main course and yard slung low, and a horrible cross swell, due apparently to a north wind beyond the second cold front not far to the north. Her company now called celestial power to their aid, in a manner typical of the age; and the way of their doing it, under the Admiral's direction, had the further merit of keeping the men busy and in a sense amused. Three successive lotteries were arranged to decide which man should represent the ship in going on a certain pilgrimage if she were saved alive. As many chick-peas as there were men aboard (excluding Indians not baptized, we presume), one pea cut with a cross, were placed in a seaman's cap; and he who drew the crossed pea must perform a pilgrimage to Santa María de Guadalupe in the mountains of Estremadura. Columbus put in his hand first, and drew the marked pea; and "henceforth regarded himself as a pilgrim and bound to fulfil the vow." As the wind and sea showed no sign of abating, the peas were shaken up again, this time for the privilege of representing *Niña* on a pilgrimage to the shrine of Santa Maria de Loreto in far-off Ancona. Pedro de Villa, a seaman of Puerto Santa María, drew the crossed pea, and the Admiral promised to pay his traveling expenses. Again, no sign that the heavenly host were paying any attention to these poor storm-tossed mariners. So a third vow was made, to watch all one night and pay for a Mass at the church of Santa Clara de Moguer, near Palos. Once more the Admiral drew the cross — is it possible that some expert gambler among the men juggled the peas against him? And still no sign of better weather. Perhaps Our Lady did not appreciate this method of playing "beano" for her favor. So all made a vow "to go in procession in their shirts" to the first shrine of the Virgin they should encounter, and say their prayers. And in addition "everyone made his special vow, because nobody expected to escape, considering themselves all lost." And after that (on February 14) the storm abated. The first cold front had crossed *Niña's* course with showers and squalls, wind changed to due W, and *Niña* scudded NE.

Columbus was man enough to admit that he was as frightened as anyone. Jotting down his impression of these terrible days of tempest, after *Niña* was safely anchored, he admitted that he should never have wavered as he did in trusting divine providence, which already had brought him safe through so many perils and tribulations, and afforded him the glory of discovering a western route to the Indies. God must have intended that discovery to be of some use to the world. But, "my weakness and anxiety would not allow my spirit to be soothed," he confessed. His greatest fear was not for loss of the discovery, since there was a good chance that *Pinta* would come through if *Niña* went down; but for the future of his lad Diego and for little Ferdinand, both of whom he had left at school in Cordova. For if he were drowned and Martín Alonso reached home with the news, they would be left orphans in a strange land with nobody to care for them, since the Pinzons undoubtedly would reap all the glory of the discovery.

So, in his cabin on that pitching and rolling vessel the Admiral got out vellum, quill and inkhorn, wrote a brief account of the voyage and of his discoveries, wrapped the parchment in a waxed cloth, ordered it to be headed up in a great wooden barrel, and cast into the sea. No more was heard of this "manuscript in a bottle" until 1892, when a fly-by-night London publisher had the impudence to claim that he had secured it, as recently picked up by a fisherman off the coast of Wales! It was written in English, he explained, because the Admiral thought that the manuscript would stand a better chance of being understood if couched in that universal maritime language. A "facsimile edition," printed in Germany in imitation script on imitation vellum, entitled "My Secrete Log Boke" and suitably adorned with genuine barnacles and seaweed, found many credulous purchasers, several of whom have tried to unload their unhappy acquisitions on the present writer.

After sunset February 14, the day of the three vows, "the sky began to show clear in the west, showing that the wind intended to blow from that quarter" — a very bad guess. But the wind moderated, the sea began to go down, and Columbus ordered the bonnet to be laced on *Niña's* course, equivalent to shaking out a reef. She continued to sail ENE at a speed of only three knots. Shortly after sunrise on Friday, February 15, a seaman named Ruy García sighted land dead ahead. The wildest conjectures were made as to what land it was. Some believed it to be Castile; others, the Rock of Sintra near Lisbon; others, Madeira. Columbus alone insisted that it was one of the Azores, and as usual he was right. It was Santa Maria, southernmost of the group, and one of the smallest.

Seventy-two hours elapsed before *Niña* came to an anchor there.

During the night of relatively moderate wind, when the ship was about 16 miles distant from the island, as they calculated, the wind whipped around to the ENE. The second cold front had passed over *Niña*, leaving her on the edge of the high-pressure area; but the sea continued high from the westward. The reason for this strange phenomenon must have been that the front, with the west winds beyond it, lay not far south in a general east and west direction. Fortunately *Niña* was a weatherly little caravel, and had sustained no important damage. So the Admiral sailed her on the wind, which veered to E February 16, and then to ESE. At sunrise February 16, just as she was coming about, they caught sight of the larger island of São Miguel over the stern, distant about 25 miles. All that day and the following night *Niña* with a fresh easterly wind was clawing her way toward the elusive Santa Maria, hidden by a great cloud rack. Columbus had his first sleep in three or four days, "and he was much crippled in the legs from always being exposed to cold and to water, and from eating little." The arthritis that the Admiral contracted on this passage stayed with him all his life, and grew more painful with advancing age.

At sunrise February 17, having overshot Santa Maria to the eastward, *Niña* took a SSW course with wind ESE, and by nightfall reached the island; but owing to the "great cloudmass" that obscured its upper slopes, the "Admiral could not recognize which island it was." After dark he came to an anchor off some houses, in the hope of hailing someone to tell him where they were; but the cable presently chafed through on the sharp rocks and parted. So the weary mariners, robbed of the quiet night's rest they anticipated, made sail and stood off-and-on all night. It had never been Columbus's intention to call at the Azores on the way home — all Portuguese islands he had carefully avoided; but ship and seamen had taken such a beating that he decided to take a chance in the hope of obtaining wood, water, fresh provisions, and a bit of rest.

Santa Maria, earliest of the Azores to be settled by the Portuguese, is only ten miles long by five wide. Mountainous, rising to 1870 feet, it contains many fertile valleys and tiny plains suitable for stock raising, but no natural harbor and only a few anchorages, none of which are tenable when the wind blows onshore.

After sunrise on Monday, February 18, Columbus again searched the northern side of the island, "and where it seemed fit anchored with one anchor and sent the boat ashore and had speech with the people, and found that it was the island of Santa Maria, one of the Azores, and they indicated the anchorage where he should moor the caravel, and the people of the island said that never had they seen such a tempest as there had been these 15 days past, and they wondered how he had escaped; and they gave many thanks to God and showed much joy at the news which they heard, that the Admiral had discovered the Indies."*

At this point, where Columbus's men first went ashore after leaving Hispaniola, the rugged mountains of Santa Maria fall away to a green coastal plain about half a mile wide. On the edge of it, where a small sand beach makes a good boat landing and a mountain stream affords fresh water, the first settlers of Santa Maria had disembarked over fifty years before Columbus's visit. Their village was called Nossa Senhora dos Anjos (Our Lady of the Angels) because the Virgin surrounded by angels had appeared to a fisherman on a rock awash at low tide; and a little chapel or hermitage dedicated to her had been built near the spot. The anchorage chosen by *Niña* off Anjos being far from safe, she shifted her position as the villagers advised to the eastward, on the other side of a high rocky cape called Punta Frades. There, in a bay open to the northeast, rimmed by high volcanic cliffs and lonely as any anchorage in the West Indies, *Niña* lay secure as long as the wind held southerly. Three men were left ashore at Anjos, a mile and a half away, in order to obtain fresh provisions and water.

All that afternoon *Niña* rode at anchor in this lonely bay, out of sight of the village, and without communication from shore. After sunset three islanders appeared on the cliff and hailed. Columbus "sent them the boat, in which they came aboard." Fortunately it was Shrovetide, so they brought fresh bread and chickens "and other things that were sent by the captain of the island, who was called João de Castanheira, saying that he knew him (the Admiral) very well, and that as it was night he did not come to call, but at

---

* "Appears fictitious this joy that the Portuguese showed," comments Las Casas sourly on the margin of the Journal for February 18.

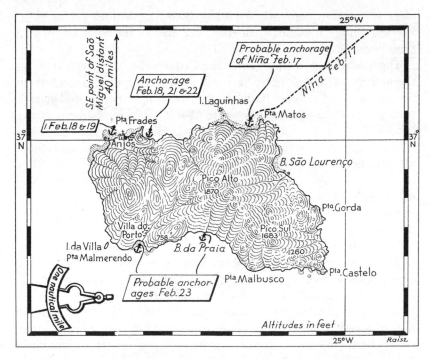

Anchorage
Feb. 18, 21 & 22

Probable anchorage
of Niña Feb. 17

I. Laguinhas

Niña Feb. 17

SE point of Saō
Miguel distant
40 miles

Pta Frades

I Feb.18 & 19

Lt.
Anjos

Pta.Matos

37
N

37
N

B. Sāo Lourenço

Pico Alto
1870

Pta.Gorda

Villa do
Porto

758

Pico Sul
1683

1260

I.da Villa
Pta Malmerendo

B. da Praia

Pta.Castelo

One nautical mile

Probable anchor-
ages Feb. 23

Pta.Malbusco

Altitudes in feet

25°W

25°W

Raisz

SANTA MARIA IN THE AZORES

daybreak he would come and bring more refreshments with the three men of the caravel who remained there, whom he did not then send back because of the great pleasure that he had with them, hearing about events of his voyage." The messengers who came aboard were given bunks for the night, as it was a long row home.

Informed by these men of a "little shrine like a hermitage which was near the sea" and dedicated to Our Lady, Columbus decided that this was the proper occasion to fulfill vow number three made at the tempest's height. This chapel, although enlarged and rebuilt in the seventeenth century, is still very small and severe in style, so that one can easily reconstruct in imagination the serio-comic scene that followed. At daybreak on Tuesday, February 19, Columbus sent half the crew ashore in *Niña's* one boat, asking the messengers who returned with them to hunt up the village priest to say Mass;

after which the men should come aboard again and act as ship-keepers while Columbus with the other half of the crew performed their vows.

The padre was routed out, and *Niña's* shore party, divesting themselves of shoes, hose and all nether garments, marched in procession, clad only in their shirts (the proper penitential garb), into the tiny chapel. As they were saying prayers of thanksgiving before the old Flemish triptych that still adorns the altar, "the whole town on horseback and afoot fell upon them and took them all prisoners"; for with nothing on but shirts, how could they resist? As Washington Irving observes, "such was the first reception of the Admiral on his return to the Old World, an earnest of the crosses and troubles with which he was to be requited through life, for one of the greatest benefits that ever man conferred upon his fellow beings."

The local official who ordered this cowardly capture of ten trouserless seamen at prayers was not the ruling captain of the island, who was absent, but his *locum tenens,* a young man named João de Castanheira. He boasted, and Columbus believed, that he had received orders from the king of Portugal to arrest him. It may be doubted whether Castanheira had any such orders, or he would have been more persistent in carrying them out; for he had already been rebuked for allowing a prisoner to escape. The Portuguese had been much troubled by Castilians poaching on the Guinea coast, contrary to the Treaty of Alcáçovas; and as the Azores were natural places of call for vessels returning from Guinea to the Peninsula, it seems probable that Castanheira suspected Columbus and his men of having been on an illicit Guinea voyage, which they were endeavoring to cover by tall tales of "The Indies."

About eleven in the morning Columbus, anxiously awaiting the return of his boat from the village that he was unable to see, decided that either the boat had been stove on the rocks or the people detained. Weighing anchor, he sailed *Niña* around Punta Frades, "and saw many horsemen who dismounted and entered the boat armed, and came out to the caravel," commanded by Castanheira. Their obvious intention was to arrest the Admiral. A parley followed between ship and boat, amusing enough for us but trying enough to Columbus. He tried to lure Castanheira aboard in order to hold him as hostage, while the Portuguese endeavored to inveigle Columbus into the boat, in order to clap him into prison with the pious pilgrims. Columbus exhibited his passport and credentials over the bulwarks, but refused to allow the Portuguese near enough to read them. High words were exchanged; Columbus "said that he was the Admiral of the Ocean Sea and Viceroy of the Indies which belong to Their Highnesses" (one can imagine Castanheira exclaiming derisively "In that little caravel!") and that he would return to Castile with half his crew if the others were not released, and see that offending Portuguese were suitably punished. Captain Castanheira replied that he knew nothing of the Sovereigns of Castile and cared less, that this was Portugal and be damned to him. Columbus then lost his temper and swore by San Fernando he would not leave until he had depopulated Santa Maria and captured a hundred Portuguese to carry home as slaves, God take them. "And so he returned to anchor in the harbor where he first lay, because wind and weather were very bad for doing anything else."

This anchorage was evidently the one off the village against which Columbus had been warned, for on the twentieth, when he was employing his remaining crew in filling casks with sea water for ballast, the cables parted and Columbus made sail for São Miguel. "Although in none of the Azores is there a good harbor in the weather that they then had, . . . he had no other recourse but to escape to sea." São Miguel is visible from Santa Maria in fair weather, but the weather was now exceedingly foul, and *Niña* was unable to make the island by nightfall. It was very difficult to handle her because of the crew left aboard only three were seamen, the rest being "idlers," landsmen or Indians who had not managed to pick up enough seamanship to be useful in a pinch. That night *Niña* lay-to "with a severe tempest and in great peril and toil," fortunately with "the sea and waves from one direction only." At sunrise on February 21, wind N and São Miguel not yet in sight, Columbus decided to bear away for Santa Maria and see what diplomacy could effect. By late afternoon he was moored by his two remaining anchors in the bay east of Punta Frades.

There, his first greeting was a defiant shout from the cliff by an officious villager. Presently, however, *Niña's* own boat came around the point, bearing five of the captured seamen, two clerics and a notary public. After such evening's entertainment aboard as the Admiral could offer, and passing the night, the priests and scribe scrutinized the Admiral's credentials, expressed themselves satisfied, and granted free entry and pratique. Castanheira had apparently repented of his rashness, and perhaps had failed to extract any evidence of poaching on the Guinea coast after giving his prisoners some sort of third degree. The boat went ashore and returned with the rest of *Niña's* crew, who said that the real reason for their release was Castanheira's failure to capture Columbus. He cared nothing for small game.

With her full crew restored *Niña* left this uneasy anchorage for the last time on February 23, and sailed around Santa Maria to the westward in search of a good place to take on wood and stone ballast. By the hour of compline (6 P.M.) she came to an anchor, in either Bahia Villa do Porto or Bahia da Praia on the southern shore of the island, there being a good landing beach and plenty of loose rocks in each. But at the passing of the first night watch (11 P.M.) the wind began to blow W, backed to SW, and as "in these islands . . . in blowing SW it presently comes S," said Columbus, and a south wind would render his anchorage untenable, it was necessary to put to sea. Columbus ordered anchors aweigh, made sail, and shaped an easterly course to steer clear of the island.

It was now Sunday, February 24. Ten days had been spent in and around Santa Maria, two or three anchors had been lost, and Columbus had nothing to show for the delay but fresh water, a few provisions, and a diplomatic victory over João de Castanheira.

CHAPTER XXIV

In Portuguese Power

FEBRUARY 24–MARCH 13, 1493

Quoniam probasti nos Deus: igne nos examinasti, sicut examinatur argentum . . . Transiuimus per ignem et aquam: et eduxisti nos in refrigerium.

For thou, O God, hast proved us; thou hast tried us, as silver is tried. . . . We went through fire and through water: but thou broughtest us out into a wealthy place.

— PSALM lxvi 10, 12

AT THE zero hour of Sunday, February 24, Columbus, "seeing it was favorable weather to go to Castile, gave up taking on wood and water, and gave orders that they lay a course to the East." Before daylight *Niña* was well beyond the inhospitable island. This easterly course was well chosen, for Santa Maria lies upon the same parallel as Cape St. Vincent, the proper landfall for a vessel approaching Palos from the westward. The distance, about 800 miles, under ordinary circumstances would not have required more than a week's sailing, for the prevailing wind at that season is north. But this stretch of water between the Azores and Portugal is a stormy one in the winter months; wind velocity beyond 100 miles per hour was reported at Lisbon in February 1941. Low-pressure areas show a tendency to "stall" in this area, along a slowly moving polar front. This means that violent storms may come close together, and may last a long time.

Another formidable tempest overtook *Niña* when she was about 250 miles out from Santa Maria; and it stayed with her right up to the bar of the Tagus. Again, the data in Columbus's Journal form a remarkable meteorological record. They show that this storm was a large well-developed cyclone, apparently with an open sector of warm air thrusting up from the tropics into cold air masses from the higher latitudes. The two whirling air masses were probably moving slowly eastward or northeastward, say at 10 knots, and took six days to pass Columbus, who was sailing along with them. This cyclone was even more of a trial to *Niña* than the storm west of the Azores, because the center passed nearer, perhaps only 150 miles or so to the northward.

The first sign of trouble came on the morning of February 26, when the zone of brisk to strong winds in the advance cold sector of the storm overtook *Niña*. Wind shifted to the SE, forcing her to head ENE, two points off her course to Cape St. Vincent. Next day the wind increased from the SE and S, the sea rose, and again Columbus could not lay his course. "It was very painful," he observed, "to have such a tempest when they were already at the doors of home." That day (February 27) Columbus "found himself 125 leagues from Cape St. Vincent and 80 from Madeira and 106 from Santa Maria." He or Vicente Yáñez or Peralonso Niño had a fairly accurate knowledge of this neck of the ocean, for if we lay off those three distances from their respective points of reference, without any deduction for overestimate, we place *Niña* on latitude 37° 05′ N, between longitudes 17° 30′ and 18° W. According to my plotting of Columbus's dead-reckoning, the longitude was about right, but the latitude, after the northing that *Niña* had been forced to make, must have been around 38° N. Madeira was probably placed too far north on Columbus's chart, which would account for his mistake in one of the three estimated distances.

On February 28 wind came SE to S with heavy seas; it was impossible to steer nearer the course than NE and ENE. So it continued for the next two days, March 1 and 2, while the slowly moving cyclone passed over *Niña*. That night the warm front of the cyclone apparently overtook her, and she entered the tropical sector of the storm. Wind shifted to SW, and it was possible to scud E by N. On the night of March 2 to 3, fifth of the storm, the cold front overtook *Niña* with a violent squall "which split all the sails, and he found himself in great peril." She could hardly have been under more than one lower course at the time; the squall must have blown the other course and mizzen out of their gaskets and stripped them off the yards.

On she drove under bare poles, rolling and pitching frightfully in a dangerous cross sea. Peas were shaken up in a cap for another shirt-clad pilgrimage, this time to the church of Santa María de la Cinta near Huelva, and as usual Columbus drew the marked pea. The seamen then vowed to spend their first Saturday night ashore fasting on bread and water, instead of feasting and carousing. A desperate state of things, indeed!

March 3 was the worst day of the entire voyage. The cold front, the squall line which *Niña* had crossed, seems to have extended almost parallel to and southward of her course, so it was almost as if she had a hostile fleet firing at her from just under the horizon. Wind rose to at least force 10 on Beaufort scale, and (in Dr. Brooks's opinion) to hurricane strength in the squalls. It was some consolation that it blew from the NW, so *Niña* drove ahead to the eastward; but the coast was coming dangerously near, and there was the same terrible cross sea as in the earlier tempest. As the dark afternoon waned, anxiety became intense; for Columbus knew by his dead-reckoning and the look of things that he was very near the land, driving toward the ironbound coast of Portugal.

Sun set at six on March 3, and shortly afterward the cyclone delivered her last tail-lashing. The wind rose to "so terrible a tempest that they thought they were lost from the seas that came aboard from two directions, and the winds which seemed to raise the caravel into the air, and the water from the sky and lightning flashes in many directions." Fortunately it was the night of full moon, which sent enough light through the storm clouds so that at 7 P.M., when the first night watch was set, the seamen sighted land dead ahead. That was a moment for quick thinking. "In order not to approach the land until he had recognized it, to see if he could pick up some port or roadstead where he could save himself," Columbus set a spare fore course that had escaped destruction in the sail locker, and clawed offshore on the starboard tack, wind NW. "And so God preserved them until day, which was accomplished with infinite toil and terror." Only one little sail to save them from crashing on Cabo da Roca, which would have meant certain death for all hands. A gallant little vessel was *Niña*, and superbly handled. Not every modern sailing ship would have come through under such conditions.

"At daybreak (March 4) he recognized the land which was the Rock of Sintra, which is next the River of Lisbon, where he decided to enter, because he could do nothing else." This Rock of Sintra is the mountainous peninsula, now studded with palaces and villas, that juts out from Portugal north of the Tagus, and makes a perfect landmark for entering Lisbon. Steep cliffs, rimmed with foam, showed the seamen what they had avoided.

Columbus, when he reached Spain, was meanly accused of having visited Lisbon with the express purpose of selling out his discovery to the king of Portugal, and a number of modern writers have repeated the ungenerous and preposterous charge. It should be clear to anyone, seaman or not, that after the cyclone had driven *Niña* north of the parallel of Cape St. Vincent, stripped her of every sail but one, and whipped around to W and NW, driving her toward a lee shore, Columbus must have entered the Tagus, as he says himself, "because he could do nothing else." Any attempt to sail 225 miles north to Galicia or south and east to Palos with his single square of canvas would have been unseamanlike and probably suicidal.

Shortly after sunrise *Niña* rounded Cabo Raso into the Tagus estuary, passed the village of Cascais, where the fishing folk were so astonished at seeing this tiny caravel come scudding in from seaward, and so alarmed for her safety, that they "spent all that morning making prayers for them." In this unusually stormy winter many vessels of the Flanders fleet had been lost, and some ships had been lying four months wind-bound in the Tagus.

Niña sailed close alongshore, safely crossed the northern channel over the bar of Lisbon, and after passing the island where D. Manuel a few years later erected the gothic Castle of Belem, came to an anchor at 9 A.M. on Monday, March 4, off Restello. This place, whose name was later changed to Belem, was the outer port of Lisbon, about four miles below the city. *Niña's* anchorage, now covered by filled-in land, was off the site of the Jeronymos Convent where lie buried Columbus's great contemporary Vasco da Gama and the poet Camoëns, who sang his praises in noble verse.

Columbus was now in a very hot spot, completely within the power of his Sovereigns' principal rival and recent enemy D. João II. His experience at Santa Maria suggested what the king's attitude might be. Powerless to resist capture or ill usage, the Admiral had to rely on his native wit and diplomacy.

Learning that the king was in the country, he dispatched a messenger with a letter requesting permission to proceed upstream to Lisbon, because he feared an attack from certain ruffians "thinking that he carried much gold," in that lonely anchorage where he was. He cited his credentials from Ferdinand and Isabella, and informed the monarch "that he came not from Guinea, but from the Indies." That was what he had to prove.

Having written to the king, Columbus wrote a postscript to the letter announcing to Ferdinand and Isabella the results of his voyage, that he had composed at sea and dated at Santa Maria.

"After having written this, and being in the Sea of Castile, there rose upon me so great a wind from the S and SE that I had to ease the ships. But today, which was the greatest wonder in the world, I made this harbor of Lisbon, whence I decided to write to Their Highnesses. In all the Indies I have always found weather as in May; thither I went in 33 days, and had returned in 28, but for those tempests which detained me 14 days running through this sea. All mariners here say that never has there been so bad a winter or so many losses of ships.

"Done on the 4th day of March."

Trouble was never far away from Columbus, whether afloat or at anchor. Moored near *Niña* was a great Portuguese man-of-war, the pride of the king's navy, equipped with sufficient artillery to blow a little caravel out of the water. Presently her master, who was none other than Bartholomew Dias, discoverer of the Cape of Good Hope, came aboard *Niña* in an armed boat and ordered Columbus to return with him and give an account of himself to the captain. Columbus stood on his dignity as Admiral of the Ocean Sea, and replied that he would not come unless by force of arms. Dias thought it would be all right with the captain if Vicente Yáñez Pinzón were sent aboard with the ship's papers. Columbus replied that neither his captain nor anyone else should go unless compelled by *force majeure;* that it was the tradition for Admirals of Castile to die before they yielded themselves or their people. Dias then asked to see his papers, which Columbus was only too glad to exhibit. The boat returned to the great ship, Dias told his story to his captain, Alvaro Damão, who then came aboard *Niña* "in great state, with drums, trumpets and pipes, making a great celebration of it," paid a visit of courtesy to the new Admiral of the Ocean Sea, and "offered to do all he commanded."

Round one for the Admiral.

All that day and the next Niña was receiving visitors from shore, including, no doubt, some of Columbus's old friends. The people were immensely impressed with the stories they heard and the captive Indians that they saw; there was much thanking God "for so great good and increase of Christianity that Our Lord had given to the Sovereigns of Castile." That was just like the kindly Portuguese. Devoid of the touchy pride and haughty jealousy of the Castilians, they seem as genuinely delighted at the good fortune of others as if it were their own. But it remained to be seen if the king would react like his subjects.

On Friday, March 8, Martin de Noronha, a young gentleman of the king's court, brought out a letter from D. João himself inviting the Admiral to come and visit him, "since the weather was not favorable for departing with the caravel." Evidently the wind still held westerly. And the king gave orders to his agents to supply *Niña* with provisions and ship chandlery at his own expense. Columbus decided to accept the invitation in order "to disarm suspicion, although he did not wish to go." Either he feared foul play, or he suspected that the purpose of his visit might be misconstrued, as it was. Mules were provided by D. Martin, a few gold noseplugs and other souvenirs of the Indies were doubtless packed in the saddlebags, and as undeniable evidence that he had been to an undiscovered country, Columbus selected some of the healthiest specimens of his ten captive Indians to share the royal week end. After being subjected to the terrors of the deep, these poor creatures were now to experience the horrors of muleback navigation in Portugal; unless, as is likely, they were required to trudge barefoot in the mud, and to be stroked and pinched by curious crowds in the streets of Lisbon. A "great pestilence" was then raging along the lower Tagus, but *Niña's* company, both white and red, fortunately escaped contamination.

What memories and thoughts must have passed through the mind of Columbus as his cavalcade threaded the narrow ways and close-built *praças* of Lisbon! His route led past the chapel of the Convento dos Santos where he had first met his wife, and below the great church of the Carmo where she had been buried in the Moniz family chapel. Perhaps he took time out to visit the tomb of Dona Felipa and say a prayer for her soul. He may even have passed the shop where Bartholomew and he had made charts for a living, while they planned the great enterprise now so brilliantly concluded. As he left the city and passed between high-walled vineyards along the road that led north by the right bank of the Tagus, Columbus must have thought out very carefully what he would say to the king, and with what fair words he might appease the monarch's irritation at his entering the service of another prince. Nightfall overtook the party at Sacavem, a pretty town on the Tagus about twelve miles from Lisbon; and there they spent the night. Next day, Saturday, March 9, the country roads were in such an execrable state after the heavy rains that it took them all day to reach the king's residence, a distance that one can now cover by car in about three quarters of an hour.

The royal house of Aviz, not provided with numerous palaces like their successors of the Bragança line, were accustomed to put up at the wealthy monasteries of their kingdom, thus saving their subjects much expense and profitably depleting the swollen ecclesiastical revenues. At that moment D. João was making a prolonged stay, to escape the pestilence, at the monastery of Santa Maria das Virtudes, situated in a pinewood at the foot of the Valle do Paraiso, a rich farming region about thirty miles from Lisbon. There is little left of that great monastery today except a large roofless gothic church, with apartments over the west end of the nave, whence royal guests could observe the celebration of Mass in privacy and seclusion. Marks on the masonry indicate that other apartments were built against the north side of the church adjoining those occupied by the king. One of these may well have been allotted to Columbus.

The meeting of king and admiral, men of high courage and

inflexible will, must have been dramatic. Columbus was forty-two years old, D. João thirty-eight. Columbus had first seen him as a suitor, and then been rejected; summoned to court in 1488, he had again been dismissed. Columbus well knew that only fear of offending the Sovereigns of Castile would prevent D. João from doing him ill; and there was always the uncomfortable feeling that *Pinta* might already have reached Spain with the news, so that Ferdinand and Isabella might not greatly care if some "accident" should cut short his inconvenient privileges of admiral, governor and viceroy.

It must have been a relief to be graciously received at Virtudes. Columbus's account of the meeting is in his Journal for March 9: —

"The king ordered him to be received very honorably by the principal officers of his household, and the king also received him with much honor and showed him much favor, and bade him be seated, and spoke very fair, offering to command all to be done freely which might be of use to the Sovereigns of Castile and for their service completely, and more than for his own, and showed that he was very pleased in the voyage having ended so favorably and having been accomplished."

Fortunately we have another account of this meeting from the pen of Rui de Pina, who as court chronicler may well have been present. According to him the king's expression of pleasure at the Admiral's success was insincere; he was irritated and inwardly enraged "because the said Admiral was somewhat elevated above his condition and in telling his tale always exceeded the bounds of truth and made the tale of gold, silver and riches much greater than it was." Moreover, the king "believed that this discovery was made within the seas and boundaries of his Lordship of Guinea; which was prohibited." He did not mean to impute that Columbus had been poaching off the West African Coast; nothing so crude as that. What the king did claim, as his subsequent diplomacy proved, was the "Ocean Sea" south of the Canaries and west of Africa as his sphere of influence, reserved exclusively for Portuguese discovery. He believed that Ferdinand and Isabella had expressly recognized this in the Treaty of Alcáçovas, which had been confirmed by the papal bull *Aeterni Regis* in 1481. D. João remarked to Columbus that if the new discovery was correctly described, "he understood from the treaty that he had with the Sovereigns, that that acquisition belonged to him." To which the Admiral replied in a placating manner that he had not seen the treaty, but the Sovereigns had ordered him "not to go to Mina or to any part of Guinea," and he had obeyed. D. João kept his poker face, said he was confident all could be amicably arranged, and handed his guest over to the Grand Prior of Crato, "who was the most eminent person there, and from whom the Admiral received many courtesies and favors."

After this first interview the courtiers, reading their king's real sentiments, crowded around and urged him to have this upstart and boastful Admiral assassinated forthwith, since "the prosecution of this enterprise by the Sovereigns of Castile would cease with the death of the Discoverer; and that this could be done discreetly if he consented and ordered it, for inasmuch as Colombo was discourteous and elated they could fix it so that any one of his shortcomings would seem to be the cause of his death. But the king like the God-fearing prince that he was, not only forbade that, but on the contrary showed him honor and much kindness."

The chronicler's tribute to his sovereign's forbearance is amusing, in view of the fact that D. João had personally assassinated his brother-in-law; but the Admiral's attitude and the king's irritation are convincing. Columbus was no longer a suppliant but a successful discoverer. Very likely he allowed himself to be carried away by pride, as was his wont, tactlessly reminded the king how he had been laughed at and told that it could never be done. Yet even the bare unvarnished truth about his First Voyage would have seemed wild and extravagant boasting to a prince whose discoveries had been made bit by bit, not in a single spectacular expedition.

Sunday morning after Mass the king "conversed long with the Admiral about his voyage, and always caused him to be seated and showed him much honor," asking all manner of questions and hearing all sorts of details, "dissimulating the chagrin that he had in his breast." The whole neighborhood flocked to view the strange people, and agreed that nothing like them had been seen in the whole world. And as Columbus boasted to the king that his Indians were intelligent, D. João arranged a test. He caused to be brought a bowl of dried beans which he scattered on a table, and

ordered an Indian to arrange them so as to make a rough map of
the lands that the Admiral claimed to have discovered. One of
them did so promptly, indicating which group of beans was Hispaniola and which Cuba, while single beans represented the Bahamas and the Lesser Antilles. The king, observing this geographical game with a gloomy countenance, as if by inadvertence
disarranged what the man had set forth, and commanded another
Indian to play map maker with the scrambled beans. The second
Indian – surely the clever "Diego Colón" – reassembled the bean

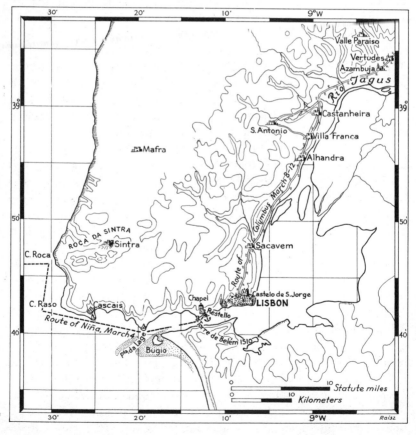

SINTRA, LISBON AND THE LOWER TAGUS VALLEY IN 1493

chart of the Antilles, and "added many more islands and lands, giving us an explanation of all that he had depicted and indicated in his own tongue, although nobody understood it. Whereupon the king, clearly apprehending the extent of the lands discovered, and the wealth that he already imagined to be in them, could no longer conceal the great chagrin, which so far he had dissembled, over the loss of things so inestimable, which by his own fault he had let slip from his hands; and in a wave of passion smote his breast and cried in a loud voice, 'O man of little comprehension!' and 'Why did I let slip an enterprise of so great importance?' — these or similar words." But he graciously concluded the scene by presenting the Arawak cartographers with some scarlet-colored clothes.

Rui de Pina introduces his account of this interview with a curious remark to the effect that "*Christovam Colombo* an Italian came from the discovery of the islands of Japan and of Antillia." Antillia, it will be recalled, was the mythical Island of the Seven Cities that so many Portuguese navigators had sought in vain. Columbus doubtless claimed that Hispaniola was Japan. He may have told the king that he had discovered Antillia, either to mislead him or to "put one over" on the Portuguese. Or, Rui de Pina may merely have reflected the king's opinion of what Columbus found, rather than the Discoverer's own claim. For it was the Portuguese who affixed the generic name *as Antilhas*, the Antilles, to the West Indies.

So with smoldering anger D. João heard a first-hand account of a voyage that gave his Castilian rivals the greatest empire in the world's history; one to which his own kingdom and all her African and Indian possessions were destined to be annexed when the seed of Aviz ran out.

This tense and exciting week end was soon over. On Monday, March 11, D. João gave Columbus certain messages for Ferdinand and Isabella, and bade him farewell, "showing him always much affection." After dinner the Admiral departed, escorted by D. Martin de Noronha and a troop of *cavaleiros*. They made a detour from the direct route for Lisbon, in order that Columbus might pay his respects to the Queen.

Dona Leonor, as her subjects addressed her, was staying at a monastery some 15 or 20 miles from Virtudes, for it was too great a strain on one establishment to entertain king and queen at the same time. News of the king's extraordinary visitors had reached her; and, as it is the privilege of royalty to hear travelers' tales from their own lips instead of waiting to read their books, Dona Leonor sent word that Columbus must not leave Portugal before calling on her.

The Convento de São Antonio de Castanheira where the queen was staying is one of the loveliest places in Portugal. The old monks chose a level plateau on the western slope of the Tagus valley, in a region evenly divided between vineyard, tillage and pasture, in order to provide themselves with every human need from their own soil. And that even fish might not be wanting, they contrived a pond between their main building and the break of the slope, edged with the *azulejos* or colored tiles that the Portuguese learned to make from the Moors. So well provided with amenities of every sort were the monks that when Portugal secularized her monasteries over a century ago, São Antonio made a perfect country estate, where a gentleman might live on his own in a land of quiet beauty. The great gothic abbey church with its elaborately sculptured tombs and chapels has been turned into a wine lodge, the choir and aisles are occupied by enormous tuns and presses, and the odor of fresh grape and fermenting wine has long since driven out the perfume of wax and incense. But the fish pond has been made into a swimming pool; and the patio where Dona Leonor took her exercise under the cloister has been preserved as on the day of the Admiral's visit.

In this cloister, or perhaps in the great hall if that March day was cold and blustery, Columbus with his suite of naked Indians knelt before Dona Leonor, kissed her hand, and "received much courtesy." With her, he says, were the father of his guide, D. Pedro de Noronha, Marquez de Villa Real, and the Queen's brother D. Manuel, Duque de Bejar and heir to the throne. If the Admiral's audience at São Antonio was small, it was interested; for the young duke, who succeeded D. João in 1495, pushed overseas enterprise with more vigor and success than any prince of that era. By D. Manuel's command Vasco da Gama sailed on a voyage more difficult in execution than that just completed by command of the Spanish Sovereigns.

Columbus did not tarry long at São Antonio. That evening he took leave of Dona Leonor, "and went to sleep at Alhandra," a town on the Tagus about 22 miles above Lisbon. The Admiral was feeling very chafed and sore after spending the better part of a third day in the saddle, and decided to charter one of the river *fregatas* the next day and be rowed or sailed down to Restello. Next morning (March 12) occurred a curious episode. Columbus, in his lodgings at Alhandra, was making arrangements about the boat when he was called upon by an *escudero* or squire of D. João, who offered on the king's behalf that, if Columbus "wished to go to Castile by land he would go with him to see to the lodging and order animals and all that he might want." Why was not this offer made at Virtudes? Had the would-be assassins won the king over, and was this a trap? It would have been easy, in the mountains between Elvas and Badajoz, to arrange an "attack by brigands" in which this boastful upstart Admiral would be "accidentally" murdered; it might even be managed on the Castilian side of the frontier, so that Portugal could evade responsibility. Or was this offer simply a belated act of courtesy? Columbus did not know, but he took no chances. What made this invitation the more suspicious was the fact that "D. João's squire ordered the Admiral to be given a mule, and presented another to his pilot, . . . and to the pilot he gave a tip of twenty *espadines*," equivalent to about fifty gold dollars. Was this messenger endeavoring to suborn the pilot? Nobody can tell. D. João had no motive but personal resentment for assassinating Columbus. Even if *Pinta* had gone down, *Niña* would have reported the discovery in Castile. Indeed the news was already on its way overland from Lisbon. But it is a privilege of tyrants to slay the bearers of ill tidings. Columbus evidently feared the worst, for, immediately after mentioning in his Journal the offer and the tips, "he says that all was told so that the Sovereigns might know of it."

At all events, Columbus refused to put his head in the bag, had himself and his suite conveyed down the Tagus, and went aboard *Niña* that night. The following morning (March 13) at eight, *Niña* got her anchors aboard, and with a swift ebb tide and a fair NNW wind passed out over the bar of Lisbon.

Now Columbus was out of Portuguese power for good and all.

CHAPTER XXV

Home Is the Sailor

MARCH 13–APRIL 20, 1493

Et deduxit eos in portum voluntatis eorum.

And so he bringeth them into the haven where they
would be.

— PSALM CVI 30

DURING the Admiral's absence the men of *Niña* had not been
idle. Indeed there was not much for them to do but work.
They had vowed to spend their first Saturday night fasting on bread
and water; and after the experience at Santa Maria, they had no
desire to see the inside of another Portuguese clink. *Niña* wanted a
new suit of sails and running rigging, not to speak of paint and
carpenter work, but with a blank check that the king had given
them on the royal shipyards, everything was quickly effected. The
filthy hold was scraped and disinfected with vinegar, new caulking
applied where she leaked, new stone ballast obtained from the
opposite shore of the Tagus; by the time the Admiral came aboard
she was all "shipshape and Bristol fashion." The whole ship's company, Christian and Indian, was aboard Tuesday night and ready
to sail.

Niña sailed from Restello at 8 A.M. Wednesday, March 13. Slow
progress was made that day, and it was not until after sunset that
she was far enough out to sea to shape a southerly course for
Cape St. Vincent. Well abaft, out of sight under the northern
horizon, *Pinta* was sailing the same course.

Martín Alonso, who had parted from his Admiral the stormy
night of February 13, did not sight the Azores. *Pinta* made port at
Bayona near Vigo, just north of the Portuguese boundary, some
450 miles from Palos and over 5 degrees of latitude north of Cape

St. Vincent. Obviously Martín Alonso shared the conviction of his brother that the caravels were near Madeira when the storm hit them on September 13, and after it was over he set a northeasterly course which missed his intended destination by several hundred miles. The date of his arrival is not recorded; but as *Pinta* was sailing while *Niña* wasted time at Santa Maria, she must have escaped the cyclone that overtook her consort on February 26, and made her unexpected Galician haven some time in the last week of February. This was another pennant for *Pinta;* first to sight America, first to reach Haiti, and first home with the news.

Columbus had always been afraid that Martín Alonso would try to beat him to the Sovereigns with the glad tidings; and that is exactly what *Pinta's* captain had in mind. He sent a message across the entire width of Spain to Ferdinand and Isabella at Barcelona, begging permission to proceed thither and acquaint Their Highnesses with the news of the discovery. The Sovereigns replied with a complete snub, declaring that they chose to hear the news from the Admiral himself. So Martín Alonso set sail from Bayona with his tail between his legs, as it were, and doubtless torn between the hope that *Niña* had gone down and fear for the safety of his brother.

In the meantime, during the night of March 13–14, refitted *Niña* was rolling southward before the "Portygee trades," covering the 85 miles between Cape Espichel and Cape St. Vincent in her usual gallant manner. Before sunrise the dark profile of the Sacred Promontory loomed up on the port bow. As Columbus wore ship, turned eastward under the lee of the cliffs, and fired the traditional salute, he must have thought of the Infante Dom Henrique, and wished that he could have reported his discovery to a sailor prince who would appreciate his dangers and difficulties. In any case, he sighted the beach where he had swum ashore with an oar seventeen years before. Wind came light on March 14, and sunset found *Niña* off Faro, southernmost harbor of the Algarves. *Pinta* must then have been rounding Cape St. Vincent.

At sunrise on the fifteenth day of March the Admiral "found himself off Saltés," took his bearings on the pine-clad summit of the Cerro del Puntal, stood off-and-on until the ebb was spent, "and at midday with a flood tide entered by the bar of Saltés within the

harbor whence he had departed on August 3 the preceding year."
The round voyage was completed in exactly thirty-two weeks.

"'Of this voyage I observe,' says the Admiral, 'that it hath
miraculously been shown . . . by the many signal miracles that
He hath shown on the voyage and for me, who for so great a
time was in the court of Your Highnesses with the opposition and
against the opinion of so many high personages of your household, who were all against me, alleging this undertaking to be
folly, which I hope in Our Lord will be to the greater glory of
Christianity, which to some slight extent already has occurred.'
These are the last words of the Admiral Don Christopher Columbus concerning his First Voyage to the Indies and their discovery."

So Columbus concluded his Journal of the First Voyage, when
Niña was fairly anchored in the Rio Tinto off the town of Palos.

Close in her wake sailed Pinta; the same tide took both caravels
across the bar and up the river. As Pinta rounded the promontory
where Nuestra Señora de la Rábida stands guard, and Martín
Alonso was straining his tired eyes for the first sight of his native
town, someone forward pointed ahead and shouted La Niña, señor
Capitán! And, by St. Iago, there she was, snugged down as pretty
as you please, might have been there a month. Thought we had
shaken off that Genoese upstart forever near the Azores; but he
beat us home with the news after all. Queen Isabella's blue-eyed
boy — probably kissing her hand now.

That finished poor old Martín Alonso. Already a sick man from
the hardships and exposure of the voyage, mortified by his snub
from the Sovereigns, he could bear no more. Without waiting
for Pinta's sails to be furled, without reporting to the flagship, or
so much as hailing Vicente Yáñez, Martín Alonso Pinzón had himself rowed ashore, went to his country house near Palos, crawled
into bed, and died.

Both caravels and their passengers and crews were the objects
of much admiring curiosity on the part of the people of Palos,
Moguer and Huelva. Many years later a citizen recalled how he
had visited Niña with a committee of inquisitors who at that time
were combing Palos for Jews and heretics; how they saw the
Indians aboard, to whom doubtless the inquisitors would have
given the "third degree" had they been able to make themselves

understood; how the Admiral had shown him some of the gold masks presented by Guacanagarí, and taken a knife and cut off a bit of pure gold and presented it to him. A highly tactful way to treat inquisitors! The Niños returned to their home town of Moguer, and many years later one Juan Roldán remembered well the *bodas y banquetes*, the parties and banquets, that were held there in honor of the heroes.

Columbus, who had already dispatched the Letter on the First Voyage to his Sovereigns overland from Lisbon, now sent another copy by way of Seville, where there was an official courier who spent his time traveling back and forth from Seville to the court. A special messenger delivered letters to the Admiral's family at Cordova, which he now considered his native city, together with a letter to the *cabildo* or municipality "concerning the islands that he had found." The city fathers were so pleased with this attention that they tipped the messenger 3351 maravedis — but unfortunately for us they lost the letter.

The Sovereigns were holding court at Barcelona diagonally across the peninsula, an overland journey of some 800 miles. Columbus, with painful memories of muleback riding in Portugal, at first intended to go there by sea. But the arrival of Martín Alonso the same afternoon put a different complexion on the matter. Haste was a consideration. Yet he could not start by land until a messenger returned from Barcelona with the desired permission to proceed. Accordingly in his letter to the Sovereigns, which was dispatched immediately, Columbus requested that the reply be sent to Seville. After performing his vows at Santa Clara de Moguer and Santa María de la Cinta at Huelva, and spending almost two weeks with Fray Juan Pérez and his other friends at La Rábida, Columbus proceeded with ten Indian captives to Seville. He entered the city "with much honor on the 31st day of March, Palm Sunday, having fully realized his object, and there was very well received." The Indians were lodged near the Gate of the Imágines, where Bartolomé de las Casas remembered staring at them as a boy; the Admiral probably put up at the Monastery of Las Cuevas, where he always stayed on subsequent visits to Seville.

Holy Week in Seville, with its alternation of abject humility and superb pride, penance and pardon, death and victory, seemed at once a symbol and a fitting conclusion to his great adventure. The daily processions of the brotherhoods with their gorgeously bedecked statues of saints, the ancient ceremonies in the Cathedral — rending of the temple veil, knocking at the great door, candles on the great *tenebrario* extinguished until only the one representing the Light of the World remained, the washing of feet on Maundy Thursday, the supreme Passion on Good Friday when the clacking of the *matraca* replaced the cheerful bells, the consecration of the paschal candle, and the supreme ecstasy of Easter morning — all that moved Columbus as no worldly honors could, and strengthened the conviction that his own toils and triumphs fitted the framework of the Passion. And it was pleasant to receive the congratulations of old friends (we always knew you would make it, old man!), to be presented to nobles and bishops, to dine with the alcalde and the archbishop and the Duke of Medina Sidonia, and to be pointed out in the crowd as the man who had sailed to the Indies and back; to have choice young *caballeros* introduced by their fathers in order to plead with Señor Almirante to take them to the Indies, and they would scrub decks or do anything he asked.

What the Indian captives thought of it all we are not told.

On or shortly after Easter Sunday, which fell on April 7, Columbus's cup of happiness overflowed on receiving this letter from the Sovereigns, addressed to "Don Cristóbal Colón, their Admiral of the Ocean Sea, Viceroy and Governor of the Islands that he hath discovered in the Indies." No quibbling about titles, no proofs of discovery required, but all that had been promised, promptly and generously conceded: —

We have seen your letters and we have taken much pleasure in learning whereof you write, and that God gave so good a result to your labors, and well guided you in what you commenced, whereof He will be well served and we also, and our realms receive so much advantage. It will please God that, beyond that wherein you serve Him, you should receive from us many favors, . . . Inasmuch as we will that that which you have commenced with the aid of God be continued and furthered, and we desire that you come here forthwith, therefore for our service make the best haste you can in your coming, so that you may be timely provided with everything you need; and because as you see the summer has begun, and you must not delay in going back there, see if something cannot be prepared in Seville or in other districts for your returning to the land which you have discovered. And write us at once in this mail which departs presently, so that things may be provided as well as may be, while you are coming and returning, in such manner that when you return hence, all will be ready. From Barcelona on the 30th day of March 1493.

I THE KING   I THE QUEEN

By order of the King and of the Queen, *Fernando Alvarez.*

That was short and to the point, with not a word too much or too little; titles and privileges confirmed, royal command to attend court, and an order to prepare a new expedition to the Indies.

Immediately after receiving this, Columbus drew up a memorial to the Sovereigns containing his ideas of how the colonization of Hispaniola should be effected and managed. This document is of the highest interest, as it shows the Admiral in a new role, that of pioneer lawgiver to the New World.

Volunteer settlers up to the number of two thousand should be accepted, and these on arrival at Hispaniola should be distributed among three or four towns to be founded at convenient places, each with an alcalde, a clerk, a church and sufficient priests or friars "for the administration of the sacraments, and for divine worship and the conversion of the Indians." Nobody should be allowed to collect gold except bona fide settlers who build houses in these towns and receive a license to do so from the governor or alcalde; and since "extreme eagerness of the colonists to gather gold may induce them to neglect all other business" (as abundantly proved to be true) there should be a close season on gold hunting during a part of every year. The licensed gold gatherers must hand over their takings to the town clerk, to be melted down, weighed and stamped, and half to be taken by the colony treasurer for the crown, and 1 per cent of the whole to be reserved for the support of religion; all gold not so melted and stamped to be forfeited. All trade between Spain and Hispaniola should be conducted between Cadiz and a selected port or ports in the island, with due regulations to see that the crown's share is not pilfered on the way home. Anyone who wishes to make further discoveries should be allowed to do so – a liberal concession, not required in his original contract with the Sovereigns, which Columbus later regretted. This document, highly realistic in so far as it recognized that gold was the only object to draw colonists to Hispaniola, but suggesting regulations that proved in practice impossible to enforce, was signed

<pre>
              · S ·
          S · A · S
          X   M   T
     :Xp̃o   FERENS. /
</pre>

Some forty-five or fifty of these signatures of Columbus have been preserved, each with the pyramid of letters arranged in exactly the same way, but the last line occasionally reading *el Almirante,* and on at least two, VIREY, the Viceroy. Columbus attached great significance to it, and in his *mayorazgo* or entail instructed his heirs to continue to "sign with my signature which I now employ which is an X with an S over it and an M with a Roman A over it and over that an S and then a Greek Y with an S over it, preserving the relation of the lines and points." The heirs did not follow his instructions, and he never revealed the meaning, which has aroused endless speculation. The problem has particularly interested those endeavoring to prove that Columbus was a Jew, a Portuguese, a Freemason, or what not; for by inverting it or reading it backward, or in some other odd manner the monogram can be twisted into almost any meaning you like. Thacher gives eight possible expansions of the initials. The third line is probably an invocation to Christ Jesus and Mary (Christe, Maria, Yesu), or to Christ, Mary and Joseph, Columbus having confused a "Greek Y" with the Greek I that begins the name of Our Lord, and of Saint Joseph. The first four letters lend themselves to almost infinite combinations, of which the simplest and most reasonable is

Servus Sum Altissimi Salvatoris

Servant I am of the Most High Saviour

The final signature, Xp̃o Ferens, is simply a Graeco-Latin form of his given name, a reminder that by baptism he was consecrated to the task of carrying the word of God overseas to heathen lands. Speculate as we may, it is unlikely that any certain solution of the cipher will be found; the exact meaning was a secret that Columbus took to his grave.

Sending this letter ahead by a swift courier, the Admiral set forth from Seville clad in the garments, and using the state, suitable to his rank. With him traveled at least one of his officers, a few men whom he had engaged as servants, and six Indians. They carried brightly colored parrots in cages, and wore their native *guayças*, ornaments and belts studded with polished fish bones "fashioned with admirable art, together with a great quantity and samples of finest gold, and many other things never before seen or heard tell of in Spain." The rumor had gone before that Columbus had discovered new lands called "Las Indias" with a strange heathen people and new things; so all along the way to Barcelona the people flocked from far and near to see the show. Nobody — not even an Irishman — loves a parade as does a Spaniard; so the Admiral did not lack popular attention and applause to enliven his long journey. In early April, moreover, Andalusia is at her fairest, with trees in full leaf, fruit in blossom, the fields green with young grain, and the pastures fresh with young grass.

Traversing the great rolling plain of Andalusia, over which Columbus had traveled on his first journey to court, the cortege on the second or third day entered Cordova by the great Moorish stone bridge over the Guadalquivir. Here Columbus saw his two sons Diego and Ferdinand, visited his mistress Beatriz Enríquez de Harana and his old friends of the apothecary-shop club; here too doubtless he was entertained by the municipality, especially informed of the discovery. The cavalcade then crossed the Sierra Morena into Murcia, reached the coast at Valencia, and followed the coastal road through Tarragona to Barcelona, where it arrived between April 15 and 20. "All the court and the city came out" to meet the Admiral, says his son.

Next day Columbus was publicly received in the Alcazar with great pomp and solemnity by the King and Queen. He entered the hall where the Sovereigns held court with a multitude of caballeros and nobles; and among the best blood of Spain his fine stature and air of authority, his noble countenance and gray hair, gave him the appearance of a Roman Senator, as he advanced with a modest smile to make his obeisance. As he approached Ferdinand

and Isabella they arose from their thrones, and when he knelt to kiss their hands they graciously bade him rise and be seated beside them and the Infante Don Juan. An hour or more passed quickly while the Sovereigns examined his plunder and the Indians and their trappings, asked him a multitude of questions about the islands, and discussed plans for the next expedition. Then all adjourned to the chapel royal where the *Te Deum* was chanted in honor of the Great Discovery, while tears of joy streamed from the Sovereigns' and the Admiral's eyes. At the close of the service, Columbus was ceremoniously conducted as a royal guest to the lodgings that had been provided for him.

This was the height of his fortunes. Never again would he know such glory, receive such praise, enjoy such favor from his Sovereigns. A more subtle man, one who worked only for material reward, would have taken it forthwith and retired, leaving others to colonize. But Columbus was not that sort of man, or he would not have made his discovery. He must hold the islands gained for Spain, extend his discoveries, meet the Grand Khan, find the mines of gold, begin the work of conversion. The task that God intended him to perform had only begun.

NOTE ON THE ORIGIN OF SYPHILIS

No problem on Columbus's voyages has been so widely discussed as the question whether he did or did not import the syphilitic spirillum from America to Europe. Evidence that syphilis existed in a mild endemic form among the American Indians before 1492 is abundant. No certain evidence of syphilis in Europe exists before 1494, although certain medical historians assert the contrary. In any case, the disease appeared in a most virulent form in Italy in 1494, and spread rapidly. By 1520 it was generally believed in Europe that syphilis came from America, because a reputed cure for it, the guaiacum or lignum vitae, had been discovered there (doctrine of specifics). In view of the excellent health aboard homecoming *Niña* in 1493, and the absence of evidence to the contrary on *Pinta*, it seems highly improbable that Columbus's crews had then contracted the disease. But Las Casas states positively that the Indians gave it to the Spaniards, Oviedo definitely assigns the European importation to the Second Voyage, and Ruy Díaz de Isla, a Spanish physician whose book on syphilis appeared in 1539, assigns it to the First Voyage. He asserts that the disease was first observed at Barcelona in 1493, and that he treated some of the victims.

Two hypotheses are tenable. (1) Syphilis existed in both America and Europe in endemic form, and was stirred up by like events on both sides of the Atlantic, simultaneously: (a) the invasion of Italy by the French army under Charles VIII in 1494–1495, (b) the Spaniards roving and raping all over Hispaniola in 1494–1496. (2) The spirillum was brought to Europe in the bloodstream of Columbus's captive Indians in 1493, and by them transmitted to public women in Barcelona, whence it crossed the Pyrenees and the Mediterranean.

The subject is discussed at length in the two-volume edition of this work, II 193–218.

CHAPTER XXVI

Diplomatic Interlude

1493–1494

*Ecce dies Domini veniunt, dicit Dominus, et diuidentur
spolia tua in medio tui.*

Behold, the day of the Lord cometh, and thy spoil shall
be divided in the midst of thee.

— ZECHARIAH xiv 1

FOR five or six weeks Columbus remained with the court at
Barcelona, taking a prominent part in the great festivals of
Whitsuntide, Trinity Sunday and Corpus Christi, attending state
dinners, receiving people who wished to go to the Indies, advising
the Sovereigns on diplomatic matters, and making plans for the
Second Voyage. Unique and memorable was the ceremony of bap-
tizing the six Indians. King, Queen and Infante D. Juan acted as
godparents; to the Indian first in rank, a relation of the cacique
Guacanagarí, they gave the name Fernando de Aragon; to another,
Don Juan de Castilla, and to a third (the clever interpreter), Don
Diego Colón. "Don Juan" remained attached to the royal household, "where he was as well behaved and circumspect," says Oviedo,
"as if he had been the son of an important caballero"; but he died
in two years' time. The others accompanied Columbus on his Second Voyage, but only two survived it.

The most important man in the kingdom after Ferdinand was
D. Pedro Gonzales de Mendoza, Archbishop of Toledo and Grand
Cardinal of Spain. Las Casas extols his wisdom and ability, his
warm and generous nature, the splendor and munificence of his
state, and the favor that he enjoyed with the Sovereigns; indeed
his character was such that no one was jealous of his power, and
it was said "that the Cardinal carried the court with him; for when
he was in the court, court was held, and when he was absent there

was no court." At a banquet given by this great man Columbus was allotted the place of honor, and treated with the ceremony of the *salva,* usually reserved for royalty; which meant that every dish offered to him was first tasted by the host, and then served covered. To this ceremonial occasion was attributed the famous egg story, the only anecdote about Columbus that everybody knows. We may as well translate the "original source" of it, Benzoni's *Historia del Mondo Nuovo,* the first Italian history of the New World, which came out in 1565: —

Columbus being at a party with many noble Spaniards, where, as was customary, the subject of the conversation was the Indies: one of them undertook to say: — "Señor Cristóbal, even if you had not undertaken this great enterprise, we should not have lacked a man who would have made the same discovery that you did, here in our own country of Spain, as it is full of great men clever in cosmography and literature." Columbus made no reply, but took an egg and had it placed on the table saying: "Gentlemen, you make it stand here, not with crumbs, salt, etc. (for anyone knows how to do it with meal or sand), but naked and without anything at all, as I will, who was the first to discover the Indies." They all tried, and no one succeeded in making it stand up. When the egg came round to the hands of Columbus, by beating it down on the table he fixed it, having thus crushed a little of one end; wherefore all remained confused, understanding what he meant: that after the deed is done, everybody knows how to do it; that they ought first to have sought for the Indies, and not laugh at him who had sought for them first.

"The universal popularity of this anecdote is a proof of its merit," says Washington Irving. Unfortunately the egg story had already done duty in several Italian biographies of other characters, including the architect Brunelleschi. Moreover, a Spanish courtier, unless very drunk, would hardly dare address an insolent query to the guest of honor of the Grand Cardinal of Spain; and a self-made admiral at his first gastronomic dinner would probably have found something better to do than juggle a hard-boiled egg.

Columbus as a newly created nobleman required a grant of arms as outward and visible sign of his rank; and on May 20, 1493, the

Sovereigns issued letters patent conferring the right to bear arms on him and his descendants. In this document they declare: —

"You may place above your arms a castle and a lion that we grant you for arms, viz. the gold castle on a green field in the upper quarter of the shield of your arms on the dexter hand and in the other upper quarter on the sinister hand a purple lion rampant with green tongue on a white field, and in the other quarter below on the dexter hand some gold islands in waves of the sea, and in the other quarter below on the sinister hand your own arms which you are accustomed to bear." No crest or motto, and no blazon of the alleged Colombo family arms.

It was a signal honor of the Sovereigns to allow Columbus to augment his arms with the gold castle of Castile and the purple lion of León; but as there was a difference in the fields, these were not, strictly speaking, the royal arms. Thus, Henry VIII of England in granting the Seymours an augmentation consisting of the lilies of France and the leopards of England, prescribed a somewhat different arrangement from that of the royal arms.

No Columbus coat of the exact description quoted above has come down to us, although doubtless every vessel on the Second Voyage had these arms of the Admiral emblazoned on her banners and waistcloths. By 1502, when Columbus compiled a Book of Privileges for the benefit of his descendants, he had made some important alterations in the blazon. The chief he made identical with the royal arms by placing the gold castle on a red field, and bringing the lion rampant in accord with the lion of León. In the lower dexter quarter there is an emerging continent as well as a cluster of islands, for by that time Columbus had discovered terra firma. A new sinister quarter is introduced, consisting of five gold anchors placed horizontally on a blue field, presumably to represent the office of Admiral of the Ocean Sea; and the family arms, blazoned as a blue bend on a gold field with a red chief, are relegated to an arched point in the base, between the third and fourth quarters. There is no particular significance in the alterations, which Columbus according to continental usage had a perfect right to make. Few people in those days adhered strictly to their original blazon.

Oviedo, in the first edition of his *Historia General de las Indias*

(Seville 1535), further augmented the Columbus arms by a crest representing a globe surmounted by a red cross, and by a white motto-ribbon encircling the shield, containing the words: —

>*Por Castilla y por Leon: Nuevo Mundo hallo Colom*
>For Castile and for León: a New World found Colón.

Both crest and motto may well have been added by the second admiral, D. Diego Colón.

ARMS OF COLUMBUS

From Oviedo

An immense amount of research has been expended by heraldic experts and others on the "family arms" of the 1502 shield in the hope that they would explain one of the numerous "secrets" or "mysteries" of Columbus invented by writers of the last century. Nothing exactly resembling them has ever been found. A dove is the feature common to all known arms of patrician Colombos of Italy, Colons of Castile and Coloms of Aragon; and none of the ingenious promoters of Portuguese, Jewish, Catalan, French and

Polish "real Columbuses" has been able to show that his favorite bore a blue bend on a gold field under a red chief. Very likely Columbus's father did use this coat; for quite humble citizens of European communes in the fifteenth century could and often did bear arms, especially when they were members of a trade gild. At least half the continental coats that have come down to us were borne by middle-class families. And this device of Columbus was a typical middle-class coat. Any freeman had a right to assume simple arms like these; if Columbus had been trying to pretend a noble origin, he would have used a flock of doves, or something more pretentious.

At the same time that they conferred the original grant of arms, the Sovereigns made the Admiral's two brothers, Bartholomew the future Adelantado and Diego whom he sent for from Genoa, "*nobles y caballeros,*" and gave them the faculty and privilege of being addressed as *Don.*"

It was also necessary, from Columbus's point of view, that the rights and privileges granted him conditionally at Granada on April 30, 1492, should be expressly and formally confirmed, now that the conditions had been fulfilled. The text of this confirmation, issued on May 28, does not prove anything (as Vignaud imagined it did) about the Sovereigns' opinion of exactly what Columbus had found, because it simply repeats the phrases "islands and mainland" used in the original document signed at Granada the previous year. That document is repeated word for word in the confirmation, which then proceeds: —

And now, forasmuch as it has pleased Our Lord that you discover many of the said islands, and as we hope with his aid that you will find and discover other islands and mainland in the said ocean sea in the said region of the Indies . . . We do by these presents confirm to you and to your children, descendants and successors, one after the other, now and forever, the said offices of Admiral of the said Ocean Sea, Viceroy and Governor of the said islands and mainland that you have found and discovered, and of the other islands and mainland that shall by you or your industry be found and discovered henceforward in the said region of the Indies.

Columbus is confirmed in his right to appoint and remove all judges and other officials in the Indies; to hear, judge and determine all suits civil or criminal, and to enjoy all other things properly appertaining to the offices of viceroy and governor including the obedience of all persons living within the said islands and terra firma; whilst all who sail upon the Ocean Sea, which is defined as all the ocean west and south of a line drawn from the Azores to the Cape Verde Islands, are required to obey him as Admiral.

This matter of the admiralty was made much more explicit in the confirmation than in the capitulations; and as Columbus preferred the sea title to those of Governor and Viceroy, and was always referred to as "The Admiral" by contemporaries, we may well inquire what it meant. *Almirante* was a title of Moorish origin, meaning simply "the sea lord," by which the medieval kings of Castile used to designate a great officer of state whose business it was to administer the royal fleets and dockyards, and to exercise what is still known as admiralty jurisdiction. It was his duty to settle disputes among fishermen and in the merchant marine between owners, mariners and merchants, and to take cognizance of piracy, mutiny and all other crimes committed on the high seas or on tidal rivers. All these matters, for the narrow seas and the Canaries, were exercised by the Admiral of Castile or High Admiral (*Almirante Mayor*), who held court at Seville, and who at that time was one Don Alfonso Enríquez. What Columbus wanted was jurisdiction over his own discoveries and the route thither, where he did not wish the Admiral of Castile to interfere. The *Almirantazgo* or office of admiral was as necessary for the control of men afloat as the viceroyalty for the government of men ashore. That is why Columbus was created Admiral "of the Ocean Sea" or "of the Indies" — both titles were used in official documents. At a line drawn from the Azores to the Cape Verdes, where the High Admiral's jurisdiction ended, that of Columbus began. I imagine that whenever the fleet crossed that meridian outward bound on the three last voyages, Columbus caused a gun to be fired and had some officer tell the seamen that they'd better behave themselves, since the Admiral now had power of life and death over them.

The office and title of Admiral had no implication of commanding a fleet. This is proved by the fact that on May 28, the same day that the privileges of Columbus were confirmed and his title defined, the Sovereigns issued letters patent appointing *D. Cristóbal Colón nuestro Almirante del Mar Océano,* also *Capitán General de la Armada,* Captain General of the fleet, which was then being prepared for the Second Voyage to the Indies.

His office of Admiral of the Ocean Sea, then, gave Columbus jurisdiction over Spanish ships bound to or from the Indies, as soon as they passed the meridian of the westernmost Azores. He also claimed, by analogy with the rights and perquisites of the Admiral of Castile (which he carefully compiled and inserted in his Book of Privileges), the exclusive right to issue letters of marque and reprisal within his jurisdiction, and a one-third rake-off on the trade to the Indies, over and above what had been promised him by the Capitulations; but he never made that pretension good. While his privileges were still intact, Columbus doubtless appointed his brother or some other officer a judge of admiralty at Isabela and Santo Domingo, and even himself heard cases involving admiralty law, such as seamen's wage disputes, mutiny and piracy. But after Bobadilla came out to Hispaniola, Columbus was so effectually prevented from exercising admiralty jurisdiction that, as he bitterly complained, he could not even punish mutineers on his own exploring fleet, once it had reached shore. He always retained the title Admiral of the Ocean Sea, but after 1500 it was a mere title and nothing more.

.   .   .   .

Columbus would have been more than human if he did not relish the favor of the Sovereigns, the friendship of the great and the admiration of lesser people at Barcelona. But he did not tarry there merely to bask in social sunshine, to have his privileges confirmed, and to indulge in his unpopular habit of saying "I told you!" to the courtiers who had made fun of the Great Enterprise. Ferdinand and Isabella wanted him on hand in order to give information and advice on a very delicate diplomatic negotiation with Portugal and with the Holy See in order to secure their title to his discoveries, and to whatever future discoveries he or others might make in the same "region of the Indies."

Even before Columbus arrived at Barcelona in mid-April, the Spanish Sovereigns, warned by their ambassador at the court of Portugal that D. João II was equipping a fleet whose rumored destination was the new discoveries, began the necessary diplomatic *démarches* at Rome to secure their exclusive title. This was in accordance with usage. The public law of Europe recognized the Pope's right to allot temporal sovereignty to any lands not possessed by a Christian prince, and the kings of Portugal had obtained a series of bulls confirming their rights to the coast of Africa "as far as the Indians who are said to worship Christ," that is, to the kingdom of Prester John. Columbus's Letter on his First Voyage, the first printed edition of which may have appeared before he arrived at Barcelona, was certainly known at Rome a few days before April 18, and a Latin translation of it by Leandro de Cosco, completed April 29, was printed at Rome very shortly. Extracts from it were included in the first bull on the subject issued by the Pope on May 3.

His Holiness Alexander VI (Rodrigo Borgia) was a Spaniard who owed his recent election as well as many earlier favors to the influence of Ferdinand and Isabella. Ferdinand had allowed him to enjoy three Aragonese bishoprics at the same time, had conferred the dukedom of Gandia on his natural son Pedro, had legitimized Pedro's more famous brother Cesare Borgia and nominated him to the bishoprics of Pampeluna and Valencia. Despite these favors the new Pope had been flirting with a group of powers on the opposite side of the balance from Spain. Eager to square himself with his royal patrons, he practically let them dictate a series of papal bulls on the new discoveries, without considering the just claims of Portugal. These four bulls were not arbitral decisions. They were acts of papal sovereignty in favor of Castile based on the Holy Father's presumed right to dispose of newly discovered lands and heathen peoples not hitherto possessed or governed by any Christian prince.

The first bull *Inter caetera*, dated May 3, 1493, declared that whereas *dilectus filius Christophorus Colon* had sailed "toward the Indians" (*versus Indos*) and discovered "certain very distant islands and even mainlands hitherto undiscovered by others, wherein dwell very many people living peaceably, going naked and not eating flesh, . . . well disposed to embrace the Christian faith," each and every island and country discovered or to be discovered by the envoys of the Sovereigns of Castile and their successors, provided they have never been in the possession of any Christian prince, are confirmed to the said monarchs and their successors in full sovereignty. This first *Inter caetera* bull was sent to Spain on May 17, and doubtless arrived before the end of the month.

By this time an ambassador from Portugal had arrived at Barcelona, to assert the claim of D. João to anything discovered west

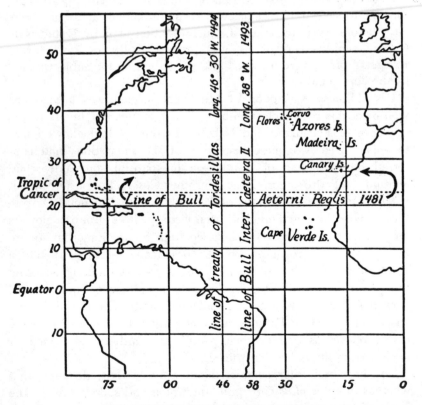

THE LINES OF DEMARCATION BETWEEN
SPAIN AND PORTUGAL

of Africa, and southward of the Canaries. We know from a subsequent remark of Columbus in the Journal of his Third Voyage
that the king of Portugal predicted the existence "of mainland
to the south," and he now wished to insure that the South Atlantic
be explicitly reserved to him as a field of discovery, as implicitly
it had been in the bull *Aeterni Regis* of 1481. In that bull the Pope
confirmed Portuguese sovereignty "over whatever islands shall be
found or acquired from beyond [south of] the Canaries, and on
this side [west] of and in the vicinity of Guinea." Whatever the
former pope's intention may have been, D. João believed that
Aeterni Regis gave Portugal a horizontal line of demarcation running through the Canaries. He was prepared to dispute Spanish
claims to anything discovered south of that latitude, no matter how
far west of Africa. In view of this Portuguese claim, the dispositions
of the bull of May 3, although clearly recognizing the Spanish title
to Cuba, Hispaniola and the Bahamas, were unsatisfactory as to
future discoveries; and Columbus intended to take a more southerly
course on his next voyage. Accordingly a fresh application was
made to Rome by Ferdinand and Isabella.

On its way to Spain, the May 3 bull *Inter caetera* crossed a
special mission from Spain to Rome. The Archbishop of Toledo
and Don Diego López de Haro were on their way to the Holy
See, for the double purpose of confirming Ferdinand's and Isabella's filial obedience to the newly elevated Supreme Pontiff, and
of insuring his loyalty to their cousin and ally, the king of Naples.
The embassy made a solemn entry into Rome on May 25. At a
consistory on June 12, López de Haro, in the name of his Sovereigns, addressed very strong language to the Pope, reproaching
him for a foreign policy which had the effect of keeping Italy in
a continual state of war, for the venality of his curia, the scandalous
auction of benefices, and even with harboring in his territory
Moors expelled from Spain. The Roman diarists who recorded
these bold words said nothing of any allusion to the Indies. But
the Great Discovery was mentioned in a sermon preached on
June 19 by the Spanish ambassador to Rome, Bernardino de Carvajal; and this sermon was promptly printed. By way of reminding
the Pope of what he and the Church owe to the Sovereigns,
Carvajal says, "Christ has subjected under them the Fortunate

[Canary] Islands, whose fertility has been proved marvellous; and he has lately given them other unknown islands toward the Indians (*versus Indos*), which may be fully regarded as the most precious things in the whole world, and it is expected that they will shortly be prepared for Christ by royal messengers."

Carvajal's warning, it is reasonable to suppose, "put the heat on" Alexander VI, who promptly issued a bull more satisfactory to Spain. It was after and not before this speech that the Pope issued two predated bulls: *Eximiae devotionis* which repeated the earlier concession in more emphatic terms, and a second *Inter caetera* which confirmed both the others and drew the famous demarcation line. The line is described as drawn from the North to the South Pole, "one hundred leagues towards the west and south from any of the islands commonly known as the Azores and Cape Verdes." West of it all future discoveries of lands not previously possessed by a Christian prince shall belong to Castile.

Columbus undoubtedly suggested this demarcation line. In the Journal of his Third Voyage, as abstracted by Las Casas, "he remembered that when he came to these Indies in past voyages, always when he reached 100 leagues toward the west from the position of the islands of the Azores, he found a change from the temperature of the north to [that of] the south." And in his Letter to the Sovereigns on the Third Voyage, Columbus says, "When I sailed from Spain to the Indies, I found straightway on passing 100 leagues to the west of the Azores a very great change in the sky, the stars, the air temperature and in the ocean; and I used much care in verifying this. I found that from North to South, in passing the said meridian of 100 leagues beyond those islands, the compass needles that formerly northeasted, now northwested a full point. And on reaching that line it is as if you had put a hill below the horizon. And also I found the sea there full of weed . . . and up to this meridian not a single spray of it was encountered. I also found the sea, on arriving there, to be very soft and smooth, it never made up even when the wind was stiff. Also I found beyond the said meridian toward the west, the temperature of the air to be very mild, and no change winter or summer."

In other words, the meridian 100 leagues west of the Azores marked the division between European and American conditions, between boisterous winds with high seas and gentle trades blowing over a "sea like the river of Seville," between cold weather and perpetual springtime. This letter to be sure was written in 1500, after Columbus had had much more experience; but that he had already reached the same conclusion on his First Voyage may be seen in his Journal. So, the second *Inter caetera* bull, prompted by Columbus, took an imaginary physical or meteorological boundary and made it a political one.

According to Las Casas, it was an entomological boundary as well. Speaking of the fauna of the Indies, he remarks on the absence of lice and fleas. "As a general rule the ships and people who follow the sea are so crawling with this 'fruit,' that for him who goeth to sea for the first time it is no small anxiety and travail; but for the Indies voyage we have a singular thing to remark: that up to the Canaries and 100 leagues beyond, or in the region of the Azores, many are the lice that breed; but from there on they all commence to die, so that upon raising the first islands [of the Indies] there be no man that breedeth or seeth one. On the homeward passage to Castile, every ship and person proceedeth clean of these creatures, until they attain the aforesaid region of the ocean, whenceforward, as if they waited upon us, they presently return in great and disturbing numbers." Undoubtedly it was an advantage to leave this "fruit" on the Portuguese side of the line. My own marine experiences indicate that the seaman's little companions which Fernández Duro humorously terms *animalejos navigantes* have since overcome their prejudice against a voyage to the Indies.

Returning to matters of deep diplomacy, Columbus left Barcelona in early June, before the last two papal bulls were executed; but the negotiations were not yet over. Evidently the Sovereigns showed the line-of-demarcation bull to the Portuguese ambassadors who arrived at Barcelona in August, and who declared themselves dissatisfied, on the ground that their royal master expected to discover lands and a continent "very profitable and richer than all the others" between this demarcation line and Africa. This news disquieted Ferdinand and Isabella, and on September 5 they wrote to Columbus at Cadiz inquiring what he thought of the rumor, and suggesting that "the bull be amended" if he thought it advisable, in order to secure these lands for Spain. In the same letter they asked for the chart of the new regions that he had promised them, and for their courses and latitudes. Columbus's reply has not been preserved, but the bull was amended. On September 26, 1493, the day after Columbus sailed from Cadiz, the Pope issued a fourth bull entitled *Dudum siquidem,* which augmented the previous grants in these words: —

"Since it may happen that your envoys and captains or subjects, while voyaging to the west or south, might land in eastern regions and there discover islands and mainlands that belong to India (*que Indie essent*) . . . we amplify and extend our aforesaid gift . . . to all islands and mainlands whatsoever, found and to be found, . . . in sailing or travelling toward the west or south, whether they be in regions occidental or meridional and oriental and of India." It further declared that all grants previously made to the regions in question, "Whether to kings, princes, infantes, religious or military orders" — Prince Henry of Portugal and his Order of Christ being obviously intended — are null and void, even if there had been previous possession.

It was now the turn of Portugal to be alarmed. This "Bull of Extension," so people called the last papal grant, was grossly unfair to her. To Spain it threw open the eastern route to the Indies, which the Portuguese had been pursuing for at least a generation. Columbus might sail around the world and plant the standard of Castile on Ceylon and Madagascar; might discover lands to the southward within striking distance of the West African coast, and assert Spanish sovereignty over them. D. João II, evidently concluding it hopeless to do business with a Spanish pope, pushed a direct negotiation with Ferdinand and Isabella for a modification of the demarcation line that would more narrowly delimit the Spanish sphere of influence. The Spanish Sovereigns were in no position to stand stiffly on their rights. They had a healthy respect for the powerful and ruthless D. João, and well knew that his navy and merchant marine, bigger and better than theirs, could render their communications with "The Indies" insecure if the two countries came to blows. Consequently, in the treaty concluded with Portugal at Tordesillas on June 7, 1494, Ferdinand and Isabella consented that the line of demarcation be moved to the meridian 370 leagues west of the Cape Verde Islands. East of this meridian all discoveries, even if made by Spanish ships, should belong to Portugal; and west of it all discoveries, even if made by the Portuguese, should belong to Spain.

How great a relief this was to the Sovereigns may be judged by a letter of theirs to Columbus at Hispaniola, dated August 16, 1494. They propose to establish a monthly packet service between Cadiz and Hispaniola, "since the affairs of Portugal are arranged, and vessels will be able to go back and forth in safety." They had already sent him a copy of the treaty, and now suggested that he come home and help them to establish the new line of demarcation.

In the Treaty of Tordesillas it was provided that each country appoint a commission of "pilots, astrologers, seamen and others," who should meet at the Grand Canary and there begin a joint cruise to the Cape Verde Islands. Thence each in its own caravel should sail due west until both parties struck land, or agreed that the correct meridian had been reached. Having decided that point, at a mid-ocean conference, they should sail due south and set up a pillar at the first land they encountered on the meridian. Considering the differences of opinion as to a ship's position among the pilots of Columbus's fleet, the impossibility of determining longitude, and the lack of knowledge of compass variation, the failure of this joint cruise to come off is a sad loss to the humors of maritime history. Instead, Spain and Portugal agreed by an exchange of notes in 1495 that this procedure would be "unprofitable," and that each would simply keep the other informed as to new discoveries and their reputed positions. That was done; and it was by virtue of the Treaty of Tordesillas, and not the papal line of demarcation, that Portugal obtained title to Brazil. Implemented by a series of royal marriages, this treaty preserved peace and friendship between the two great colonizing powers until Magellan's circumnavigation intruded on the sphere that Portugal rightly believed to be hers. Never in modern history has so vast a colonial expansion been carried out with so little friction between rivals.

CHAPTER XXVII

Spreading the News

1493–1494

Epistola Cristoferi Colom (cui etas nostra multum debet: de Insulis in mari Indico nuper inuentis. Ad quas perquirendas octauo antea mense: auspicijs et ere Inuictissimi Fernandi Hispaniarum Regis missus fuerat) ad Magnificum dominum Raphaelem Sanxis: eiusdem serenissimi Regis Thesaurarium missa. Quam nobilis ac litteratus vir Aliander de Cosco: ab Hispano ydeomate in latinum conuertit: tercio kalendas Maij. M.cccc.xciij. Pontificatus Alexandri Sexti Anno Primo.

Letter of Christopher Columbus (to whom our era oweth much, concerning the Islands newly discovered in the Indian Ocean, for the discovery whereof eight months before he had been sent under the auspices and in the pay of the most unconquerable Ferdinand King of the Spains), sent to the magnificent Don Raphael Sánchez Treasurer of the said most serene king. The which a noble man of letters Leandro Cosco hath turned into Latin from the Spanish on the 29th of April 1493, in the first year of the Pontificate of Alexander VI.

— Introduction to First Latin Edition of COLUMBUS LETTER

H IGHLY entertaining and significant are the traces of how the news of Columbus's discovery spread, and what people thought about it. For Columbus gave a new world not only to Castile and to León, but to European curiosity.

Earliest evidence that the news had reached Spain is the Duke of Medina Celi's letter of March 19, 1493, written from his castle about fifty miles northeast of Madrid, and stating that Columbus had arrived in Lisbon, after finding all that he went to seek. This is the only private letter about the First Voyage by a Spaniard that we have. The duke must have received word from Lisbon, where Columbus arrived March 6, and not from Palos, where the voyage ended on March 15.

Many Italians were then established in Spain as merchants, diplomats or churchmen, and a number of their letters written to their friends and patrons in Italy mentioning the Great Discovery have been preserved. As early as the last week of March, 1493, according to a contemporary chronicler named Tribaldo de Rossi, the Signory of Florence received a letter from Spain stating that certain youths with three caravels had gone in search of new countries "not already seen by the King of Portugal," and had discovered a very great island inhabited by naked people "wearing certain leaves about their genitals but nothing more," and using spears "tipped with porcupine quills instead of iron, of which they had no knowledge." The discoverers found considerable gold and a river whose sand was mixed with it, as well as cotton, pines, cypress trees and spicery.

The earliest Italian letter about Columbus to be preserved intact was written by a Barcelona merchant named Hannibal Zenaro or Januarius to his brother at Milan on April 9, 1493: —

Last August these Lord Sovereigns, on the plea of a certain *Colomba*, were content that the aforesaid should equip four caravels, because he said he wanted to pass over the Great Sea and sail directly to the west, in order to reach the Orient; since, the world being spherical, he would have to turn and find the oriental region. And so he did; the said caravels were accordingly equipped and the westward course was taken from outside the Straits, according to the letter which he wrote and which I have seen. In 34 days he arrived at a great island inhabited by naked people of olive complexion without any skill in fighting and very timorous. And, some having landed, they took some by force, so as to have knowledge of them, and to learn their language, in order that they might understand. [The natives] having thus lost their fear, for they were men of intelligence, [Columbus and his men] accomplished their object, and by signs and other means it was learned that they were among islands of India. And so the said captives went through the houses and towns of their neighbors, saying that there had come into that region a man sent from God. And, therefore, all these people, being of good faith, contracted warm friendship and amity with the said *Collomba* and his men. From this island

they then passed on to other islands, so far that in taking that course
they have found a great number of islands, two of which are each of
greater extent than England or Scotland, and the other greater than
all Spain. The aforesaid *Colomba* has left there some of his men. And
before departing he built a fort furnished with victual and artillery,
and carried off thence six men who are learning our language. In that
island they say they have found pepper, lignum aloes, and a mine of
gold in the rivers, i.e., a river, which has sand with many grains of
gold. And the people there, it is said, navigate with *canne* which are
so big that the largest hold 70 and 80 men. *Collomba* aforesaid has
returned directly and made land in Lisbon, and has written this to the
Lord King, who has written to him to come here at once. I expect
to have a copy of that letter which he has written, and shall send it
to you, and when he has come and I learn anything further I shall
let you know. And this is regarded as certain in this court; and, as I
have said, I have seen the letter which says, furthermore, that he has
not observed among those people any law or religion, except that they
believe that all things come from Heaven, and that there is the creator
of all things; whence cometh hope of their easy conversion to the Holy
Catholic Faith. He says further that he was afterwards in a province
where men are born with a tail.

Including the last item, which was a slight exaggeration of
Columbus's hearsay report that Sir John Mandeville's tailed men
grew in the Province of Havana, Zenaro's information was derived
from Columbus's Letter on the First Voyage, either a manuscript
copy or the first printed edition. The recipient of Zenaro's letter
gave a copy of it to Jacome Trotti, the Ferraran envoy at Milan,
who sent it on April 21 to his master the duke. This was none
other than the famous Ercole d'Este, who was keenly interested
in voyages and discoveries. He replied promptly, demanding more
detail; and on May 10 Trotti wrote again enclosing another "letter
come from Spain," probably the copy of Columbus's Letter that
Zenaro had promised to procure. As the court of Ercole d'Este
was a center of scientific inquiry as well as of humanist learning,
we may be certain that news of the discovery spread fast among
the *cognoscenti* of Northern Italy.

A copy of Columbus's own Letter on the First Voyage reached
Rome a few days before April 18, as it is mentioned in a Venetian
chronicle on that day. On the twenty-seventh the Milanese envoy

at Venice sends a copy of the Letter to his master, the famous Ludovico il Moro. On April 22 an architect named Luca Fancelli writes from Florence about the discovery to his patron, the Marquis of Mantua. Fancelli does not mention the name of Columbus. He says that in sixteen (!) days vessels of the King of Spain "discovered certain islands, among others a very large island toward the Orient which had very great rivers and terrible mountains and a most fertile country, inhabited by handsome men and women, but they all go naked, except that some wear a leaf of cotton over their genitals, . . . the country is most abounding in gold, . . . from it one sees neither the Arctic nor the Antarctic Pole." Allegretto Allegretti, a Sienese diarist, noted on April 25 that he had heard "from many letters of our merchants in Spain, and from the lips of many people," that *Cristoforo Colombo* (the first time his name is given correctly) had found islands with gold, spicery, and people of strange customs, and had left a garrison of eighty men on one island; "they consider our men as gods." And he has heard that a second voyage is already being planned. The Duke of Milan's agent at Bologna reported on June 17 that *Columbo* had found some "southern islands in the crossing of the Indian Ocean" inhabited by "simple and naked people whom they tried to capture, treating them with liberality and humanity." Battista Fregoso, a former doge of Genoa, noted in his "Chronicle of Memorable Words and Deeds" for 1493 that *Christophorus Columbus natione Genuensis* had safely returned from India, having reached it in 31 days from Cadiz, as he proposed to do.

Columbus's Letter on the First Voyage (the one usually described as "to Santangel" or "to Sanxis") must have been printed at Barcelona as early as April 1, before Columbus came to court, to circulate so quickly. The first Latin translation, dated April 29, made by a Catalan named Leandro de Cosco, was printed at Rome in May in news-letter form, as a pamphlet of eight pages, entitled *De Insulis inuentis. Epistola Cristoferi Colom.* This became a "best seller"; it ran through three Roman editions in 1493, and six different editions were printed at Paris, Basle and Antwerp in 1493–1494. Giuliano Dati, a Florentine theologian and poet who was living in Rome, translated the Latin Letter into Tuscan verse, a poem of sixty-eight stanzas which was printed at Rome on

June 15, and at Florence twice in 1493. A German translation was printed at Strassburg in 1497, and the second Spanish edition appeared at Valladolid about the same time.

News of the First Voyage must have reached Northern Europe slowly. The great *Nuremberg Chronicle* was printed on July 12, 1493, without any mention of the discovery; and two days later a Nuremberg scientist wrote to D. João II, urging him to undertake a western voyage to the Indies, in complete ignorance that Columbus had taken the trick. As for England, the earliest evidence that anyone there had heard about Columbus's First Voyage is in a letter from Ferdinand and Isabella of March 28, 1496, to their ambassador at London, referring to news from him that "one like Columbus" (John Cabot) was trying to persuade the king "to enter upon another undertaking like that of the Indies." One would suppose that Ferdinand and Isabella would have seen that copies of the Pope's bulls reached the kings of every seafaring nation; but no copies of any such communications have been found in the archives of any European state except Portugal.

It is clear, then, that news of the Great Discovery traveled very quickly from Spain to Italy, partly through private letters of Italian merchants and partly through the efforts of Ferdinand and Isabella to secure their title from the Pope. But beyond the Alps and the Pyrenees it traveled very slowly indeed; three months after it was known at Rome and in Northern Italy, almost four months after it was known at Barcelona, the *Gelehrten* of Nuremberg, center of geographical studies in Northern Europe, had no word of Columbus's First Voyage. Indeed the news seems to have aroused very little interest outside Italy and the Iberian peninsula. Not until after a colony had been planted in the New World did the learned people in France, the Low Countries, Germany and England take notice that something important had happened. And the first nation after Spain to seek a western route to the Indies did so on the initiative of another Genoese, John Cabot.

From such letters and chronicles as we have quoted, and the few others that have been discovered, it is clear that Columbus's discovery struck the European imagination as a unique combination of the marvelous united to the truth. Scientific and literary curiosity were equally aroused. The points in Columbus's dis-

covery that chiefly interested people were the new things that
recalled something very old, like Adam and Eve in the garden of
Eden. The one touch of nature that made all newsmongers kin was
the naked natives, especially the women who wore nothing but
a leaf. Naked women were much less common in 1493 than today.
All Europeans of that era were overdressed, according to our
notions; and women were not accustomed to strip or bathe in
public. Completely naked Negroes had been seen by the Portuguese discoverers in equatorial Africa; but whatever the Portuguese
saw in the Dark Continent they did not tell. So Columbus's story
of men and women going winter and summer without clothes was
news indeed. Another group of facts that aroused comment were
the lack of religion among these natives, their timid and generous
nature, and ignorance of lethal weapons; these characteristics,
combined with their prelapsarian innocence, suggested to anyone
with a classical education that the Golden Age still existed in far-
off corners of the globe. Fascinating to all was Columbus's statement that "most of the rivers" in Hispaniola "yield gold," for
everyone knew the legend of King Midas and the River Pactolus,
for which the Portuguese had been vainly searching the west coast
of Africa. Europe was short of specie, and any new gold strike,
as in our own day, made a story of universal appeal. The exact
location of these marvelous discoveries apparently interested nobody; and the possibility that Columbus had opened up a new sea
route to the Indies, and thus damaged the commerce of Italian
seaports, did not occur to any letter writer of that nation.

One minor reaction to the news is an interesting illustration of
the adage that the truth does not matter so much as "who has the
telling of it." Owing to the news being broadcast from the capital
of Aragon, and to a Catalan making the first Latin translation of
the Columbus Letter, King Ferdinand gained all the credit that
should have gone to the Queen. Cosco prefaced his edition with
an introductory paragraph stating that *Colom* (the Catalan form
of the name) had sailed by command of "the unconquerable
Ferdinand King of the Spains," and the illustrated editions have
a woodcut of *Fernandus rex hyspania* [*rum*] clad in armor, bearing the pomegranates of Aragon on one arm and the castle and
lion of Castile and León on the other. Queen Isabella receives a

credit line in later editions; but in the Italian letters we have quoted, the Voyage is represented as a purely Aragonese enterprise.

To what extent did public opinion support Columbus's own view of his discoveries? As the news spread largely through copies, digests and translations of the Letter, his own claim that he had really reached "The Indies" was generally accepted. Ferdinand and Isabella adopted it officially, as it was their interest to do; and the Pope accepted their claim at its face value. The Admiral's great delusion is perpetuated by the name "Indian," by which we still call the natives of the New World. Until the latter half of the eighteenth century Spain officially called her overseas empire "The Indies." With the qualification "West" this name still persists. Yet there were skeptics even from the first. The king of Portugal, first European of any importance to whom Columbus communicated his news, refused to believe that the Genoese had discovered anything but islands in the ocean like the fabled Antillia; and the West Indies were always called "Las Antilhas" in Portugal and "Les Antilles" in France. Indeed any learned man who had read Ptolemy and accepted his approximately correct idea of the size of the globe must have concluded that Columbus could not possibly have reached Asia in thirty-three days' sailing from the Canaries. Either that, or Ptolemy was wrong — a proposition difficult for any man of learning to entertain.

This dilemma, which was not solved until the conclusion of Magellan's circumnavigation in 1521, is first seen in the letters of Peter Martyr d'Anghiera. That young Italian humanist in the Spanish service was with the court at Barcelona when Columbus arrived there in April 1493. He was not very prompt to inform his correspondents about Columbus, but gradually became more and more interested, and within a year decided to write a history of the discoveries. On May 14, 1493, at least seven weeks after the news reached Barcelona, Martyr wrote to his friend Count Borromeo: —

A few days afterward there returned from the western antipodes a certain *Christophorus Colonus* of Genoa who had with difficulty obtained from my Sovereigns three ships [to visit] this province, for they considered what he said fabulous; he has returned and brought proofs of many precious things, especially of gold, which these regions naturally produce.

So far, Peter Martyr does not question Columbus's claim that he had reached the "antipodes," meaning Asia. And in a letter dated September 13 to Count Tendilla and the Archbishop of Granada, he writes: —

Listen, you two very wise old gentlemen, and consider a new discovery. You remember how *Colonus* the Genoese, in camp with the Sovereigns, demanded permission to pass over to a new hemisphere by the western antipodes; you certainly should. Because in some measure it is owing to you. Nor without your advice, so I think, did he undertake the thing. He has returned safe and sound and declares that he has discovered marvels.

There then follows an accurate digest of Columbus's Letter on the First Voyage. Peter Martyr's letter of the same date, September 13, to Cardinal Ascanio Sforza, also declares that "a certain *Christophorus Colonus* Genoese" had reached the Antipodes. By October 1, Peter Martyr begins to be doubtful. In a letter of that date to the Archbishop of Braga he writes: —

A certain *Colonus* has sailed to the western antipodes, even to the Indian coast, as he believes. He has discovered many islands which are thought to be those of which mention is made by cosmographers, beyond the eastern ocean and adjacent to India. I do not wholly deny this, *although the size of the globe seems to suggest otherwise,* for there are not wanting those who think the Indian coast to be a short distance from the end of Spain. . . . Enough for us that the hidden half of the globe is brought to light, and the Portuguese daily go farther and farther beyond the equator. Thus shores hitherto unknown will soon become accessible. For one in emulation of another sets forth on labors and mighty perils.

One month later Peter Martyr seems at first glance to have decided that Columbus had *not* reached the Indies; for in a letter to Cardinal Sforza of November 1, 1493, he speaks of *Colonus ille Novi Orbis repertor,* "that famous Columbus the discoverer of a New World." This is the first recorded mention of the discoveries as constituting a new world. But in Peter Martyr's mind *novus orbis* was not incompatible with "The Indies." For, in a letter to Count

Giovanni Borromeo, written late in 1494 after the first news of the Second Voyage to Cuba had arrived, he says: —

Daily more and more marvels from the New World are reported through that Genoese *Colonus* the Admiral. . . . He says that he has run over the globe so far from Hispaniola toward the west that he has reached the Golden Chersonese, which is the furthest extremity of the known globe in the east. He thinks he has left behind only two hours of the four and twenty in which the Sun in its course encircles the universe. . . . I have begun to write books about this great discovery.

The Golden Chersonese was the Ptolemaic name for the Malay Peninsula. Consequently Peter Martyr, when describing Columbus's discoveries as a new world, means to suggest that they were new-found islands lying off Asia, in much the same position as the Moluccas. This mistake is important, for Columbus made the same error and obstinately adhered to it all his life. We are so used to considering the Americas as the New World that we find it hard to understand how educated men could consider outlying parts of Asia as a new world; but so almost everyone thought in Columbus's lifetime, and many continued in that opinion until Magellan's circumnavigation proved that Ptolemy and not Columbus was right about the extent of the globe. Columbus himself, in his Letter on the Third Voyage, employed *otro mundo* ("an other world") in exactly the same sense as Peter Martyr did *novus orbis:* a hitherto undiscovered appendage of Asia. Amerigo Vespucci, in his "Medici" letter which was printed in 1503 or 1504 under the title *Mundus Novus,* declares that the South American coasts which he had sailed along in 1501 "we may rightly call a new world because our ancestors had no knowledge of them, and it will be a matter wholly new to all those who hear about them." Yet even he probably conceived of South America as having much the same relation to Southeastern Asia as Australia has. Vespucci's admirer Waldseemüller announced in 1508 that Amerigo had discovered a "fourth part of the world" which therefore should be named *America;* but it was some years before the new name and the new geographical conception were accepted. Alessandro Geraldini, writing reminiscently in 1522 of Columbus's original project which he had heard discussed in court, speaks on the same sentence of the Admiral's proposition "for discovering a new world" and his belief that by crossing the ocean he could reach "the Antipodes" of Eastern Asia. He saw· no incompatibility between a new world and the Indies. All the learned quibbling of modern historians over the phrase *mundus novus,* as though it necessarily meant America, is a waste of words.

Columbus's discoveries, then, were taken at his own valuation; he had discovered a new world of islands "in" or "toward" the Indies, and everyone expected that on the next voyage something definitely Asiatic as described by Ptolemy or Marco Polo would be reached. Neither he nor anyone else suspected in 1493 or 1494 that the prophecy of Seneca had been fulfilled, and a vast continent lay revealed. Before Peter Martyr had finished the history *de Orbe Novo* that he told his friend had already been begun, he well knew that it was a new world indeed; but Columbus was not so easily convinced. The very pertinacity which had· made him push his Grand Enterprise during ten discouraging years, the screne confidence that kept him steadfast, prevented him from ever altering his conviction that he had discovered a western route to Asia. In his cosmographical ideas Columbus remained stubbornly and obstinately, to the end of his life, absolutely and completely wrong.